# Beowulf Cluster Computing with Windows

NOUS·SOMMES·PRETS

## Scientific and Engineering Computation
Janusz Kowalik, editor

# Beowulf Cluster Computing with Windows

Thomas Sterling

The MIT Press
Cambridge, Massachusetts
London, England

This book was set in LATEX by the authors and was printed and bound in the United States of America.

Library of Congress Control Number 2001095384
ISBN: 0–262–69275–9

Dedicated with respect and appreciation to the memory of
Seymour R. Cray
1925–1996

# Contents

# Series Foreword

The world of modern computing potentially offers many helpful methods and tools to scientists and engineers, but the fast pace of change in computer hardware, software, and algorithms often makes practical use of the newest computing technology difficult. The Scientific and Engineering Computation series focuses on rapid advances in computing technologies, with the aim of facilitating transfer of these technologies to applications in science and engineering. It will include books on theories, methods, and original applications in such areas as parallelism, large-scale simulations, time-critical computing, computer-aided design and engineering, use of computers in manufacturing, visualization of scientific data, and human-machine interface technology.

The series is intended to help scientists and engineers understand the current world of advanced computation and to anticipate future developments that will affect their computing environments and open up new capabilities and modes of computation.

This volume in the series describes the increasingly successful distributed/parallel system called Beowulf. A Beowulf is a cluster of PC's interconnected by network technology and employing the message-passing model for parallel computation. Key advantages of this approach are high performance for low price, system scalability, and rapid adjustment to new technological advances.

This book includes how to build, program, and operate a Beowulf system based on the Windows 2000 operating system. A companion volume in the series provides the same information for Beowulf clusters based on the Linux operating system.

Beowulf hardware, operating system software, programming approaches and libraries, and machine management software are all covered here. The book can be used as an academic textbook as well as a practical guide for designing, implementing, and operating a Beowulf for those in science and industry who need a powerful system but are reluctant to purchase an expensive massively parallel processor or vector computer.


Janusz S. Kowalik

# Foreword

We know two things about progress in parallel programming:

1. Like nearly all technology, progress comes when effort is headed in a common, focused direction with technologists competing and sharing results.

2. Parallel programming remains very difficult and should be avoided if at all possible. This argues for a single environment and for someone else to do the programming through built-in parallel function (e.g., databases, vigorous applications sharing, and an applications market).

After 20 years of false starts and dead ends in high-performance computer architecture, "the way" is now clear: Beowulf clusters are becoming the platform for many scientific, engineering, and commercial applications. Cray-style supercomputers from Japan are still used for legacy or unpartitionable applications code; but this is a shrinking fraction of supercomputing because such architectures aren't scalable or affordable. But if the code cannot be ported or partitioned, vector supercomputers at larger centers are required. Likewise, the Top500 share of proprietary MPPs[1] (massively parallel processors), SMPs (shared memory, multiple vector processors), and DSMs (distributed shared memory) that came from the decade-long government-sponsored hunt for *the* scalable computer is declining. Unfortunately, the architectural diversity created by the hunt assured that a standard platform and programming model could not form. Each platform had low volume and huge software development costs and a lock-in to that vendor.

Just two generations ago based on Moore's law (1995[2]), a plethora of vector supercomputers, nonscalable multiprocessors, and MPP clusters built from proprietary nodes and networks formed the market. That made me realize the error of an earlier prediction that these exotic shared-memory machines were supercomputing's inevitable future. At the time, several promising commercial off-the-shelf (COTS) technology clusters using standard microprocessors and networks were beginning to be built. Wisconsin's Condor to harvest workstation cycles and Berkeley's NOW (network of workstations) were my favorites. They provided one to two orders of

---

[1] MPPs are a proprietary variant of clusters or multicomputers. Multicomputers is the name Allen Newell and I coined in our 1971 book, *Computer Structures*, to characterize a single computer system comprising connected computers that communicate with one another via message passing (versus via shared memory). In the 2001 list of the world's Top500 computers, all except a few shared-memory vector and distributed shared-memory computers are multicomputers. "Massive" has been proposed as the name for clusters over 1,000 computers.

[2] G. Bell, "1995 Observations on Supercomputing Alternatives: Did the MPP Bandwagon Lead to a Cul-de-Sac?", *Communications of the ACM* 39, no. 3 (March 1996) 11–15.

magnitude improvement in performance/price over the proprietary systems, including their higher operational overhead.

In the past five years, the "Beowulf way" has emerged. It developed and integrated a programming environment that operates on scalable clusters built on commodity parts—typically based on Intel but sometimes based on Alphas or PowerPCs. It also leveraged a vendor-neutral operating system (Linux) and helped mature tools such as GNU, MPI, PVM, Condor, and various schedulers. The introduction of Windows Beowulf leverages the large software base, for example, applications, office and visualization tools, and clustered SQL databases.

Beowulf's lower price and standardization attracted a large user community to a common software base. Beowulf follows the personal computer cycle of innovation: platform availability attracts applications; applications attract users; user demand attracts platform competition and more applications; lower prices come with volume and competition. Concurrently, proprietary platforms become less attractive because they lack software, and hence live in niche markets.

Beowulf is the hardware vendor's worst nightmare: there is little profit in Beowulf clusters of commodity nodes and switches. By using COTS PCs, networks, *free* Linux/GNU-based operating systems and tools, or Windows, Beowulf enables any group to buy and build its own supercomputer. Once the movement achieved critical mass, the world *tipped* to this new computing paradigm. No amount of government effort to prop up the ailing domestic industry, and no amount of industry lobbying, could reverse that trend. Today, traditional vector supercomputer companies are gone from the United States, and they are a vanity business in Japan, with less than 10% of the Top500 being vector processors. Clusters beat vector supercomputers, even though about eight scalar microprocessors are still needed to equal the power of a vector processor.

The Beowulf movement unified the cluster community and changed the course of technical computing by "commoditizing" it. Beowulf enabled users to have a common platform and programming model independent of proprietary processors, interconnects, storage, or software base. An applications base, as well as an industry based on many low-cost "killer microprocessors," is finally forming.

You are the cause of this revolution, but there's still much to be done! There is cause for concern, however. Beowulf is successful because it is a common base with critical mass.

There will be considerable pressure to create Linux/Beowulf dialects (e.g., 64-bit flavor and various vendor binary dialects), which will fragment the community, user attention span, training, and applications, just as proprietary-platform Unix dialects sprang from hardware vendors to differentiate and lock in users. The community must balance this pseudo- and incremental innovation against standardization, because standardization is what gives the Beowulf its huge advantage.

Having described the inevitable appearance of Linux/Beowulf dialects, and the associated pitfalls, I am strongly advocating Windows Beowulf. Instead of fragmenting the community, Windows Beowulf will significantly increase the Beowulf community. A Windows version will support the large community of people who want the Windows tools, layered software, and development style. Already, most users of large systems operate a heterogeneous system that runs both, with Windows (supplying a large scalable database) and desktop Visual-X programming tools. Furthermore, competition will improve both. Finally, the big gain will come from cross-fertilization of .NET capabilities, which are leading the way to the truly distributed computing that has been promised for two decades.

## Beowulf Becomes a Contender

In the mid-1980s an NSF supercomputing centers program was established in response to Digital's VAX minicomputers.[3] Although the performance gap between the VAX and a Cray could be as large as 100,[4] the performance per price was usually the reverse: VAX gave much more bang for the buck. VAXen soon became the dominant computer for researchers. Scientists were able to own and operate their own computers and get more computing resources with their own VAXen, including those that were operated as the first clusters. The supercomputer centers were used primarily to run jobs that were too large for these personal or departmental systems.

In 1983 ARPA launched the Scalable Computing Initiative to fund over a score of research projects to design, build, and buy scalable, parallel computers. Many of these were centered on the idea of the emerging "killer microprocessor." Over forty startups were funded with venture capital and our tax dollars to build different parallel computers. *All of these efforts failed.* (I estimate these efforts cost between one and three billion dollars, plus at least double that in user programming that is best written off as training.) The vast funding of all the different species, which varied only superficially, guaranteed little progress and no applications market. The user community did, however, manage to *defensively* create lowest common

---

[3]The VAX 780 was introduced in 1978.

[4]VAXen lacked the ability to get 5–20 times the performance that a large, shared Cray provided for single problems.

denominator standards to enable programs to run across the wide array of varying architectures.

In 1987, the National Science Foundation's new computing directorate established the goal of achieving parallelism of 100X by the year 2000. The goal got two extreme responses: Don Knuth and Ken Thompson said that parallel programming was too hard and that we shouldn't focus on it; and others felt the goal should be 1,000,000X! Everyone else either ignored the call or went along quietly for the funding. This call was accompanied by an offer (by me) of yearly prizes to reward those who achieved extraordinary parallelism, performance, and performance/price. In 1988, three researchers at Sandia obtained parallelism of 600X on a 1000-node system, while indicating that 1000X was possible with more memory. The announcement of their achievement galvanized others, and the Gordon Bell prizes continue, with gains of 100% nearly every year.

Interestingly, a factor of 1000 scaling seems to continue to be the limit for most scalable applications, but 20–100X is more common. In fact, at least half of the Top500 systems have fewer than 100 processors! Of course, the parallelism is determined largely by the fact that researchers are budget limited and have only smaller machines costing $1,000–$3,000 per node or parallelism of < 100. If the nodes are in a center, then the per node cost is multiplied by at least 10, giving an upper limit of 1000–10,000 nodes per system. If the nodes are vector processors, the number of processors is divided by 8–10 and the per node price raised by 100X.

In 1993, Tom Sterling and Don Becker led a small project within NASA to build a gigaflops workstation costing under $50,000. The so-called Beowulf project was outside the main parallel-processing research community: it was based instead on commodity and COTS technology and publicly available software. The Beowulf project succeeded: a 16-node, $40,000 cluster built from Intel 486 computers ran in 1994. In 1997, a Beowulf cluster won the Gordon Bell Prize for performance/price. The recipe for building one's own Beowulf was presented in a book by Sterling et al. in 1999.[5] By the year 2000, several thousand-node computers were operating. In June 2001, 33 Beowulfs were in the Top500 supercomputer list (www.top500.org). Today, in the year 2001, technical high schools can buy and assemble a supercomputer from parts available at the corner computer store.

Beowulfs formed a do-it-yourself cluster computing community using commodity microprocessors, local area network Ethernet switches, Linux (and now Windows 2000), and tools that have evolved from the user community. This vendor-neutral

---

[5]T. Sterling, J. Salmon, D. J. Becker, and D. V. Savarese, *How to Build a Beowulf: A Guide to the Implementation and Application of PC Clusters,* MIT Press, Cambridge, MA, 1999.

platform used the MPI message-based programming model that scales with additional processors, disks, and networking.

Beowulf's success goes beyond the creation of an "open source" model for the scientific software community. It utilizes the two decades of attempts by the parallel processing community to apply these mutant multicomputers to a variety of applications. Nearly all of these efforts, like Beowulf, have been created by researchers outside the traditional funding stream (i.e., "pull" versus "push" research). Included among these efforts are the following:

- Operating system primitives in Linux and GNU tools that support the platform and networking hardware to provide basic functions
- Message Passing Interface (MPI) programming model
- Various parallel programming paradigms, including Linda, the Parallel Virtual Machine (PVM), and Fortran dialects.
- Parallel file systems, awaiting transparent database technology
- Monitoring, debugging, and control tools
- Scheduling and resource management (e.g., Wisconsin's Condor, the Maui scheduler)
- Higher-level libraries (e.g., LINPACK, BLAS)

## Challenges of "Do-It-Yourself Supercomputers"

Will the supercomputer center's role change in light of personal Beowulfs? Beowulfs are even more appealing than VAXen because of their ubiquity, scalability, and extraordinary performance/price. A supercomputer center user usually gets no more than 64–128 nodes[6] for a single problem—comparable to the size that researchers have or can build up in their labs. At a minimum, centers will be forced to rethink and redefine their role.

An interesting scenario arises when Gigabit and 10 Gigabit Ethernets become the de facto LAN. As network speed and latency increase more rapidly than processing, message passing looks like memory access, making data equally accessible to all nodes within a local area. These match the speed of the next-generation Internet. This would mean any LAN-based collection of PCs would become a de facto Beowulf! Beowulfs and Grid computing technologies will become more closely

---

[6]At a large center with over 600 processors, the following was observed: 65%, of the users were assigned < 16 processors; 24%<32; 4%<64; 4%<128; and 1%<256.

related to each other than they are now. I can finally see the environment that I challenged the NSF computer science research community to build in 1987!

By 2010 we can expect several interesting paths that Beowulf could host for more power through parallelism:

- In situ Condor-scheduled workstations providing de facto clusters, with scaleup of 100–10,000X in many environments
- Large on-chip caches, with multiple processors to give much more performance for single nodes
- Disks with embedded processors in a network attached storage architecture, as opposed to storage area networking that connects disks to nodes and requires a separate system area network to interconnect nodes

Already in 2001, a relatively large number of applications can utilize Beowulf technology by "avoiding" parallel programming, including the following:

- Web and Internet servers that run embarrassingly parallel to serve a large client base
- Commercial transaction processing, including inherent, parallelized databases
- Monte Carlo simulation and image rendering that are embarrassingly parallel

Great progress has been made in parallelizing applications (e.g., $n$-body problems) that had challenged us in the past. The most important remaining challenge is to continue on the course to parallelize those applications heretofore deemed the province of shared-memory multiprocessors. These include problems requiring random variable access and adaptive mesh refinement. For example, automotive and aerodynamic engineering, climate and ocean modeling, and applications involving heterogeneous space remain the province of vector multiprocessors. We need to have a definitive list of challenges to log progress; but, unfortunately, the vector supercomputer community have not provided this list.

Another challenge must be to make the use of multicomputers for parallel operation as easy as scalar programming. Although great progress has been made by computational scientists working with computer scientists, the effort to adopt, understand, and train computer scientists in this form of parallelism has been minimal. Few computer science departments are prepared to take on this role.

Based on two decades of "no surprises" in overall architectures, will there be any unforeseen advances outside of Moore's law to help achieve petaflops? What will high-performance systems look like in two or four more generations of Moore's law, considering processing, storage, networking, and user connections? Will Beowulf evolve to huge (100,000-node) clusters built from less costly nodes? Or will clusters be just part of the international computing "Grid"?

Gordon Bell
Microsoft Research

# Preface

Within the past three years, there has been a rapid increase in the deployment and application of computer clusters to expand the range of available system capabilities beyond those of conventional desktop and server platforms. By leveraging the development of hardware and software for these widely marketed and heavily used mainstream computer systems, clusters deliver order of magnitude or more scaling of computational performance and storage capacity without incurring significant additional R&D costs. Beowulf-class systems, which exploit mass-market PC hardware and software in conjunction with cost-effective commercial network technology, provide users with the dual advantages of unprecedented price/performance and configuration flexibility for parallel computing. Beowulf-class systems may be implemented by the end users themselves from available components. But with their growth in popularity, so has evolved industry support for commercial Beowulf systems. Today, depending on source and services, Beowulf systems can be installed at a cost of between one and three dollars per peak megaflops and of a scale from a few gigaflops to half a teraflops. Equally important is the rapid growth in diversity of application. Originally targeted to the scientific and technical community, Beowulf-class systems have expanded in scope to the broad commercial domain for transaction processing and Web services as well as to the entertainment industry for computer-generated special effects. Right now, the largest computer under development in the United States is a commodity cluster that upon completion will be at a scale of 30 teraflops peak performance. It is quite possible that, by the middle of this decade, commodity clusters in general and Beowulf-class systems in particular may dominate middle and high-end computing for a wide range of technical and business workloads. It also appears that for many students, their first exposure to parallel computing is through hands-on experience with Beowulf clusters.

The publication of *How to Build a Beowulf* by MIT Press marked an important milestone in commodity computing. For the first time, there was an entry-level comprehensive book showing how to implement and apply a PC cluster. The initial goal of that book, which was released almost two years ago, was to capture the style and content of the highly successful tutorial series that had been presented at a number of conferences by the authors and their colleagues. The timeliness of this book and the almost explosive interest in Beowulf clusters around the world made it the most successful book of the MIT Press Scientific and Engineering Computation series last year. While other books have since emerged on the topic of assembling clusters, it still remains the most comprehensive work teaching hardware, software, and programming methods. Nonetheless, in spite of its success, *How to Build a Beowulf* addressed the needs of only a part of the rapidly growing commodity cluster community. And because of the rapid evolution in hardware and software, aspects of its contents have grown stale in a very short period of time. *How to Build a Beowulf* is still a very useful introduction to commodity clusters and has been widely praised for its accessibility to first-time users. It has even found its way into a number of high schools across the country. But the community requires a much more extensive treatment of a topic that has changed dramatically since that book was introduced.

In addition to the obvious improvements in hardware, over the past two years there have been significant advances in software tools and middleware for managing cluster resources. The early Beowulf systems ordinarily were employed by one or a few closely associated workers and applied to a small easily controlled workload, sometimes even dedicated to a single application. This permitted adequate supervision through direct and manual intervention, often by the users themselves. But as the user base has grown and the nature of the responsibilities for the clusters has rapidly diversified, this simple "mom-and-pop" approach to system operations has proven inadequate in many commercial and industrial-grade contexts. As one reviewer somewhat unkindly put it, *How to Build a Beowulf* did not address the hard problems. This was, to be frank, at least in part true, but it reflected the state of the community at the time of publication. Fortunately, the state of the art has progressed to the point that a new snapshot of the principles and practices is not only justified but sorely needed.

The book you are holding is far more than a second addition of the original *How to Build a Beowulf;* it marks a major transition from the early modest experimental Beowulf clusters to the current medium- to large-scale, industrial-grade PC-based clusters in wide use today. Instead of describing a single depth-first minimalist path to getting a Beowulf system up and running, this new reference work reflects a range of choices that system users and administrators have in programming and managing what may be a larger user base for a large Beowulf clustered system. Indeed, to support the need for a potentially diverse readership, this new book comprises three major parts. The first part, much like the original *How to Build a Beowulf,* provides the introductory material, underlying hardware technology, and assembly and configuration instructions to implement and initially use a cluster. But even this part extends the utility of this basic-level description to include discussion and tutorial on how to use existing benchmark codes to test and evaluate new clusters. The second part focuses on programming methodology. Here we have given equal treatment to the two most widely used programming frameworks: MPI and PVM. This part stands alone (as do the other two) and provides detailed presentation of parallel programming principles and practices, including some of the most widely used libraries of parallel algorithms. The largest and third part of the new book describes software infrastructure and tools for managing cluster resources. This includes some of the most popular of the readily available software packages for distributed task scheduling, as well as tools for monitoring and administering system resources and user accounts.

To provide the necessary diversity and depth across a range of concepts, topics, and techniques, I have developed a collaboration among some of the world's experts in cluster computing. I am grateful to the many contributors who have added their expertise to the body of this work to bring you the very best presentation on so many subjects. In many cases, the contributors are the original developers of the software component being described. Many of the contributors have published earlier works on these or other technical subjects and have experience conveying sometimes difficult issues in readable form. All are active participants in the cluster community. As a result, this new book is a direct channel to some of the most influential drivers of this rapidly moving field.

One of the important changes that has taken place is in the area of node operating system. When Don Becker and I developed the first Beowulf-class systems in 1994, we adopted the then-inchoate Linux kernel because it was consistent with other Unix-like operating systems employed on a wide range of scientific compute platforms from workstations to supercomputers and because it provided a full open source code base that could be modified as necessary, while at the same time providing a vehicle for technology transfer to other potential users. Partly because of these efforts, Linux is the operating system of choice for many users of Beowulf-class systems and the single most widely used operating system for technical computing with clusters. However, during the intervening period, the single widest source of PC operating systems, Microsoft, has provided the basis for many commercial clusters used for data transaction processing and other business-oriented workloads. Microsoft Windows 2000 reflects years of development and has emerged as a mature and robust software environment with the single largest base of targeted independent software vendor products. Important path-finding work at NCSA and more recently at the Cornell Theory Center has demonstrated that scientific and technical application workloads can be performed on Windows-based systems. While heated debate continues as to the relative merit of the two environments, the market has already spoken: both Linux and Windows have their own large respective user base for Beowulf clusters.

As a result of attempting to represent the PC cluster community that clearly embodies two distinct camps related to the node operating system, my colleagues and I decided to simultaneously develop two versions of the same book. *Beowulf*

*Cluster Computing with Linux* and *Beowulf Cluster Computing with Windows* are essentially the same book except that, as the names imply, the first assumes and discusses the use of Linux as the basis of a PC cluster while the second describes similar clusters using Microsoft Windows. In spite of this marked difference, the two versions are conceptually identical. The hardware technologies do not differ. The programming methodologies vary in certain specific details of the software packages used but are formally the same. Many but not all of the resource management tools run on both classes of system. This convergence is progressing even as the books are in writing. But even where this is not true, an alternative and complementary package exists and is discussed for the other system type. Approximately 80 percent of the actual text is identical between the two books. Between them, they should cover the vast majority of PC clusters in use today.

On behalf of my colleagues and myself, I welcome you to the world of low-cost Beowulf cluster computing. This book is intended to facilitate, motivate, and drive forward this rapidly emerging field. Our fervent hope is that you are able to benefit from our efforts and this work.

## Acknowledgments

I thank first the authors of the chapters contributed to this book:

David Bailey, Lawrence Berkeley National Laboratory
Al Geist, Oak Ridge National Laboratory
William Gropp, Argonne National Laboratory
David B. Jackson, University of Utah
James Patton Jones, Veridian
Jim Kohl, Oak Ridge National Laboratory
David Lifka, Cornell Theory Center
Miron Livny, University of Wisconsin
Ewing Lusk, Argonne National Laboratory
Karen Miller, University of Wisconsin
Bill Nitzberg, Veridian
Mark Russinovich, Winternals Software
Stephen Scott, Oak Ridge National Laboratory
David Solomon, David Solomon Expert Seminars
Todd Tanenbaum, University of Wisconsin
Derek Wright, University of Wisconsin

Many other people helped in various ways to put this book together. Thanks are due to David Ashton, Michael Brim, Anthony Chan, Andrew Lusk, Richard Lusk, John Mugler, Thomas Naughton, and Dan Nurmi.

Jan Lindheim of Caltech provided substantial information related to networking hardware. Narayan Desai of Argonne provided invaluable help with both the node and network hardware chapters.

David Solomon (author of Chapter 4) and Mark Russinovich (author of Chapter 6) would like to thank the Microsoft Windows 2000 development team for their support in writing the book Inside Windows 2000, 3rd edition (Microsoft Press), from which their chapters were condensed. In particular, Dave Cutler, Rob Short, Landy Wang, Richard Ward, John Vert, Neil Clift, Tim Moore, Ryszard Kott, Mario Goertzel, Yun Lin, Steven Nelson, Ilan Caron, Gurdeep Singh Pall, and David Orbits.

Paul Angelino of Caltech contributed the assembly instructions for the Beowulf nodes. Susan Powell of Caltech performed the initial editing of several chapters of the book.

The authors would like to respectfully acknowledge the important initiative and support provided by George Spix, Svetlana Verthein, and Todd Needham of Microsoft that were critical to the development of this book. Dr. Sterling would like to thank Gordon Bell and Jim Gray for their advice and guidance in its formulation.

Gail Pieper, technical writer in the Mathematics and Computer Science Division at Argonne, was an indispensable guide in matters of style and usage and vastly improved the readability of the prose.

# Beowulf Cluster Computing with Windows

# 1 Introduction

*Thomas Sterling*

Clustering is a powerful concept and technique for deriving extended capabilities from existing classes of components. In nature, clustering is a fundamental mechanism for creating complexity and diversity through the aggregation and synthesis of simple basic elements. The result is no less than the evolution and structure of the universe, the compound molecules that dictate the shape and attributes of all materials and the form and behavior of all multicellular life, including ourselves. To accomplish such synthesis, an intervening medium of combination and exchange is required that establishes the interrelationships among the constituent elements and facilitates their cooperative interactions from which is derived the emergent behavior of the compound entity. For compound organizations in nature, the binding mechanisms may be gravity, coulombic forces, or synaptic junctions. In the field of computing systems, clustering is being applied to render new systems structures from existing computing elements to deliver capabilities that through other approaches could easily cost ten times as much. In recent years clustering hardware and software have evolved so that today potential user institutions have a plethora of choices in terms of form, scale, environments, cost, and means of implementation to meet their scalable computing requirements. Some of the largest computers in the world are cluster systems. But clusters are also playing important roles in medium-scale technical and commerce computing, taking advantage of low-cost, mass-market PC-based computer technology. These Beowulf-class systems have become extremely popular, providing exceptional price/performance, flexibility of configuration and upgrade, and scalability to provide a powerful new tool, opening up entirely new opportunities for computing applications.

## 1.1 Definitions and Taxonomy

In the most general terms, a cluster is any ensemble of independently operational elements integrated by some medium for coordinated and cooperative behavior. This is true in biological systems, human organizations, and computer structures. Consistent with this broad interpretation, computer clusters are ensembles of independently operational computers integrated by means of an interconnection network and supporting user-accessible software for organizing and controlling concurrent computing tasks that may cooperate on a common application program or workload. There are many kinds of computer clusters, ranging from among the world's largest computers to collections of throwaway PCs. Clustering was among the first computer system architecture techniques for achieving significant improvements in overall performance, user access bandwidth, and reliability. Many research clusters have been implemented in industry and academia, often with proprietary networks and/or custom processing nodes.

Commodity clusters are local ensembles of computing nodes that are commercially available systems employed for mainstream data-processing markets. The interconnection network used to integrate the compute nodes of a commodity cluster is dedicated to the cluster system and is also commercially available from its manufacturer. The network is dedicated in the sense that it is used internally within the cluster supporting only those communications required between the compute nodes making up the cluster, its host or master nodes, which are themselves "worldly," and possibly the satellite nodes responsible for managing mass storage resources that are part of the cluster. The network of a commodity cluster must not be proprietary to the cluster product of a single vendor but must be available for procurement, in general, for the assembly of any cluster. Thus, all components of a commodity cluster can be bought by third-party systems integrators or the end-user installation site itself. Commodity clusters employ software, which is also available to the general community. Software can be free, repackaged and distributed for modest cost, or developed by third-party independent software vendors (ISVs) and commercially marketed. Vendors may use and distribute as part of their commodity cluster products their own proprietary software as long as alternate external software is available that could be employed in its place. The twin motivating factors that drive and restrict the class of commodity computers is (1) their use of nonspecialty parts that exploits the marketplace for cost reduction and stable reliability and (2) the avoidance of critical unique solutions restricted to a specific cluster product that if unavailable in the future would disrupt end-user productivity and jeopardize user investment in code base.

Beowulf-class systems are commodity clusters that exploit the attributes derived from mass-market manufacturing and distribution of consumer-grade digital electronic components. Beowulfs are made of PCs, sometimes lots of them; cheap EIDE (enchanced integrated drive electronics) (usually) hard disks; and low-cost DIMMs (dual inline memory modules) for main memory. A number of different microprocessor families have been used successfully in Beowulfs, including the long-lasting Intel X86 family (80386 and above), their AMD binary compatible counterparts, the Compaq Alpha 64-bit architecture, and the IBM PowerPC series. Beowulf systems deliver exceptional price/performance for many applications. They use low cost/no cost software to manage the individual nodes and the ensemble as a whole. A large part of the scientific and technical community using Beowulf has employed the Linux open source operating system, while many of the business and commercial users of Beowulf support the widely distributed commercial Microsoft Windows operating system. Both types of Beowulf system use middleware that is a combination of free open software and commercial ISV products. Many of these tools have been ported to both environments, although some still are restricted to one or the other environment. The nodes of Beowulfs are either uniprocessor or symmetric multiprocessors (SMPs) of a few processors. The price/performance sweet spot appears to be the dual-node SMP systems, although performance per microprocessor is usually less than for single-processor nodes. Beowulf-class systems are by far the most popular form of commodity cluster today.

At the other end of the cluster spectrum are the constellations. A constellation is a cluster of large SMP nodes scaled such that the number of processors per node is greater than the number of such nodes making up the entire system. This is more than an arbitrary distinction. Performance of a cluster for many applications is derived through program and system parallelism. For most commodity clusters and Beowulf systems, the primary parallelism exploited is the internode parallelism. But for clusters, the primary parallelism is intranode, meaning most of the parallelism used is within the node. Generally, processors within an SMP node are more tightly coupled through shared memory and can exploit finer-grained parallelism than can Beowulf clusters. But shared-memory systems require the use of a different programming model from that of distributed-memory systems, and therefore programming constellations may prove rather different from programming Beowulf clusters for optimal performance. Constellations are usually restricted to the largest systems.

## 1.2   Opportunities and Advantages

Commodity clusters and Beowulf-class systems bring many advantages to scalable parallel computing, opening new opportunities for users and application domains. Many of these advantages are a consequence of superior price/performance over many other types of system of comparable peak capabilities. But other important attributes exhibited by clusters are due to the nature of their structure and method of implementation. Here we highlight and expand on these, both to motivate the deployment and to guide the application of Beowulf-class systems for myriad purposes.

**Capability Scaling.** More than even cost effectiveness, a Beowulf system's principle attribute is its scalability. Through the aggregation of commercial off-the-shelf components, ensembles of specific resources deemed critical to a particular mode of operation can be integrated to provide a degree of capability not easily acquired through other means. Perhaps most well known in high-end computing circles is peak performance measured in flops (floating-point operations per second). Even modest Beowulf systems can attain a peak performance between 10 and 100 gigaflops. The largest commodity cluster under development will achieve 30 teraflops peak performance. But another important capability is mass storage, usually through collections of hard disk drives. Large commodity disks can contain more than 100 gigabytes, but commercial database and scientific data-intensive applications both can demand upwards of 100 terabytes of on-line storage. In addition, certain classes of memory intensive applications such as those manipulating enormous matrices of multivariate data can be processed effectively only if sufficient hardware main memory is brought to bear on the problem. Commodity clusters provide one method of accumulating sufficient DRAM (dynamic random access memory) in a single composite system for these large datasets. We note that while clusters enable aggregation of resources, they do so with limited coupling, both logical and physical, among the constituent elements. This fragmentation within integrated systems can negatively impact performance and ease of use.

**Convergence Architecture.** Not anticipated by its originators, commodity clusters and Beowulf-class systems have evolved into what has become the de facto standard for parallel computer structure, having converged on a communitywide system architecture. Since the mid-1970s, the high-performance computing industry has dragged its small user and customer base through a series of often-disparate parallel architecture types, requiring major software rework across successive generations. These changes were often a consequence of individual vendor decisions and resulted in low customer confidence and a strong reticence to invest in porting codes to a system that could easily be obsolete before the task was complete and incompatible with any future generation systems. Commodity clusters employing communitywide message-passing libraries offer a common structure that crosses vendor boundaries and system generations, ensuring software investment longevity and providing customer confidence. Through the evolution of clusters, we have witnessed a true convergence of parallel system architectures, providing a shared framework in which hardware and software suppliers can develop products with the assurance of customer acceptance and application developers can devise advanced user programs with the confidence of continued support from vendors.

**Price/Performance.** No doubt the single most widely recognized attribute of Beowulf-class cluster systems is their exceptional cost advantage compared with other parallel computers. For many (but not all) user applications and workloads,

Beowulf clusters exhibit a performance-to-cost advantage of as much as an order of magnitude or more compared with massively parallel processors (MPPs) and distributed shared-memory systems of equivalent scale. Today, the cost of Beowulf hardware is approaching one dollar per peak megaflops using consumer-grade computing nodes. The implication of this is far greater than merely the means of saving a little money. It has caused a revolution in the application of high-performance computing to a range of problems and users who would otherwise be unable to work within the regime of supercomputing. It means that for the first time, computing is playing a role in industry, commerce, and research unaided by such technology. The low cost has made Beowulfs ideal for educational platforms, enabling the training in parallel computing principles and practices of many more students than previously possible. More students are now learning parallel programming on Beowulf-class systems than all other types of parallel computer combined.

**Flexibility of Configuration and Upgrade.** Depending on their intended user and application base, clusters can be assembled in a wide array of configurations, with very few constraints imposed by commercial vendors. For those systems configured at the final site by the intended administrators and users, a wide choice of components and structures is available, making possible a broad range of systems. Where clusters are to be dedicated to specific workloads or applications, the system structure can be optimized for the required capabilities and capacities that best suit the nature of the problem being computed. As new technologies emerge or additional financial resources are available, the flexibility with which clusters are imbued is useful for upgrading existing systems with new component technologies as a midlife "kicker" to extend the life and utility of a system by keeping it current.

**Technology Tracking.** New technologies most rapidly find their way into those products likely to provide the most rapid return: mainstream high-end personal computers and SMP servers. Only after substantial lag time might such components be incorporated into MPPs. Clustering, however, provides an immediate path to integration of the latest technologies, even those that may never be adopted by other forms of high-performance computer systems.

**High Availability.** Clusters provide multiple redundant identical resources that, if managed correctly, can provide continued system operation through graceful degradation even as individual components fail.

**Personal Empowerment.** Because high-end cluster systems are derived from readily available hardware and software components, installation sites, their system administrators, and users have more control over the structure, elements, operation, and evolution of this system class than over any other system. This sense of control and flexibility has provided a strong attractor to many, especially those in the research community, and has been a significant motivation for many installations.

**Development Cost and Time.** The emerging cluster industry is being fueled by the very low cost of development and the short time to product delivery. Based on existing computing and networking products, vendor-supplied commodity clusters can be developed through basic systems integration and engineering, with no component design required. Because the constituent components are manufactured for a much larger range of user purposes than is the cluster market itself, the cost to the supplier is far lower than custom elements would otherwise be. Thus commodity clusters provide vendors with the means to respond rapidly to diverse customer needs, with low cost to first delivery.

## 1.3   A Short History

Cluster computing originated within a few years of the inauguration of the modern electronic stored-program digital computer. SAGE was a cluster system built for NORAD under Air Force contract by IBM in the 1950s based on the MIT Whirlwind computer architecture. Using vacuum tube and core memory technologies, SAGE consisted of a number of separate standalone systems cooperating to manage early warning detection of hostile airborne intrusion of the North American continent. Early commercial applications of clusters employed paired loosely coupled computers, with one computer performing user jobs while the other managed various input/output devices.

Breakthroughs in enabling technologies occurred in the late 1970s, both in hardware and software, which were to have significant long-term effects on future cluster computing. The first generations of microprocessors were designed with the initial development of VLSI (very large scale integration) technology, and by the end of the decade the first workstations and personal computers were being marketed. The advent of Ethernet provided the first widely used local area network technology, creating an industry standard for a modestly priced multidrop interconnection medium and data transport layer. Also at this time, the multitasking Unix operating system was created at AT&T Bell Labs and extended with virtual memory and network interfaces at the University of California–Berkeley. Unix was adopted in its various commercial and public domain forms by the scientific and technical computing community as the principal environment for a wide range of computing system classes from scientific workstations to supercomputers.

During the decade of the 1980s, increased interest in the potential of cluster computing was marked by important experiments in research and industry. A collection of 160 interconnected Apollo workstations was employed as a cluster to perform certain computational tasks by the National Security Agency. Digital Equipment Corporation developed a system comprising interconnected VAX 11/750 computers, coining the term "cluster" in the process. In the area of software, task management tools for employing workstation farms were developed, most notably the Condor software package from the University of Wisconsin. Different strategies for parallel processing were explored during this period by the computer science research community. From this early work came the communicating sequential processes model more commonly referred to as the message-passing model, which has come to dominate much of cluster computing today.

An important milestone in the practical application of the message-passing model was the development of PVM (Parallel Virtual Machine), a library of linkable functions that could allow routines running on separate but networked computers to exchange data and coordinate their operation. PVM (developed by Oak Ridge National Laboratory, Emery University, and the University of Tennessee) was the first widely deployed distributed software system available across different platforms. By the beginning of the 1990s, a number of sites were experimenting with clusters of workstations. At the NASA Lewis Research Center, a small cluster of IBM workstations was used to simulate the steady-state behavior of jet aircraft engines in 1992. The NOW (network of workstations) project at UC Berkeley began operating the first of several clusters there in 1993, which led to the first cluster to be entered on the Top500 list of the world's most powerful computers. Also in 1993, Myrinet, one of the first commercial system area networks, was introduced for commodity clusters, delivering improvements in bandwidth and latency an order of magnitude better than the Fast Ethernet local area network (LAN) most widely used for the purpose at that time.

The first Beowulf-class PC cluster was developed at the NASA Goddard Space Flight center in 1994 using early releases of the Linux operating system and PVM running on 16 Intel 100 MHz 80486-based personal computers connected by dual 10 Mbps Ethernet LANs. The Beowulf project developed the necessary Ethernet driver software for Linux and additional low-level cluster management tools and demonstrated the performance and cost effectiveness of Beowulf systems for real-world scientific applications. That year, based on experience with many other message-passing software systems, the first Message-Passing Interface (MPI) stan-

dard was adopted by the parallel computing community to provide a uniform set
of message-passing semantics and syntax. MPI has become the dominant parallel computing programming standard and is supported by virtually all MPP and
cluster system vendors. Workstation clusters running Sun Microsystems Solaris operating system and NCSA's PC cluster running the Microsoft NT operating system
were being used for real-world applications.

In 1996, the DOE Los Alamos National Laboratory and the California Institute of
Technology with the NASA Jet Propulsion Laboratory independently demonstrated
sustained performance of over 1 Gflops for Beowulf systems costing under $50,000
and was awarded the Gordon Bell Prize for price/performance for this accomplishment. By 1997, Beowulf-class systems of over a hundred nodes had demonstrated
sustained performance of greater than 10 Gflops, with a Los Alamos system making
the Top500 list. By the end of the decade, 28 clusters were on the Top500 list with
a best performance of over 200 Gflops. In 2000, both DOE and NSF announced
awards to Compaq to implement their largest computing facilities, both clusters of
30 Tflops and 6 Tflops, respectively.

## 1.4   Elements of a Cluster

A Beowulf cluster comprises numerous components of both hardware and software.
Unlike pure closed-box turnkey mainframes, servers, and workstations, the user or
hosting organization has considerable choice in the system architecture of a cluster,
whether it is to be assembled on site from parts or provided by a systems integrator
or vendor. A Beowulf cluster system can be viewed as being made up of four major
components, two hardware and two software. The two hardware components are the
compute nodes that perform the work and the network that interconnects the node
to form a single system. The two software components are the collection of tools
used to develop user parallel application programs and the software environment
for managing the parallel resources of the Beowulf cluster. The specification of a
Beowulf cluster reflects user choices in each of these domains and determines the
balance of cost, capacity, performance, and usability of the system.

The hardware node is the principal building block of the physical cluster system.
After all, it is the hardware node that is being clustered. The node incorporates the
resources that provide both the capability and capacity of the system. Each node
has one or more microprocessors that provide the computing power of the node
combined on the node's motherboard with the DRAM main memory and the I/O
interfaces. In addition the node will usually include one or more hard disk drives

for persistent storage and local data buffering although some clusters employ nodes that are diskless to reduce both cost and power consumption as well as increase reliability.

The network provides the means for exchanging data among the cluster nodes and coordinating their operation through global synchronization mechanisms. The subcomponents of the network are the network interface controllers (NIC), the network channels or links, and the network switches. Each node contains at least one NIC that performs a series of complex operations to move data between the external network links and the user memory, conducting one or more transformations on the data in the process. The channel links are usually passive, consisting of a single wire, multiple parallel cables, or optical fibers. The switches interconnect a number of channels and route messages between them. Networks may be characterized by their topology, their bisection and per channel bandwidth, and the latency for message transfer.

The software tools for developing applications depend on the underlying programming model to be used. Fortunately, within the Beowulf cluster community, there has been a convergence of a single dominant model: communicating sequential processes, more commonly referred to as message passing. The message-passing model implements concurrent tasks or processes on each node to do the work of the application. Messages are passed between these logical tasks to share data and to synchronize their operations. The tasks themselves are written in a common language such as Fortran or C++. A library of communicating services is called by these tasks to accomplish data transfers with tasks being performed on other nodes. While many different message-passing languages and implementation libraries have been developed over the past two decades, two have emerged as dominant: PVM and MPI (with multiple library implementations available for MPI).

The software environment for the management of resources gives system administrators the necessary tools for supervising the overall use of the machine and gives users the capability to schedule and share the resources to get their work done. Several schedulers are available and discussed in this book. For coarse-grained job stream scheduling, the popular Condor scheduler is available. PBS, the Maui scheduler, and the CTC Cluster Controller handle task scheduling for interactive concurrent elements. PBS also provides many of the mechanisms needed to handle user accounts.

## 1.5   Description of the Book

*Beowulf Cluster Computing* is offered as a fully comprehensive discussion of the foundations and practices for the operation and application of commodity clusters with an emphasis on those derived from mass-market hardware components and readily available software. The book is divided into three broad topic areas. Part I describes the hardware components that make up a Beowulf system and shows how to assemble such a system as well as take it out for an initial spin using some readily available parallel benchmarks. Part II discusses the concepts and techniques for writing parallel application programs to run on a Beowulf using the two dominant communitywide standards, PVM and MPI. Part III explains how to manage the resources of Beowulf systems, including system administration and task scheduling. Each part is standalone; any one or pair of parts can be used without the need of the others. In this way, you can just jump into the middle to get to the necessary information fast. To help in this, Chapter 2 (the next chapter) provides an overview and summary of all of the material in the book. A quick perusal of that chapter should give enough context for any single chapter to make sense without your having to have read the rest of the book.

The Beowulf book presents three kinds of information to best meet the requirements of the broad and varied cluster computing community. It includes foundation material for students and people new to the field. It also includes reference material in each topic area, such as the major library calls to MPI and PVM or the basic controls for PBS. And, it gives explicit step-by-step guidance on how to accomplish specific tasks such as assembling a processor node from basic components or installing the Maui scheduler.

This book can be used in many different ways. We recommend just sitting down and perusing it for an hour or so to get a good feel for where the information is that you would find most useful. Take a walk through Chapter 2 to get a solid overview. Then, if you're trying to get a job done, go after that material germane to your immediate needs. Or if you are a first-time Beowulf user and just learning about cluster computing, use this as your guide through the field. Every section is designed both to be interesting and to teach you how to do something new and useful.

One major challenge was how to satisfy the needs of the majority of the commodity cluster community when a major division exists across the lines of the operating system used. In fact, at least a dozen different operating systems have been used for cluster systems. But the majority of the community use either Linux or Windows. The choice of which of the two to use depends on many factors, some of them purely subjective. We therefore have taken the unprecedented action of offering a choice: we've crafted two books, mostly the same, but differing between the two operating systems. So, you are holding either *Beowulf Cluster Computing with Windows* or *Beowulf Cluster Computing with Linux.* Whichever works best for you, we hope you find it the single most valuable book on your shelf for making clusters and for making clusters work for you.

# I ENABLING TECHNOLOGIES

# 2 An Overview of Cluster Computing

*Thomas Sterling*

Commodity cluster systems offer an alternative to the technical and commercial computing market for scalable computing systems for medium- and high-end computing capability. For many applications they replace previous-generation monolithic vector supercomputers and MPPs. By incorporating only components already developed for wider markets, they exploit the economy of scale not possible in the high-end computing market alone and circumvent significant development costs and lead times typical of earlier classes of high-end systems resulting in a price/performance advantage that may exceed an order of magnitude for many user workloads. In addition, users have greater flexibility of configuration, upgrade, and supplier, ensuring longevity of this class of distributed system and user confidence in their software investment. Beowulf-class systems exploit mass-market components such as PCs to deliver exceptional cost advantage with the widest space of choice for building systems. Beowulfs integrate widely available and easily accessible low-cost or no-cost system software to provide many of the capabilities required by a system environment. As a result of these attributes and the opportunities they imply, Beowulf-class clusters have penetrated almost every aspect of computing and are rapidly coming to dominate the medium to high end.

Computing with a Beowulf cluster engages four distinct but interrelated areas of consideration:

1. hardware system structure,

2. resource administration and management environment,

3. distributed programming libraries and tools, and

4. parallel algorithms.

Hardware system structure encompasses all aspects of the hardware node components and their capabilities, the dedicated network controllers and switches, and the interconnection topology that determines the system's global organization. The resource management environment is the battery of system software and tools that govern all phases of system operation from installation, configuration, and initialization, through administration and task management, to system status monitoring, fault diagnosis, and maintenance. The distributed programming libraries and tools determine the paradigm by which the end user coordinates the distributed computing resources to execute simultaneously and cooperatively the many concurrent logical components constituting the parallel application program. Finally, the domain of parallel algorithms provides the models and approaches for organizing a user's application to exploit the intrinsic parallelism of the problem while operating within the practical constraints of effective performance.

This chapter provides a brief and top-level overview of these four main domains that constitute Beowulf cluster computing. The objective is to provide sufficient context for you to understand any single part of the remaining book and how its contribution fits in to the broader form and function of commodity clusters.

## 2.1    A Taxonomy of Parallel Computing

The goal of achieving performance through the exploitation of parallelism is as old as electronic digital computing itself, which emerged from the World War II era. Many different approaches and consequent paradigms and structures have been devised, with many commercial or experimental versions being implemented over the years. Few, however, have survived the harsh rigors of the data processing marketplace. Here we look briefly at many of these strategies, to better appreciate where commodity cluster computers and Beowulf systems fit and the tradeoffs and compromises they represent.

A first-tier decomposition of the space of parallel computing architectures may be codified in terms of coupling: the typical latencies involved in performing and exploiting parallel operations. This may range from the most tightly coupled fine-grained systems of the systolic class, where the parallel algorithm is actually hard-wired into a special-purpose ultra-fine-grained hardware computer logic structure with latencies measured in the nanosecond range, to the other extreme, often referred to as distributed computing, which engages widely separated computing resources potentially across a continent or around the world and has latencies on the order of a hundred milliseconds. Thus the realm of parallel computing structures encompasses a range of $10^8$, when measured by degree of coupling and, by implication, granularity of parallelism. In the following list, the set of major classes in order of tightness of coupling is briefly described. We note that any such taxonomy is subjective, rarely orthogonal, and subject to debate. It is offered only as an illustration of the richness of choices and the general space into which cluster computing fits.

**Systolic** computers are usually special-purpose hardwired implementations of fine-grained parallel algorithms exploiting one-, two-, or three-dimensional pipelining. Often used for real-time postsensor processors, digital signal processing, image processing, and graphics generation, systolic computing is experiencing a revival through adaptive computing, exploiting the versatile FPGA (field programmable gate array) technology that allows different systolic algorithms to be programmed into the same FPGA medium at different times.

**Vector** computers exploit fine-grained vector operations through heavy pipelining of memory bank accesses and arithmetic logic unit (ALU) structure, hardware support for gather-scatter operations, and amortizing instruction fetch/execute cycle overhead over many basic operations within the vector operation. The basis for the original supercomputers (e.g., Cray), vector processing is still a formidable strategy in certain Japanese high end systems.

**SIMD** (single instruction, multiple data) architecture exploits fine-grained data parallelism by having many (potentially thousands) or simple processors performing the same operation in lock step but on different data. A single control processor issues the global commands to all slaved compute processors simultaneously through a broadcast mechanism. Such systems (e.g., MasPar-2, CM-2) incorporated large communications networks to facilitate massive data movement across the system in a few cycles. No longer an active commercial area, SIMD structures continue to find special-purpose application for postsensor processing.

**Dataflow** models employed fine-grained asynchronous flow control that depended only on data precedence constraints, thus exploiting a greater degree of parallelism and providing a dynamic adaptive scheduling mechanism in response to resource loading. Because they suffered from severe overhead degradation, however, dataflow computers were never competitive and failed to find market presence. Nonetheless, many of the concepts reflected by the dataflow paradigm have had a strong influence on modern compiler analysis and optimization, reservation stations in out-of-order instruction completion ALU designs, and multithreaded architectures.

**PIM** (processor-in-memory) architectures are only just emerging as a possible force in high-end system structures, merging memory (DRAM or SRAM) with processing logic on the same integrated circuit die to expose high on-chip memory bandwidth and low latency to memory for many data-oriented operations. Diverse structures are being pursued, including system on a chip, which places DRAM banks and a conventional processor core on the same chip; SMP on a chip, which places multiple conventional processor cores and a three-level coherent cache hierarchical structure on a single chip; and Smart Memory, which puts logic at the sense amps of the DRAM memory for in-place data manipulation. PIMs can be used as standalone systems, in arrays of like devices, or as a smart layer of a larger conventional multiprocessor.

**MPPs** (massively parallel processors) constitute a broad class of multiprocessor architectures that exploit off-the-shelf microprocessors and memory chips in custom designs of node boards, memory hierarchies, and global system area networks. Ironically, "MPP" was first used in the context of SIMD rather than MIMD (multiple instruction, multiple data) machines. MPPs range from distributed-memory machines such as the Intel Paragon, through shared memory without coherent caches such as the BBN Butterfly and CRI T3E, to truly CC-NUMA (non-uniform memory access) such as the HP Exemplar and the SGI Origin2000.

**Clusters** are an ensemble of off-the-shelf computers integrated by an interconnection network and operating within a single administrative domain and usually within a single machine room. Commodity clusters employ commercially available networks (e.g., Ethernet, Myrinet) as opposed to custom networks (e.g., IBM SP-2). Beowulf-class clusters incorporate mass-market PC technology for their compute nodes to achieve the best price/performance.

**Distributed** computing, once referred to as "metacomputing", combines the processing capabilities of numerous, widely separated computer systems via the Internet. Whether accomplished by special arrangement among the participants, by means of disciplines referred to as Grid computing, or by agreements of myriad workstation and PC owners with some commercial (e.g., DSI, Entropia) or philanthropic (e.g., SETI@home) coordinating host organization, this class of parallel computing exploits available cycles on existing computers and PCs, thereby getting something for almost nothing.

In this book, we are interested in commodity clusters and, in particular, those employing PCs for best price/performance, specifically, Beowulf-class cluster systems. Commodity clusters may be subdivided into four classes, which are briefly discussed here.

**Workstation clusters** — ensembles of workstations (e.g., Sun, SGI) integrated by a system area network. They tend to be vendor specific in hardware and software. While exhibiting superior price/performance over MPPs for many problems, there can be as much as a factor of 2.5 to 4 higher cost than comparable PC-based clusters.

**Beowulf-class systems** — ensembles of PCs (e.g., Intel Pentium 4) integrated with commercial COTS local area networks (e.g., Fast Ethernet) or system area networks (e.g., Myrinet) and run widely available low-cost or no-cost software for managing system resources and coordinating parallel execution. Such systems exhibit exceptional price/performance for many applications.

**Cluster farms** — existing local area networks of PCs and workstations serving either as dedicated user stations or servers that, when idle, can be employed to perform pending work from outside users. Exploiting job stream parallelism, software systems (e.g., Condor) have been devised to distribute queued work while precluding intrusion on user resources when required. These systems are of lower performance and effectiveness because of the shared network integrating the resources, as opposed to the dedicated networks incorporated by workstation clusters and Beowulfs.

**Superclusters** — clusters of clusters, still within a local area such as a shared machine room or in separate buildings on the same industrial or academic campus, usually integrated by the institution's infrastructure backbone wide area netork. Although usually within the same internet domain, the clusters may be under separate ownership and administrative responsibilities. Nonetheless, organizations are striving to determine ways to enjoy the potential opportunities of partnering multiple local clusters to realize very large scale computing at least part of the time.

## 2.2   Hardware System Structure

The most visible and discussed aspects of cluster computing systems are their physical components and organization. These deliver the raw capabilities of the system, take up considerable room on the machine room floor, and yield their excellent price/performance. The two principal subsystems of a Beowulf cluster are its constituent compute nodes and its interconnection network that integrates the nodes into a single system. These are discussed briefly below.

### 2.2.1   Beowulf Compute Nodes

The compute or processing nodes incorporate all hardware devices and mechanisms responsible for program execution, including performing the basic operations, holding the working data, providing persistent storage, and enabling external communications of intermediate results and user command interface. Five key components make up the compute node of a Beowulf cluster: the microprocessor, main memory, the motherboard, secondary storage, and packaging.

The *microprocessor* provides the computing power of the node with its peak performance measured in Mips (millions of instructions per second) and Mflops (millions of floating-point operations per second). Although Beowulfs have been implemented with almost every conceivable microprocessor family, the two most prevalent today are the 32-bit Intel Pentium 3 and Pentium 4 microprocessors and the 64-bit Compaq Alpha 21264 family. We note that the AMD devices (including the Athlon), which are binary compatible with the Intel Pentium instruction set, have also found significant application in clusters. In addition to the basic floating-point and integer arithmetic logic units, the register banks, and execution pipeline and control logic, the modern microprocessor, comprising on the order of 20 to 50 million transistors, includes a substantial amount of on-chip high-speed memory called cache for rapid access of data. Cache is organized in a hierarchy usually with two or three layers, the closest to the processor being the fastest but smallest and the most distant being relatively slower but with much more capacity. These caches buffer data and instructions from main memory and, where data reuse or spatial locality of access is high, can deliver a substantial percentage of peak performance. The microprocessor interfaces with the remainder of the node usually by two external buses: one specifically optimized as a high-bandwidth interface to main memory, and the other in support of data I/O.

*Main memory* stores the working dataset and programs used by the microprocessor during job execution. Based on DRAM technology in which a single bit is stored as a charge on a small capacitor accessed through a dedicated switching transistor, data read and write operations can be significantly slower to main memory than to cache. However, recent advances in main memory design have improved memory access speed and have substantially increased memory bandwidth. These improvements have been facilitated by advances in memory bus design such as RAMbus.

The *motherboard* is the medium of integration that combines all the components of a node into a single operational system. Far more than just a large printed circuit board, the motherboard incorporates a sophisticated chip set almost as complicated as the microprocessor itself. This chip set manages all the interfaces between components and controls the bus protocols. One important bus is PCI, the primary interface between the microprocessor and most high-speed external devices. Initially a 32-bit bus operating at 33 MHz, the most recent variation operates at 66 MHz on 64-bit data, thus quadrupling its potential throughput. Most system area network interface controllers are connected to the node by means of the PCI bus. The motherboard also includes a substantial read-only memory (which can be updated) containing the system's BIOS (basic input/output system), a set of low-level services, primarily related to the function of the I/O and basic bootstrap tasks, that defines the logical interface between the higher-level operating system software and the node hardware. Motherboards also support several other input/output ports such as the user's keyboard/mouse/video monitor and the now-ubiquitous universal serial bus (USB) port that is replacing several earlier distinct interface types. Nonetheless, the vestigial parallel printer port can still be found, whose specification goes to the days of the earliest PCs more than twenty years ago.

*Secondary storage* provides high-capacity persistent storage. While main memory loses all its contents when the system is powered off, secondary storage fully retains its data in the powered-down state. While many standalone PCs include several classes of secondary storage, some Beowulf-systems may have nodes that keep only something necessary for holding a boot image for initial startup, all other data being downloaded from an external host or master node. Secondary storage can go a long way to improving reliability and reducing per node cost. However, it misses the opportunity for low-cost, high-bandwidth mass storage. Depending on how the system ultimately is used, either choice may be optimal. The primary medium for secondary storage is the hard disk, based on a magnetic medium little different from an audio cassette tape. This technology, almost as old as digital computing itself, continues to expand in capacity at an exponential rate, although access speed and bandwidths have improved only gradually. Two primary contenders, SCSI (small computer system interface) and EIDE (enhanced integrated dual electronics), are differentiated by somewhat higher speed and capacity in the first case, and lower cost in the second case. Today, a gigabyte of EIDE disk storage costs the user a few dollars, while the list price for SCSI in a RAID (redundant array of independent disks) configuration can be as high as $100 per gigabyte (the extra cost does buy more speed, density, and reliability). Most workstations use SCSI, and most PCs employ EIDE drives, which can be as large as 100 GBytes per drive. Two other forms of secondary storage are the venerable floppy disk and the optical disk. The modern 3.5-inch floppy (they don't actually flop anymore, since they now come in a hard rather than a soft case), also more than twenty years old, holds only 1.4 MBytes of data and should have been retired long ago. Because of its ubiquity, however, it continues to hang on and is ideal as a boot medium for Beowulf nodes. Largely replacing floppies are the optical CD (compact disk), CD-RW (compact disk-read/write), and DVD (digital versatile disk). The first two hold approximately 600 MBytes of data, with access times of a few milliseconds. (The basic CD is read only, but the CD-RW disks are writable, although at a far slower rate.) Most commercial software and data are now distributed on CDs because they are very cheap to create (actually cheaper than a glossy one-page double-sided commercial flyer). DVD technology also runs on current-generation PCs, providing direct access to movies.

*Packaging* for PCs originally was in the form of the "pizza boxes": low, flat units, usually placed on the desk with a fat monitor sitting on top. Some small early Beowulfs were configured with such packages, usually with as many as eight of these boxes stacked one on top of another. But by the time the first Beowulfs were implemented in 1994, tower cases—vertical floor-standing (or sometimes on the desk next to the video monitor) components—were replacing pizza boxes because of their greater flexibility in configuration and their extensibility (with several heights available). Several generations of Beowulf clusters still are implemented using this low-cost, robust packaging scheme, leading to such expressions as "pile of PCs" and "lots of boxes on shelves" (LOBOS). But the single limitation of this strategy was its low density (only about two dozen boxes could be stored on a floor-to-ceiling set of shelves) and the resulting large footpad of medium- to large-scale Beowulfs. Once the industry recognized the market potential of Beowulf clusters, a new generation of rack-mounted packages was devised and standardized (e.g., 1U, 2U, 3U, and 4U, with 1U boxes having a height of 1.75 inches) so that it is possible to install a single floor-standing rack with as many as 42 processors, coming close to doubling the processing density of such systems. Vendors providing complete turnkey systems as well as hardware system integrators ("bring-your-own software") are almost universally taking this approach. Yet for small systems where cost is critical and simplicity a feature, towers will pervade small labs, offices, and even homes for a long time. (And why not? On those cold winter days, they make great space heaters.)

Beowulf cluster nodes (i.e., PCs) have seen enormous, even explosive, growth over the past seven years since Beowulfs were first introduced in 1994. We note that the entry date for Beowulf was not arbitrary: the level of hardware and software technologies based on the mass market had just (within the previous six months) reached the point that ensembles of them could compete for certain niche applications with the then-well-entrenched MPPs and provide price/performance benefits (in the very best cases) of almost 50 to 1. The new Intel 100 MHz 80486 made it possible to achieve as much as 5 Mflops per node for select computationally intense problems and the cost of 10 Mbps Ethernet network controllers and network hubs had become sufficiently low that their cost permitted them to be employed as dedicated system area networks. Equally important was the availability of the inchoate Linux operating system with the all-important attribute of being free and open source and the availability of a good implementation of the PVM message-passing library. Of course, the Beowulf project had to fill in a lot of the gaps, including writing most of the Ethernet drivers distributed with Linux and other simple tools, such as channel bonding, that facilitated the management of these early modest systems. Since then, the delivered floating-point performance per processor has grown by more than two orders of magnitude while memory capacity has grown by more than a factor of ten. Disk capacities have expanded by as much as 1000X. Thus, Beowulf compute nodes have witnessed an extraordinary evolution in capability. By the end of this decade, node floating-point performance, main memory size, and disk capacity all are expected to grow by another two orders of magnitude.

One aspect of node structure not yet discussed is symmetric multiprocessing. Modern microprocessor design includes mechanisms that permit more than one processor to be combined, sharing the same main memory while retaining full coherence across separate processor caches, thus giving all processors a consistent view of shared data in spite of their local copies in dedicated caches. While large industrial-grade servers may incorporate as many as 512 processors in a single SMP unit, a typical configuration for PC-based SMPs is two or four processors per unit. The ability to share memory with uniform access times should be a source of improved performance at lower cost. But both design and pricing are highly complicated, and the choice is not always obvious. Sometimes the added complexity of SMP design offsets the apparent advantage of sharing many of the node's resources. Also, performance benefits from tight coupling of the processors may be outweighed by the contention for main memory and possible cache thrashing. An added difficulty is attempting to program at the two levels: message passing between nodes and shared memory between processors of the same node. Most users don't bother, choosing to remain with a uniform message-passing model even between processors within the same SMP node.

### 2.2.2 Interconnection Networks

Without the availability of moderate-cost short-haul network technology, Beowulf cluster computing would never have happened. Interestingly, the two leaders in cluster dedicated networks were derived from very different precedent technologies. Ethernet was developed as a local area network for interconnecting distributed single user and community computing resources with shared peripherals and file servers. Myrinet was developed from a base of experience with very tightly coupled processors in MPPs such as the Intel Paragon. Together, Fast and Gigabit Ethernet and Myrinet provide the basis for the majority of Beowulf-class clusters.

A network is a combination of physical transport and control mechanisms associated with a layered hierarchy of message encapsulation. The core concept is the "message." A message is a collection of information organized in a format (order and type) that both the sending and the receiving processes understand and can

correctly interpret. One can think of a message as a movable record. It can be
as short as a few bytes (not including the header information) or as long as many
thousands of bytes. Ordinarily, the sending user application process calls a library
routine that manages the interface between the application and the network. Performing a high-level send operation causes the user message to be packaged with
additional header information and presented to the network kernel driver software.
Additional routing information and additional converges are performed prior to
actually sending the message. The lowest-level hardware then drives the communication channel's lines with the signal, and the network switches route the message
appropriately in accordance with the routing information encoded bits at the header
of the message packet. Upon receipt at the receiving node, the process is reversed
and the message is eventually loaded into the user application name space to be
interpreted by the application code.

The network is characterized primarily in terms of its bandwidth and its latency.
Bandwidth is the rate at which the message bits are transferred, usually cited in
terms of peak throughput as bits per second. Latency is the length of time required
to sends the message. Perhaps a fairer measure is the time from sending to receiving an application process, taking into consideration all of the layers of translation,
conversions, and copying involved. But vendors often quote the shorter time between their network interface controllers. To complicate matters, both bandwidth
and latency are sensitive to message length and message traffic. Longer messages
make better use of network resources and deliver improved network throughput.
Shorter messages reduce transmit, receive, and copy times to provide an overall
lower transfer latency but cause lower effective bandwidth. Higher total network
traffic (i.e., number of messages per unit time) increases overall network throughput, but the resulting contention and the delays they incur result in longer effective
message transfer latency.

More recently, an industrial consortium has developed a new networking model
known as VIA. The goal of this network class is to support a zero-copy protocol,
avoiding the intermediate copying of the message in the operating system space
and permitting direct application-to-application message transfers. The result is
significantly reduced latency of message transfer. Emulex has developed the cLAN
network product, which provides a peak bandwidth in excess of 1 Gbps and for
short messages exhibits a transfer latency on the order of 7 microseconds.

## 2.3   Node Software

A node in a cluster is often (but not always) an autonomous computing entity, complete with its own operating system. Beowulf clusters exploit the sophistication of modern operating systems both for managing the node resources and for communicating with other nodes by means of their interconnection network.

The world's most widely used PC operating system is the family from Microsoft loosely referred to as NT. Over the past decade the series of offerings has culminated in Windows 2000. This full-featured operating system is both low cost and highly robust. It includes virtual memory, multiuser capabilities, multiprocessing, security protection, a powerful graphical user interface, and network control. Windows is the dominant PC operating system in the commercial community and is making rapid inroads into the technical computing community. A number of major supercomputing centers including the Cornell Theory Center and NCSA employ major Windows-based Beowulf clusters.

## 2.4   Resource Management

Except in the most restrictive of cases, matching the requirements of a varied workload and the capabilities of the distributed resources of a Beowulf cluster system demands the support and services of a potentially sophisticated software system for resource management. The earliest Beowulfs were dedicated systems used by (at most) a few people and controlled explicitly, one application at a time. But today's more elaborate Beowulf clusters, possibly comprising hundreds or even thousands of processors and shared by a large community of users, both local and at remote sites, need to balance contending demands and available processing capacity to achieve rapid response for user programs and high throughput of cluster resources. Fortunately, several such software systems are available to provide systems administrators and users alike with a wide choice of policies and mechanisms by which to govern the operation of the system and its allocation to user tasks.

The challenge of managing the large set of compute nodes that constitute a Beowulf cluster involves several tasks to match user-specified workload to existing resources.

**Queuing.** User jobs are submitted to a Beowulf cluster by different people, potentially from separate locations, who are possibly unaware of requirements being imposed on the same system by other users. A queuing system buffers the randomly submitted jobs, entered at different places and times and with varying requirements, until system resources are available to process each of them. Depending on priorities and specific requirements, different distributed queues may be maintained to facilitate optimal scheduling.

**Scheduling.** Perhaps the most complex component of the resource manager, the scheduler has to balance the priorities of each job, with the demands of other jobs, the existing system compute and storage resources, and the governing policies dictated for their use by system administrators. Schedulers need to contend with such varied requirements as large jobs needing all the nodes, small jobs needing only one or at most a few nodes, interactive jobs during which the user must be available and in the loop for such things as real-time visualization of results or performance debugging during program development, or high-priority jobs that must be completed quickly (such as medical imaging). The scheduler determines the order of execution based on these independent priority assessments and the solution to the classic bin-packing problem: What jobs can fit on the machine at the same time?

**Resource Control.** A middleware component, resource control puts the programs on the designated nodes, moves the necessary files to the respective nodes, starts jobs, suspends jobs, terminates jobs, and offloads result files. It notifies the scheduler when resources are available and handles any exception conditions across the set of nodes committed to a given user job.

**Monitoring.** The ongoing status of the Beowulf cluster must be continuously tracked and reported to a central control site such as a master or host node of the system. Such issues as resource availability, task status on each node, and operational health of the nodes must be constantly monitored to aid in the successful management of the total system in serving its incident user demand. Some of this information must continuously update the system operators status presentation, while other statistics and status parameters must be directly employed by the automatic resource management system.

**Accounting.** In order to assess billing or at least to determine remaining user allocation of compute time (often measured in node hours), as well as to assess overall system utilization, availability, and demand response effectiveness, records must be automatically kept of user accounts and system work. This is the primary tool by which system administrators and managers assess effectiveness of scheduling policies, maintenance practices, and user allocations.

While no single resource management system addresses all of these functions optimally for all operational and demand circumstances, several tools have proven useful in operational settings and are available to users and administrators of Beowulf-class cluster systems. An entire chapter is dedicated to each of these in Part III of this book; here they are discussed only briefly.

**Condor** supports distributed job stream resource management emphasizing capacity or throughput computing. Condor schedules independent jobs on cluster nodes to handle large user workloads and provides many options in scheduling policy. This venerable and robust package is particularly well suited for managing both workloads and resources at remote sites.

**PBS** is a widely used system for distributing parallel user jobs across parallel Beowulf cluster resources and providing the necessary administrative tools for professional systems supervision. Both free and commercially supported versions of this system are available, and it is professionally maintained, providing both user and administrator confidence.

**Maui** is an advanced scheduler incorporating sophisticated policies and mechanisms for handling a plethora of user demands and resource states. This package actually sits on top of other lower-level resource managers, providing added capability.

**Cluster Controller** is a fully operational system that manages the Beowulf cluster resources at the Cornell Theory Center, one of the foremost sites applying Windows Beowulf clusters to a broad range of technical computing applications. This system provides all of the basic tools required for managing the resources of a large Beowulf-based computer center, exploiting the advantages of the Windows environment.

## 2.5   Distributed Programming

Exploitation of the potential of Beowulf clusters relies heavily on the development of a broad range of new parallel applications that effectively takes advantage of the parallel system resources to permit larger and more complex problems to be explored in a shorter time. Programming a cluster differs substantially from that of programming a uniprocessor workstation or even an SMP. This difference is in part due to the fact that the sharing of information between nodes of a Beowulf cluster can take a lot longer than between the nodes of a tightly coupled system, because the fragmented memory space reflected by the distributed-memory Beowulfs imposes substantially more overhead than that required by shared-memory systems, and because a Beowulf may have many more nodes than a typical 32-processor SMP. As a consequence, the developer of a parallel application code for a Beowulf must take into consideration these and other sources of performance degradation to achieve effective scalable performance for the computational problem.

A number of different models have been employed for parallel programming and execution, each emphasizing a particular balance of needs and desirable traits. The models differ in part by the nature and degree of abstraction they present to the user of the underlying parallel system. These vary in generality and specificity of control. But one model has emerged as the dominant strategy. This is the "communicating sequential processes" model, more often referred to as the message-passing model. Through this methodology, the programmer partitions the problem's global data among the set of nodes and specifies the processes to be executed on each node, each working primarily on its respective local data partition. Where information from other nodes is required, the user establishes logical paths of communication between cooperating processes on separate nodes. The application program for each process explicitly sends and receives messages passed between itself and one or more other remote processes. A message is a packet of information containing one or more values in an order and format that both processes involved in the exchange understand. Messages are also used for synchronizing concurrent processes in order to coordinate the execution of the parallel tasks on different nodes.

Programmers can use low-level operating system kernel interfaces to the network, such as Winsock or remote procedure calls. Fortunately, however, an easier way exists. Two major message-passing programming systems have been developed to facilitate parallel programming and application development. These are in the form of linkable libraries that can be used in conjunction with conventional languages such as Fortran or C. Benefiting from prior experiences with earlier such tools, PVM has a significant following and has been used to explore a broad range of semantic constructs and distributed mechanisms. PVM was the first programming system to be employed on a Beowulf cluster and its availability was critical to this early work. MPI, the second and more recently distributed programming system, was developed as a product of a communitywide consortium. MPI is the model of choice for the majority of the parallel programming community on Beowulf clusters and other forms of parallel computer as well, even shared-memory machines. There are a number of open and commercial sources of MPI with new developments, especially in the area of parallel I/O, being incorporated in implementations of MPI-2. Together, MPI and PVM represent the bulk of parallel programs being developed around the world, and both languages are represented in this book.

Of course, developing parallel algorithms and writing parallel programs involves a lot more than just memorizing a few added constructs. Entire books have been dedicated to this topic alone (including threein this series), and it is a focus of active research. A detailed and comprehensive discourse of parallel algorithm design is beyond the scope of this book. Instead, we offer specific and detailed examples that provide templates that will satisfy many programming needs. Certainly not exhaustive, these illustrations nonetheless capture many types of problem.

## 2.6   Conclusions

Beowulf cluster computing is a fascinating microcosm of parallel processing, providing hands-on exposure and experience with all aspects of the field, from low-level hardware to high-level parallel algorithm design and everything in between. While many solutions are readily available to provide much of the necessary services required for effective use of Beowulf clusters in many roles and markets, many challenges still remain to realizing the best of the potential of commodity clusters. Research and advanced development is still an important part of the work surrounding clusters, even as they are effectively applied to many real-world workloads. The remainder of this book serves two purposes: it represents the state of the art for those who wish ultimately to extend Beowulf cluster capabilities, and it guides those who wish immediately to apply these existing capabilities to real-world problems.

# 3 Node Hardware

*Thomas Sterling*

Beowulf is a network of nodes, with each node a low-cost personal computer. Its power and simplicity is derived from exploiting the capabilities of the mass-market systems that provide both the processing and the communication. This chapter explores all of the hardware elements related to computation and storage. Communication hardware options will be considered in detail in Chapter 5.

Few technologies in human civilization have experienced such a rate of growth as that of the digital computer and its culmination in the PC. Its low cost, ubiquity, and sometimes trivial application often obscure its complexity and precision as one of the most sophisticated products derived from science and engineering. In a single human lifetime over the fifty-year history of computer development, performance and memory capacity have grown by a factor of almost a million. Where once computers were reserved for the special environments of carefully structured machine rooms, now they are found in almost every office and home. A personal computer today outperforms the world's greatest supercomputers of two decades ago at less than one ten-thousandth the cost. It is the product of this extraordinary legacy that Beowulf harnesses to open new vistas in computation.

Hardware technology changes almost unbelievably rapidly. The specific processors, chip sets, and three-letter acronyms (TLAs) we define today will be obsolete in a very few years. The prices quoted will be out of date before this book reaches bookstore shelves. On the other hand, the organizational design of a PC and the functions of its primary components will last a good deal longer. The relative strengths and weaknesses of components (e.g., disk storage is slower, larger, cheaper and more persistent than main memory) should remain valid for nearly as long. Fortunately, it is now easy to find up-to-date prices on the Web; see Appendix C for some places to start.

This chapter concentrates on the practical issues related to the selection and assembly of the components of a Beowulf node. You can assemble the nodes of the Beowulf yourself, let someone else (a system integrator) do it to your specification, or purchase a turnkey system. In either case, you'll have to make some decisions about the components. Many system integrators cater to a know-nothing market, offering a few basic types of systems, for example, "office" and "home" models with a slightly different mix of hardware and software components. Although these machines would work in a Beowulf, with only a little additional research you can purchase far more appropriate systems for less money. Beowulf systems (at least those we know of) have little need for audio systems, speakers, joysticks, printers, frame grabbers, and the like, many of which are included in the standard "home" or "office" models. High-performance video is unnecessary except for specialized applications where video output is the primary function of the system. Purchasing just the components you need, in the quantity you need, can be a tremendous advantage. Fortunately, customizing your system this way does not mean that you have to assemble the system yourself. Many system integrators, both large and small, will assemble custom systems for little or no price premium. In fact, every system they assemble is from component parts, so a custom system is no more difficult for them than a standard one.

An enormous diversity of choice exists both in type and quantity of components. More than one microprocessor family is available, and within each family are multiple versions. There is flexibility in both the amount and the type of main memory. Disk drives, too, offer a range of interface, speed, capacity, and number. Choices concerning ancillary elements such as floppy disk drives and CD-ROM drives have to be considered. Moreover, the choice of the motherboard and its chip set provide yet another dimension to PC node implementation. This chapter examines each of these issues individually and considers their interrelationships. A step-by-step procedure for the assembly of a processor node is provided to guide the initiate and protect the overconfident.

We reiterate that we make no attempt to offer a complete or exhaustive survey. Far more products are available than can be explicitly presented in any single book, and new products are being offered all the time. In spite of the impossibility of exhaustive coverage, however, the information provided here should contain most of what is required to implement a Beowulf node. Final details can be acquired from documentation provided by the parts vendors.

## 3.1   Overview of a Beowulf Node

The Beowulf node is responsible for all activities and capabilities associated with executing an application program and supporting a sophisticated software environment. These fall into four general categories:

1. instruction execution,
2. high-speed temporary information storage,
3. high-capacity persistent information storage, and
4. communication with the external environment, including other nodes.

The node is responsible for performing a set of designated instructions specified by the application program code or system software. The lowest-level binary encoding of the instructions and the actions they perform are dictated by the microprocessor instruction set architecture (ISA). Both the instructions and the data upon which they act are stored in and loaded from the node's random access memory (RAM). The speed of a processor is often measured in megahertz, indicating that its clock ticks so many million times per second. Unfortunately, data cannot be loaded into or stored in memory at anywhere near the rate necessary to feed a modern microprocessor (1 GHz and higher rates are now common). Thus, the processor often waits for memory, and the overall rate at which programs run is usually governed as much by the memory system as by the processor's clock speed.

Microprocessor designers employ numerous ingenious techniques to deal with the problem of slow memories and fast processors. Usually, a memory hierarchy is incorporated that includes one or more layers of very fast but very small and very expensive cache memories, which hold copies of the contents of the slower but much larger main memory. The order of instruction execution and the access patterns to memory can profoundly affect the performance impact of the small high-speed caches. In addition to holding the application dataset, memory must support the operating system and provide sufficient space to keep the most frequently used functions and system management tables and buffers coresident for best performance.

Except for very carefully designed applications, a program's entire dataset must reside in RAM. The alternative is to use disk storage either explicitly (out-of-core calculations) or implicitly (virtual memory swapping), but this usually entails a severe performance penalty. Thus, the size of a node's memory is an important parameter in system design. It determines the size of problem that can practically be run on the node. Engineering and scientific applications often obey a rule of thumb that says that for every floating-point operation per second, one byte of RAM is necessary. This is a gross approximation at best, and actual requirements can vary by many orders of magnitude, but it provides some guidance; for example, a 1 GHz processor capable of sustaining 200 Mflops should be equipped with approximately 200 MBytes of RAM.

Information stored in RAM is not permanent. When a program finishes execution, the RAM that was assigned to it is recovered by the operating system and reassigned to other programs. The data is not preserved. Thus, if one wishes to permanently store the results of a calculation, or even the program itself, a persistent storage device is needed. Hard disk devices that store data on a rotating magnetic medium are the most common storage device in Beowulf nodes. Data stored on hard disk is persistent even under power failures, a feature that makes the hard disk the preferred location for the operating system and other utilities that are required to restart a machine from scratch. A widely held guideline is that the

local disk capacity be at least ten times the main memory capacity to provide an
adequate area for virtual-memory swap space; more room is required for software
and user-generated data. With the low cost of hard disk, a single drive can provide
this capacity at a small fraction of the overall system cost. An alternative is to provide permanent storage capability off-node, providing access via the system area
network to remote storage resources (e.g., an NFS server on one of the nodes). This
may be a practical solution for small Beowulf systems, but as the system grows, a
single server can easily be overwhelmed.

The results of computational activities performed on a Beowulf node must be
presented to the node's external environment during and after a computation. This
requires communication with peripheral devices such as video monitors, printers,
and external networks. Furthermore, users need access to the system to start jobs
and to monitor and control jobs in progress. System managers may need console
access, the ability to install software distributions on CD-ROMs or other media, or
backup data to tape or other archival storage. The requirements are served by the
I/O subsystem of the node. On today's PCs, these devices usually share the PCI
bus, with some low-performance devices using the older ISA bus. In fact, some
systems no longer have an ISA bus.

In a Beowulf system typically only one or two nodes have extensive I/O capabilities beyond communication on the system area network. All external interaction
is then funneled through these *worldly* nodes. The specific I/O requirements vary
greatly from installation to installation, so a precise specification of the peripherals
attached to a worldly node is impossible. We can, however, make firm recommen-
dations about the I/O requirements of internal or *compute* nodes. The majority of
nodes in a Beowulf system lack the personality of a worldly node. They have one
major I/O requirement, which is to communicate with one another. The hardware
and software involved in interprocessor communication are discussed in Chapters 5
and 6, respectively. For now, we will simply observe that the processor communicates with the network through the network interface controller attached to a
high-speed bus.

### 3.1.1   Principal Specifications

In selecting the proper node configuration for a new Beowulf, the choices can appear
overwhelming. Fortunately, only a small number of critical parameters largely
characterize a particular Beowulf node. These parameters usually relate to a few
peak capabilities or capacities and are only roughly predictive of the performance of
any given application or workload. Nonetheless, they are widely used and provide
a reasonable calibration of the price/performance tradeoff space.

**Processor clock rate** — the frequency (MHz or GHz) of the primary signal within the processor that determines the rate at which instructions are issued

**Peak floating-point performance** — the combination of the clock rate and the number of floating-point operations that can be issued and/or retired per instruction (Mflops)

**Cache size** — the storage capacity (KBytes) of the high-speed buffer memory between the main memory and the processor

**Main memory capacity** — the storage capacity (MBytes) of the primary system node memory in which resides the global dataset of the applications as well as myriad other supporting program, buffering, and argument data

**Disk capacity** — the storage capacity (GBytes) of the permanent secondary storage internal to the processing node

**SAN network port peak bandwidth** — the bandwidth (Mbps) of the network control card and system area network communication channel medium

Other parameters that are sometimes of interest are the number of processors included in symmetric multiprocessing configurations, memory latency and bandwidth, measured performance of various benchmarks, and seek and access times to disks.

### 3.1.2 Basic Elements

The general Beowulf node is a complex organization of multiple subsystems that support the requirements for computation, communication, and storage discussed above. Figure 3.1 shows a block diagram of a node architecture representative of the general structures found in today's PCs adapted to the purpose of Beowulf-class computing.

**Microprocessor** — all of the logic required to perform instruction execution, memory management and address translation, integer and floating-point operations, and cache management. Processor clock speeds can be as low as 100 MHz found on previous-generation Intel Pentium processors to as high as 1.7 GHz on the Intel Pentium 4 with an 800 MHz Pentium 3 representing near the sweet spot in price/performance.

**Cache** — a small but fast buffer for keeping recently used data. Cache provides the illusion of a much higher-speed memory than is actually available. Multiple

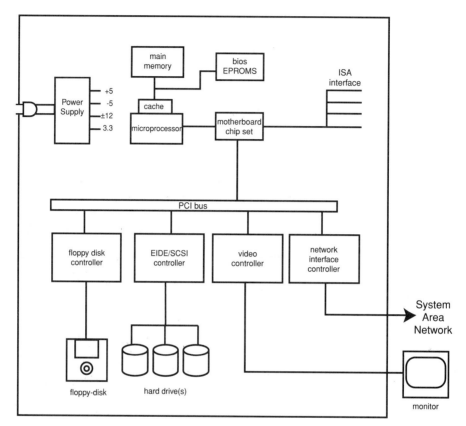

**Figure 3.1**
Block diagram of a typical Beowulf node. Some additional components, e.g., keyboard, mouse, additional network interfaces, graphics adaptors, CD-ROM drive, will be necessary on nodes responsible for I/O services.

layers of cache may be employed; 16 KBytes of Level 1 (L1) and 256 KBytes of Level 2 (L2) cache are common. The effect of cache can be dramatic, but not all programs will benefit. Memory systems are so complex that often the only reliable way to determine the effectiveness of cache for a given application is to test the application on machines with different amounts of cache.

**Main memory** — high-density storage with rapid read/write access. Typical access times of 70 nanoseconds can be found with DIMM memory modules with memory capacities between 64 MBytes and 512 MBytes. This memory is often optimized for throughput, delivering successive data items every 10 nanoseconds or less after an initial setup step.

**EIDE/SCSI disk controller** — a sophisticated unit that manages the operation of the hard disk and CD-ROM drives, buffers data blocks, and controls the transfer of data directly to or from main memory.

**Hard drive** — persistent storage, even after processor power cycling, and backing store to the main memory for problems requiring datasets larger than the main memory can hold. Disk capacities range from 1 GByte to over 100, but the most common and cost effective sizes today are between 20 and 80 GBytes. Hard disks conform to either the EIDE or SCSI interface standards. Access times of a few milliseconds are usual for these electromechanical rotating magnetic storage devices.

**Floppy disk controller** — a very low cost and low capacity storage medium of nominally 1.4 MBytes capacity (double sizes are available). Floppies are used primarily at boot time to install a minimal system capable of bootstrapping itself into a full configuration. Access times are long, and the small capacity makes them unsuitable for other data storage roles. Nevertheless, their historical role as a boot medium makes them a valuable part of every Beowulf node.

**Motherboard chip set** — a sophisticated special-purpose controller that manages and coordinates the interactions of the various components of the PC through PCI, USB, and other interfaces. It plays an important role in memory management, especially for symmetric multiprocessors where cache coherence is maintained through snooping cache protocols.

**BIOS ROM memory** — the minimum set of functional binary routines needed to perform rudimentary functionality of the motherboard and its interfaces, including bootstrap and diagnostic functions. Modern systems include writable BIOS EEPROMs (electronically erasable, programmable ROMs) that can have their contents directly upgraded from newer versions of the BIOS programs with replacement on the actual chips.

**PCI bus** — the universal industry standard for high-speed controllers. The common PCI bus operates a 32-bit data path at 33 MHz; PCI buses with 64-bit data paths at 66 MHz are also available.

**Video controller** — a card that converts digital signals from the processor into analog signals suitable for driving a video display. Modern high-end video cards contain powerful on-board processors and often have many megabytes of memory and sophisticated programmable interfaces. Such a card might be appropriate for an I/O or interactive node intended to drive a high-resolution monitor for data visualization and interactive display. Other Beowulf nodes, however, have little need for video output. Indeed, were it were not for the fact that most BIOS software will not boot without a video card, such cards would be unnecessary on the majority of Beowulf nodes. Video cards are available with either PCI or AGP connections.

**Network interface controller** — an interface that provide communication access to the node's external environment. One or more such interfaces couple the node to the Beowulf's system area network. A second network interface card (not shown) on a worldly node can provide the link between the entire Beowulf machine and the local area network that connects it to other resources in the user's environment, such as file servers, printers, terminals, and the Internet.

**Power supply** — not part of the logical system, but an important component to the overall operation. It provides regulated output voltages of 5 volts, −5 volts, 12 volts, and −12 volts to support system operation. Power supplies are rated in watts and have a general range of between 200 and 400 watts per node.

**Cooling systems** — typically a fan mounted on the CPU carrier itself, for dissipating heat from the processor. Other fans cool the rest of a node. Because fans are mechanical devices, they are among the most likely components to fail in a Beowulf cluster.

## 3.2   Processors

The microprocessor is the critical computational component of the PC-based node and Beowulf-class systems. In the seven-year period since the first Beowulf was completed in early 1994, central processing unit (CPU) clock speed has increased by a factor of 16. More impressive is the single-node floating-point performance sustained on scientific and engineering problems which has improved by two orders of magnitude during the same period. A single PC today outperforms the entire 16-processor first-generation Beowulf of 1994.

With the proliferation of Linux ports to a wide array of processors, Beowulf-like clusters are being assembled with almost every conceivable processor type. Primary attention has been given to Intel processors and their binary compatible siblings from AMD. The Compaq Alpha family of processors has also been effectively applied in this arena. Compaq has recently announced that development of the Alpha family will continue only through 2003, with Compaq contributing the Alpha technology to the development of future Intel IA64 processors.

This section presents a brief description of the most likely candidates of microprocessors for future Beowulf-class systems. The choice is constrained by three factors: performance, cost, and software compatibility. Raw performance is important to building effective medium- and high-end parallel systems. To build an effective parallel computer, you should start with the best uniprocessor. Of course, this tendency must be tempered by cost. The overall price/performance ratio for your favorite application is probably the most important consideration. The highest performance processor at any point in time rarely has the best price/performance ratio. Usually it is the processor one generation or one-half generation behind the cutting edge that is available with the most attractive ratio of price to performance. Recently, however, the Compaq Alpha has delivered both best performance and best price/performance for many applications. The third factor of software compatibility is an important practical consideration. If a stable software environment is not available for a particular processor family, even if it is a technical pacesetter, it is probably inappropriate for Beowulf. Some key features of current processors are summarized in Table 3.1.

### 3.2.1   Intel Pentium Family

The Pentium 4 implements the IA32 instruction set but uses an internal architecture that diverges substantially from the old P6 architecture. The internal architecture is geared for high clock speeds; it produces less computing power per clock cycle but is capable of extremely high frequencies.

The Pentium III is based on the older Pentium Pro architecture. It is a minor upgrade from the Pentium II; it includes another optimized instruction set called SSE for three-dimensional instructions and has moved the L2 cache onto the chip, making it synchronized with the processor's clock. The Pentium III can be used within an SMP node with two processors; a more expensive variant, the Pentium III Xeon, can be used in four-processor SMP nodes.

### 3.2.2   AMD Athlon

The AMD Athlon platform is similar to the Pentium III in its processor architecture but similar to the Compaq Alpha in its bus architecture. It has two large 64 KByte L1 caches and a 256 KByte L2 cache that runs at the processor's clock speed. The performance is a little ahead of the Pentium III in general, but either can be faster

| Chip | Vendor | Speed (MHz) | L1 Cache Size I/D (KBytes) | L2 Cache Size (KBytes) |
|---|---|---|---|---|
| Pentium III | Intel | 1000 | 16K/16K | 256K |
| Pentium 4 | Intel | 1700 | 12K/8K | 256K |
| Itanium | Intel | 800 | 16K/16K | 96K |
| Athlon | AMD | 1330 | 64K/64K | 256K |
| Alpha 21264B | Compaq | 833 | 64K | 64K |

**Table 3.1**
Key features of selected processors, mid-2001.

(at the same clock frequency) depending on the application. The Athlon supports dual-processor SMP nodes.

### 3.2.3  Compaq Alpha 21264

The Compaq Alpha processor is a true 64-bit architecture. For many years, the Alpha held the lead in many benchmarks, including the SPEC benchmarks, and was used in many of the fastest supercomputers, including the Cray T3D and T3E, as well as the Compaq SC family.

The Alpha uses a Reduced Instruction Set Computer (RISC) architecture, distinguishing it from Intel's Pentium processors. RISC designs, which have dominated the workstation market of the past decade, eschew complex instructions and addressing modes, resulting in simpler processors running at higher clock rates, but executing somewhat more instructions to complete the same task.

### 3.2.4  IA64

The IA64 is Intel's first 64-bit architecture. This is an all-new design, with a new instruction set, new cache design, and new floating-point processor design. With clock rates approaching 1 GHz and multiway floating-point instruction issue, Itanium should be the first implementation to provide between 1 and 2 Gflops peak performance. The first systems with the Itanium processor were released in the middle of 2001 and have delivered impressive results. For example, the HP Server rx4610, using a single 800 MHz Itanium, delivered a SPECfp2000 of 701, comparable to recent Alpha-based systems. The IA64 architecture does, however, require significant help from the compiler to exploit what Intel calls EPIC (explicitly parallel instruction computing).

## 3.3  Motherboard

The motherboard is a printed circuit board that contains most of the active electronic components of the PC node and their interconnection. The motherboard provides the logical and physical infrastructure for integrating the subsystems of the Beowulf PC node and determines the set of components that may be used. The motherboard defines the functionality of the node, the range of performance that can be exploited, the maximum capacities of its storage, and the number of subsystems that can be interconnected. With the exception of the microprocessor itself, the selection of the motherboard is the most important decision in determining the qualities of the PC node to be used as the building block of the Beowulf-class system. It is certainly the single most obvious piece of the Beowulf node other than the case or packaging in which it is enclosed.

While the motherboard may not be the most interesting aspect of a computer, it is, in fact, a critical component. Assembling a Beowulf node primarily involves the insertion of modules into their respective interface sockets, plugging power and signal cables into their ports, and placing configuration jumpers across the designated posts. The troubleshooting of nonfunctioning systems begins with verification of these same elements associated with the motherboard.

The purpose of the motherboard is to integrate all of the electronics of the node in a robust and configurable package. Sockets and connectors on the motherboard include the following:

- Microprocessor(s)
- Memory
- Peripheral controllers on the PCI bus
- AGP port
- Floppy disk cables
- EIDE cables for hard disk and CD-ROM
- Power
- Front panel LEDs, speakers, switches, etc.
- External I/O for mouse, keyboard, joystick, serial line, USB, etc.

Other chips on the motherboard provide

- the system bus that links the processor(s) to memory,
- the interface between the peripheral buses and the system bus, and
- programmable read-only memory (PROM) containing the BIOS software.

The motherboard restricts as well as enables functionality. In selecting a motherboard as the basis for a Beowulf node, several requirements for its use should be considered, including

- processor family,
- processor clock speed,
- number of processors,
- memory capacity,
- memory type,
- disk interface,
- required interface slots, and
- number of interface buses (32- and 64-bit PCI).

Currently the choice of processor is likely to be the Intel Pentium III, AMD Athlon, or the Compaq Alpha 21264B. More processors, including native 64-bit processors, will continue to be released. In most cases, a different motherboard is required for each choice. Clock speeds for processors of interest range from 733 MHz to almost 2 GHz, and the selected motherboard must support the desired speed. Motherboards containing multiple processors in symmetric multiprocessor configurations are available, adding to the diversity of choices. Nodes for compute intensive problems often require large memory capacity with high bandwidth. Motherboards have a limited number of memory slots, and memory modules have a maximum size. Together, these will determine the memory capacity of your system. Memory bandwidth is a product of the width and speed of the system memory bus.

Several types of memory are available, including conventional DRAM, EDO RAM (extended data output RAM), SDRAM (synchronous DRAM), and RDRAM (Rambus DRAM). The choice of memory type depends on your application needs. While RDRAM currently provides the highest bandwidth, other types of memory, such as SDRAM and DDR SDRAM (double data rate SDRAM) can provide adequate bandwidth at a significantly reduced cost. The two disk interfaces in common use are EIDE and SCSI. Both are good with the former somewhat cheaper and the latter slightly faster under certain conditions. Most motherboards come with EIDE interfaces built in, and some include an SCSI interface as well, which can be convenient and cost effective if you choose to use SCSI. On the other hand, separate SCSI controllers may offer more flexibility and options. Motherboards have a fixed number of PCI slots, and it is important to select one with enough slots to meet your needs. This is rarely a consideration in Beowulf compute nodes but can become an issue in a system providing I/O services.

## 3.4  Memory

The memory system of a personal computer stores the data upon which the processor operates. We would like a memory system to be fast, cheap, and large, but available components can simultaneously deliver only two (any two) of the three. Modern memory systems use a hierarchy of components implemented with different technologies that together, under favorable conditions, achieve all three. When purchasing a computer system, you must select the size and type of memory to be used. This section provides some background to help with that choice.

### 3.4.1  Memory Capacity

Along with processor speed, memory capacity has grown at a phenomenal rate, quadrupling in size approximately every three years. Prices for RAM have continued to decline and now are about ten cents per megabyte (a little more for higher-speed/capacity SDRAMs). A general principle is that faster processors require more memory. With increasingly sophisticated and demanding operating systems, user interfaces, and advanced applications such as multimedia, there is demand for ever-increasing memory capacity. As a result of both demand and availability, the size of memory in Beowulf-class systems has progressively expanded. Today, a typical Beowulf requires at least 256 MBytes of main memory, and this can be expected to grow to 2 GBytes within the next two to three years.

### 3.4.2  Memory Speed

In addition to the capacity of memory, the memory speed can significantly affect the overall behavior and performance of a Beowulf node. Speed may be judged by the latency of memory access time and the throughput of data provided per unit time. While capacities have steadily increased, access times have progressed only slowly. However, new modes of interfacing memory technology to the processor managed system bus have significantly increased overall throughput of memory systems. This increase is due to the fact that the memory bandwidth internal to the memory chip is far greater than that delivered to the system bus at its pins. Significant advances in delivering these internal acquired bits to the system bus in rapid succession have been manifest in such memory types as EDO-DRAM, SDRAM, and Rambus DRAM. Further improvement to the apparent performance of the entire memory system as viewed by the processor comes from mixing small memories of fast technology with high-capacity memory of slower technology.

### 3.4.3  Memory Types

Semiconductor memory is available in two fundamental types. Static random access memory (SRAM) is high speed but moderate density, while dynamic random access memory (DRAM) provides high-density storage but operates more slowly. Each plays an important role in the memory system of the Beowulf node.

**SRAM**  is implemented from bit cells fabricated as multitransistor flipflop circuits. These active circuits can switch state and be accessed quickly. They are not as high density as are DRAMs and consume substantially more power. They are reserved for those parts of the system principally requiring high speed and are employed regularly in L1 and L2 caches. Current-generation processors usually include SRAMs directly on the processor chip. L2 caches may be installed on the motherboard of the system or included as part of the processor module.

Earlier SRAM was asynchronous (ASRAM) and provided access times of between 12 and 20 nanoseconds. Motherboards operating up to 66 MHz or better use synchronous burst SRAM (SBSRAM) providing access times on the order of ten nanoseconds.

**DRAM**  is implemented from bit cells fabricated as a capacitor and a single bypass transistor. The capacitor stores a charge passively. The associated switching transistor deposits the state of the capacitor's charge on the chip's internal memory bus when the cell is addressed. Unlike SRAM, reading a DRAM cell is destructive, so after a bit is accessed, the charged state has to be restored by recharging the capacitor to its former condition. As a consequence, DRAM can have a shorter access time (the time taken to read a cell) than cycle time (the time until the same cell may be accessed again). Also, isolation of the cell's storage capacitor is imperfect and the charge leaks away, requiring it to be refreshed (rewritten) every few milliseconds. Finally, because the capacitor is a passive, nonamplifying device, it takes longer to access a DRAM than an SRAM cell. However, the benefits are substantial. DRAM density can exceed ten times that of SRAM, and its power consumption is much lower. Also, new techniques for moving data from the DRAM internal memory row buffers to the system bus have narrowed the gap in terms of memory bandwidth between DRAM and SRAM. As a result, main memory for all Beowulf nodes is provided by DRAM in any one of its many forms.

Of the many forms of DRAM, the two most likely to be encountered in Beowulf nodes are EDO DRAM and SDRAM. Both are intended to increase memory throughput. EDO DRAM provides a modified internal buffering scheme that maintains data at the output pins longer than conventional DRAM, improving memory data transfer rates. While many current motherboards support EDO DRAM, the higher-speed systems likely to be used as Beowulf nodes in the immediate future will employ SDRAM instead. SDRAM is a significant advance in memory interface design. It supports a pipeline burst mode that permits a second access cycle to begin before the previous one has completed. While one cycle is putting output data on the bus, the address for the next access cycle is simultaneously applied to the memory. Effective access speeds of 10 nanoseconds can be achieved with systems using a 100 MHz systems bus; such memory is labeled PC100 SDRAM. Faster versions are available, including PC133 SDRAM.

Other, even higher-performance forms of DRAM memory are appearing. Two of the most important are Rambus DRAM and DDR SDRAM. These may be described as "PC1600" or "PC2100" memory. These are not 16 or 21 times as fast as PC100; in these cases, the number refers to the peak transfer rate (in Mbps) rather than the system bus clock speed. It is important to match both the memory type (e.g., SDRAM or RDRAM) and the system bus speed (e.g., PC133) to the motherboard.

### 3.4.4  Memory Hierarchy and Caches

The modern memory system is a hierarchy of memory types. Figure 3.2 shows a typical memory hierarchy. Near the processor at the top of the memory system are the high-speed Level-1 (L1) caches. Usually a separate cache is used for data and instructions for high bandwidth to load both data and instructions into the processor on the same cycle. The principal requirement is to deliver the data and instruction words needed for processing on every processor cycle. These memories run fast and hot, are relatively expensive, and now often incorporated directly on the processor chip. For these reasons, they tend to be very small, with a typical size of 16 KBytes. Because L1 caches are so small and the main memory requires long access times, modern architectures usually include a second-level (L2) cache to hold both data and instructions. Access time to acquire a block of L2 data may take several processor cycles. A typical L2 cache size is 256 KBytes. Some systems add large external caches (either L2 or L3) with sizes of up to 8 MBytes.

Cache memory is usually implemented in SRAM technology, which is fast (a few nanoseconds) but relatively low density. Only when a datum required by the processor is not in cache does the processor directly access the main memory. Main memory is implemented in one of the DRAM technologies. Beowulf nodes will often include between 256 MBytes and 512 MBytes of SDRAM memory.

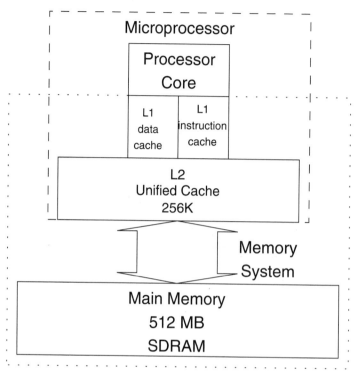

**Figure 3.2**
A node memory hierarchy with sizes typical of Beowulf nodes in 2001.

### 3.4.5  Package Styles

The packaging of memory has evolved along with the personal computers in which they were installed and has converged on a few industrywide standards. Dual Inline Memory Modules (DIMMs) are the primary means of packaging DRAMs, and most modern motherboards use one or more of these forms. The most common form factors are 168-pin and 184-pin DIMMs.

## 3.5  BIOS

Even with effective industrywide standardization, hardware components will differ in detail. In order to avoid the necessity of customizing a different operating system for each new hardware system, a set of low-level service routines is provided, incorporated into read-only memory on the motherboard. This basic I/O system

(BIOS) software is a logical interface to the hardware, giving a layer of abstraction that facilitates and makes robust higher-level support software. Besides the system BIOS that is hardwired to the motherboard, additional BIOS ROMs may be provided with specific hardware peripherals. These include the video BIOS, the drive controller BIOS, the network interface controller BIOS, and the SCSI drive controller BIOS. The BIOS contains a large number of small routines organized in three groups: startup or POST (for power-on self-test), setup, and system services.

The POST startup BIOS routines manage initialization activities, including running diagnostics, setting up the motherboard chip set, organizing scratchpad memory for the BIOS data area (BDA), identifying optional equipment and their respective BIOS ROMs, and then bootstrapping the operating system. The CMOS (complementary metal oxide semiconductor) setup routine provides access to the system configuration information, which is stored in a small CMOS RAM. The system services routines are called through interrupts directly from hardware on the motherboard, from the processor itself, or from software. They allow access to low-level services provided by the system including the CPU, memory, motherboard chip set, integrated drive electronics, PCI, USB, boot drives, plug-n-play capability, and power control interfaces.

## 3.6   Secondary Storage

With the exception of the BIOS ROM, all information in memory is lost during power cycling except for that provided by a set of external (to the motherboard) devices that fall under the category of secondary storage. Of these, disk drives, floppy drives, and CD-ROM drives are most frequently found on Beowulf nodes. Disk and floppy drives are spinning magnetic media, while CD-ROM drives (which are also spinning media) use optical storage to hold approximately 650 MBytes of data. The newer DVD technology is replacing CD-ROMs with greater storage capacity. Besides persistence of storage, secondary storage is characterized by very high capacity and low cost per bit. While DRAM may be purchased at about ten cents per megabyte, disk storage costs less than half a cent per megabyte, and the price continues to fall. For the particular case of Beowulf, these three modes of secondary storage play very different roles.

CD-ROMs provide an easy means of installing large software systems but are used for little else. Even for this purpose, only one or two nodes in a system are likely to include a CD-ROM drive because installation of software on most of the nodes is performed over the system area network.

Floppy discs are fragile and slow and don't hold very much data (about 1.44 MBytes). They would be useless except that they were the primary means of persistent storage on early PCs, and PC designers have maintained backward compatibility that allows systems to boot from a program located on floppy disk. Occasionally, something goes terribly wrong with a node (due either to human or to system error), and it is necessary to restore the system from scratch. A floppy drive and an appropriate "boot floppy" can make this a quick, painless, and trouble-free procedure. Although other means of recovery are possible, the small price of about $15 per node for a floppy drive is well worth the investment.

The hard drive serves three primary purposes. It maintains copies of system wide programs and data so that these do not have to be repeatedly acquired over the network. It provides a large buffer space to hold very large application datasets. And it provides storage space for demand paging as part of the virtual memory management system. When the user or system memory demands exceed the available primary memory, page blocks can be automatically migrated to hard disk, making room in memory for other information to be stored.

Between the hard disk drive and the motherboard are two dominant interface types: EIDE and SCSI. The earlier IDE interface evolved from the PC industry, while SCSI was a product of the workstation and server industry. Today, both are available. In the past, SCSI performance and cost were both significantly greater than those of IDE. The EIDE standard closed the performance gap a few years ago, but the price difference still exists. Perhaps equally important is that many motherboards now include EIDE interfaces as integral components so that no separate control card is required to be purchased or to take up a PCI socket. SCSI drive capacities can run a little higher than IDE drives, a factor that may be important for some installations. Several different SCSI standards exist, including Wide, UltraWide, SCSI-2, and SCSI-3. Systems are usually downwards compatible, but it is safest to match the drive's capabilities with that of your SCSI controller. Beowulf-class systems have been implemented with both types, and your needs or preferences should dictate your choice. (We have continued to rely on EIDE drives because of their lower cost.)

The primary performance characteristic of a hard drive is its capacity. EIDE hard drives with 80 GByte capacities are available for under $300, and 40 GByte drives cost around $100. Also of interest is the rotation speed, measured in revolutions per minute, which governs how quickly data can be accessed. The fastest rotation speeds are found on SCSI drives, and are now around 15000 rpm and deliver transfer rates in excess of 50 MBytes per second.

## 3.7   PCI Bus

While the PC motherboard determines many of the attributes of the PC node, it also provides a means for user-defined configuration through the Peripheral Component Interconnect. This interface is incorporated as part of virtually every modern motherboard, providing a widely recognized standard for designing separate functional units. PCI is replacing the ISA and EISA buses as the principal means of adding peripherals to personal computers.

The PCI standard permits rapid data transfer of 132 MBytes per second peak using a 33 MHz clock and 32-bit data path. A 64-bit extension is defined, enabling peak throughput of 264 MBytes per second when used. A extension with a bus clock rate of 66 MHz provides a peak transfer bandwidth of 528 MBytes per second. A new version, PCI-X, is expected toward the end of 2001.

The PCI bus permits direct interconnection between any pair of PCI devices, between a PCI device and the system memory, or between the system processor and the PCI devices. PCI supports multiple bus masters, allowing any PCI device to take ownership of the bus and permitting (among other things) direct memory access transfers without processor intervention. Arbitration among the pending PCI masters for the next transfer action can be overlapped with the current PCI bus operation, thereby hiding the arbitration latency and ensuring high sustained bus throughput.

High throughput is enabled by a process called linear burst transfer. A block of data being sent from one device to another on the PCI bus is moved without having to send the address of each word of data. Instead, the length of the block is specified along with the initial address of the location where the block is to be moved. Each time a word is received, the accepting unit increments a local address register in preparation for the next word of the block. PCI bus transfers can be conducted concurrently with operation of the processor and its system bus to avoid processor delays caused by PCI operation.

Although bus loading limits the number of PCI sockets to three or four, each connected board can logically represent as many as eight separate PCI functions for a total of 32. Up to 256 PCI buses can be incorporated into one system, although rarely are more than two present.

The PCI standard includes complete bit-level specification of configuration registers. This makes possible the automatic configuration of connected peripheral devices for plug-n-play reconfigurability.

## 3.8   Example of a Beowulf Node

The majority of Beowulfs (over five generations of systems in the past seven years) have employed microprocessors from Intel or AMD. This is because they have been among the least expensive systems to build, the system architectures are open providing a wealth of component choices, and the Linux operating system was first available on them. While not the fastest processors in peak performance, their overall capability has been good, and their price/performance ratios are excellent. The most recent microprocessors in this family and their motherboards support clock speeds of over 1 GHz.

The following table shows a snapshot of current costs for an AMD Athlon-based node and illustrates the amazing value of commodity components. These prices were taken from a variety of sources, including online retailers and Web pages about recent Beowulf clusters. We note that, as discussed earlier, a CD-ROM is not included in the list because it is assumed that system installation will be performed over the network. A floppy drive is included to facilitate initial installation and crash recovery. Moreover, since the BIOS requires a video card to boot, a very inexpensive one is included on every system.

Many other choices exist, of course, and the products of other vendors in many cases are as worthy of consideration as the ones listed here.

| | | |
|---|---|---|
| Processor | AMD Athlon 1GHz | $102 |
| Processor Fan | | $8.50 |
| Motherboard | Generic | $117.50 |
| Memory | 512 MB PC100 SDRAM | $74 |
| Hard Disk | 40GB | $141 |
| Floppy Disk | Sony 1.44MB | $13.50 |
| Network Interface Controller | 100Mb/s Ethernet | $16.50 |
| Video Card | Generic VGA | $25 |
| Package | Generic tower case with power supply and cables | $58 |
| Total | | $556 |

## 3.9   Boxes, Shelves, Piles, and Racks

A review of Beowulf hardware would be incomplete without some mention of the technology used to physically support (i.e., keep it off the floor) a Beowulf system. Packaging is an important engineering domain that can significantly influence the cost and practical aspects of Beowulf implementation and operation. Packaging of Beowulfs has taken two paths: the minimalist "lots of boxes on shelves" strategy, captured so well by the acronym of the NIH LOBOS system, and the "looks count" strategy, adopted by several projects including the Hive system at NASA Goddard Space Flight Center and the Japanese Real World Computing Initiative. The minimalist approach was driven by more than laziness. It is certainly the most economical approach and is remarkably reliable as well. This is due to the same economies of scale that enable the other low-cost, high-reliability subsystems in Beowulf. In the minimalist approach, individual nodes are packaged in exactly the same "towers" that are found deskside in homes and offices. These towers incorporate power supplies, fan cooling, and cabling and cost less than a hundred dollars. Towers provide uniform configuration, standardized interface cabling, effective cooling, and a structurally robust component mounting framework but are flexible enough to support a variety of internal node configurations. Industrial-grade shelving, usually of steel framework and particle board shelves, is strong, readily available, easily assembled, and inexpensive. It is also flexible, extensible, and easily reconfigured. You can find it at your nearest home and garden center.

When assembling such a system, care should be taken to design tidy power distribution and networking wire runs. Extension cords and power strips work fine but should be physically attached to the shelving with screws or wire-ties so that the system does not become an unmaintainable mess. Similar considerations apply to the Ethernet cables. Labeling cables so the ends can be identified without laboriously tracing the entire run can save hours of headache.

Different approaches are possible for video and keyboard cables. In our systems, most nodes do not have dedicated keyboard and video cables. Instead, we manually attach cables to nodes in the very rare circumstances when necessary maintenance cannot be carried out remotely.

Rack mounting is considerably more expensive but offers the possibility of much higher physical densities. New motherboards with rack-mountable form factors that incorporate a Fast Ethernet controller, SCSI controller, and video controller offer the possibility of building Beowulf nodes that can be packaged very tightly because they don't require additional daughter cards. These systems probably will be important in the future, as larger Beowulf systems are deployed and machine room space becomes a major consideration.

## 3.10   Node Assembly

We conclude this chapter with a checklist for building a Beowulf node. Building Beowulf nodes from component parts may not be the right choice for everyone. Some will feel more comfortable with systems purchased from a system integrator, or they simply won't have the manpower or space for in-house assembly. Nevertheless, the cost should not be overlooked; a node can be several hundred dollars. You should carefully weigh the luxury of having someone else wield the screwdriver vs. owning 25 percent more computer power. Keep in mind that cables often come loose in shipping, and there is no guarantee that the preassembled system will not require as much or more on-site troubleshooting as the homemade system.

Although targeted at the reader who is building a Beowulf node from parts, this checklist will also be useful to those who purchase preassembled systems. Over the lifetime of the Beowulf system, technology advances will probably motivate upgrades in such things as memory capacity, disk storage, or improved networking. There is also the unavoidable problem of occasional maintenance. Yes, once in a while, something breaks. Usually it is a fan, a memory module, a power supply, or a disk drive, in that order of likelihood. More often than not, such a break will occur in the first few weeks of operation. With hundreds of operational nodes in a large Beowulf, some parts replacement will be required. The checklist below will get you started if you decide to replace parts of a malfunctioning node.

To many, the list below will appear obvious, but, in fact, experience has shown that a comprehensive list of steps is not only convenient but likely to simplify the task and aid in getting a system working the first time. Many sites have put together such procedures, and we offer the one used at Caltech as a helpful example.

Before you initiate the actual assembly, it helps to get organized. Five minutes of preparation can save half an hour during the process. If you're assembling a Beowulf, you will probably build more than one unit at one time, and the preparation phase is amortized over the number of units built.

- Collect and organize the small set of tools you will be using:
  - #2 Phillips head screwdriver
  - Antistatic wrist strap
  - Antistatic mat on which to place assembly
  - Needlenose pliers
  - 1/8-inch blade flat blade screwdriver
  - Small high-intensity flashlight

- Organize all parts to be assembled. If more than one unit is to be built, collect like parts together bin-style.
- Provide sufficient flat space for assembly, including room for keyboard, mouse, and monitor used for initial check-out.
- Work in a well-lighted environment.
- Follow the same order of tasks in assembling all units; routine leads to reliability.
- Have a checklist, like this one, handy, even if it is used only as a reference.
- When first opening a case, collect screws and other small items in separate containers.
- Keep food and drink on another table to avoid the inevitable accident.

After you have done one or two systems, the process becomes much quicker. We find that we can assemble nodes in well under an hour once we become familiar with the idiosyncrasies of any particular configuration.

Many of the instructions below may not apply in every case. Included are directions for such subassemblies as monitors, keyboards, and sound cards that rarely show up in the majority of Beowulf nodes. Usually, however, at least one such node is more heavily equipped to support user interface, operations support, and external connections for the rest of the system.

In a number of cases, the specific action is highly dependent on the subsystems being included. Only the documentation for that unit can describe exactly what actions are to be performed. For example, every motherboard will have a different set and positioning of jumpers, although many of the modern boards are reducing or almost eliminating these. In these instances, all we can say is: "do the right thing," but we still indicate in general terms the class of action to take place.

### 3.10.1   Motherboard Preassembly

- Set every jumper on the motherboard properly.
- Look through your motherboard manual and verify every setting, since the default may not work for your CPU, memory, or cache configuration.
- Locate every jumper and connector: floppy, hard drive, PS/2, COM port, LPT port, sound connectors, speaker connector, hard disk LED, power LED, reset switch, keyboard lock switch, and so forth.
- Install the CPU.
  - Processors are designed so that they can only be inserted correctly. Don't force.
  - Whatever the chip, match the notched corner of the CPU with the notched corner of the socket.

- When using a ZIF socket, lift the handle 90 degrees, insert the CPU, and then return the handle back to its locked position.
- Install the memory.
  - Main memory DIMM. Note pin 1 on the DIMM, and find the pin 1 mark on the motherboard. It is difficult to install 164-pin DIMMs incorrectly, but it is possible. Begin by placing the DIMM at a 45 degree angle to the socket of bank 0. The DIMM will be angled toward the rest of the DIMM sockets (and away from any DIMMs previously installed). Insert the DIMM firmly into the socket; then rotate the DIMM until it sits perpendicular to the motherboard and the two clips on each edge have snapped around the little circuit board. There may or may not be a "snap," but you should verify that the two clips are holding the DIMM fast and that it doesn't jiggle in the socket. Repeat this until you fill one, two, or more banks.
  - Cache memory (if so equipped). Some older units may have L2 caches on the motherboard, while newer processors include them within the processor module. Cache memory may be DIMM or SIMM; in any case, install it now.

### 3.10.2   The Case

- Open the case, remove all the internal drive bays, and locate all the connectors: speaker, hard disk LED, power LED, reset switch, keyboard lock switch, mother board power, peripheral power, and so forth.
- Mount the motherboard in the case.
  - ATX-style cases use only screws to mount the motherboard, and it is very straightforward.
- Plug in the keyboard, and see whether it fits.
- Plug in an adapter card, and see whether it fits.
- Start connecting the case cables to the motherboard.
  - Pull out floppy cables, hard disk cables, PS/2 mouse cable, and lights. Line up each pin 1 to the red side of cables.
  - Install the speaker. It usually is a 4-pin connector with two wires (one red, one black, which can be installed either way on the motherboard).
  - If your case has holes for COM ports and LPT ports, punch these out, and save a card slot by unscrewing the connectors that came on the slot-filler strip of metal, removing the connector, and mounting it directly on the case.
  - Attach power cables to the motherboard.
    - ATX-style cases have only one power connector, which is keyed to only fit one way.

- The AT-style power connector comes in two pieces and must be connected properly. The black wires *must be placed together* when they are plugged into the motherboard.
- Ensure that the CPU cooling fan is connected to the power supply. This is usually a 4-pin male connector that goes to one of the power supply connectors.

### 3.10.3  Minimal Peripherals

- Floppy disk drive
  - Mechanical
    - It may be necessary to reinstall the floppy mounting bay (if it was taken out previously).
    - The floppy drive must protrude from the front of the case. Take off one of the 3.5 inch plastic filler panels from the front of the case. Then slide the floppy drive in from the front until the front of the drive is flush with the front of the case. Using two small screws that are supplied with the case, attach the floppy drive's left side. If the floppy drive bay is detachable, remove the bay with the floppy half installed, and with the drive bay out, install the screws for the right side.
    - If the drive bay is going to contain hard disks in addition to floppy drives, leave the drive bay out for now, and go to the hard disk installation section before putting the drive bay back into the case.
  - Electrical
    - The floppy disk needs two connections: one to the power supply, and one to the motherboard or floppy controller. The power supply connector is shaped to prevent you from getting it backwards.
    - Some floppy power connectors are smaller than the standard connector, and most power supplies come with one of these plugs. These connectors can be installed in only one way.
    - For data, a flat ribbon cable is needed. It is gray with 34 conductors and a red stripe to indicate pin 1. One end of the cable will usually have a twist in it. The twisted portion connects to a second floppy drive (drive B:). The end farthest from the twist connects to the motherboard or floppy controller.
- VGA card installation
  - If the motherboard has an integrated video adapter, skip the next step.
  - Plug the VGA card into the appropriate slot, depending on the type of card purchased (PCI slot for a PCI card, ISA slot for an ISA card).
  - Screw the top of the metal bracket that is attached to the adapter into the case, using one of the screws supplied with the case.

- Monitor
  - Plug the monitor into a wall power outlet.
  - Plug the video input plug, which is a 15-pin connector, into the back of the video card.

### 3.10.4 Booting the System

Setup involves configuring the motherboard's components, peripherals, and controllers. The setup program is usually in ROM and can be run by pressing a certain key during POST. Check the CMOS settings using the setup program before booting for the first time. If you make changes, you will need to exit setup and save changes to CMOS for them to take effect. You will be able to change the date and time kept by the real time clock. Memory configuration such as shadow RAM and read/write wait states can be changed from their defaults. IDE hard disks can be detected and configured. Boot sequence and floppy drives can be configured and swapped. PCI cards and even ISA cards can be configured, and plug-n-play disabled (which should be done if running a non-Windows operating system). ISA bus speed can be changed and ports can be enabled or disabled.

IDE disks are almost always configured as auto detect or user-defined type. Use shadow video unless you have problems. Shadow the ROM of your network interface card (NIC) or SCSI card for better speed. For better speed and if you have EDO memory, you can usually use the most aggressive memory settings—just try it out before you stick with it to avoid corrupting data files.

Minimum requirements for booting the system are as follows:

- A bootable floppy disk
- Motherboard with CPU and memory installed
- Video card on the motherboard
- Floppy drive with one cable connected to it and power to it
- Monitor plugged into the wall and the video card
- Keyboard attached

To boot the system, proceed as follows:

- Making sure that the power switch is off, attach a power cord from the case to the wall.
- Turn on the monitor.
- Turn on the power to the PC, and get ready to shut it off if you see, hear, or smell any problems.
- Look for signs that all is working properly:

- The speaker may make clicks or beeps.
- The monitor should fire up and show something.
- Make sure all of the memory counts.
- The floppy drive light should come on one time during POST.

To set up the system, proceed as follows:

- Enter setup by hitting the appropriate key (delete, F1, F10, Esc, or whatever the motherboard manual specifies), and check the CMOS settings.
- Change the CMOS settings, and see whether the computer will remember them.
- Update the date and time.
- View every setup screen, and look at each of the settings.
- Make sure the first boot device is set to be the floppy drive.
- If you have EDO RAM, optimize the memory settings (if you wish) or make any other changes you see fit.
- Save your changes and reboot; rerun setup, and make sure the updates were made.
- Save any changes after the rerun. Make sure the bootable floppy is in the drive, and let it try to boot from the floppy. If it does not boot, or there is some error message—or nothing—on the screen, go to the troubleshooting section (Section 3.10.6).

### 3.10.5  Installing the Other Components

If your PC boots and runs setup, you're almost done. Now you can install all of the other components. First, unplug your PC and wait a few minutes. You should begin to mount the drives if you have not already done so.

**IDE Hard disk installation**

- Mechanical. This is similar to the floppy installation above, with the exception that the drive will not be visible from outside of the case.
- Electrical
  - Most motherboard BIOS systems today can read the IDE drive's specifications and automatically configure them. If it does not, you will have to get the drive's parameters (usually written on the drive), which include number of cylinders, number of heads, and number of sectors per track, and enter them in the drive parameter table in the CMOS setup.
  - A ribbon cable and power connector attach to each hard disk. The power cable has four wires in it and is keyed so it cannot be installed incorrectly.

- The documentation that came with the hard disk indicates how the jumpers are set, if you are installing one disk and no other IDE device, the jumpers can usually be removed. If you are installing more than one disk, decide which disk will be booted. The boot disk should go on the primary hard disk controller. Move the jumper(s) on the hard disk to make it a MASTER or PRIMARY. Many newer hard disks will use pins labeled MA, SL, and CS; you will jumper the MA pins. The second hard disk or CD-ROM will be configured as a SLAVE or SECONDARY drive. You will jumper the SL pins on this device. Use your drive's manual or call the manufacturer's 800 number for proper jumper settings. If the CD-ROM drive will be alone on its own controller, follow the manufacturer's directions (usually it is okay to jumper it as a slave). Once jumpered properly, the drives can be connected with the 18-inch 40-pin ribbon cables and powered up. Pin 1 usually goes next to the power connector.

**SCSI hard disk installation**

- Mechanical. Follow the floppy installation above, with the exception that the drive will not be visible from outside of the case.
- Electrical
  - Unless the motherboard has the SCSI controller built in, the BIOS will not read a SCSI drive, and the drive table should be set up with "not installed."
  - A ribbon cable and power connector attach to each hard disk. The power cable has four wires in it and is keyed so it cannot be installed incorrectly. The other end of the ribbon cable plugs into the SCSI controller itself.
  - The documentation that came with the hard disk explains how the jumpers are set. If you are installing one disk and no other SCSI devices, the jumpers can usually be removed so that the disk will be set to ID 0. Each SCSI device on the chain (ribbon cable) must have its own unique ID number, usually 0 through 7, with 7 being reserved for the controller itself.
  - The last physical device on the cable has to be terminated, depending on the device, either with a jumper or with some type of resistor networks that are plugged in. This is very important.

**NIC installation**

- This is similar to the VGA card installation described previously. If any jumpers are to be set, do that now, and write the settings down. Read the installation manual that came with the card.

**Sound card installation**

- See NIC installation above. If you are setting jumpers, make sure you don't set two cards to the same resource (interrupt request, direct memory access, or port address). Keep all settings distinct.

At this point, you are ready to begin installing the operating system. Don't forget to connect the mouse and external speakers and to make a network hookup, if you have these options installed.

### 3.10.6   Troubleshooting

Each time you boot, you should connect at least the following four components to your PC:

- Speaker
- Keyboard
- Floppy drive
- Monitor

What should a normal boot look and sound like?

- First, LEDs will illuminate everywhere—the motherboard, the hard disks, the floppy drive, the case, the NIC, the printer, the CD-ROM, the speakers, the monitor, and the keyboard.
- The hard disks usually spin up, although some disks, especially SCSIs, may wait for a cue from the controller or may simply wait a fixed amount of time to begin spinning to prevent a large power surge during boot.
- The P/S and CPU fans will start to spin.
- The first thing displayed on the monitor usually will be either memory counting or a video card BIOS display.
- During the memory count, the PC speaker may click.
- When the memory is done counting, the floppy disk often screeches as its LED comes on (called floppy seek).
- The monitor may have messages from the BIOS, including BIOS version, number of CPUs, a password prompt, and nonfatal error messages.
- The last part of the power-on self-test is often a chart that lists the components found during POST, such as CPU and speed, VGA card, serial ports, LPT ports, IDE hard disks, and floppy disks. If no system files are found, either on a bootable floppy or hard disk, you may get a message from the BIOS saying, "Insert Boot disk and press any key" or something similar. This is a nonfatal error, and you can put a bootable floppy in the drive and press a key.

If the above happens, you will know that your motherboard is at least capable of running the ROM's POST. The POST has many potential problems, most of which are nonfatal errors. Any consistent error, however, is a cause for concern. The fatal POST errors will normally generate no video, so you need to listen to the speaker and count beeps. The number of beeps and their length indicate codes for a technician to use in repairing the PC.

At this point, the POST is done, and the boot begins.

What should I do if there is no video or bad video during boot?

• Check the monitor's power and video connection.
• Try reseating the video card or putting it in a new socket (turn off the system first!).
• Make sure the speaker is connected, in case you are getting a fatal POST message that could have nothing to do with video.
• Swap out the video card and/or the monitor.

The two most notable and common POST messages are as follows:

• HDD (or FDD) controller error. Usually this is a cabling issue, such as a reversed connector.
• Disk drive 0 failure. You forgot power to the hard disk, or you've got the wrong drive set in CMOS (rerun setup). Also make sure the disk is properly connected to the controller.

What about floppy problems?

• If the light stays on continuously after boot, you probably have the connector on backwards.

If you are still experiencing problems, try the following:

• Check the cables or try someone else's cables.
• Recheck all the jumper settings on the motherboard.
• Remove secondary cache, or disable it in setup. This can fix many problems.
• Slow down the CPU: it may have been sold to you at the wrong speed.
• Replace SIMMs with known working ones.
• Replace the video card.
• Remove unnecessary components such as extra RAM, sound card, mouse, modem, SCSI card, extra hard disks, tape drives, NIC, or other controller card.
• Remove all hard disks, and try booting from floppy.
• Remove the motherboard from the case, and run it on a piece of cardboard. This will fix a problem caused by a motherboard grounded to the case.

# 4 Windows 2000

*David Solomon*

This chapter introduces the architecture of the Windows 2000 operating system. Before delving into the internals of the system, let's review the origin of the system and its various flavors.

## 4.1 Introduction to Windows 2000

Windows 2000 is actually the fifth version of the Windows NT-based operating system family. The original version, Windows NT 3.1, was released in 1993. From the initial announcement of Windows NT, Microsoft has always made it clear that this operating system was to be their single strategic operating system platform for the future. The next version, Windows XP, is the first NT-based release to be aimed not just at the business desktop and server market, but also at the consumer or home market. It replaces Windows 95, Windows 98, Windows Millennium Edition, and Windows 2000.

NT stands for "new technology." While NT represents a modern 32-bit operating system platform (and with Windows XP, a 64-bit version is available as well), it is not "new" when compared with most modern-day Unix systems. The core system calls and networking capabilities are quite similar.

There are four editions of Windows 2000: Windows 2000 Professional, Windows 2000 Server, Windows 2000 Advanced Server, and Windows 2000 Datacenter Server. These editions differ by

- the number of processors supported,
- the amount of physical memory supported,
- the number of concurrent network connections supported, and
- layered services that come with Server editions that don't come with the Professional edition.

These differences are summarized in Table 4.1.

## 4.2 Operating System Model

To provide a framework for understanding Windows 2000, let's first review the requirements and goals that shaped the original design and specification of the

| Edition | Number of Processors Supported | Physical Memory Supported | Number of Concurrent Client Network Connections[1] | Additional Layered Services |
|---|---|---|---|---|
| Windows 2000 Professional | 2 | 4 GBytes | 10 | |
| Windows 2000 Server | 4 | 4 GBytes | Unlimited | Ability to be a domain controller, Active Directory service, software-based RAID, Dynamic Host Configuration Protocol (DHCP) server, Domain Name System (DNS) server, Distributed File System (DFS) server, Certificate Services, remote install, and terminal services |
| Windows 2000 Advanced Server | 8 | 8 GBytes | Unlimited | Two-node clusters |
| Windows 2000 Datacenter Server | 32 | 64 GBytes[2] | Unlimited | Four-node clusters, Process Control Manager tool |

**Table 4.1**
Differences between Windows 2000 Professional and Server editions.

system. These requirements included the following

- Provide a true 32-bit, preemptive, reentrant, virtual memory operating system.
- Run on multiple hardware architectures and platforms.
- Run and scale well on symmetric multiprocessing systems.

---

[1]The End-User License Agreement for Windows 2000 Professional (contained in \Winnt\ System32\ Eula.txt) states, "You may permit a maximum of ten (10) computers or other electronic devices (each a "Device") to connect to the Workstation Computer to utilize the services of the Product solely for file and print services, internet information services, and remote access (including connection sharing and telephony services)." This limit is enforced for file and print sharing and remote access but not for Internet Information Services.

[2]Theoretical limit—the supported limit might be less than this because of availability of commercial hardware.

- Be a great distributed computing platform, both as a network client and as a server.
- Run most existing 16-bit MS-DOS and Microsoft Windows 3.1 applications.
- Meet government requirements for POSIX 1003.1 compliance.
- Meet government and industry requirements for operating system security.
- Be easily adaptable to the global market by supporting Unicode.

The following sections expand on how these goals were met by the design and implementation of the system.

### 4.2.1 Memory Protection Model

Windows 2000 is similar to most Unix systems in that it is a monolithic operating system in the sense that the bulk of the operating system and device driver code shares the same protected memory space. Windows 2000 isn't a microkernel-based operating system in the classic definition of microkernel (although some claim it as such), where the principal operating system components (such as the memory manager, process manager, and I/O manager) run as separate processes in their own private address spaces, layered on a primitive set of services the microkernel provides.

All these operating system components are, of course, fully protected from errant applications because applications don't have direct access to the code and data of the privileged part of the operating system (though they can quickly call other kernel services).

In most multiuser operating systems, applications are separated from the operating system itself—the operating system code runs in a privileged processor mode (referred to as *kernel mode* in this book), with access to system data and to the hardware; application code runs in a nonprivileged processor mode (called *user mode*), with a limited set of interfaces available, limited access to system data, and no direct access to hardware. When a user-mode program calls a system service, the processor traps the call and then switches the calling thread to kernel mode. When the system service completes, the operating system switches the thread context back to user mode and allows the caller to continue.

This protection is one of the reasons that Windows 2000 has the reputation for being robust and stable both as an application server and as a workstation platform, yet fast and nimble from the perspective of core operating system services, such as virtual memory management, file I/O, and networking.

The kernel-mode components of Windows 2000 also embody basic object-oriented design principles. For example, they don't reach into one another's data structures to access information maintained by individual components. Instead, they use formal interfaces to pass parameters and access and/or modify data structures.

Despite its pervasive use of objects to represent shared system resources, Windows 2000 is not an object-oriented system in the strict sense. Most of the operating system code is written in C because C enables portability and because C development tools are widely available. C doesn't directly support object-oriented constructs, such as dynamic binding of data types, polymorphic functions, or class inheritance. Therefore, the C-based implementation of objects in Windows 2000 borrows from, but doesn't depend on, features of particular object-oriented languages.

### 4.2.2   Portability

Windows 2000 was designed to run on a variety of hardware architectures, including Intel-based CISC systems as well as RISC systems. The initial release of Windows NT supported the x86 and MIPS architecture. Support for the Digital Equipment Corporation (DEC) Alpha AXP was added shortly thereafter. Support for a fourth processor architecture, the Motorola PowerPC, was added in Windows NT 3.51. Because of changing market demands, however, support for the MIPS and PowerPC architectures was dropped before development began on Windows 2000. Later Compaq withdrew support for the Alpha AXP architecture, resulting in Windows 2000 being supported only on the x86 architecture. The 64-bit version of Windows XP supports the new Intel Itanium processor family, the first implementation of the 64-bit architecture family being jointly developed by Intel and Hewlett-Packard, called IA-64 (for Intel Architecture 64). The 64-bit version of Windows XP will provide a much larger address space for both user processes and the system.

Windows 2000 achieves portability across hardware architectures and platforms in two primary ways:

•  Windows 2000 has a layered design, with low-level portions of the system that are processor-architecture specific or platform specific isolated into separate modules so that upper layers of the system can be shielded from the differences between architectures and among hardware platforms. The two key components that provide operating system portability are the kernel (contained in `Ntoskrnl.exe`) and the hardware abstraction layer (contained in `Hal.dll`). (Both these components are described in more detail later in this chapter.) Functions that are architecture specific (such as thread context switching and trap dispatching) are implemented in the kernel. Functions that can differ among systems within the same architecture (for example, different motherboards) are implemented in the hardware abstraction layer (HAL).

- The vast majority of Windows 2000 is written in C, with some portions in C++. Assembly language is used only for those parts of the operating system that need to communicate directly with system hardware (such as the interrupt trap handler) or that are extremely performance sensitive (such as context switching). Assembly language code exists not only in the kernel and the HAL but also in a few other places within the core operating system (such as the routines that implement interlocked instructions as well as one module in the local procedure call facility), in the kernel-mode part of the Win32 subsystem, and even in some user-mode libraries, such as the process startup code in Ntdll.dll (a system library explained later in this chapter).

### 4.2.3   Symmetric Multiprocessing

Windows 2000 is a *symmetric multiprocessing* (SMP) operating system. In a multiprocessor configuration, there is no master processor—the operating system as well as user threads can be scheduled to run on any processor. Also, all the processors share just one memory space. This model contrasts with *asymmetric multiprocessing* (ASMP), in which the operating system typically selects one processor to execute operating system code while other processors run only user code. The differences in the two multiprocessing models are illustrated in Figure 4.1.

Although Windows NT was originally designed to support up to 32 processors, nothing inherent in the multiprocessor design limits the number of processors to 32—that number is simply an obvious and convenient limit because 32 processors can easily be represented as a bit mask using a native 32-bit data type.

The actual number of supported processors depends on the edition of Windows 2000 installed. For example, Windows 2000 Professional supports up to two processors, whereas Windows 2000 Datacenter Server supports up to 32 processors. This number is stored in the registry value

```
HKLM\SYSTEM\CurrentControlSet\Control\Session\Manager\LicensedProcessors.
```

Tampering with that data is a violation of the software license and will likely result in a system crash upon rebooting, because modifying the registry to allow use of more processors involves more than changing just this value.

One of the key issues with multiprocessor systems is *scalability*. To run correctly on an SMP system, operating system code must adhere to strict guidelines and rules. Resource contention and other performance issues are more complicated in

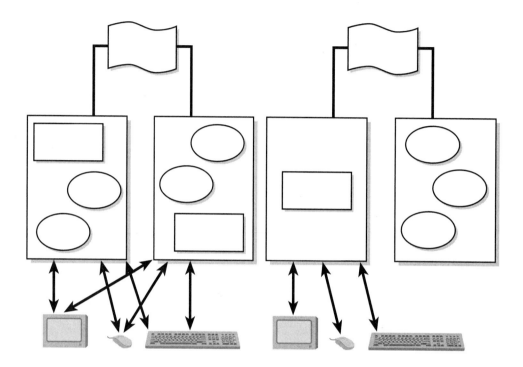

**Figure 4.1**
Symmetric vs. asymmetric multiprocessing.

multiprocessing systems than in uniprocessor systems and must be accounted for in the system's design. Windows 2000 incorporates several features that are crucial to its success as a multiprocessor operating system:

• The ability to run operating system code on any available processor and on multiple processors at the same time

• Multiple threads of execution within a single process, each of which can execute simultaneously on different processors

• Fine-grained synchronization within the kernel as well as within device drivers and server processes, which allows more components to run concurrently on multiple processors

In addition, Windows 2000 provides mechanisms (such as I/O completion ports) that facilitate the efficient implementation of multithreaded server processes that can scale well on multiprocessor systems.

### 4.2.4   Virtual Memory

Windows 2000 implements a virtual memory system based on a flat (linear) 32-bit address space. Thirty-two bits of address space translates into 4 GBytes of virtual memory. On most systems, Windows 2000 allocates half this address space (the lower half of the 4 GByte virtual address space, from x00000000 through x7FFFFFFF) to processes for their unique private storage and uses the other half (the upper half, addresses x80000000 through xFFFFFFFF) for its own protected operating system memory utilization. The mappings of the lower half change to reflect the virtual address space of the currently executing process, but the mappings of the upper half always consist of the operating system's virtual memory. Windows 2000 Advanced Server and Datacenter Server support a boot-time option (the /3GB qualifier in Boot.ini) that gives processes running specially marked programs (the large address space aware flag must be set in the header of the executable image) a 3 GByte private address space (leaving 1 GByte for the operating system). This option allows applications such as database servers to keep larger portions of a database in the process address space, thus reducing the need to map subset views of the database. Figure 4.2 shows the two virtual address space layouts supported by Windows 2000.

Although 3 GBytes is better than 2 GBytes, it's still not enough virtual address space to map very large (multigigabyte) databases. To address this need, Windows 2000 has a new mechanism called *Address Windowing Extensions* (AWE), which allows a 32-bit application to allocate up to 64 GBytes of physical memory and then map views, or windows, into its 2 GByte virtual address space. Although using AWE puts the burden of managing mappings of virtual to physical memory on the programmer, it does solve the immediate need of being able to directly access more physical memory than can be mapped at any one time in a 32-bit process address space. The long-term solution to this address space limitation is 64-bit Windows.

Recall that a process's virtual address space is the set of addresses available for the process's threads to use. Virtual memory provides a logical view of memory that might not correspond to its physical layout. At run time the memory manager, with assistance from hardware, translates, or *maps,* the virtual addresses into physical addresses, where the data is actually stored. By controlling the protection and mapping, the operating system can ensure that individual processes don't bump into one another or overwrite operating system data. Figure 4.3 illustrates three virtually contiguous pages mapped to three discontiguous pages in physical memory.

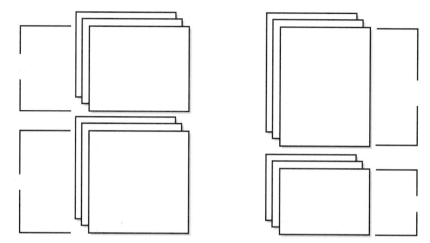

**Figure 4.2**
Address space layouts supported by Windows 2000.

Because most systems have much less physical memory than the total virtual memory in use by the running processes (2 GBytes or 3 GBytes for each process), the memory manager transfers, or *pages,* some of the memory contents to disk. Paging data to disk frees physical memory so that it can be used for other processes or for the operating system itself. When a thread accesses a virtual address that has been paged to disk, the virtual memory manager loads the information back into memory from disk. Applications don't have to be altered in any way to take advantage of paging because hardware support enables the memory manager to page without the knowledge or assistance of processes or threads.

### 4.2.5   Processes, Threads, and Jobs

A Windows 2000 process comprises the following:

• A private *virtual address space,* which is a set of virtual memory addresses that the process can use
• An executable program, which defines initial code and data and is mapped into the process's virtual address space
• A list of open handles to various system resources, such as semaphores, communication ports, and files, that are accessible to all threads in the process

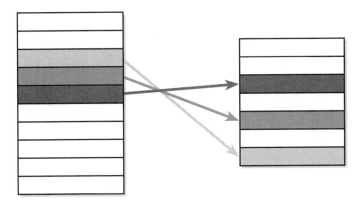

**Figure 4.3**
Mapping virtual memory to physical memory.

- A security context called an *access token* that identifies the user, security groups, and privileges associated with the process
- A unique identifier called a *process ID* (internally called a *client ID*)
- At least one thread of execution

A *thread* is the entity within a process that Windows 2000 schedules for execution. Without it, the process's program can't run. A thread includes the following essential components:

- The contents of a set of CPU registers representing the state of the processor
- Two stacks, one for the thread to use while executing in kernel mode and one for executing in user mode
- A private storage area called thread-local storage for use by subsystems, runtime libraries, and dynamic-link libraries (DLLs)
- A unique identifier called a *thread ID* (also internally called a *client ID*—process IDs and thread IDs are generated out of the same namespace, so they never overlap)

Threads sometimes have their own security context, which often is used by multithreaded server applications that impersonate the security context of the clients that they serve

The volatile registers, the stacks, and the private storage area are called the thread's *context*. Because this information is different for each machine architecture that Windows 2000 runs on, this structure, by necessity, is architecture specific. In fact, the CONTEXT structure returned by the Win32 *GetThreadContext* function is the only public data structure in the Win32 API that is machine dependent.

Although threads have their own execution context, every thread within a process shares the process's virtual address space (in addition to the rest of the resources belonging to the process); hence, all the threads in a process can write to and read from each other's memory. Threads can't reference the address space of another process, however, unless the other process makes available part of its private address space as a *shared memory section* (called a *file mapping object* in the Win32 API) or unless one process opens another process and uses the *ReadProcessMemory* and *WriteProcessMemory* functions.

Every process has a security context that is stored in an object called an *access token*. The process access token contains the security identification and credentials for the process. By default, threads don't have their own access token, but they can obtain one, thus allowing individual threads to impersonate the security context of another process—including processes running on a remote Windows 2000 system—without affecting other threads in the process.

The virtual address descriptors (VADs) are data structures that the memory manager uses to keep track of the virtual addresses the process is using.

Windows 2000 introduces an extension to the process model called a *job*. A job object's main function is to allow groups of processes to be managed and manipulated as a unit. A job object allows control of certain attributes and provides limits for the process or processes associated with the job. It also records basic accounting information for all processes associated with the job and for all processes that were associated with the job but have since terminated. In some ways, the job object compensates for the lack of a structured process tree in Windows 2000, yet in many other ways is more powerful than a Unix-style process tree.

### 4.2.6 Security

Windows 2000 supports C2-level security as defined by the U.S. Department of Defense Trusted Computer System Evaluation Criteria (DoD 5200.28–STD, December 1985). This standard includes discretionary (need-to-know) protection for all sharable system objects (such as files, directories, processes, and threads), security auditing (for accountability of subjects, or users, and the actions they initiate), password authentication at logon, and the prevention of one user from accessing uninitialized resources (such as free memory or disk space) that another user has deallocated.

Windows NT 4 was formally evaluated at the C2 level and is on the U.S. government Evaluated Products List. (Windows 2000 is still in the evaluation process.) Also, Windows NT 4 has met the European organization ITSEC (IT Security Evaluation Criteria) at the FC2/E3 (functional level C2 and assurance level E3, something normally associated only with B-level systems) security level. Achieving a government-approved security rating allows an operating system to compete in that arena. Of course, many of these required capabilities are advantageous features for any multiuser system.

Windows 2000 has two forms of access control over objects. The first form—discretionary access control—is the protection mechanism that most people think of when they think of protection under Windows 2000. It's the method by which owners of objects (such as files or printers) grant or deny access to others. When users log in, they are given a set of security credentials, or a security context. When they attempt to access objects, their security context is compared with the access control list on the object they are trying to access to determine whether they have permission to perform the requested operation.

Privileged access control is necessary for those times when discretionary access control isn't enough. It's a method of ensuring that someone can get to protected objects if the owner isn't available. For example, if an employee leaves a company, the administrator needs a way to gain access to files that might have been accessible only to that employee. In that case, under Windows 2000, the administrator can take ownership of the file and manage its rights as necessary.

Security pervades the interface of the Win32 API. The Win32 subsystem implements object-based security in the same way the operating system does; the Win32 subsystem protects shared Windows objects from unauthorized access by placing Windows 2000 security descriptors on them. The first time an application tries to access a shared object, the Win32 subsystem verifies the application's right to do so. If the security check succeeds, the Win32 subsystem allows the application to proceed.

The Win32 subsystem implements object security on a number of shared objects, some of which were built on top of native Windows 2000 objects. The Win32 objects include desktop objects, window objects, menu objects, files, processes, threads, and several synchronization objects.

### 4.2.7   Unicode

Windows 2000 differs from most other operating systems in that most internal text strings are stored and processed as 16-bit-wide Unicode characters. Unicode is an international character set standard that defines unique 16-bit values for most of the world's known character sets. (For more information about Unicode, see `www.unicode.org` as well as the programming documentation in the MSDN Library.)

Because many applications deal with 8-bit (single-byte) ANSI character strings, Win32 functions that accept string parameters have two entry points: a Unicode (wide, 16-bit) and an ANSI (narrow, 8-bit) version. The Windows 95, Windows 98, and Windows Millennium Edition implementations of Win32 don't implement all the Unicode interfaces to all the Win32 functions, so applications designed to run on one of these operating systems as well as Windows 2000 typically use the narrow versions. If you call the narrow version of a Win32 function, input string parameters are converted to Unicode before being processed by the system and output parameters are converted from Unicode to ANSI before being returned to the application. Thus, if you have an older service or piece of code that you need to run on Windows 2000 but this code is written using ANSI character text strings, Windows 2000 will convert the ANSI characters into Unicode for its own use. Windows 2000 never converts the *data* inside files, however; it's up to the application to decide whether to store data as Unicode or as ANSI.

In previous editions of Windows NT, Asian and Middle East editions were a superset of the core U.S. and European editions and contained additional Win32 functions to handle more complex text input and layout requirements (such as right to left text input). In Windows 2000, all language editions contain the same Win32 functions. Instead of having separate language versions, Windows 2000 has a single worldwide binary so that a single installation can support multiple languages (by adding various language packs). Applications can also take advantage of Win32 functions that allow single worldwide application binaries that can support multiple languages.

## 4.3   System Architecture

Now that we've looked at the goals that shaped the design of Windows 2000, let's look at the internal system architecture. Figure 4.4 illustrates the relationship of the key operating system components.

In the figure is a line dividing the user-mode and kernel-mode parts of the Windows 2000 operating system. The boxes above the line represent user-mode processes, and the components below the line are kernel-mode operating system services. As mentioned earlier, user-mode threads execute in a protected process address space (although while they are executing in kernel mode, they have access to system space). Thus, system support processes, service processes, user applications, and environment subsystems each have their own private process address space.

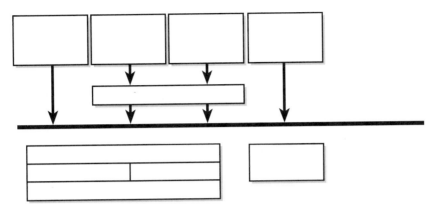

**Figure 4.4**
Simplified Windows 2000 architecture.

The four basic types of user-mode processes are described as follows:

- Fixed (or hardwired) *system support processes,* such as the logon process and the session manager, that are not Windows 2000 services (that is, not started by the service control manager).
- *Service processes* that host Win32 services, such as the Task Scheduler and Spooler services. Many Windows 2000 server applications, such as Microsoft SQL Server and Microsoft Exchange Server, also include components that run as services.
- *User applications,* which can be one of five types: Win32, Windows 3.1, MS-DOS, POSIX, or OS/2 1.2.
- *Environment subsystems,* which expose the native operating system services to user applications through a set of callable functions, thus providing an operating system *environment,* or personality. Windows 2000 ships with three environment subsystems: Win32, POSIX, and OS/2.

In Figure 4.4, notice the "Subsystem DLLs" box below the "Service processes" and "User applications" boxes. Under Windows 2000, user applications don't call the native Windows 2000 operating system services directly; rather, they go through one or more *subsystem dynamic-link libraries.* The role of the subsystem DLLs is to translate a documented function into the appropriate internal (and undocumented) Windows 2000 system service calls. This translation might or might not involve sending a message to the environment subsystem process that is serving the user application.

The kernel-mode components of Windows 2000 include the following:

- The Windows 2000 *executive* contains the base operating system services, such as memory management, process and thread management, security, I/O, and interprocess communication.
- The Windows 2000 *kernel* consists of low-level operating system functions, such as thread scheduling, interrupt and exception dispatching, and multiprocessor synchronization. It also provides a set of routines and basic objects that the rest of the executive uses to implement higher-level constructs.
- *Device drivers* include hardware device drivers that translate user I/O function calls into specific hardware device I/O requests, as well as file system and network drivers.
- The *hardware abstraction layer* is a layer of code that isolates the kernel, device drivers, and the rest of the Windows 2000 executive from platform-specific hardware differences (such as differences between motherboards).
- The *windowing and graphics system* implements the graphical user interface (GUI) functions (better known as the Win32 USER and graphics device interface, or GDI, functions), such as dealing with windows, user interface controls, and drawing.

Figure 4.5 is a more detailed and complete diagram of the Windows 2000 system architecture and components than was shown earlier in Figure 4.4. The following sections elaborate on each major element of this diagram.

### 4.3.1   Environment Subsystems and Subsystem DLLs

As shown in Figure 4.4, Windows 2000 has three environment subsystems: OS/2, POSIX, and Win32. As we'll explain shortly, of the three, the Win32 subsystem is special in that Windows 2000 can't run without it. (It owns the keyboard, mouse, and display, and it is required to be present even on server systems with no interactive users logged in.) In fact, the other two subsystems are configured to start on demand, whereas the Win32 subsystem must always be running.

The role of an environment subsystem is to expose some subset of the base Windows 2000 executive system services to application programs. Each subsystem can provide access to different subsets of the native services in Windows 2000. That means that some things can be done from an application built on one subsystem that can't be done by an application built on another subsystem. For example, a Win32 application can't use the POSIX *fork* function.

Each executable image (`.exe`) is bound to one and only one subsystem. When an image is run, the process creation code examines the subsystem type code in the image header so that it can notify the proper subsystem of the new process. This type code is specified with the `/SUBSYSTEM` qualifier of the *link* command in

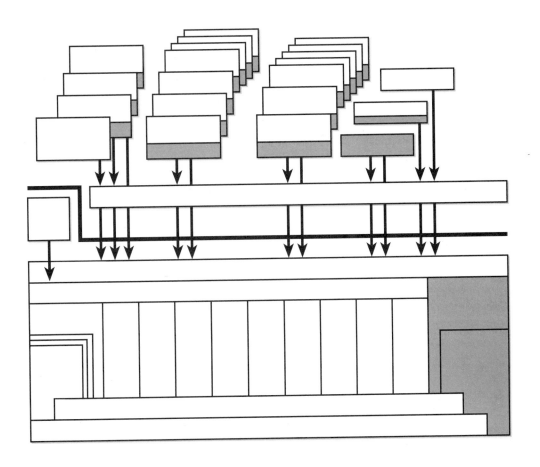

**Figure 4.5**
Windows 2000 architecture.

Microsoft Visual C++ and can be viewed with the Exetype tool in the Windows 2000 resource kits.

Function calls can't be mixed between subsystems. In other words, a POSIX application can call only services exported by the POSIX subsystem, and a Win32 application can call only services exported by the Win32 subsystem. As you'll see later, this restriction is the reason that the POSIX subsystem, which implements a very limited set of functions (only POSIX 1003.1), isn't a useful environment for porting Unix applications.

As mentioned earlier, user applications don't call Windows 2000 system services directly. Instead, they go through one or more subsystem DLLs. These libraries export the documented interface that the programs linked to that subsystem can call. For example, the Win32 subsystem DLLs (such as Kernel32.dll, Advapi32.dll, User32.dll, and Gdi32.dll) implement the Win32 API functions. The POSIX subsystem DLL implements the POSIX 1003.1 API.

When an application calls a function in a subsystem DLL, one of three things can occur:

- The function is entirely implemented in user mode inside the subsystem DLL. In other words, no message is sent to the environment subsystem process, and no Windows 2000 executive system services are called. The function is performed in user mode, and the results are returned to the caller. Examples of such functions include *GetCurrentProcess* (which always returns −1, a value that is defined to refer to the current process in all process-related functions) and *GetCurrentProcessId* (the process ID doesn't change for a running process, so this ID is retrieved from a cached location, thus avoiding the need to call into the kernel).
- The function requires one or more calls to the Windows 2000 executive. For example, the Win32 *ReadFile* and *WriteFile* functions involve calling the underlying internal (and undocumented) Windows 2000 I/O system services *NtReadFile* and *NtWriteFile*, respectively.
- The function requires some work to be done in the environment subsystem process. (The environment subsystem processes, running in user mode, are responsible for maintaining the state of the client applications running under their control.) In this case, a client/server request is made to the environment subsystem via a message sent to the subsystem to perform some operation. The subsystem DLL then waits for a reply before returning to the caller.

Some functions can be a combination of the second and third items above, such as the Win32 *CreateProcess* and *CreateThread* functions.

Although Windows 2000 was designed to support multiple, independent environment subsystems, from a practical perspective, having each subsystem implement all the code to handle windowing and display I/O would result in a large amount of duplication of system functions that, ultimately, would negatively affect both system size and performance. Because Win32 was the primary subsystem, the Windows 2000 designers decided to locate these basic functions there and have the other subsystems call on the Win32 subsystem to perform display I/O. Thus, the

POSIX and OS/2 subsystems call services in the Win32 subsystem to perform display I/O. (In fact, if you examine the subsystem type for these images, you'll see that they are Win32 executables.)

Let's take a closer look at each of the environment subsystems.

**Win32 Subsystem.**  The Win32 subsystem consists of the following major components:

- The environment subsystem process (`Csrss.exe`) contains support for
  - console (text) windows,
  - creating and deleting processes and threads,
  - portions of the support for 16-bit virtual DOS machine (VDM) processes, and
  - other miscellaneous functions, such as *GetTempFile DefineDosDevice, ExitWindowsEx*, and several natural language support functions.
- The kernel-mode device driver (`Win32k.sys`) contains two components:
  - The window manager, which controls window displays; manages screen output; collects input from keyboard, mouse, and other devices; and passes user messages to applications.
  - The Graphics Device Interface (GDI), which is a library of functions for graphics output devices. It includes functions for line, text, and figure drawing and for graphics manipulation.
- Subsystem DLLs (such as `Kernel32.dll`, `Advapi32.dll`, `User32.dll`, and `Gdi32.dll`) translate documented Win32 API functions into the appropriate undocumented kernel-mode system service calls to `Ntoskrnl.exe` and `Win32k.sys`.
- Graphics device drivers are hardware-dependent graphics display drivers, printer drivers, and video miniport drivers.

Applications call the standard USER functions to create user interface controls, such as windows and buttons, on the display. The window manager communicates these requests to the GDI, which passes them to the graphics device drivers, where they are formatted for the display device. A display driver is paired with a video miniport driver to complete video display support.

The GDI provides a set of standard two-dimensional functions that let applications communicate with graphics devices without knowing anything about the devices. GDI functions mediate between applications and graphics devices such as display drivers and printer drivers. The GDI interprets application requests for graphic output and sends the requests to graphics display drivers. It also provides a standard interface for applications to use varying graphics output devices. This interface enables application code to be independent of the hardware devices and their drivers. The GDI tailors its messages to the capabilities of the device, often dividing the request into manageable parts. For example, some devices can understand directions to draw an ellipse; others require the GDI to interpret the command as a series of pixels placed at certain coordinates. For more information about the graphics and video driver architecture, see the "Design Guide" section of the book *Graphics Drivers* in the Windows Device Driver Kit (DDK), available at `www.microsoft.com/ddk`.

**POSIX Subsystem.**   POSIX, an acronym loosely defined as "a portable operating system interface based on Unix," refers to a collection of international standards for Unix-style operating system interfaces. The POSIX standards encourage vendors implementing Unix-style interfaces to make them compatible so that programmers can move their applications easily from one system to another.

Windows 2000 implements only one of the many POSIX standards, POSIX.1, formally known as ISO/IEC 9945-1:1990 or IEEE POSIX standard 1003.1-1990. This standard was included primarily to meet U.S. government procurement requirements set in the mid-to-late 1980s that mandated POSIX.1 compliance as specified in Federal Information Processing Standard (FIPS) 151-2, developed by the National Institute of Standards and Technology. Windows NT 3.5, 3.51, and 4 have been formally tested and certified according to FIPS 151-2.

Because POSIX.1 compliance was a mandatory goal for Windows 2000, the operating system was designed to ensure that the required base system support was present to allow for the implementation of a POSIX.1 subsystem (such as the *fork* function, which is implemented in the Windows 2000 executive, and the support for hard file links in the Windows 2000 file system). However, because POSIX.1 defines a limited set of services (such as process control, interprocess communication, and simple character cell I/O), the POSIX subsystem that comes with Windows 2000 isn't a complete programming environment. And because applications can't mix calls between subsystems on Windows 2000, by default, POSIX applications are limited to the strict set of services defined in POSIX.1. This restriction means that a POSIX executable on Windows 2000 can't create a thread or a window or use remote procedure calls (RPCs) or sockets.

To address this limitation, Microsoft provides a product called Interix, which includes an enhanced POSIX subsystem environment that provides nearly 2000 Unix functions and 300 Unix-like tools and utilities. (See `www.microsoft.com/windows2000/interix/default.asp` for more information on Microsoft Interix.) With this enhancement, it is more viable to port Unix applications to the POSIX subsystem. However, because the programs are still linked as POSIX executables, they cannot call Win32 functions.

To port Unix applications to Windows 2000 and allow the use of Win32 functions, you can purchase a Unix-to-Win32 porting library, such as the one included with the MKS N*u*TCRACKER Professional product available from Mortice Kern Systems Inc. (www.mks.com). With this approach, a Unix application can be recompiled and relinked as a Win32 executable and can slowly start to integrate calls to native Win32 functions. Another such library is available from www.cygwin.com. This site also provides ports of popular GNU development tools and utilities for Windows.

To compile and link a POSIX application in Windows 2000 requires the POSIX headers and libraries from the Platform SDK. POSIX executables are linked against the POSIX subsystem library, Psxdll.dll. Because by default Windows 2000 is configured to start the POSIX subsystem on demand, the first time you run a POSIX application, the POSIX subsystem process (Psxss.exe) must be started. It remains running until the system reboots.

For more information about the POSIX subsystem and about porting Unix applications to Windows 2000, do a search for POSIX and Unix in MSDN Library (msdn.microsoft.com).

**OS/2 Subsystem.** The OS/2 environment subsystem, like the built-in POSIX subsystem, is fairly limited in usefulness in that it supports only OS/2 1.2 16-bit character-based or video I/O (VIO) applications. Although Microsoft did sell a replacement OS/2 1.2 Presentation Manager subsystem for Windows NT 4, it didn't support OS/2 2.*x* (or later) applications (and the replacement isn't available for Windows 2000).

### 4.3.2  Ntdll.dll

Ntdll.dll is a special system support library primarily for the use of subsystem DLLs. It contains two types of function:

- System service dispatch stubs to Windows 2000 executive system services
- Internal support functions used by subsystems, subsystem DLLs, and other native images

The first group of functions provides the interface to the Windows 2000 executive system services that can be called from user mode. There are more than two hundred such functions, such as *NtCreateFile* and *NtSetEvent*. As noted earlier, most of the capabilities of these functions are accessible through the Win32 API. (A number are not, however, and are for Microsoft internal use only.)

For each of these functions, `Ntdll` contains an entry point with the same name. The code inside the function contains the architecture-specific instruction that causes a transition into kernel mode to invoke the system service dispatcher, which, after verifying some parameters, calls the actual kernel-mode system service that contains the real code inside `Ntoskrnl.exe`.

`Ntdll` also contains many support functions, such as the image loader (functions that start with *Ldr*), the heap manager, and Win32 subsystem process communication functions (functions that start with *Csr*), as well as general runtime library routines (functions that start with *Rtl*). It also contains the user-mode exception dispatcher.

### 4.3.3 Executive

The Windows 2000 executive is the upper layer of `Ntoskrnl.exe`. (The kernel is the lower layer.) The executive includes the following types of function:

- Functions that are exported and callable from user mode. These functions are called *system services* and are exported via `Ntdll`. Most of the services are accessible through the Win32 API or the APIs of another environment subsystem. A few services, however, aren't available through any documented subsystem function. (Examples include LPCs and various query functions such as *NtQueryInformationxxx* and specialized functions such as *NtCreatePagingFile*. on.)
- Functions that can be called only from kernel mode that are exported and documented in the Windows 2000 DDK or Windows 2000 Installable File System (IFS) Kit. (For information on the Windows 2000 IFS Kit, go to `www.microsoft.com/ddk/ifskit`.)
- Functions that are exported and callable from kernel mode but are not documented in the Windows 2000 DDK or IFS Kit (such as the functions called by the boot video driver, which start with *Inbv*).
- Functions that are defined as global symbols but are not exported. These include internal support functions called within `Ntoskrnl`, such as those that start with *Iop* (internal I/O manager support functions) or *Mi* (internal memory management support functions).
- Functions that are internal to a module that are not defined as global symbols.

The executive contains the following major components:

- The *configuration manager* is responsible for implementing and managing the system registry.

- The *process and thread manager* creates and terminates processes and threads. The underlying support for processes and threads is implemented in the Windows 2000 kernel; the executive adds additional semantics and functions to these lower-level objects.
- The *security reference monitor* enforces security policies on the local computer. It guards operating system resources, performing runtime object protection and auditing.
- The *I/O manager* implements device-independent I/O and is responsible for dispatching to the appropriate device drivers for further processing.
- The *Plug and Play* (PnP) *manager* determines which drivers are required to support a particular device and loads those drivers. It retrieves the hardware resource requirements for each device during enumeration. Based on the resource requirements of each device, the PnP manager assigns the appropriate hardware resources such as I/O ports, IRQs, DMA channels, and memory locations. It is also responsible for sending proper event notification for device changes (addition or removal of a device) on the system.
- The *power manager* coordinates power events and generates power management I/O notifications to device drivers. When the system is idle, the power manager can be configured to reduce power consumption by putting the CPU to sleep. Changes in power consumption by individual devices are handled by device drivers but are coordinated by the power manager.
- The *WDM Windows Management Instrumentation routines* enable device drivers to publish performance and configuration information and receive commands from the user-mode WMI service. Consumers of WMI information can be on the local machine or remote across the network.
- The *cache manager* improves the performance of file-based I/O by causing recently referenced disk data to reside in main memory for quick access (and by deferring disk writes by holding the updates in memory for a short time before sending them to the disk). As described shortly, it does this by using the memory manager's support for mapped files.
- The *virtual memory manager* implements *virtual memory,* a memory management scheme that provides a large, private address space for each process that can exceed available physical memory. The memory manager also provides the underlying support for the cache manager.

In addition, the executive contains four main groups of support functions that are used by the executive components just listed.

- The *object manager,* which creates, manages, and deletes Windows 2000 executive objects and abstract data types that are used to represent operating system resources such as processes, threads, and the various synchronization objects.
- The *LPC facility* passes messages between a client process and a server process on the same computer. LPC is a flexible, optimized version of remote procedure call, an industry-standard communication facility for client and server processes across a network.
- A broad set of common *runtime library* functions, such as string processing, arithmetic operations, data type conversion, and security structure processing.
- *Executive support routines,* such as system memory allocation (paged and nonpaged pool), interlocked memory access, as well as two special types of synchronization objects: resources and fast mutexes.

About a third of these support functions are documented in the DDK because device drivers also use them.

### 4.3.4   Kernel

The kernel consists of a set of functions in `Ntoskrnl.exe` that provide fundamental mechanisms (such as thread scheduling and synchronization services) used by the executive components, as well as low-level hardware architecture-dependent support (such as interrupt and exception dispatching), that are different on each processor architecture. The kernel code is written primarily in C, with assembly code reserved for those tasks that require access to specialized processor instructions and registers not easily accessible from C.

Like the various executive support functions mentioned in the preceding section, a number of functions in the kernel are documented in the DDK (search for functions beginning with *Ke*) because they are needed to implement device drivers.

**Kernel Objects.**   The kernel provides a low-level base of well-defined, predictable operating system primitives and mechanisms that allow higher-level components of the executive to do what they need to do. The kernel separates itself from the rest of the executive by implementing operating system mechanisms and avoiding policy making. It leaves nearly all policy decisions to the executive, with the exception of thread scheduling and dispatching, which the kernel implements.

Outside the kernel, the executive represents threads and other sharable resources as objects. These objects require some policy overhead, such as object handles to manipulate them, security checks to protect them, and resource quotas to be deducted when they are created. This overhead is eliminated in the kernel, which implements a set of simpler objects, called *kernel objects,* that help the kernel control central processing and support the creation of executive objects. Most executive-level objects encapsulate one or more kernel objects, incorporating their kernel-defined attributes.

One set of kernel objects, called *control objects,* establishes semantics for controlling various operating system functions. This set includes the APC object, the *deferred procedure call* (DPC) object, and several objects the I/O manager uses, such as the interrupt object.

Another set of kernel objects, known as *dispatcher objects,* incorporates synchronization capabilities that alter or affect thread scheduling. The dispatcher objects include the kernel thread, mutex (called *mutant* internally), event, kernel event pair, semaphore, timer, and waitable timer. The executive uses kernel functions to create instances of kernel objects, to manipulate them, and to construct the more complex objects it provides to user mode.

**Hardware Support.**   The other major job of the kernel is to abstract or isolate the executive and device drivers from variations between the hardware architectures supported by Windows 2000. This job includes handling variations in functions such as interrupt handling, exception dispatching, and multiprocessor synchronization.

Even for these hardware-related functions, the design of the kernel attempts to maximize the amount of common code. The kernel supports a set of interfaces that are portable and semantically identical across architectures. Most of the code that implements this portable interface is also identical across architectures.

Some of these interfaces are implemented differently on different architectures, however, or some of the interfaces are partially implemented with architecture-specific code. These architecturally independent interfaces can be called on any machine, and the semantics of the interface will be the same whether or not the code varies by architecture.

The kernel also contains a small amount of code with x86-specific interfaces needed to support old MS-DOS programs. These x86 interfaces aren't portable in the sense that they can't be called on a machine based on any other architecture; they won't be present. This x86-specific code, for example, supports calls to manipulate global descriptor tables (GDTs) and LDTs, hardware features of the x86.

Another example of architecture-specific code in the kernel is the interface to provide translation buffer and CPU cache support. This support requires different code for the different architectures because of the way caches are implemented. Still another example is context switching. Although at a high level the same algorithm is used for thread selection and context switching (the context of the previous

| HAL File Name | Systems Supported |
|---|---|
| Hal.dll | Standard PCs |
| Halacpi.dll | Advanced Configuration and Power Interface(ACPI) PCs |
| Halapic.dll | Advanced Programmable Interrupt Controller (APIC) PCs |
| Halaacpi.dll | APIC ACPI PCs |
| Halmps.dll | Multiprocessor PCs |
| Halmacpi.dll | Multiprocessor ACPI PCs |
| Halborg.dll | Silicon Graphics Workstation (no longer marketed) |
| Halsp.dll | Compaq SystemPro |

**Table 4.2**
List of HALs

thread is saved, the context of the new thread is loaded, and the new thread is started), there are architectural differences among the implementations on different processors. Because the context is described by the processor state (registers and so on), what is saved and loaded varies depending on the architecture.

### 4.3.5  Hardware Abstraction Layer

As mentioned at the beginning of this chapter, one of the crucial elements of the Windows 2000 design is its portability across a variety of hardware platforms. The hardware abstraction layer is a key part of making this portability possible. The HAL is a loadable kernel-mode module (Hal.dll) that provides the low-level interface to the hardware platform on which Windows 2000 is running. It hides hardware-dependent details such as I/O interfaces, interrupt controllers, and multiprocessor communication mechanisms—any functions that are both architecture-specific and machine dependent.

Thus, rather than access hardware directly, Windows 2000 internal components as well as user-written device drivers maintain portability by calling the HAL routines when they need platform-dependent information. For this reason, the HAL routines are documented in the Windows 2000 DDK. To find out more about the HAL and its use by device drivers, refer to the DDK.

Although several HALs are included on the Windows 2000 CD (see Table 4.2), only one is chosen at installation time and copied to the system disk with the filename Hal.dll. Therefore, you can't assume that a system disk from one x86 installation will boot on a different processor if the HAL that supports the other processor is different.

### 4.3.6   Device Drivers

This section provides a brief overview of the types of drivers and explains how to list the drivers installed and loaded on your system.

Device drivers are loadable kernel-mode modules (typically ending in.sys) that interface between the I/O manager and the relevant hardware. They run in kernel mode in one of three contexts:

- In the context of the user thread that initiated an I/O function
- In the context of a kernel-mode system thread
- As a result of an interrupt (and therefore not in the context of any particular process or thread—whichever process or thread was current when the interrupt occurred)

As stated in the preceding section, device drivers in Windows 2000 don't manipulate hardware directly; rather, they call functions in the HAL to interface with the hardware. Drivers are typically written in C (sometimes C++) and therefore, with proper use of HAL routines, can be source code portable across the CPU architectures supported by Windows 2000 and binary portable within an architecture family.

Several types of device drivers exist:

- *Hardware device drivers* manipulate hardware (using the HAL) to write output to or retrieve input from a physical device or network. There are many types of hardware device drivers, such as bus drivers, human interface drivers, and mass storage drivers.
- *File system drivers* are Windows 2000 drivers that accept file-oriented I/O requests and translate them into I/O requests bound for a particular device.
- *File system filter drivers,* such as those that perform disk mirroring and encryption, intercept I/Os and perform some added-value processing before passing the I/O to the next layer.
- *Network redirectors* and *servers* are file system drivers that transmit file system I/O requests to a machine on the network and receive such requests, respectively.
- *Protocol drivers* implement a networking protocol such as TCP/IP, NetBEUI, or IPX/SPX.
- *Kernel streaming filter drivers* are chained together to perform signal processing on data streams, such as recording or displaying audio and video.

Windows 2000 adds support for PnP, Power Options, and an extension to the Windows NT driver model called the Windows Driver Model (WDM). Windows

2000 can run legacy Windows NT 4 drivers, but because these don't support PnP and Power Options, systems running these drivers will have reduced capabilities in these two areas.

From the WDM perspective, there are three kinds of drivers:

- A *bus driver* services a bus controller, adapter, bridge, or any device that has child devices. Bus drivers are required drivers, and Microsoft generally provides them; each type of bus (such as PCI, PCMCIA, and USB) on a system has one bus driver. Third parties can write bus drivers to provide support for new buses, such as VMEbus, Multibus, and Futurebus.

- A *function driver* is the main device driver and provides the operational interface for its device. It is a required driver unless the device is used raw (an implementation in which I/O is done by the bus driver and any bus filter drivers, such as SCSI PassThru). A function driver is by definition the driver that knows the most about a particular device, and it is usually the only driver that accesses device-specific registers.

- A *filter driver* is used to add functionality to a device (or existing driver) or to modify I/O requests or responses from other drivers (often used to fix hardware that provides incorrect information about its hardware resource requirements). Filter drivers are optional and can exist in any number, placed above or below a function driver and above a bus driver. Usually, system original equipment manufacturers (OEMs) or independent hardware vendors supply filter drivers.

In the WDM driver environment, no single driver controls all aspects of a device: a bus driver is concerned with reporting the devices on its bus to the PnP manager, while a function driver manipulates the device.

In most cases, lower-level filter drivers modify the behavior of device hardware. For example, if a device reports to its bus driver that it requires 4 I/O ports when it actually requires 16 I/O ports, a lower-level device-specific function filter driver could intercept the list of hardware resources reported by the bus driver to the PnP manager, and update the count of I/O ports.

Upper-level filter drivers usually provide added-value features for a device. For example, an upper-level device filter driver for a keyboard can enforce additional security checks.

### 4.3.7  System Processes

The following system processes appear on every Windows 2000 system. (Two of these—Idle and System—are not full processes, as they are not running a user-mode executable.)

- Idle process (contains one thread per CPU to account for idle CPU time)
- System process (contains the majority of the kernel-mode system threads)
- Session manager (`Smss.exe`)
- Win32 subsystem (`Csrss.exe`)
- Logon process (`Winlogon.exe`)
- Service control manager (`Services.exe`) and the child service processes it creates
- Local security authentication server (`Lsass.exe`)

To help you understand the relationship of these processes, use the *tlist /t* command in the Windows 2000 Support Tools to display the process "tree," that is, the parent/child relationship between processes. Here is a partial annotated output from *tlist /t*:

```
System Process (0)        Idle process
System (8)                System process (default home for system threads)
  smss.exe (144)          Session Manager
    csrss.exe (172)       Win32 subsystem process
    winlogon.exe (192)    Logon process (also contains NetDDE service)
      services.exe (220)  Service control manager
        svchost.exe (384) Generic service host image
        spoolsv.exe (480) Spooler service
        regsvc.exe (636)  Remote registry service
        mstask.exe (664)  Task Scheduler service
      lsass.exe (232)     Local security authentication server
```

The next sections explain the key system processes shown in this output.

**Idle Process.** Despite the name shown, the first process listed in the preceding sample *tlist /t* output (process ID 0) is actually the System Idle process. Processes are identified by their image name. However, this process (as well as process ID 8, named System) isn't running a real user-mode image. Hence, the names shown by the various system display utilities differ from utility to utility. Although most utilities call process ID 8 "System," not all do.

Now let's look at system threads and the purpose of each of the system processes that are running real images.

**System Process and System Threads.** The System process (always process ID 8) is the home for a special kind of thread that runs only in kernel mode: a *kernel-mode system thread*. System threads have all the attributes and contexts of regular user-mode threads (such as a hardware context and priority) but are different in that they run only in kernel mode executing code loaded in system space, whether that is in `Ntoskrnl.exe` or in any other loaded device driver. In addition, system threads don't have a user process address space and hence must allocate any dynamic storage from operating system memory heaps, such as paged or nonpaged pool.

System threads are created by the *PsCreateSystemThread* function (documented in the DDK), which can be called only from kernel mode. Windows 2000 as well as various device drivers create system threads during system initialization to perform operations that require thread context, such as issuing and waiting for I/Os or other objects or polling a device. For example, the memory manager uses system threads to implement such functions as writing dirty pages to the page file or mapped files, swapping processes in and out of memory, and so forth. The kernel creates a system thread called the *balance set manager* that wakes up once per second to possibly initiate various scheduling and memory management–related events. The cache manager also uses system threads to implement both read-ahead and write-behind I/Os. The file server device driver (`Srv.sys`) uses system threads to respond to network I/O requests for file data on disk partitions shared to the network. Even the floppy driver has a system thread to poll the floppy device (polling is more efficient in this case because an interrupt-driven floppy driver consumes a large amount of system resources).

By default, system threads are owned by the System process, but a device driver can create a system thread in any process. For example, the Win32 subsystem device driver (`Win32k.sys`) creates system threads in the Win32 subsystem process (`Csrss.exe`) so that they can easily access data in the user-mode address space of that process.

**Session Manager (Smss).** The Session Manager (\Winnt\System32\Smss.exe) is the first user-mode process created in the system. The kernel-mode system thread that performs the final phase of the initialization of the executive and kernel creates the actual `Smss` process.

The Session Manager is responsible for a number of important steps in starting Windows 2000, such as opening additional page files, performing delayed file rename and delete operations, and creating system environment variables. It also launches the subsystem processes (normally just `Csrss.exe`) and the Winlogon process, which in turn creates the rest of the system processes.

Much of the configuration information in the registry that drives the initialization steps of `Smss` can be found under

```
HKLM\SYSTEM\CurrentControlSet\Control\Session Manager .
```

You'll find it interesting to examine the kinds of data stored there. (For a description of the keys and values, see the Registry Entries help file, `Regentry.chm`, in the Windows 2000 resource kits.)

After performing these initialization steps, the main thread in `Smss` waits forever on the process handles to Csrss and Winlogon. If either of these processes terminates unexpectedly, `Smss` crashes the system, since Windows 2000 relies on their existence. Meanwhile, `Smss` waits for requests to load subsystems, new subsystems starting up, and debug events. It also acts as a switch and monitor between applications and debuggers.

**Logon (Winlogon).** The Windows 2000 logon process (\Winnt\System32\ Winlogon.exe) handles interactive user logons and logoffs. Winlogon is notified of a user logon request when the *secure attention sequence* (SAS) keystroke combination is entered. The default SAS on Windows 2000 is the combination `Ctrl+Alt+Delete`. The SAS protects users from password-capture programs that simulate the logon process. Once the username and password have been captured, they are sent to the local security authentication server process (described in the next section) to be validated. If they match, Winlogon extracts the value of the Userinit registry value under the registry key HKLM\SOFTWARE\ Microsoft\Windows NT\CurrentVersion\Winlogon and creates a process to run each executable image listed in that value. The default is to run a process named `Userinit.exe`.

This process performs some initialization of the user environment (such as restoring mapped drive letters, running the login script, and applying group policies), looks in the registry at the Shell value (under the same Winlogon key referred to previously), and creates a process to run the system-defined shell (by default, `Explorer.exe`). Then Userinit exits. This is the reason `Explorer.exe` is shown with no parent—its parent has exited, and (as explained earlier), tlist left-justifies processes whose parent isn't running. (Another way of looking at it is that Explorer is the grandchild of Winlogon.)

The identification and authentication aspects of the logon process are implemented in a replaceable DLL named GINA (Graphical Identification and Authentication). The standard Windows 2000 GINA, Msgina.dll, implements the default Windows 2000 logon interface. Developers can, however, provide their own GINA DLL to implement other identification and authentication mechanisms in place of the standard Windows 2000 username/password method (such as one based on a voice print). In addition, Winlogon can load other network provider DLLs that need to perform secondary authentication. This capability allows multiple network providers to gather identification and authentication information all at one time during normal logon.

Winlogon is active not only during user logon and logoff but also whenever it intercepts the SAS from the keyboard. For example, when you press Ctrl+Alt+Delete while logged in, the Windows Security dialog box comes up, providing the options to log off, start the Task Manager, lock the workstation, shut down the system, and so forth. Winlogon is the process that handles this interaction.

**Local Security Authentication Server (LSASS).** The local security authentication server process (\Winnt\System32\Lsass.exe) receives authentication requests from Winlogon and calls the appropriate authentication package (implemented as a DLL) to perform the actual verification, such as checking whether a password matches what is stored in the active directory or the SAM (the part of the registry that contains the definition of the users and groups).

Upon a successful authentication, LSASS generates an access token object that contains the user's security profile. Winlogon then uses this access token to create the initial shell process. Processes launched from the shell then by default inherit this access token.

**Service Control Manager (SCM).** The service control manager is a special system process running the image \Winnt\System32\Services.exe that is responsible for starting, stopping, and interacting with service processes. Service processes are like Unix daemon processes in that they can be configured to start automatically at system boot time without requiring an interactive logon. Service processes run normal Win32 images that call special Win32 functions to interact with the service control manager to perform such actions as registering the service's successful startup, responding to status requests, or pausing or shutting down the service. Services are defined in the registry under HKLM\SYSTEM\CurrentControlSet\Services.

To map a service process to the services contained in that process, use the *tlist /s* command. Note that there isn't always one-to-one mapping between service process and running services, however, because some services share a process with other services. In the registry, the type code indicates whether the service runs in its own process or shares a process with other services in the image.

A number of Windows 2000 components are implemented as services, such as the spooler, event log, task scheduler, and various other networking components. To list the installed services, select Administrative Tools from the Control Panel, and then select Services.

## 4.4   Win32 API

The Win32 application programming interface is the primary programming interface to the Microsoft Windows operating system family, including Windows 2000, Windows 95, Windows 98, Windows Millennium Edition, and Windows CE. Each operating system implements a different subset of Win32. For the most part, Windows 2000 is a superset of all Win32 implementations.

Although Windows 2000 was designed to support multiple programming interfaces, Win32 is the primary, or preferred, interface to the operating system. Win32 has this position because, of the three environment subsystems (Win32, POSIX, and OS/2), it provides the greatest access to the underlying Windows 2000 system services.

The Win32 API documentation can be viewed on line at `msdn.microsoft.com`. It can also be installed by downloading the Platform SDK (available for free at *msdn.microsoft.com*). The Platform SDK contains the C header files and libraries necessary to compile and link Win32 applications. (Although Microsoft Visual C++ comes with a copy of these header files, the versions contained in the Platform SDK always match the latest version of the Windows operating systems, whereas the version that comes with Visual C++ might be an older version that was current when Visual C++ was released.)

The following is an overview of the major groups of Win32 system calls:

- *Base services:* processes and threads, memory management, synchronization, device and file I/O, error handling, debugging, event Logging, interprocess communication, power management, and system configuration
- *Graphics:* functions that deal with graphical output, such as bitmaps, pens, brushes, fonts, text, and colors
- *Window management:* windows, desktops, mouse and keyboard input, buttons, cursors, dialog boxes, icons, menus, scroll bars, and other controls

Note that these represent only the core system calls—the Platform SDK describes over 100 groups of functions for building applications, such as COM+ (a framework for building *n*-tier distributed applications), data services, multimedia, and Web services.

## 4.5   Tools to Explore Windows 2000

Many details about the internals of Windows 2000 can be exposed and demonstrated by using a variety of available tools, such as those that come with Windows

2000, the Windows 2000 Support Tools, the Windows 2000 resource kits, and the Windows debugging tools. These tool packages are briefly introduced next.

### 4.5.1   Windows 2000 Support Tools

The Windows 2000 Support Tools consist of about forty tools useful in administering and troubleshooting Windows 2000 systems. Many of these tools were formerly part of the Windows NT 4 resource kits. You can install the Support Tools by running `Setup.exe` in the \Support\Tools folder on any Windows 2000 product distribution CD. (That is, the Support Tools are the same on Windows 2000 Professional, Server, and Advanced Server.)

### 4.5.2   Windows 2000 Resource Kits

The Windows 2000 resource kits supplement the Support Tools, adding some two hundred additional tools. Besides including many tools useful for displaying internal system state, they contain useful internals documentation, such as the Registry Reference and Performance Counters help files. There are two editions of the resource kits: the Windows 2000 Professional Resource Kit and the Windows 2000 Server Resource Kit. For updates to tools, as well as for new tools, see the Web site `www.reskit.com`.

### 4.5.3   Debugging Tools

The Debugging Tools for Windows package, available for download from `www.microsoft.com/ddk/debugging`, contains tools and documentation for advanced debugging and troubleshooting. For example, the package includes the Microsoft kernel debuggers, which, although used mainly for analyzing crash dumps or debugging device drivers, can also be used to investigate Windows 2000 internals because they can display internal system information not visible through any standard utility. For example, they can dump internal data structures such as thread blocks, process blocks, page tables, I/O, and pool structures. For more information, see the debugging tools help file included with this package. It explains how to set up and use the kernel debuggers (as well as other debugging and support tools that are part of the package).

### 4.5.4   Device Driver Kit

The Windows 2000 DDK is part of the MSDN Professional (and Universal) subscription, but it is also available for free download at `www.microsoft.com/ddk`. Although the DDK is aimed at device driver developers, the DDK is an abundant source of Windows 2000 internals information. For example, the DDK documentation contains a comprehensive description of the Windows 2000 I/O system in both a tutorial and reference form, including the internal system routines and data structures used by device drivers. Besides the documentation, the DDK contains header files that define key internal data structures and constants as well as interfaces to many internal system routines (in particular, `Wdm.h`).

### 4.5.5  Sysinternals Tools

Another source of useful troubleshooting and analysis tools is `www.sysinternals.com`.

# 5 Network Hardware

*Thomas Sterling*

Networking converts a shelf full of PCs into a single system. Networking also allows a system to be accessed remotely and to provide services to remote clients. The incredible growth of both the Internet and enterprise-specific intranets has resulted in the availability of high-performance, low-cost networking hardware that Beowulf systems use to create a single system from a collection of nodes. This chapter reviews networking hardware, with a particular emphasis on Fast Ethernet because of its superb price/performance ratio.

For Beowulf systems, the most demanding communication requirements are not with the external environment but with the other nodes on the system area network. In a Beowulf system, every Beowulf node may need to interact with every other node, independently or together, to move a wide range of data types between processors. Such data may be large blocks of contiguous information representing subpartitions of very large global data sets, small packets containing single values, or synchronization signals in support of collective operation. In the former case, a high bandwidth communication path may be required. In the latter case, low latency communication is required to expedite execution. Requirements in both cases are highly sensitive to the characteristics of the parallel program being executed. In any case, communications capability will determine the generality of the Beowulf-class system and the degree of difficulty in constructing efficient programs. The choice of network hardware and software dictates the nature of this capability.

Section 5.1 introduces some of the most popular networking technologies for Beowulf clusters. In Section 5.2, we take a detailed look at the most popular networking choice, Fast Ethernet (and Gigabit Ethernet). We conclude in Section 5.3 with comments on interconnect technology choice and some other practical issues

## 5.1 Interconnect Technologies

In spite of its popular use in existing Beowulfs, Ethernet-based networking is not the only technology choice for enabling internode communication. Other solutions exist that can deliver equal or better performance depending on the application. Fast Ethernet is a popular choice because of its ubiquity and consequent low price. A Fast Ethernet card costs only about 2 percent of the price of today's $1,000 Beowulf nodes. Only the network switches have a significant impact on the overall price of the system. With other networking technologies, each network interface card can cost as much as a 16-port Fast Ethernet switch. So you have to think carefully before committing to an alternative network. If the kinds of applications you intend to run require specific properties, such as low latency, which are not provided by Fast Ethernet, then it is likely worth the additional cost. For example, real-time image processing, parallel video streaming, and real-time transaction processing all require low latencies and do not work well with Fast Ethernet. We will briefly discuss the most common networking technologies used by Beowulf systems. Not enough data has been collected on application performance in systems using these technologies for us to comment on when each should be used.

### 5.1.1   The Ethernets

The most popular and inexpensive networking choice for Beowulfs is Ethernet, particularly Fast Ethernet. Ethernet, first developed at Xerox PARC in the early 1970s and standardized by the IEEE in the early 1980s, is the most widely used technology for local area networks. Ethernet continues to be an evolving technology: 10 Gigabit Ethernet (10 Gbps) has entered vendor field testing and should be available in quantity by early 2002. With the very low cost of Fast Ethernet and the rapid emergence of Gigabit and 10 Gigabit Ethernet, Ethernet will continue to play a critical role in Beowulf-class computing for some time to come.

**Fast Ethernet.**   Beowulf was enabled by the availability of a low-cost, moderate-bandwidth networking technology. Ethernet, operating initially at 10 megabits per second (Mbps) for early Beowulfs and shortly thereafter at 100 Mbps peak bandwidth, provided a cost-effective means of interconnecting PCs to form an integrated cluster. Used primarily for commercial local area network technology, Ethernet supplied the means of implementing a system area network at about 20 percent of the cost of the total system, even when employing low-cost personal computers. Fast Ethernet with TCP/IP provides 90–95 Mbps to applications with latencies in the hundreds of microseconds. Drivers for Fast Ethernet and TCP/IP have been integrated into the mainline Linux kernel sources for quite some time and are well tested, with a large user base. Cost of Fast Ethernet interfaces has dropped to the point that many motherboard vendors have begun to integrate single- or dual-port interfaces into their products. While other networking continues to be available (and used in some Beowulfs), Fast Ethernet will continue to be a mainstay of many Beowulf implementations because of its extremely low cost.

**Gigabit Ethernet.**   The success of 100 base-T Fast Ethernet and the growing demands imposed on networks by high-resolution image data, real-time data browsing, and Beowulf-class distributed applications have driven the industry to establish a new set of standards for Ethernet technology capable of 1 Gbps. Referred to as "Gigabit Ethernet," a backward-compatible network infrastructure has been devised, and products are available from various vendors. A number of changes were required to Fast Ethernet, including the physical layer and a large part of the data exchange protocols. However, to maintain compatibility with Fast Ethernet, or 100-baseT systems, means for mixed-mode operation has been provided. Currently, Gigabit Ethernet is not quite cost effective for Beowulf-class computing. The early product offerings for Gigabit Ethernet, as the early offerings for 10 Gigabit Ethernet will be, were for backbone service and traffic aggregation rather than for direct host connections; hence, the demand for NICs was assumed to be low, and a large market has not yet emerged to amortize development costs. Both switches and NICs are substantially more expensive than their Fast Ethernet equivalents.

Several factors will motivate the migration of next-generation Gigabit Ethernet into the role of system area networks for Beowulf-class systems. While Fast Ethernet served well for 200 MHz Intel Pentium Pro processor-based Beowulf nodes, current Pentium 4 processors are available at speeds of 1.7 GHz. The PCI bus now supports a data path twice as wide and twice the clock rate, permitting high-bandwidth data transfers to peripheral devices including Gigabit NICs. A broader range of Beowulf applications can be supported with higher bandwidth. Unfortunately, Gigabit Ethernet with TCP/IP does not provide substantially better latencies than does Fast Ethernet. Some Beowulf installations have already experimented with Gigabit Ethernet, and the Beowulf project has already delivered drivers to the Linux operating system for several Gigabit Ethernet cards. Some vendors have even begun to supply high-performance, open source gigabit drivers for their NICs. The experience with Fast Ethernet demonstrated that a rapid and dramatic drop in price can be expected once the technology is adopted by the mass market. With the introduction of inexpensive combination ethernet/Fast Ethernet/Gigabit Ethernet ASICs, motherboard integration and low-cost gigabit adapters are beginning to appear. Gigabit switch prices have also begun to fall. The 1 Gbps technology is in place, and experience by manufacturers is leading to rapid improvements and cost cutting. With these advances, we expect that Gigabit Ethernet will become a leader in interconnect price/performance in the next one to two years.

### 5.1.2   Myrinet

Myrinet is a system area network (SAN) designed by Myricom, Inc. On November 2, 1998, it was approved as American National Standard ANSI/VITA 26-1998. It is designed around simple low-latency blocking switches. The path through these switches is implemented with "header-stripping" source routing, where the sending node prepends the route through the network, and each switch removes the first byte of the message and uses it as the output port. Packets can be of arbitrary length.

The bandwidth of the adapter and switch is hidden from the application and has regularly increased over time from the original 640 Mbps to the current 2.4 Gbps. Myrinet delivers between 10 and 7 microseconds, depending on the generation of adapter and switch. A limitation of Myrinet is that the switches are incrementally blocking. If a destination port is busy in a multistage network, the packet is stalled, and that stalled packet potentially blocks other packets traveling the network, even to unrelated source and destination nodes. This problem is mitigated, however, by the network's high speed and the ability to construct topologies with rich interconnects. Blocking is minimized by higher-density switches that reduce the number of a stages traversed by a typical message in a network of fixed size.

While Myrinet is the strongest provider of high-bandwidth SANs, it has the limitation of being provided by a single vendor. The price of the network adapters and per port costs of switches has remained high, typically exceeding the price of the entire computing node. Myrinet's big advantage is its customized protocols. These protocols are designed to yield high performance and low latency by offloading as much work as possible to the NIC itself and bypassing the operating system whenever possible. Myrinet NICs effectively provide a second processor that can do much of the protocol work and avoid interrupting the host CPU during communication. This advantage could also be obtained for less money by adding a second primary processor. This advantage is most significant with active messages, where the on-board processor can handle the message and generate a reply without and interrupting the host CPU. In order for the hardware to be used in this way, Myricom provides a substantial amount of open source software, both drivers and a tuned version of MPICH. Using customized protocols also encourages user-level access to the hardware. This strategy has also been pursued with commodity hardware (see Section 5.3.3 for a brief discussion of MVIA, an implementation for commodity hardware by the Virtual Interface Architecture, VIA). Unfortunately, user-level access protocols have the disadvantage of precluding clusters from transparently scaling from standard TCP and Ethernet on small-scale machines to alternative hardware such as Myrinet on big clusters.

### 5.1.3   cLAN

The cLAN high-performance cluster switches provide a native implementation of the VIA (see www.viarch.org). Eight port and thirty port switches are available, offering 1.25 Gbps per port (2.5 Gbps bidirectional). Because these implement the

VIA directly in hardware, latencies are low (around 0.5 microsecond) and bandwidths are high (comparable to the other high-end networking solutions). The developer of cLAN was Giganet, which was acquired by Emulex in March 2001.

While VIA is defined by a consortium and is not a single-vendor design, the VIA standard specifies only a set of concepts and operations. There is no specification of the signals (they can be electrical, optical, or anything else) or the interfaces to individual computers. There is also no standard programmer interface, although most VIA efforts (including cLAN) use the sample application programming interface provided in the VIA specification. However, because the VIA standard does not specify the hardware over which VIA is used, there is no possibility of interoperable VIA solutions. Infiniband, discussed below, addresses this issue.

### 5.1.4    Scalable Coherent Interface

The Scalable Coherent Interface is an IEEE standard originally designed to provide an interconnect for cache-coherent shared-memory systems. One of the first major deployments of SCI was on the Convex Exemplar SPP-1000 in 1994. SCI has not been able to gain ground in traditional networking markets, despite its ability to serve as a general-purpose interconnect. The main reason Beowulf designers choose to use SCI is for its low latency of well under 10 $\mu$s. Current PC motherboard chip sets do not support the coherency mechanisms required to construct an SCI-based shared-memory Beowulf. But if that functionality is ever added to commodity motherboards, we may see an increase in the popularity of SCI as researchers experiment with shared-memory Beowulf systems. Seven years ago, SCI delivered many clear advantages, but today commodity network technology has caught up, although SCI still delivers significantly lower latency. Dolphin Interconnect offers an SCI-based interconnect for Beowulf systems along with closed-source binary drivers and an implementation of MPI tuned for the SCI network.

### 5.1.5    QsNet

Another high-performance network, called QsNet, is produced by Quadrics. This network provides a bandwidth of 340 Mbps and an MPI latency of around 5 $\mu$s. While this network is one the costliest, it has been chosen by some of the largest clusters, including Compaq SC systems for the ASCI Q system and the NSF teraflops system at the Pittsburg Supercomputing Center. To provide high performance, Quadrics uses many techniques similar to those mentioned above for Myrinet.

| Preamble 1010.....1010 | SYNCH 11 | DESTINATION ADDRESS | SOURCE ADDRESS | TYPE | DATA | FRAME CHECK SEQUENCE |
|---|---|---|---|---|---|---|
| 62 BITS | 2 BITS | 6 BYTES | 6 BYTES | 2 BYTES | 16-1500 BYTES | 4 BYTES |

**Figure 5.1**
Ethernet packet format.

### 5.1.6   Infiniband

Infiniband (`www.infinibandta.org`) combines many of the concepts of VIA with a detailed electrical and interface specification that will allow vendors to produce interoperable components. This addresses the major limitation of the VIA specification. One goal of the Infiniband trade organization (with over two hundred members) is to increase the rate at which networking performance improves.

As of early 2001, no Infiniband products were available. Many are under development, however, and by 2002 Infiniband may become an important alternative to the other networks described here. Intel has committed to delivering integrated Infiniband interfaces on its motherboards in the next one to two years. This should provide another high-bandwidth, low-latency interconnect at a relatively low price point.

## 5.2   A Detailed Look at Ethernet

Ethernet was originally developed as a packet-based, serial multidrop network requiring no centralized control. All network access and arbitration control is performed by distributed mechanisms. Variable-length message packets comprise a sequence of bits including a header, data, and error-detecting nodes. A fixed-topology (no switched line routing) network passes packets from the source to destination through intermediate elements known as hubs or switches. The next step through the network is determined by addressing information in the packet header. The topology can be a shared multidrop passive cable to which many Ethernet controllers are attached, a tree structure of hubs or switches, or some more complicated switching technology for high bandwidths and low latency under heavy loads.

### 5.2.1   Packet Format

The Ethernet message packet comprises a sequence of seven multibit fields, one of which is variable length. The fields include a combination of network control information and data payload. The structure of the Ethernet packet is shown in

Figure 5.1 and is described below. The packet's variable length allows improved overall network performance across a wide range of payload requirements. Thus, a transfer of only a few words between nodes does not impose the full burden of the longest possible packet. However, even with this capability, sustained data transfer throughput is sensitive to packet length and can vary by more than an order of magnitude depending on payload size, even in the absence of network contention.

**Preamble.** Arrival of a message packet at a receiving node (whether or not the message is addressed for that node) is asynchronous. Prior to data assimilation, the node and the incident packet must first synchronize. The preamble field is a 62-bit sequence of alternating 1s and 0s that allows the phase lock loop circuitry of the node receiver to lock on to the incoming signal and synchronize with the bit stream.

**Synch.** The synch field is a 2-bit sequence of 1s (11) that breaks the sequence of alternating 1s and 0s provided by the preamble and indicates where the remaining information in the packet begins. If the preamble provides carrier-level synchronization, the synch field provides bit field registration.

**Destination Address.** The destination address field is 6 bytes (or 48 bits) in length and specifies the network designation of the network node intended to receive the packet. A message packet may be intended for an individual node or a group of nodes. If the first bit of the destination address field is 0, then the message is intended for a single receiving node. If the first bit is 1, then the message is multicast, intended for some or all network nodes. In the case of multicast communications, a group address is employed providing a logical association among some subset of all receiving nodes. Any node that is a member of a group specified by the message destination address field (with the first bit equal to 1) must accept the message. In the case of a multicast transmitted packet, a destination address field of all 1s indicates that the packet is a broadcast message intended for all nodes on the network. Ethernet node receivers must be capable of receiving, detecting, and accepting broadcast messages.

In addition to distinguishing among single destination and multicast transmission, the destination address also determines whether the specified address is a globally or locally administered address. A globally administered address is unique and is provided by an industrywide assignment process. The address is built into the network adaptor (interface card) by the manufacturer. A locally administered address is provided by the local systems administrator and can be changed by the organization managing the network. The second bit of the destination address field is a 0 if globally administered and a 1 if the address designation is locally administered. The sequence of bits of the destination address field is sent least significant bit first.

**Source Address.** The source address is a 48-bit field that indicates the address of the transmitting node. The format of the source address is the same as that of the destination address. The source address is always the individual address and never a group address of the node sending a packet. Therefore, the least significant bit is always 0. Likewise, the broadcast address is never used in this field.

**Type.** The type field is 16 bits in length and designates the message protocol type. This information is used at higher levels of message-handling software and does not affect the actual exchange of data bits across the network. The most significant of the two bytes is sent first, with the least significant bit of each byte of the type field being sent first.

**Data.** The message payload of the packet is included in the data field. The data field is variable length. It may have as few as 46 bytes and as many as 1,500 bytes. Thus, a packet may be as small as 72 bytes or as long as 1,526 bytes. The contents of the data field are passed to higher-level software and do no affect the network transfer control. Data is transferred least significant bit first.

**Frame Check Sequence.** Error detection for message corruption in transmission is provided by computing a cyclic redundancy check (CRC) for the destination address, source address, type, and data fields. The four-byte CRC value is provided as the last field of the message packet. It is computed by both the transmitting and receiving nodes and compared by the receiving node to determine that the integrity of the packet has been retained in transmission.

### 5.2.2 NIC Architecture

The Network Interface Controller accepts message data from the host node processor and presents an encapsulated and encoded version of the data to the physical network medium for transmission. While there have been many different implementations of the Ethernet NIC hardware, with some enhancements, their basic architecture is the same. Figure 5.2 shows a block diagram of the typical Ethernet NIC architecture. The Data Link Layer of the architecture is responsible for constructing the message packet and controlling the logical network interface functions. The Physical Layer is responsible for encoding the message packet in a form that can actually be applied to the transmission medium.

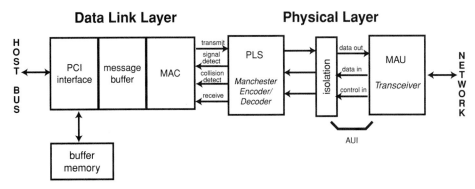

**Figure 5.2**
Ethernet NIC architecture.

**Data Link Layer.** The Data Link Layer provides the logical interface between the host processor and the Physical Layer of the Ethernet. When a message is to be transmitted, the Data Link Layer accepts, temporarily stores, and encapsulates the message and controls the transmission process of the Physical Layer. When a message is being received, it accepts the packet from the Physical Layer, determines whether the node is the correct destination, verifies bit integrity, unpacks the data into byte sequence, temporarily buffers the data, and passes it on to the processor. The Data Link Layer is made up of the Logical Link Control sublayer and the Media Access Control sublayer.

For most current-generation Beowulf nodes, the Logical Link Control sublayer incorporates an interface to the PCI bus. This element of the Ethernet controller provides all logical control required to accept commands from the host processor and to provide direct memory access to the node main memory for rapid data transfers between memory and the network. Usually included is some form of FIFO buffering within the Data Link Layer to hold one or more incoming or outgoing messages in the node. The Logical Link Control sublayer presents variable-length byte sequences to the Media Access Control sublayer and accepts data byte sequences from it. The exact form and operation of the Logical Link Control sublayer is not standardized, and manufacturer differences are a source of headaches for device driver writers.

The Media Access Controller (MAC) is largely responsible for conducting the Ethernet protocol for both transmitted and received messages. Its two principal tasks are message encapsulation and packet collision handling. To transmit a message, the MAC accepts the byte sequence of the data to be sent, as well as the destination address, from the Logical Link Controller. It formats the message packet including the preamble, synch bits, destination address, its own address in the source address field, and the protocol type provided by the logical link controller as well as the data field. It then computes the CRC value and appends it to the message packet. When receiving an Ethernet packet from the Physical Layer, the MAC strips away the preamble and synch bits and determines if the destination address is that of its host node. If not, the rest of the message is discarded and the receive process terminates. If the Destination Address field matches the local address, the MAC accepts the data, reformatting it into the correctly ordered byte sequence for the Logical Link Controller. The MAC computes the cyclic redundancy check and compares it with the value included in the message to verify transmission integrity.

The MAC is also responsible for handling the CSMA/CD (Carrier Sense Multiple Access/Collision Detect) arbitration protocol. The Physical Layer provides signals to the MAC indicating whether there is packet transmission on the data link and whether there is a collision among two or more packets on the link. When a signal is available, the MAC operates as above to determine whether the message is for the host node and, if so, acquires the data. In the case of a collision, the MAC simply discards any partial incoming messages and waits for new packet data. When transmitting, the MAC is responsible for handling collision avoidance and resolution. As described above, the MAC waits for access to the data link and supplies the packet to the physical layer that begins transmission. If in the process of packet transmission the MAC receives a collision signal from the Physical Layer, after briefly continuing transmission (to overcome the network propagation delay) it terminates the message and begins its random roll-back sequence to determine a new time when it will again attempt to transmit the message.

**Physical Layer.** The Physical Layer encodes the message packet provided by the Data Link Layer and converts it to electrical signals appropriate for the physical transmission medium. Upon receiving messages transmitted by other nodes, the Physical Layer acquires the electrical signals from the transmission medium, converts them to digital signals, and decodes them into the message's binary bit sequence. The Physical Layer includes two major stages: the transceiver and the Physical Line Signaling (PLS) sublayer. The transceiver, also referred to as the Medium Attachment Unit (MAU), performs the electrical conversion from transmission media signals to logical signal levels.

The interface between the PLS sublayer of the Physical Layer and the MAC sublayer of the Data Link Layer exchanges data with bits represented as discrete voltage levels. This form of information representation is inadequate for Ethernet for two reasons. First, in a highly noisy (in the electrical sense) environment such as presented by a local area network, signal levels can be significantly attenuated and distorted. Second, in a single bit-serial communication protocol such as that employed by the Ethernet interconnect, both data and timing information need to be incorporated in the signal. For this reason, Manchester encoding is used to convey the information with the value of a bit specified by the sense (direction) of the signal transition rather than a specific range of values. With data fixed at the point of signal transition, the timing information is provided simultaneously.

The actual Ethernet signal is differential; that is, one line is high when the other is low and vice versa. The PLS sublayer converts the message packet provided by the MAC first into its Manchester encoded representation and then into differential form. The PLS layer performs the decoding task for incoming signals from the transceiver, converting Manchester sequences into regular bit strings. The PLS layer also provides the collision detect signal to the MAC.

### 5.2.3 Hubs and Switches

The Network Interface Controllers provide the connection between the processor node and the system area network. The effectiveness of the SAN and its scalability depend on the means by which the nodes are interconnected. These include passive multidrop coaxial cable, active repeaters, and intelligent routing switches, as well as more complicated through-the-node store and forward techniques.

**Repeaters and Hubs.** An early advantage of Ethernet was that the medium of communication was a passive multidrop coaxial cable. Over a limited distance and number of nodes, such a cable located all expensive logic and electronics in the NICs. As technology costs dropped and demands on network performance increased, other approaches could compete. Ironically, the coax cables that had helped keep costs down became the dominant cost driver. Twisted-pair connections using inexpensive repeaters or hubs have now replaced coaxial cables in all but the oldest installations. Logically, hubs provide the same NIC interface. All nodes are visible from all other nodes, and the CSMA/CD arbitration protocol is still employed. A repeater is an active unit that accepts signals from the distributed nodes on separate twisted pair wires, actively cleans up the signals, amplifies them to desired levels, and then redistributes them to all of the attached nodes.

**Switches.** The demand for higher sustained bandwidths and the need to include larger number of nodes on a single network spurred development of more sophisticated means of exchanging messages among nodes. Switches, like hubs or repeaters, accept packets on twisted-pair wires from the nodes. Unlike repeaters, however, these signals are not broadcast to all connected nodes. Instead, the destination address fields of the message packets are interpreted and the packet is sent only to the target node or nodes. This functionality is much more complicated than that of a simple repeater, requiring buffer space and logic not required by a hub. At the time of the earliest Beowulfs, the cost of switches was prohibitive. By the third generation of Beowulf systems (based on Intel Pentium Pro processors), however, the cost of switches was sufficiently low that they became standard Beowulf components.

Today, 16-way switches have dropped in price another factor of four or more, and they are the backbone of many moderate-sized systems. Moderate-cost switches with up to 48 connections are widely available. For greater connectivity, multiple switches can be interconnected. There is a catch, however. The network must be a tree; it may not contain any cycles.

A problem occurs with the tree topology. The bisection bandwidth of the root or top level switch becomes a communication bottleneck. All the traffic might have to go through this channel. A typical bandwidth for low-cost, 16-way Fast Ethernet switches is near or at 1.6 Gbps. Backplane saturation with Fast Ethernet switches is not a serious problem at this point. Current generation of gigabit switches provides much higher backplane bisection bandwidth and therefore the possibility of many more network ports without contention. With a properly sized core gigabit switch, the network core can be easily (with money) scaled to 192 Gbps or more. With these, use of Fast Ethernet switches with dual or quad gigabit uplinks scale properly, without serious contention in the network to a scale easily upwards of 1,000 nodes.

## 5.3   Network Practicalities: Interconnect Choice

Network choice for a system area network can be a difficult process. In this section we consider various factors and present two examples illustrating how different choices can affect performance.

### 5.3.1   Importance of the Interconnect

The cost for the NIC and switch complex can equal or exceed the cost of node hardware on a large cluster: it is not a factor that should be taken lightly.

In the absence of financial considerations, however, the most important factor when choosing an interconnect technology is the communication patterns of the intended workload for the cluster. While the peak CPU performance of the processors in a cluster tends to add up rather quickly, a given application may or may not be able to effectively utilize it without a high bandwidth and/or low latency interconnect. This can account for up to a 95% penalty when comparing theoretical speed with achieved performance. Because of this fact, and the high cost of interconnect hardware, it is important to build a properly sized system area network for a given workload.

If a cluster is being built for a small number of applications, thorough application benchmarking is in order. The spectrum of communication patterns exhibited by applications ranges from occasional communication from one node to another to consistent communication from all nodes to all other nodes. At one extreme are applications that behave like Seti@Home, wherein compute nodes infrequently query a master node for a work unit to process for hours or days. At the other extreme are applications like MILC (MIMD Lattice Computation), where nodes are in constant communication with one or more other nodes and the speed of the computation is limited by the performance of the slowest node. As is obvious from the communication pattern description, basically any interconnect would perform admirably in the first case, while the fastest interconnect possible is desirable in the second case.

### 5.3.2   Differences between the Interconnect Choices

As seen in the preceding descriptions, interconnects vary wildly with respect to bandwidth, latency, scalability, and cost. Available interconnect bandwidth can range from a shared 10 Mbps network segment for the entire cluster to upwards to 340 Mbps available to all nodes simultaneously. Latency delivered to applications can range from in the hundreds of microseconds down to half a microsecond. This is near the latency cost of using the PCI bus. Various interconnects scale to different levels. Switched Ethernet-based interconnects, for example, basically work for any number of nodes on a network segment, as reliable packet delivery is provided by the TCP/IP layer. For this reason, Ethernet switch complexes deal well with congestion. Interconnect networks do not universally possess these characteristics, however; various interconnect types have topology scalability issues, and others basically require a full bisectional bandwidth switch complex to be built to minimize switch congestion. The cost of these technologies ranges from practically free to into the thousands of dollars per node of up-front cost. This does not take into consideration the substantial, recurring effort of integration, software, and hardware debugging. Variance in the types of drivers provided can also affect difficulty in integration. Some vendors provide binary drivers only for particular versions of the Linux kernel. These cause clusters using these interconnects to become kernel "version locked." In many cases, the kernel bugs that cluster administrators are likely to encounter are fixed by subsequent releases of the kernel. Hence, version-locked machines are harder to support.

### 5.3.3 Strategies to Improve Performance over Ethernet

Realistically, financial considerations are fairly important while designing a cluster. This is clearly indicated by the high frequency of clusters with Ethernet as an interconnect. As this is the slowest interconnect on the above list, performance optimization is of the utmost importance. The simplest approach is to tune the system's Ethernet and TCP/IP stacks; these changes are fairly nonintrusive and straightforward to implement, and there is a fairly good document detailing this tuning process at `www.psc.edu/networking/perf_tune.html`. Other approaches can be more intrusive. These fall into three categories: hardware choice, software features, and other network topologies.

Ethernet card performance will be heavily influenced by the characteristics of the NIC chosen. Higher-quality Ethernet NICs will deliver better throughput and latency at a lower host CPU utilization. This better performance is achieved through a number of techniques. Use of jumbo frames is one way to reduce host CPU utilization. By using a large MTU setting of 9,000 bytes as opposed to the usual 1,500 bytes, the NIC has to package up a considerably smaller number of Ethernet frames. Jumbo frames are supported only in Gigabit networks, but their use can significantly increase network throughput. Some NICs support TCP checksum calculation in hardware on the NIC itself. This removes one of the most expensive tasks from the host CPU. Some NICs also support interrupt coalescing. This means that the NIC has some quantity of local memory into which received packets can be stored temporarily, to reduce the interrupt load of NIC use. Without interrupt coalescing, heavy network use can induce enough context switching for interrupt servicing that computational throughput of the host CPU drops substantially. This feature is also really used only on Gigabit networks. Substantial differences in the feature set are supported by Gigabit network adapters.

On the other hand, Fast Ethernet NICs have a basically comparable hardware feature set and depend on drivers to deliver outstanding performance. There is a large variation in the quality of Gigabit drivers as well. All of the hardware features mentioned above need to be supported in software as well as in hardware in order to be used. Alternatively, TCP/IP may not be used at all. All of the properties a network protocol provides, such as reliable delivery and out-of-order packet reassembly, come at the cost of latency and bandwidth penalties. Some of these properties are important, some not. The VIA specification (`www.viarch.org`) describes an architecture that implements only those properties that are required in cluster communication. This provides a protocol with far less overhead than Ethernet's CSMA/CD and TCP/IP have. By using the MVIA implementation (`www.nersc.gov/research/FTG/via/`) of the VIA specification and its drivers for Fast Ethernet or Gigabit Ethernet NICs, more bandwidth is delivered to applications with less latency using commodity hardware. (This is the same protocol mentioned in Section 5.1.3.)

The final approach taken to maximize Ethernet performance is to use a different network topology. One of these topologies is to use EtherChannel, or Ethernet bonding. This software makes multiple physical Ethernet interfaces negotiate a virtual aggregated connection from the switch (there is no benefit to doing this in a shared network segment) to the client. This can increase the amount of bandwidth available to applications by integer multiples based on the number of physical interfaces available. Unfortunately, this has no positive effect on latency, as the logical path that a message takes from end to end has bonding routines to go through as well. Another topology designed to improve bisectional bandwidth and latency is FNN (`www.aggregate.org/FNN`), or Flat Network Neighborhoods. In this topology, hosts have multiple network interfaces that each home on a different switch. In a properly setup network, each host will have a NIC on the same switch as an interface on any given other host in the network. This technique attempts to leverage the large performance difference between backplanes and uplinks in a cost-effective manner.

### 5.3.4   Cluster Network Pitfalls

Linux gigabit support doesn't interact well with switch autonegotiation and time-sensitive protocols such as DHCP. We have had several problems with gigabit switch port initialization time. These long initialization times cause DHCP requests to time out. We have tracked this problem to a number of factors on the switch, all of which had to do with autonegotiation. Gigabit switches try to autonegotiate a number of settings when link comes up. The list of settings that are autonegotiated by default includes flow control, port negotiation, etherchannel (bonding), and 802.1q trunking. Then a spanning tree check is run to determine whether any switching loops exist in the network. All said, this process can take up to a minute to complete. This is certainly longer than the default DHCP request timeout. On Fast Ethernet networks, a number of these same settings are autonegotiated. While this list is shorter, and the port setup time is considerably less than on Gigabit Ethernet, problems can still result if many hosts are brought up in parallel.

To this end, disabling autonegotiation whenever possible will immensely simplify the network itself and reduce the number of problems encountered.

As Fast Ethernet is the most common interconnect, and Ethernet is the most common sort of Linux host networking, internode communication and cluster administrative processes may compete with one another for resources. This event should be avoided if at all possible. With the heavy usage of transparent network-based services like NFS, it is possible to unintentionally use large quantities of network bandwidth with fairly innocuous operations. Extraneous processes, even administrative tasks, should be avoided if possible while user jobs are running.

The nature of cluster administrative operations, whether synchronous, like `pdsh`, or asynchronous, like cron jobs, is that they run in a loosely parallel fashion. While these jobs are not synchronized internally, their methods of invocation cause them to be started in very small time windows. When these administrative operations are performed in parallel, the load pattern on servers is more bursty than normal Unix servers. In these cases, peak capacity is important more often than sustained throughput.

### 5.3.5   An Example of an Ethernet Interconnected Beowulf

The Clemson Mini-grid Beowulf employs four switches. The processor pool utilizes a Foundry Networks FastIron III with a backplane throughput of 480 Gbps and supports up to 336 Fast Ethernet ports or up to 120 Gigabit Ethernet ports. The configuration used in the Clemson machine includes 16 Gigabit Ethernet ports and 264 Fast Ethernet ports. The Mini-grid processor pool includes 130 nodes each with two Fast Ethernet NICs connected to this switch. In addition, the processor pool's switch is connected to three primary clusters one of which employs a Foundry Networks FastIron II Plus with a backplane throughput of 256 Gbps connected to 66 dual-NIC nodes, and two of which employ a Foundry Networks FastIron II with a backplane throughput of 128 Gbps connected to 34 dual-NIC nodes. The switches in the Mini-grid are connected by multiple trunked Gigabit Ethernet links. There are four trunked links between the pool and the larger cluster and two trunked links each between the pool and the two smaller clusters. The dual-NIC nodes in the pool and the clusters use Linux channel bonding to double the throughput of a normal Fast Ethernet NIC. The Foundry Networks switches use a similar technique to trunk up to eight Gigabit Ethernet links between any two switches. Using this approach one could build a Fast Ethernet switching system with up to 1080 ports with no bottlenecks. In practice, considerably larger networks can be built, though not with full bisection bandwidth. For many applications somewhat less bandwidth may be adequate. Other vendors with large Fast Ethernet switches include Hewlett Packard, Cisco, and Extreme.

### 5.3.6   An Example of a Myrinet Interconnected Cluster

The Chiba City cluster at Argonne National Laboratory has two discrete networks: (1) a Myrinet network consisting of 5 Clos switches, 4 Spine switches, and 320 host ports, and (2) a Fast/Gigabit Ethernet network consisting of 10 Cisco Catalyst 4000s and a Catalyst C6509 with 480 Fast Ethernet ports and 102 Gigabit Ethernet ports. The Myrinet network is used primarily as the system interconnect; however, if need be, Ethernet can be used as well. The Myrinet topology is symmetric, as is the Ethernet topology. Each spine switch has 128 network ports, with connections to all of the Clos switches in the network, but no connections to other spines. Each Myrinet Clos switch has 64 host ports and 64 network (switch interconnect) ports. Each Clos has its network ports distributed across all four spine switches. This yields 4096 potential routes from any given node to any other node in the network. This is required to guarantee full bisectional bandwidth for all possible workloads.

The Ethernet network is also fairly symmetric. Each group of 32 nodes and their management node are connected to a Catalyst 4000. Each of the 32 nodes is connected with Fast Ethernet, and the manager is connected with Gigabit Ethernet. Each of these switches has dual gigabit uplinks to the core Catalyst C6509. Because of the oversubscription of uplinks between each Catalyst 4000 and the core C6509, this network does not have full bisectional bandwidth. If this were primarily an interconnect network, and full bisectional bandwidth were important, this could be remedied by upgrading all switch uplinks from dual to quad gigabit connections.

# 6 Windows 2000 Networking

*Mark Russinovich*

Microsoft Windows 2000 was designed with networking in mind, and it includes broad networking support that is integrated with the I/O system and the Win32 API. The four basic types of networking software are services, APIs, protocols, and network adapter device drivers, and each is layered on the next to form a network stack. Windows 2000 has well-defined interfaces for each layer, so in addition to using the wide variety of different APIs, protocols, and adapter device drivers that ship with Windows 2000, third parties can extend the operating system's networking capabilities by developing their own.

In this chapter, we take you from the top of the Windows 2000 networking stack to the bottom. First, we present the Windows 2000 networking software components and define their roles in supporting network operations. Then we briefly describe the networking APIs available on Windows 2000 and explain how they are implemented. You'll learn how network-resource name resolution works and how protocol drivers are implemented. The chapter concludes by describing the Windows 2000 network adapter driver model.

## 6.1 Windows 2000 Networking Components

Figure 6.1 provides an overview of the components of Windows 2000 networking, showing how each component fits into the OSI reference model and which protocols are used between layers. The mapping between OSI layers and networking components isn't precise, which is the reason that some components cross layers. The various components include the following:

- *Networking APIs* provide a protocol-independent way for applications to communicate across a network. Networking APIs can be implemented in user mode or in both user mode and kernel mode, and in some cases are wrappers around another networking API that implements a specific programming model or provides additional services. (Note that the term *networking API* also describes any programming interfaces provided by networking-related software.)
- *Transport Driver Interface* (TDI) *clients* are kernel-mode device drivers that usually implement the kernel-mode portion of a networking API's implementation. TDI clients get their name from the fact that the I/O request packets (IRPs) they send to protocol drivers are formatted according to the Windows 2000 Transport Driver Interface standard (documented in the DDK). This standard specifies a common programming interface for kernel-mode device drivers.

- *TDI transports,* also known as *transports, Network Driver Interface Specification* (NDIS) *protocol drivers,* and *protocol drivers,* are kernel-mode protocol drivers. They accept IRPs from TDI clients and process the requests these IRPs represent. This processing might require network communications with a peer, prompting the TDI transport to add protocol-specific headers (such as TCP, UDP, IPX) to data passed in the IRP and to communicate with adapter drivers using NDIS functions (also documented in the DDK). TDI transports generally facilitate application network communications by transparently performing message operations such as segmentation and reassembly, sequencing, acknowledgment, and retransmission.

- The *NDIS library* (`Ndis.sys`) provides encapsulation for adapter drivers, hiding from them specifics of the Windows 2000 kernel-mode environment. The NDIS library exports functions for use by TDI transports as well as support functions for adapter drivers.

- *NDIS miniport drivers* are kernel-mode drivers that are responsible for interfacing TDI transports to particular network adapters. NDIS miniport drivers are written so that they are wrapped by the Windows 2000 NDIS library. The encapsulation provides cross-platform compatibility with Microsoft Consumer Windows. NDIS miniport drivers don't process IRPs; rather, they register a call-table interface to the NDIS library that contains pointers to functions corresponding to ones that the NDIS library exports to TDI transports. NDIS miniport drivers communicate with network adapters by using NDIS library functions that resolve to hardware abstraction layer (HAL) functions.

As the figure shows, the OSI layers don't correspond to actual software. TDI transports, for example, frequently cross several boundaries. In fact, the bottom four layers of software are often referred to collectively as "the transport." Software components residing in the upper three layers are referred to as "users of the transport."

In the remainder of this chapter, we examine the networking components shown in Figure 6.1 (as well as others not shown in the figure), looking at how they fit together and how they relate to Windows 2000 as a whole.

## 6.2  Networking APIs

Windows 2000 implements multiple networking APIs to provide support for legacy applications and compatibility with industry standards. In this section, we briefly look at the networking APIs and describe how applications use them. It's important to keep in mind that the decision about which API an application uses depends on

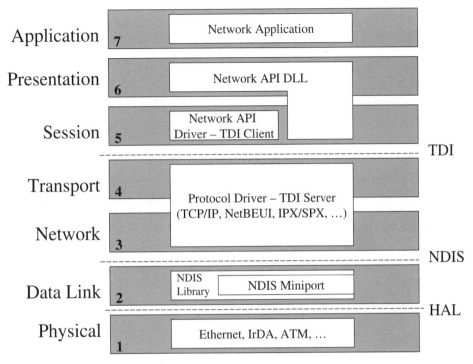

**Figure 6.1**
OSI model and Windows 2000 networking components.

characteristics of the API, such as which protocols the API can layer over, whether the API supports reliable or bidirectional communication, and how portable the APIs are to other Windows platforms the application might run on. We discuss the following networking APIs:

- Named pipes and mailslots
- Windows Sockets (Winsock)
- Remote procedure call (RPC)

In addition, we briefly describe several APIs that build on the APIs listed here and that are widely used on a typical Windows 2000 system.

### 6.2.1 Named Pipes and Mailslots

Named pipes and mailslots are programming APIs that Microsoft originally developed for OS/2 LAN Manager and then ported to Windows NT. Named pipes

provide for reliable bidirectional communications, whereas mailslots provide unreliable unidirectional data transmission. An advantage of mailslots is that they
support broadcast capability. In Windows 2000, both APIs take advantage of Windows 2000 security, which allows a server to control precisely which clients can
connect to it.

The names servers assign to named pipes and clients conform to the Windows
2000 Universal Naming Convention (UNC), which is a protocol-independent way
to identify resources on a Windows network. The implementation of UNC names
is described later in the chapter.

**Named Pipe Operation.**   Named pipe communication consists of a named pipe
server and a named pipe client. A named pipe server is an application that creates
a named pipe to which clients can connect. A named pipe's name has the format \\
Server\Pipe\PipeName. The *Server* component of the name specifies the computer
on which the named pipe server is executing (a named pipe server can't create a
named pipe on a remote system), and the name can be a DNS name (for example,
*mspress. microsoft.com*), a NetBIOS name (*mspress*), or an IP address (255.0.0.0).
The *Pipe* component of the name must be the string "Pipe", and *PipeName* is
the unique name assigned to a named pipe. The unique portion of the named
pipe's name can include subdirectories; an example of a named pipe name with a
subdirectory is \\MyComputer\Pipe\MyServerApp\ConnectionPipe.

A named pipe server uses the *CreateNamedPipe* Win32 function to create a
named pipe. One of the function's input parameters is a pointer to the named
pipe name, in the form\\.\Pipe\PipeName. The "\\.\" is a Win32-defined alias
for "this computer." Other parameters the function accepts include an optional
security descriptor that protects access to the named pipe, a flag that specifies
whether the pipe should be bidirectional or unidirectional, a value indicating the
maximum number of simultaneous connections the pipe supports, and a flag specifying whether the pipe should operate in byte mode or message mode.

Most networking APIs operate only in *byte mode,* which means that a message
sent with one send function might require the receiver to perform multiple receives,
building up the complete message from fragments. Named pipes operating in *message mode* simplify the implementation of a receiver because there is a one-to-one
correspondence between sends and receives. A receiver therefore obtains an entire
message each time it completes a receive and doesn't have to concern itself with
keeping track of message fragments.

The first call to *CreateNamedPipe* for a particular name creates the first instance
of that name and establishes the behavior of all named pipe instances having that

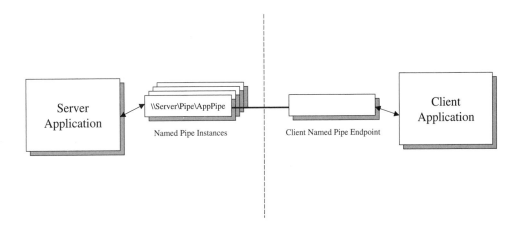

**Figure 6.2**
Named pipe communications.

name. A server creates additional instances, up to the maximum specified in the
first call, with additional calls to *CreateNamedPipe*. After creating at least one
named pipe instance, a server executes the *ConnectNamedPipe* Win32 function,
which enables the named pipe the server created to establish connections with
clients. *ConnectNamedPipe* can be executed synchronously or asynchronously, and
it doesn't complete until a client establishes a connection with the instance (or an
error occurs).

A named pipe client uses the Win32 *CreateFile* or *CallNamedPipe* function, specifying the name of the pipe a server has created, to connect to a server. If the server
has performed a *ConnectNamedPipe* call, the client's security profile and the access
it requests to the pipe (read, write) are validated against the named pipe's security
descriptor. If the client is granted access to a named pipe, it receives a handle
representing the client side of a named pipe connection, and the server's call to
*ConnectNamedPipe* completes.

After a named pipe connection is established, the client and server can use the
*ReadFile* and *WriteFile* Win32 functions to read from and write to the pipe. Named
pipes support both synchronous and asynchronous operation for message transmit-
tal. Figure 6.2 shows a server and client communicating through a named pipe
instance.

A unique characteristic of the named pipe networking API is that it allows a
server to impersonate a client by using the *ImpersonateNamedPipeClient* function.

**Mailslot Operation.** Mailslots provide an unreliable unidirectional broadcast mechanism. One example of an application that can use this type of communication is a time synchronization service, which might broadcast a source time across the domain every few seconds. Receiving the source-time message isn't crucial for every computer on the network and is therefore a good candidate for the use of mailslots.

Like named pipes, mailslots are integrated with the Win32 API. A mailslot server creates a mailslot by using the *CreateMailslot* function. *CreateMailslot* accepts a name of the form "\\.\Mailslot\MailslotName" as an input parameter. Again like named pipes, a mailslot server can create mailslots only on the machine it's executing on, and the name it assigns to a mailslot can include subdirectories. *CreateMailslot* also takes a security descriptor that controls client access to the mailslot. The handles returned by *CreateMailslot* are *overlapped,* which means that operations performed on the handles, such as sending and receiving messages, are asynchronous.

Because mailslots are unidirectional and unreliable, *CreateMailslot* doesn't take many of the parameters that *CreateNamedPipe* does. After it creates a mailslot, a server simply listens for incoming client messages by executing the *ReadFile* function on the handle representing the mailslot.

Mailslot clients use a naming format similar to that used by named pipe clients but with variations that make it possible to broadcast messages to all the mailslots of a given name within the client's domain or a specified domain. To send a message to a particular instance of a mailslot, the client calls *CreateFile*, specifying the computer-specific name. An example of such a name is \\Server\ Mailslot\ MailslotName. (The client can specify \\.\ to represent the local computer.) If the client wants to obtain a handle representing all the mailslots of a given name on the domain it's a member of, it specifies the name in the format \\*\Mailslot\ MailslotName, and if the client wants to broadcast to all the mailslots of a given name within a different domain, the format it uses is \\DomainName\Mailslot\ MailslotName.

After obtaining a handle representing the client side of a mailslot, the client sends messages by calling *WriteFile*. Because of the way mailslots are implemented, only messages smaller than 425 bytes can be broadcast. If a message is larger than 425 bytes, the mailslot implementation uses a reliable communications mechanism that requires a one-to-one client/server connection, which precludes broadcast capability. Also, a quirk of the mailslot implementation causes messages of 425 or 426 bytes to be truncated to 424 bytes. These limitations make mailslots generally unsuitable for messages larger than 424 bytes. Figure 6.3 shows an example of a client broadcasting to multiple mailslot servers within a domain.

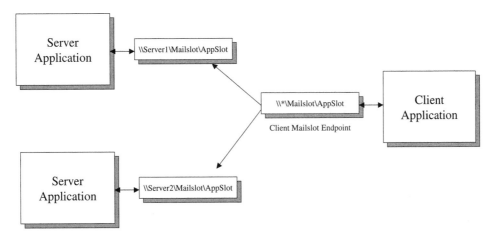

**Figure 6.3**
Mailslot broadcast.

**Named Pipe and Mailslot Implementation.** As evidence of their tight integration with Win32, named pipe and mailslot functions are all implemented in the `Kernel32.dll` Win32 client-side DLL. *ReadFile* and *WriteFile*, which are the functions applications use to send and receive messages using named pipes and mailslots, are the primary Win32 I/O routines. The *CreateFile* function, which a client uses to open either a named pipe or a mailslot, is also a standard Win32 I/O routine. However, the names specified by named pipe and mailslot applications specify file system namespaces managed by the named pipe file system driver (\Winnt\System32\Drivers\Npfs.sys) and the mailslot file system driver (\Winnt\System32\Drivers\Msfs.sys), as shown in Figure 6.4. The named pipe file system driver creates a device object named \Device\NamedPipe and a symbolic link to that object named \??\Pipe, and the mailslot file system driver creates a device object named \Device\Mailslot and a symbolic link named \??\Mailslot that points to that object. Names passed to *CreateFile* of the form \\.\Pipe\... and \\.\Mailslot\ ...have their prefix of \\.\ translated to \??\ so that the names resolve through a symbolic link to a device object. The special functions *CreateNamedPipe* and *CreateMailslot* use the corresponding native functions *NtCreateNamedPipeFile* and *NtCreateMailslotFile*.

Later in the chapter, we discuss how the redirector file system driver is involved when a name that specifies a remote named pipe or mailslot resolves to a remote system. However, when a named pipe or mailslot is created by a server or opened by a client, the appropriate file system driver (FSD) on the machine where the named

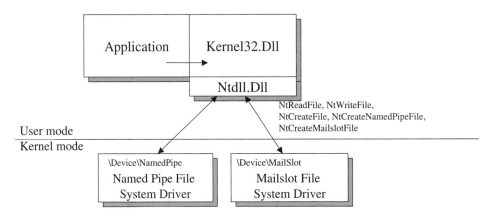

**Figure 6.4**
Named pipe and mailslot implementation.

pipe or mailslot is located is eventually invoked. There are several reasons why FSDs in kernel mode implement named pipes and mailslots, the main one being that they integrate with the object manager namespace and can use file objects to represent opened named pipes and mailslots. This integration results in several benefits:

• The FSDs use kernel-mode security functions to implement standard Windows 2000 security for named pipes and mailslots.
• Applications can use *CreateFile* to open a named pipe or mailslot because FSDs integrate with the object manager namespace.
• Applications can use Win32 functions such as *ReadFile* and *WriteFile* to interact with named pipes and mailslots.
• The FSDs rely on the object manager to track handle and reference counts for file objects representing named pipes and mailslots.
• The FSDs can implement their own named pipe and mailslot namespaces, complete with subdirectories.

Because named pipes and mailslot name resolution use the redirector FSD to communicate across the network, they indirectly rely on the Common Internet File System (CIFS) protocol (which is based on the Server Message Blocks—SMB—protocol). CIFS works by using the IPX, TCP/IP, and NetBEUI protocols, so applications running on systems that have at least one of these in common can use named pipes and mailslots.

### 6.2.2   Windows Sockets

Windows Sockets (Winsock) is Microsoft's implementation of BSD (Berkeley Software Distribution) Sockets, a programming API that became the standard by which Unix systems have communicated over the Internet since the 1980s. Support for sockets on Windows 2000 makes the task of porting Unix networking applications to Windows 2000 relatively straightforward. Winsock includes most of the functionality of BSD Sockets but also includes Microsoft-specific enhancements, which continue to evolve. Winsock supports reliable-connection-oriented communication as well as unreliable-connectionless communication. Windows 2000 provides Winsock 2.2, which is also either included with or available as an add-on for all versions of Consumer Windows.

Winsock includes the following features:

- Support for scatter-gather and asynchronous application I/O.
- Quality of service (QoS) conventions so that applications can negotiate latency and bandwidth requirements when the underlying network supports QoS.
- Extensibility so that Winsock can be used with protocols other than those Windows 2000 requires it to support.
- Support for integrated namespaces other than those defined by a protocol an application is using with Winsock. A server can publish its name in Active Directory, for example, and using namespace extensions, a client can look up the server's address in Active Directory.
- Support for multipoint messages where messages transmit to multiple receivers simultaneously.
- Support for Server Area Networks (SANs). A SAN, not to be confused with Storage Area Networks, connects computers through highly reliable, low-latency, high-speed interconnect. Winsock's Windows Sockets Direct (WSD) architecture allows TCP-based socket applications to access the SAN hardware without going through the TCP/IP stack.

We next examine typical Winsock operation and then describe ways that Winsock can be extended. The section concludes with a look at WSDP's use in SANs.

**Winsock Operation.**   After initializing the Winsock API with a call to an initialization function, the first step a Winsock application takes is to create a *socket* that will represent a communications endpoint. Since a socket must be *bound* to an address on the local computer, binding is the second step the application performs. Winsock is a protocol-independent API, so an address can be specified for any protocol installed on the system over which Winsock operates (NetBEUI, TCP/IP,

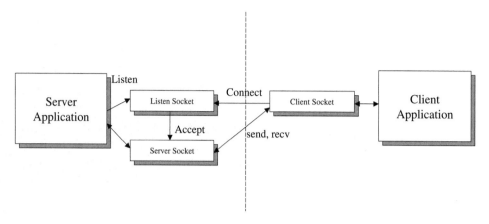

**Figure 6.5**
Connection-oriented Winsock operation.

IPX). After binding is complete, the steps taken by a server and client diverge, as do steps for connection-oriented and connectionless socket operation.

A connection-oriented Winsock server performs a *listen* operation on the socket, indicating the number of connections that it can support for the socket. Then it performs an *accept* operation to allow a client to connect to the socket. If there is a pending connection request, the accept call completes immediately; otherwise, it completes when a connection request arrives. When a connection is made, the *accept* function returns a new socket that represents the server's end of the connection. The server can perform receive and send operations by using functions such as *recv* and *send*.

Connection-oriented clients connect to a server by using the Winsock *connect* function that specifies a remote address. When a connection is established, the client can send and receive messages over its socket. Figure 6.5 shows connection-oriented communication between a Winsock client and server.

After binding an address, a connectionless server is no different from a connectionless client: it can send and receive messages over the socket simply by specifying the remote address with each message. When using connectionless messages, which are also called *datagrams,* a sender learns that a message wasn't received when the sender obtains an error code the next time a receive operation is performed.

**Winsock Extensions.**   A powerful feature from a Windows programming point of view is that the Winsock API is integrated with Windows messages. A Winsock application can take advantage of this feature to perform asynchronous socket operations and receive notification of an operation's completion via a standard Windows message or through the execution of a callback function. This capability simplifies the design of a Windows application because the application doesn't need to be multithreaded or manage synchronization objects to both perform network I/O and respond to user input or requests from the window manager to update the application windows. The names of message-based versions of BSD-style Winsock functions usually begin with the prefix *WSA*—for example, *WSAAccept*.

In addition to supporting functions that correspond directly to those implemented in BSD Sockets, Microsoft has added a handful of functions that aren't part of the Winsock standard. Two of these functions, *AcceptEx* and *TransmitFile*, are worth describing because many Web servers on Windows 2000 use them to achieve high performance. *AcceptEx* is a version of the *accept* function that, in the process of establishing a connection with a client, returns the client's address and the client's first message. With this function, a Web server avoids executing multiple Winsock functions that would otherwise be required.

After establishing a connection with a client, a Web server usually sends a file, such as a Web page, to the client. The *TransmitFile* function's implementation is integrated with the Windows 2000 cache manager so that a client can send a file directly from the file system cache. Sending data in this way is called *zero-copy* because the server doesn't have to touch the file data to send it; it simply specifies a handle to a file and the ranges of the file to send. In addition, *TransmitFile* allows a server to prepend or append data to the file's data so that the server can send header information, which might include the name of the Web server and a field that indicates to the client the size of the message the server is sending. Internet Information Services (IIS) 5.0, which is bundled with Windows 2000, uses both *AcceptEx* and *TransmitFile*.

**Extending Winsock.** Winsock is an extensible API on Windows 2000 because third parties can add a *transport service provider* that interfaces Winsock with other protocols as well as a *namespace service provider* to augment Winsock's name-resolution facilities. Service providers plug in to Winsock using the Winsock *service provider interface*. When a transport service provider is registered with Winsock, Winsock uses the transport service provider to implement socket functions, such as *connect* and *accept*, for the address types that the provider indicates it implements. There are no restrictions on how the transport service provider implements the functions, but the implementation usually involves communicating with a transport driver in kernel mode.

A requirement of any Winsock client/server application is for the server to make its address available to clients so that the clients can connect to the server. Standard services that execute on the TCP/IP protocol use "well-known addresses" to make their addresses available. As long as a browser knows the name of the computer a Web server is running on, it can connect to the Web server by specifying the well-known Web server address (the IP address of the server concatenated with :80, the port number used for HTTP). Namespace service providers make it possible for servers to register their presence in other ways. For example, one namespace service provider might, on the server side, register the server's address in Active Directory and, on the client side, look up the server's address in Active Directory. Namespace service providers supply this functionality to Winsock by implementing standard Winsock name-resolution functions such as *gethostbyaddr*, *getservbyname*, and *getservbyport*.

**Winsock Implementation.** Winsock's implementation is shown in Figure 6.6. Its application interface consists of an API DLL, Ws2_32.dll (\Winnt\System32\ Ws2_32.dll), which provides applications access to Winsock functions. Ws2_32.dll calls on the services of namespace and transport service providers to carry out name and message operations. The Msafd.dll library acts as a transport service provider for the protocols Microsoft provides support for in Winsock, and Msafd.dll uses *Winsock Helper* libraries that are protocol specific to communicate with kernel-mode protocol drivers. For example, Wshtcpip.dll is the TCP/IP helper, and Wshnetbs.dll is the NetBEUI helper. Mswsock.dll (\Winnt\ System32\Mswsock.dll) implements the Microsoft Winsock extension functions, such as *TransmitFile*, *AcceptEx*, and *WSARecvEx*. Windows 2000 ships with helper DLLs for TCP/IP, NetBEUI, AppleTalk, IPX/SPX, ATM, and IrDA (Infrared Data Association) and namespace service providers for DNS (TCP/IP), Active Directory, and IPX/SPX.

Like the named pipe and mailslot APIs, Winsock integrates with the Win32 I/O model and uses file handles to represent sockets. This support requires the aid of a kernel-mode file system driver, so Msafd.dll uses the services of the Ancillary Function Driver (AFD - \Winnt\System32\Drivers\Afd.sys) to implement socket-based functions. AFD is a TDI client and executes network socket operations, such as sending and receiving messages, by sending TDI IRPs to protocol drivers. AFD isn't coded to use particular protocol drivers; instead, Msafd.dll informs AFD of the name of the protocol used for each socket so that AFD can open the device object representing the protocol.

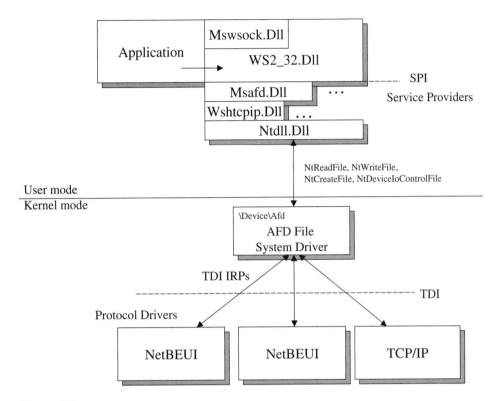

**Figure 6.6**
Winsock implementation

### 6.2.3   Windows Sockets Direct

Windows Sockets Direct is an interface that allows Winsock applications to take advantage of server area networks without application modification. The high-performance characteristics of SANs make them ideal for a applications ranging from distributed computation to three-tier e-commerce architectures like the one shown in Figure 6.7. In the system depicted, SANs connect the front-end Web servers with business logic servers and connects the business logic servers with backend database servers to provide high-speed data movement through the data-processing layers. WSD is available on Windows XP and Windows 2002, Windows 2000 Data Center Server, Windows 2000 Advanced Server with Service Pack (SP) 2 or higher, and Windows Server Appliance Kit with SP2 or higher.

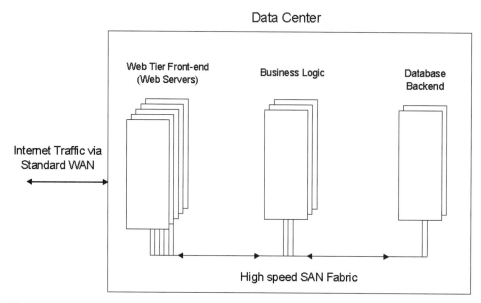

**Figure 6.7**
Use of a SAN in a 3-tier e-commerce architecture

**SAN Interconnect.**   Server area networks usually achieve their high-performance characteristics by relying on specialized network interconnect and switching hardware.   Common SAN interconnect types include InfiniBand, Gigabit Ethernet, FiberChannel, and proprietary solutions.  Physical memory shared between two computers can also serve as SAN interconnect. Vendors that currently sell SAN hardware supported by Windows include Emulex (`http://www.emulex.com`) with its cLAN host adapters and switches that deliver throughput of 1.25 Gbs/ (2.5 Gbs/ bidirectional).

SAN switching hardware implements a nonroutable protocol that provides TCP-like guarantees such as reliable, in-order message delivery.  They also support a SAN feature called remote direct memory access (RDMA) that allows messages to be transmitted directly from physical memory of source computer to that of a destination computer without the intermediate memory copy operation that normally takes place on the receive end of a message transmission. RDMA thus frees both CPU and memory bus bandwidth that a copy operation consumes.

SAN implementations also permit applications to bypass kernel-mode components altogether, sending and receiving data directly from or to user applications. This strategy minimizes the number of system calls applications make and further reduces time spent in operating system networking code.

**WSD Architecture.** Most SAN implementations require application changes for the applications to interface with SAN network protocols and take advantage of SAN hardware-implemented network protocols and SAN features such as RDMA, but Windows Sockets Direct allows any Winsock-based application that uses the TCP protocol to take advantage of SANs without modification. WSD gets its name from the fact that it gives applications direct access to SAN hardware, bypassing the TCP/IP stack. This shortcut to the network hardware gives applications a performance improvement of 2-2.5.

WSD achieves its shortcut to SAN hardware by using a software switch beneath the Winsock DLL and WSPs, as shown in Figure 6.8. The switch routes SAN network activity to a vendor-supplied SAN WSP. The WSP acts as the user-mode equivalent of an NDIS driver, with the capability to map SAN hardware registers into user-mode memory and then manipulate the hardware without going through kernel-mode components. Some network activity does require the aid of a kernel-mode component (for instance, to map hardware into user-mode memory), which is also provided by the SAN vendor. Finally, the SAN vendor supplies an NDIS miniport driver to interface the TCP/IP stack to SAN hardware for applications that use Winsock networking features not supported natively by the SAN.

### 6.2.4   Remote Procedure Call

Remote procedure call is a network programming standard originally developed in the early 1980s. The Open Software Foundation (now The Open Group) made RPC part of the distributed computing environment (DCE) distributed computing standard. Although there is a second RPC standard, SunRPC, the Microsoft RPC implementation is compatible with the OSF/DCE standard. RPC builds on other networking APIs, such as named pipes or Winsock, to provide an alternate programming model that in some sense hides the details of networking programming from an application developer.

**RPC Operation.** A remote procedure call allows a programmer to create an application consisting of any number of procedures, some that execute locally and others that execute on remote computers via a network. It provides a procedural view of networked operations rather than a transport-centered view, thus simplifying the development of distributed applications.

Networking software is traditionally structured around an I/O model of processing. In Windows 2000, for example, a network operation is initiated when an

Traditional Model                    WSD Model

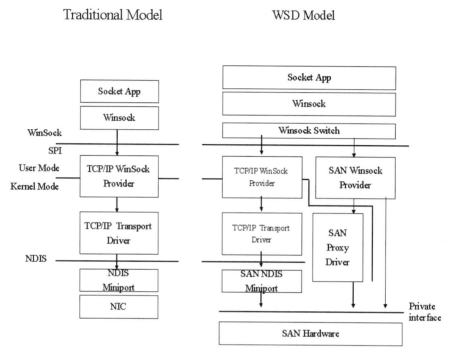

**Figure 6.8**
Traditional Winsock model versus WSD model.

application issues a remote I/O request. The operating system processes it accordingly by forwarding it to a *redirector,* which acts as a remote file system by making the client interaction with the remote file system invisible to the client. The redirector passes the operation to the remote file system, and after the remote system fills the request and returns the results, the local network card interrupts. The kernel handles the interrupt, and the original I/O operation completes, returning results to the caller.

Remote procedure call takes a different approach altogether. RPC applications are like other structured applications, with a main program that calls procedures or procedure libraries to perform specific tasks. The difference between RPC applications and regular applications, however, is that some of the procedure libraries in an RPC application execute on remote computers, as shown in Figure 6.9, whereas others execute locally.

To the RPC application, all the procedures appear to execute locally. In other words, instead of making a programmer actively write code to transmit compu-

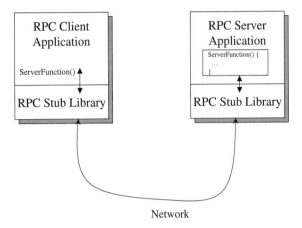

**Figure 6.9**
RPC operation.

tational or I/O-related requests across a network, handle network protocols, deal with network errors, wait for results, and so forth, RPC software handles these tasks automatically. And the Windows 2000 RPC facility can operate over any available transports loaded into the system.

To write an RPC application, you decides which procedures will execute locally and which will execute remotely. For example, suppose an ordinary workstation has a network connection to a Cray supercomputer or to a machine designed specifically for high-speed vector operations. If you were writing an application that manipulated large matrices, it would make sense from a performance point of view to offload the mathematical calculations to the remote computer by writing the program as an RPC application.

RPC applications work as follows. As an application runs, it calls local procedures as well as procedures that aren't present on the local machine. To handle the latter case, the application is linked to a local static-link library or dynamic-link library that contains *stub procedures,* one for each remote procedure. For simple applications, the stub procedures are statically linked with the application, but for bigger components the stubs are included in separate DLLs. In the Distributed Component Object Model (DCOM), covered later in the chapter, the latter method is typically used. The stub procedures have the same name and use the same interface as the remote procedures, but instead of performing the required operations, the stub takes the parameters passed to it and *marshals* them for transmission across the network. Marshaling parameters means ordering and packaging them in a particular way to suit a network link, such as resolving references and picking up a copy of any data structures that a pointer refers to.

The stub then calls RPC run-time procedures that locate the computer where the remote procedure resides, determine which transport mechanisms that computer uses, and send the request to it using local transport software. When the remote server receives the RPC request, it *unmarshals* the parameters (the reverse of marshaling them), reconstructs the original procedure call, and calls the procedure. When the server finishes, it performs the reverse sequence to return results to the caller.

In addition to the synchronous function-call-based interface described here, Windows 2000 RPC also supports *asynchronous RPC*. Asynchronous RPC lets an RPC application execute a function but not wait until the function completes to continue processing. Instead, the application can execute other code; and later, when a response has arrived from the server, the RPC run time signals an event object the client associates with the asynchronous call. The client can use standard Win32 functions, such as *WaitForSingleObject*, to learn of the function's completion.

Besides the RPC run time, Microsoft's RPC facility includes a compiler, called the *Microsoft Interface Definition Language* (MIDL) compiler. The MIDL compiler simplifies the creation of an RPC application. The programmer writes a series of ordinary function prototypes (assuming a C or C++ application) that describe the remote routines and then places the routines in a file. The programmer then adds some additional information to these prototypes, such as a network-unique identifier for the package of routines and a version number, plus attributes that specify whether the parameters are input, output, or both. The embellished prototypes form the developer's *Interface Definition Language* (IDL) file.

Once the IDL file is created, the programmer compiles it with the MIDL compiler, which produces both client-side and server-side stub routines, mentioned previously, as well as header files to be included in the application. When the client-side application is linked to the stub routines file, all remote procedure references are resolved. The remote procedures are then installed, using a similar process, on the server machine. A programmer who wants to call an existing RPC application need only write the client side of the software and link the application to the local RPC run-time facility.

The RPC run time uses a generic *RPC transport provider interface* to talk to a transport protocol. The provider interface acts as a thin layer between the RPC facility and the transport, mapping RPC operations onto the functions provided by the transport. The Windows 2000 RPC facility implements transport provider DLLs for named pipes, NetBIOS, and TCP/IP. You can write new provider DLLs to support additional transports. In a similar fashion, the RPC facility is designed to work with different network security facilities.

Most of the Windows 2000 networking services are RPC applications, which means that both local processes and processes on remote computers can call them. Thus, a remote client computer can call the server service to list shares, open files, write to print queues, or activate users on your server, or it can call the messenger service to direct messages to you (all subject to security constraints, of course).

*Server name publishing,* which is the ability of a server to register its name in a location accessible for client lookup, is in RPC and is integrated with Active Directory. If Active Directory isn't installed, the RPC name locator services fall back on NetBIOS broadcast. This behavior ensures interoperability with Windows NT 4 systems and allows RPC to function on standalone servers and workstations.

**RPC Implementation.**  RPC implementation is depicted in Figure 6.10, which shows that an RPC-based application links with the RPC runtime DLL (\Winnt\ System32\Rpcrt4.dll). The RPC runtime DLL provides marshaling and unmarshaling functions for use by an application's RPC function stubs as well as functions for sending and receiving marshaled data. The RPC runtime DLL includes support routines to handle RPC over a network as well as a form of RPC called *local RPC.* Local RPC can be used for communication between two processes located on the same system, and the RPC runtime DLL uses the local procedure call (LPC) facilities in kernel mode as the local networking API. When RPC is based on nonlocal communication mechanisms, the RPC runtime DLL uses the Winsock, named pipe, or Message Queuing APIs.

For name registry and lookup, RPC applications link with the RPC name services DLL (\Winnt\System32\Rpcns4.dll). The DLL communicates with the RPC Subsystem (RPCSS - \Winnt\System32\Rpcss.dll), which is implemented as a Win32 service. RPCSS is itself an RPC application that communicates with instances of itself on other systems to perform name lookup and registration. (For clarity, Figure 6.10 doesn't show RPCSS link with the RPC runtime DLL.)

### 6.2.5  Other Networking APIs

Windows 2000 includes other networking APIs that are used less frequently or are layered on the APIs already described (and outside the scope of this book). These include Telephony API (TAPI), Distributed Component Object Model (DCOM),

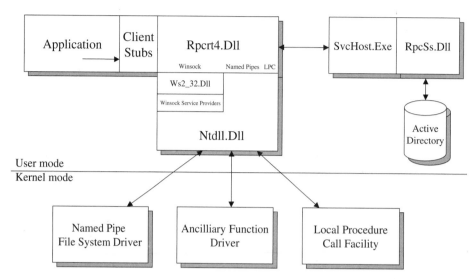

**Figure 6.10**
RPC implementation.

and Message Queuing, all of which are important to the operation of a Windows 2000 system and many applications.

## 6.3   Network-Resource Name Resolution

Applications can examine or access resources on remote systems in two ways. One way is by using the UNC standard with Win32 functions to directly address a remote resource; the second way is by using the Windows Networking (WNet) API to enumerate computers and resources that those computers export for sharing. Both these approaches use the capabilities of a redirector to find their way to the network. As we stated earlier, to access CIFS servers from a client, Microsoft supplies a CIFS redirector, which has a kernel-mode component called the redirector FSD and a user-mode component called the Workstation service. Microsoft also makes available a redirector that can access resources shared by Novell NetWare servers, and third parties can add their own redirectors to Windows 2000. In this section, we examine the software that decides which redirector to invoke when remote I/O requests are issued. The responsible components are as follows:

• *Multiple provider router* (MPR) is a DLL that determines which network to access when an application uses the Win32 WNet API for browsing remote file systems.

- *Multiple UNC Provider* (MUP) is a driver that determines which network to access when an application uses the Win32 I/O API to open remote files.

We conclude this section by describing Domain Name System, the heart of computer name resolution in Windows 2000.

### 6.3.1   Multiple Provider Router

The Win32 WNet functions allow applications (including the Windows Explorer My Network Places) to connect to network resources, such as file servers and printers, and to browse the contents of any type of remote file system. Because the WNet API can be called to work across different networks using different transport protocols, software must be present to send the request correctly over the network and to understand the results that the remote server returns. Figure 6.11 shows the redirector software responsible for these tasks.

A *provider* is software that establishes Windows 2000 as a client of a remote network server. Rhe operations a WNet provider performs include making and breaking network connections, printing remotely, and transferring data. The built-in WNet provider includes a DLL, the Workstation service, and the redirector. Other network vendors need to supply only a DLL and a redirector.

When an application calls a WNet routine, the call passes directly to the MPR DLL. MPR takes the call and determines which WNet provider recognizes the resource being accessed. Each provider DLL beneath MPR supplies a set of standard functions collectively called the *provider interface*. This interface allows MPR to determine which network the application is trying to access and to direct the request to the appropriate WNet provider software. The redirector's provider is \Winnt\System32\Ntlanman.dll, as directed by the ProviderPath value under the HKLM\SYSTEM\CurrentControlSet\Services\ lanmanworkstation\NetworkProvider registry key.

When called by the *WNetAddConnection* API function to connect to a remote network resource, MPR checks the HKLM\SYSTEM\CurrentControlSet\Control\ NetworkProvider\Order\ProviderOrder registry value to determine which network providers are loaded. It polls them one at a time in the order in which they're listed in the registry until a redirector recognizes the resource or until all available providers have been polled. You can change the ProviderOrder by using the Advanced Settings dialog box, shown in Figure 6.12. (Only one provider is installed on the system from which the screen shot was taken.) This dialog box is accessible from the Advanced menu of the Network And Dial-Up Connections application. You can

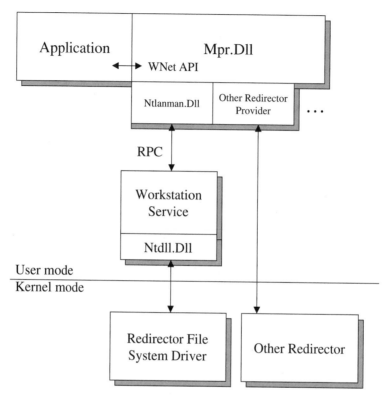

**Figure 6.11**
MPR components.

access the Network And Dial-Up Connections application by right-clicking the My Network Places icon on the desktop and selecting Properties from the pop-up menu or by selecting it from the Settings option from the Start menu.

The *WNetAddConnection* function can also assign a drive letter or device name to a remote resource. When called to do so, *WNetAddConnection* routes the call to the appropriate network provider. The provider, in turn, creates a symbolic-link object in the object manager namespace that maps the drive letter being defined to the redirector (that is, the remote FSD) for that network.

Figure 6.13 shows the \?? directory, where you can see several driver letters representing connections to remote file shares. The figure shows that the redirector creates a device object named \Device\LanmanRedirector and that the additional

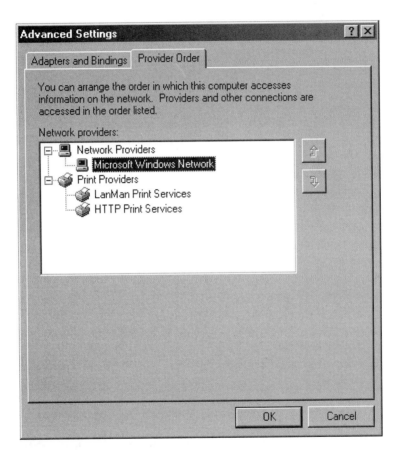

**Figure 6.12**
The provider order editor.

text included in the symbolic link's value indicates to the redirector which remote resource the drive letter corresponds to. When you open X:\Book\Chap13.doc, the redirector is passed the unparsed portion of the path that resolves through the symbolic link, which is ";X:0\dual\e\Book\Chap13.doc". The redirector notes that the resource being accessed is located on the E share of server *dual*.

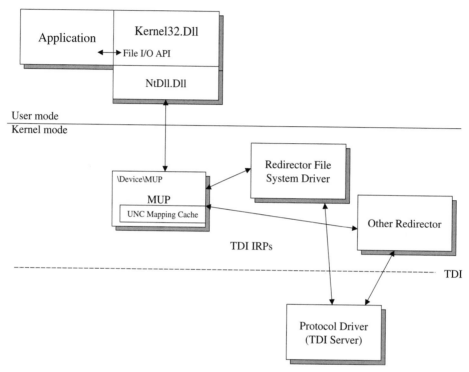

**Figure 6.13**
Resolving a network resource name.

Like the built-in redirector, other redirectors create a device object in the object manager namespace when they are loaded into the system and initialized. Then, when the WNet or other API calls the object manager to open a resource on a different network, the object manager uses the device object as a jumping-off point into the remote file system. It calls an I/O manager parse method associated with the device object to locate the redirector FSD that can handle the request.

### 6.3.2  Multiple UNC Provider

The Multiple UNC Provider (MUP) is a networking component similar to MPR. It fields I/O requests destined for a file or a device that has a UNC name (names beginning with the characters \\, indicating that the resource exists on the network).

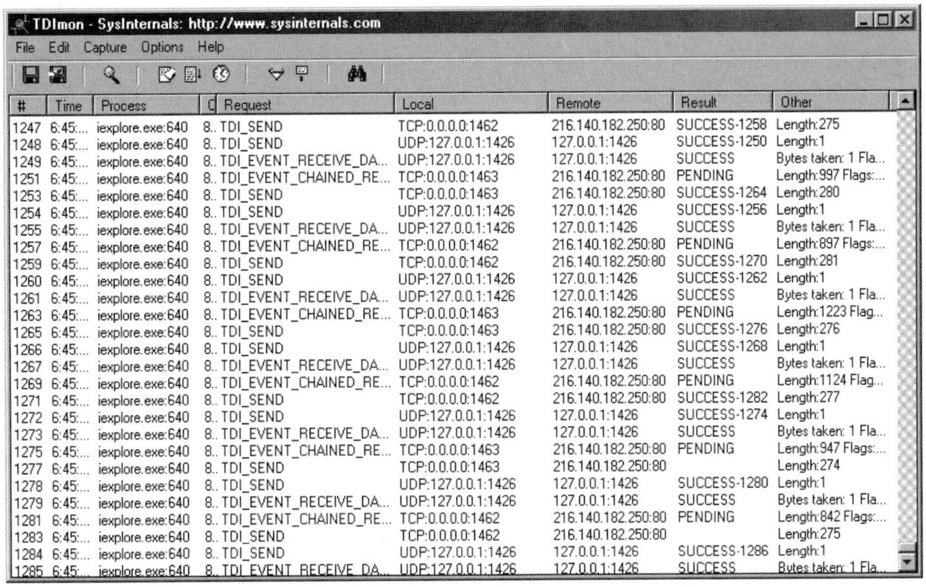

**Figure 6.14**
Multiple UNC Provider (MUP).

MUP takes such requests and, like MPR, determines which local redirector recognizes the remote resource. Unlike MPR, however, MUP is a device driver (loaded at system boot time) that issues I/O requests to lower-layer drivers, in this case to redirectors, as shown in Figure 6.14.

The MUP driver is activated when an application first attempts to open a remote file or device by specifying a UNC name (instead of a redirected drive letter, as described earlier). When the Win32 client-side DLL Kernel32.dll (which is the DLL that exports file-I/O-related APIs) receives such a request, the subsystem appends the UNC name to the string \??\UNC and then calls the *NtCreateFile* system service to open the file. This object name is the name of a symbolic link that resolves to \Device\Mup, a device object that represents the MUP driver.

The MUP driver receives the request and sends an IRP asynchronously to each registered redirector, waiting for one of them to recognize the resource name and reply. When a redirector recognizes the name, it indicates how much of the name is unique to it. For example, if the name is \\WIN2KSERVER\ PUBLIC\insidew2k\ chap13.doc, the redirector recognizes it and claims the string \\WIN2KSERVER\ PUBLIC as its own. The MUP driver caches this information and thereafter sends requests beginning with that string directly to the redirector, skipping the polling operation. The MUP driver's cache has a timeout feature, so after a period of inactivity, a string's association with a particular redirector expires. If more than one redirector claims a particular resource, the MUP driver uses the registry's ProviderOrder value's list of loaded redirectors to determine which redirector takes precedence.

### 6.3.3 Domain Name System

Domain Name System (DNS) is a standard by which Internet names (such as www. microsoft.com) are translated to their corresponding IP addresses. A network application that wants to resolve a DNS name to an IP address sends a DNS lookup request using the TCP/IP protocol to a DNS server. DNS servers implement a distributed database of name/IP address pairs that are used to perform translations, and each server maintains the translations for a particular *zone*. Describing the details of DNS is outside the scope of this book, but DNS is the foundation of naming in Windows 2000 and hence is the primary Windows 2000 name resolution protocol.

The Windows 2000 DNS server is implemented as a Win32 service (\Winnt\ System32\Dns.exe) that is included in server versions of Windows 2000. Standard DNS server implementation relies on a text file as the translation database, but the Windows 2000 DNS server can be configured to store zone information in Active Directory.

## 6.4  Protocol Drivers

Networking API drivers must take API requests and translate them into low-level network protocol requests for transmission across the network. The API drivers rely on transport protocol drivers in kernel mode to do the actual translation. Separating APIs from underlying protocols gives the networking architecture the flexibility of letting each API use a number of different protocols. The protocol drivers that Windows 2000 includes are Data Link Control (DLC), NetBEUI, TCP/IP, and NWLink, although other protocols might be present as options, such as the AppleTalk protocol installed with Services For Macintosh on Windows 2000 servers.

So that networking API drivers don't need to employ various interfaces for each transport protocol they might want to use, Microsoft established the Transport Driver Interface standard. As mentioned earlier in this chapter, a TDI interface is essentially a convention for the way network requests format into IRPs and for the way network addresses and communications are allocated. Transport protocols that adhere to the TDI standard export the TDI interface to their clients, which include networking API drivers such as AFD and the redirector. A transport protocol implemented as a Windows 2000 device driver is known as a TDI transport. Because TDI transports are device drivers, they format requests they receive from clients as IRPs.

TDI transports in Windows 2000 generally implement all the protocols associated with their primary protocol. For example, the TCP/IP driver (\Winnt\System32\Drivers\Tcpip.sys) implements TCP, UDP, IP, ARP, ICMP, and IGMP. A TDI transport generally creates device objects that represent particular protocols so that clients can obtain a file object representing a protocol and issue network I/O to the protocol by using IRPs. The TCP/IP driver creates three device objects that represent various TDI-client accessible protocols: \Device\Tcp, \Device\Udp, and \Device\Ip.

The TDI interface is made up of support functions in the \Winnt\System32\Drivers\Tdi.sys library, along with definitions developers include in their drivers. The TDI programming model is similar to that of Winsock. A TDI client executes the following steps to establish a connection with a remote server:

1.   The client allocates and formats an *address open* TDI IRP to allocate an address. The TDI transport returns a file object, which is known as an *address object,* that represents the address. This step is the equivalent of using the *bind* Winsock function.

2.   The client then allocates and formats a *connection open* TDI IRP, and the TDI transport returns a file object, which is known as a *connection object,* that represents the connection. This step is the equivalent of the use of the Winsock *socket* function.

3.   The client associates the connection object to the address object with an *associate address* TDI IRP. (There's no equivalent to this step in Winsock.)

4.   A TDI client that accepts remote connections issues a *listen* TDI IRP specifying the number of connections supported for a connection object and then issues an *accept* TDI IRP, which completes when a remote system establishes a connection

(or an error occurs). These operations are equivalent to the use of the Winsock *listen* and *accept* functions.

5. A TDI client that wants to establish a connection with a remote server issues a *connect* TDI IRP, specifying the connection object, that the TDI transport completes when a connection is established (or an error occurs). Issuing a *connect* TDI IRP is the equivalent of using the *connect* Winsock function.

TDI also supports connectionless communications for connectionless protocols such as UDP. In addition, TDI provides a means whereby a TDI client can register *event callbacks* (that is, functions that are directly invoked) with TDI transports. When it receives data from across the network, a TDI transport can invoke a registered client receive callback, for example. This event-based callback feature of TDI allows the TDI transport to notify its clients of network events. Clients that rely on event callbacks don't need to preallocate resources such as buffers when receiving network data because they can view the contents of the buffers supplied by a TDI protocol driver.

**Watching TDI Activity.** TDImon, a free utility available from the Sysinternals Web site (`www.sysinternals.com`), is a form of filter driver that attaches to the \ Device\Tcp and \Device\Udp device objects that the TCP/IP driver creates. After attaching, TDImon sees every IRP that TDI clients issue to these protocols. By intercepting TDI client event callback registration, it also monitors event callbacks. The TDImon driver sends information about the TDI activity for display in its GUI, where you can see the time of an operation, the type of TDI activity that took place, the local and remote addresses of a TCP connection or the local address of a UDP endpoint, the resulting status code of the IRP or event callback, and additional information such as the number of bytes sent or received. Following is a screen shot of TDImon watching the TDI activity that is generated when Microsoft Internet Explorer browses a Web page.

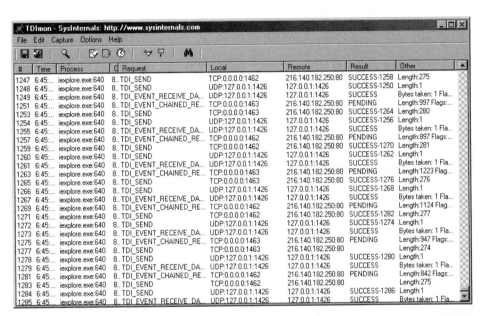

As evidence that TDI operations are inherently asynchronous, the PENDING codes in the Result column indicate that an operation initiated but that the IRP defining the operation hasn't yet completed. To accurately show the order of completions with respect to the start of other operations, the issuing of each IRP or event callback is tagged with a sequence number. If other IRPs are issued or completed before an IRP completes, the IRP's completion is also tagged with a sequence number that is shown in the Result column. For example, the IRP that was tagged with sequence number 1278 in the screen shot completed after the one tagged with 1279 was issued, so you see 1280 in the Result column for IRP 1278.

## 6.5   NDIS Drivers

When a protocol driver wants to read or write messages formatted in its protocol's format from or to the network, the driver must do so using a network adapter. Because expecting protocol drivers to understand the nuances of every network adapter on the market (proprietary network adapters number in the thousands) isn't feasible, network adapter vendors provide device drivers that can take network messages and transmit them via the vendors' proprietary hardware. In 1989, Microsoft and 3Com jointly developed the Network Driver Interface Specification, which lets protocol drivers communicate with network adapter drivers in a device-independent manner. Network adapter drivers that conform to NDIS are called NDIS drivers or NDIS miniport drivers. The version of NDIS that ships with Windows 2000 is NDIS 5.

On Windows 2000, the NDIS library (\Winnt\System32\Drivers\Ndis.sys) implements the NDIS boundary that exists between TDI transports (typically) and NDIS drivers. As is `Tdi.sys`, the NDIS library is a helper library that NDIS driver clients use to format commands they send to NDIS drivers. NDIS drivers interface with the library to receive requests and send back responses. Figure 6.15 shows the relationship between various NDIS-related components.

One of Microsoft's goals for its network architecture was to let network adapter vendors easily develop NDIS drivers and take driver code and move it between Consumer Windows and Windows 2000. Thus, instead of merely providing the NDIS boundary helper routines, the NDIS library provides NDIS drivers an entire execution environment. NDIS drivers aren't genuine Windows 2000 drivers because they can't function without the encapsulation the NDIS library gives them. This insulation layer wraps NDIS drivers so thoroughly that NDIS drivers don't accept and process IRPs. Rather, the NDIS library receives NDIS packets, the NDIS equivalent of an IRP, from TDI servers and translates the packets into calls into the NDIS driver. NDIS drivers also don't have to worry about reentrancy, in which the NDIS library invokes an NDIS driver with a new request before the driver has finished servicing a previous request. Exemption from reentrancy means that NDIS driver writers don't need to worry about complex synchronization, which is made even more tricky because of the parallel execution possible on a multiprocessor.

Although the NDIS library's serialization of NDIS drivers simplifies development, serialization can hamper multiprocessor scalability. Standard NDIS 4 drivers (the Windows NT 4 version of the NDIS library) don't scale well for certain operations on multiprocessors. Microsoft gave developers a deserialized operation option in NDIS 5. NDIS 5 drivers can indicate to the NDIS library that they don't want to be serialized; the NDIS library will then forward requests to the driver as fast as it receives the IRPs that describe the requests. Responsibility for queuing and managing multiple simultaneous requests falls on the NDIS driver, but deserialization confers the benefit of higher multiprocessor performance.

NDIS 5 also includes the following features:

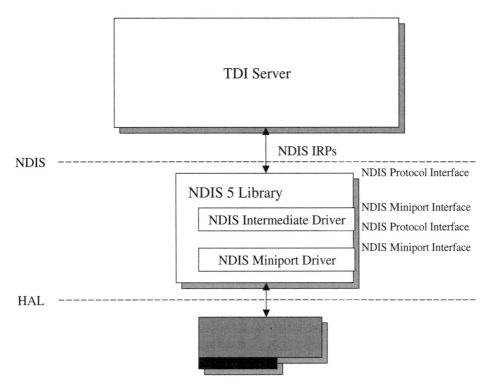

**Figure 6.15**
NDIS components.

- NDIS drivers can report whether or not their network medium is active, which allows Windows 2000 to display a network connected/disconnected icon on the taskbar. This feature also allows protocols and other applications to be aware of this state and react accordingly. The TCP/IP transport, for example, will use this information to determine when it should reevaluate addressing information it receives from DHCP.
- TCP/IP task offloading allows a miniport to use advanced features of a network adapter to perform operations such as packet checksums and Internet Protocol security (IPSec). This task offloading can improve system performance by relieving the CPU from these operations.

- Fast packet forwarding allows the network adapter hardware to route packets not destined for a computer to remote systems without ever delivering them to the CPU.

- Wake-on-LAN allows a wake-on-LAN-capable network adapter to bring Windows 2000 out of a suspend power state. Events that can trigger the network adapter to signal the system include media connections (such as plugging a network cable into the adapter), the receipt of protocol-specific patterns registered by a protocol (the TCP/IP transport asks to be woken for ARP requests), and, for Ethernet adapters, the receipt of a *magic* packet (a network packet that contains 16 contiguous copies of the adapter's Ethernet address).

- Connection-oriented NDIS allows NDIS drivers to manage connection-oriented media such as Asynchronous Transfer Mode (ATM) devices. (Connection-oriented NDIS is described in more detail shortly.)

The interfaces that the NDIS library provides for NDIS drivers to interface with network adapter hardware are available via functions that translate directly to corresponding functions in the HAL.

### 6.5.1   Variations on the NDIS Miniport

The NDIS model also supports hybrid TDI transport-NDIS drivers, called *NDIS intermediate drivers.* These drivers lie between TDI transports and NDIS drivers. To an NDIS driver, an NDIS intermediate driver looks like a TDI transport; to a TDI transport, an NDIS intermediate driver looks like an NDIS driver. NDIS intermediate drivers can see all network traffic taking place on a system because the drivers lie between protocol drivers and network drivers. Software that provides fault-tolerant and load-balancing options for network adapters, such as Microsoft's Network Load Balancing Provider, are based on NDIS intermediate drivers. The packet scheduler that is part of Microsoft's QoS implementation is another example of an NDIS intermediate driver.

### 6.5.2   Connection-Oriented NDIS

NDIS 5 introduces a new type of NDIS driver: a connection-oriented NDIS miniport driver. Support for connection-oriented network hardware (for example, ATM) is therefore native in Windows 2000, which makes connection management and establishment standard in the Windows 2000 network architecture. Connection-oriented NDIS drivers use many of the same APIs that standard NDIS drivers use; however, connection-oriented NDIS drivers send packets through established network connections rather than place them on the network medium.

In addition to miniport support for connection-oriented media, NDIS 5 includes definitions for drivers that work to support a connection-oriented miniport driver:

• Call managers are NDIS drivers that provide call setup and teardown services for connection-oriented clients (described shortly). A call manager uses a connection-oriented miniport to exchange signaling messages with other network entities such as network switches or other call managers. A call manager supports one or more signaling protocols, such as ATM User-Network Interface (UNI) 3.1.

• An integrated miniport call manager (MCM) is a connection-oriented miniport driver that also provides call manager services to connection-oriented clients. An MCM is essentially an NDIS miniport driver with a built-in call manager.

• A connection-oriented client uses the call setup and teardown services of a call manager or MCM and the send and receive services of a connection-oriented NDIS miniport driver. A connection-oriented client can provide its own protocol services to higher levels in the network stack, or it can implement an emulation layer that interfaces connectionless legacy protocols and connection-oriented media. An example of an emulation layer fulfilled by a connection-oriented client is a LAN emulation (LANE), which hides the connected-oriented characteristics of ATM and presents a connectionless media (such as Ethernet) to protocols above it.

Figure 6.16 shows the relationships between these components.

**Using Network Monitor to Capture Network Packets.** Windows 2000 Server comes with a tool named Network Monitor that lets you capture packets that flow through one or more NDIS miniport drivers on your system by installing an NDIS intermediate driver. Before you can use Network Monitor, you need to have the Windows 2000 Network Monitor Tools installed on your system. To install these tools, open Add/Remove Programs in the Control Panel, and select Add/Remove Windows Components. Select Management And Monitoring Tools, click Details, select Network Monitor Tools, and click OK.

After you've installed Network Monitor Tools, you install Network Monitor by following these steps:

1.   Bring up the Network And Dial-Up Connections application by right-clicking on the My Network Places icon on the desktop and selecting Properties, or by selecting Network And Dial-Up Connections from the Settings option on the Start menu.

2.   Right-click on a local adapter, select Properties, and click the Install button in the Local Area Connection Properties dialog box.

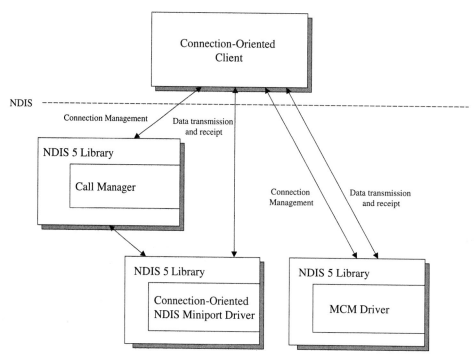

**Figure 6.16**
Connection-oriented NDIS drivers.

3.  Select Protocol, and click the Add button.

4.  Choose Network Monitor Driver, and click OK.

After the Network Monitor driver has been installed, you can launch Network Monitor by selecting it from the Programs, Administrative Tools folder in the Start menu.

Network Monitor might ask you which network connection you want to monitor. After selecting one, begin monitoring by pressing the Start Capture button in the toolbar. Perform operations that generate network activity on the connection you're monitoring, and after you see that Network Monitor has captured packets, stop monitoring by clicking the Stop And View Capture button (the stop button that has glasses next to it). Network Monitor will present a view of the capture data like the following screen shot.

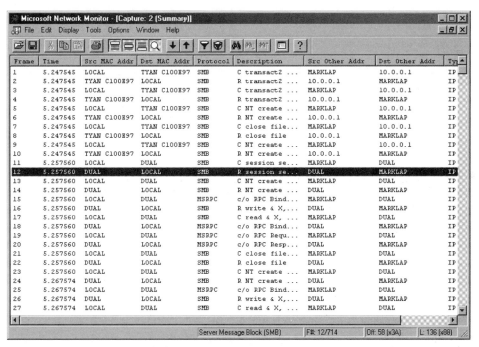

The screen shot shows the SMB (CIFS) packets that Network Monitor captured as remote files were accessed from the system. If you double-click on a line, Network Monitor will switch to a view of the packet that breaks it apart to show various layered application and protocol headers, as shown in the following screen shot.

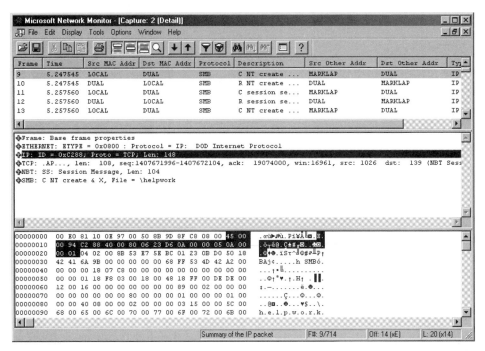

Network Monitor also includes a number of other features, such as capture triggers and filters, that make it a powerful tool for troubleshooting network problems.

## 6.6  Conclusion

The Windows 2000 network architecture provides a flexible infrastructure for networking APIs, network protocol drivers, and network adapter drivers. The Windows 2000 networking architecture takes advantage of I/O layering to give networking support the extensibility to evolve as computer networking evolves. When new protocols appear, developers can write a TDI transport to implement the protocol on Windows 2000. Similarly, new APIs can interface to existing Windows 2000 protocol drivers. Finally, the range of networking APIs implemented on Windows 2000 affords network application developers a range of possible implementations, each with different programming models and protocol support.

# 7 Setting Up Clusters: Installation and Configuration

*David Lifka*

The true beauty of a Windows 2000 cluster installation is that, at its heart, it is simply a customization of a standard Windows 2000 domain installation. If you already have a Windows domain of workstations or servers set up, you have at least 80 percent of the knowledge required to set up a Windows cluster. High-performance computing is now a very real option for the masses. Indeed, the ease of installing and running a Windows 2000 cluster will ultimately be the reason Windows will revolutionize the high-performance computing industry—much as the Windows operating system did the workstation market.

In this chapter we discuss important issues to consider when planning a Windows cluster installation, and we provide detailed installation instructions that relate to these issues. Many of the concepts presented in this chapter are discussed in far greater detail elsewhere in this book; our objective here is to provide you with a complete picture for planning your Windows cluster installation.

## 7.1 Resource Considerations

When planning a Windows 2000 cluster installation, you must consider several key components. These include the Windows domain configuration, file server setup, use of login nodes, compute node configuration, and interconnect.

### 7.1.1 Domain Controllers

The first step in any Windows cluster installation is considering the domain structure in which the cluster will reside. For example, do you want a separate domain for the cluster, a separate subdomain, or a trusted domain, or do you want the cluster completely integrated with your current domain (which may include a mix of workstations, laptops, and servers)? Certainly the most popular choice is to integrate the cluster resources into an existing domain, thereby providing easy accessibility for domain users. In general, the integrated approach works well, but it does raise some management considerations. You must, for example, consider who will have access to the domain and where they will be accessing it from. If you allow outside users without domain accounts to access the cluster from a network, you may want to have the cluster domain separate from your production desktop environment to shield it from potential security problems.

## 7.1.2   File Servers

File servers under Windows work differently from the way they work in a Unix
environment. In particular, remote file access is built into the operating system,
without requiring mounted file systems like NFS, for example. Windows files may
be accessed remotely via their Universal Naming Convention (UNC) or by mapping
the share to a local drive via Windows Explorer. For example, if you have a file
server with the name of "fileserver1" and it has a shared folder called "tools," you
can access this folder remotely from the command line by UNC as follows:

```
c:\ dir \\fileserver1\tools
```

or you can map it to a drive letter from the command line as follows:

```
c:\ net use Z: \\fileserver\tools
```

After issuing this command the local Z: will appear as if it were a local file system.

Storage on several file servers can be logically aggregated into a single logical
volume via Microsoft's distributed file system (DFS). DFS allows multiple physical
disk volumes to be accessed through a single shared volume. All cluster nodes can
map this share as the same drive letter to provide a consistent interface across
all cluster resources. Of course, this configuration does raise a potential problem:
normally all mapped drives are disconnected when you log off the machine console.
To work around this, you have two options. The first is to lock the screen and leave
the console logged in with the drive mapped. This is sufficient if you have a secure
machine room, but it is not the most elegant solution. The second option is to use
a Windows service to map the drive, which will continue running even when you
are not logged in at the console. The following simple Perl script uses a special
module called Win32::Daemon (from Roth Consulting) that allows the script to act
as a Windows service. You can download this module from **www.roth.net/perl/**.

```perl
#!perl

use Win32::Daemon;

%ModelHash =
 (
  name    => 'Model',
  display => 'Model Perl Service',
  path    => 'c:\perl\bin\perl.exe',
```

```
  user      =>  '',
  pwd       =>  '',
  parameters =>'C:\temp\model.pl',
 );

if ($ARGV[0] eq "-h")      { &Help;    exit; }
if ($ARGV[0] eq "-help")   { &Help;    exit; }
if ($ARGV[0] eq "help")    { &Help;    exit; }
if ($ARGV[0] eq "install") { &Install; exit; }
if ($ARGV[0] eq "remove")  { &Remove;  exit; }


#============================================================================
$sleep_interval = 5;
$hostname = Win32::NodeName();
$LogDir = $ENV{"TEMP"};      # log folder

Win32::Daemon::StartService();
while( SERVICE_STOPPED != ( $State = Win32::Daemon::State() ) )
 {
  if (( SERVICE_START_PENDING == $State ) || ( SERVICE_STARTING == $State ))
   {
    Win32::Daemon::State( SERVICE_RUNNING );
    &Log("Service STARTING -> RUNNING");
   }
  elsif ( SERVICE_PAUSE_PENDING == $State )
   {
    Win32::Daemon::State( SERVICE_PAUSED );
    &Log("Service PAUSE_PENDING -> PAUSE");
   }
  elsif ( SERVICE_CONTINUE_PENDING == $State )
   {
    Win32::Daemon::State( SERVICE_RUNNING );
    &Log("Service CONTINUE_PENDING -> RUNNING");
   }
  elsif ( SERVICE_STOP_PENDING == $State )
   {
    Win32::Daemon::State( SERVICE_STOPPED );
    &Log("Service STARTING -> STOPPED");
   }
  elsif ( SERVICE_CONTROL_SHUTDOWN == $State )
   {
    # Request 45 seconds to shut down...
    Win32::Daemon::State( SERVICE_STOP_PENDING, 45);
    # Add code here to shut down
```

```
        Win32::Daemon::State( SERVICE_STOPPED );
        &Log("Service CONTROL_SHUTDOWN -> STOP_PENDING -> STOPPED");
      }
    elsif ( SERVICE_RUNNING == $State )
     {
      # Add code for the running state
      &Log("Service RUNNING");
     }
    else
     {
      # Un-handled control messages
      &Log("Service UNHANDLED");
     }
   sleep($sleep_interval);
  }
Win32::Daemon::StopService();


#===============================================================================

sub Help
 {
  print "Usage: Model.pl <option>\n";
  print "Options: install\n";
  print "         remove\n";
  print "         help\n";
 }

sub Install
 {
  if( Win32::Daemon::CreateService(\%ModelHash))
   {
    print "Successfully added.\n";
   }
  else
   {
    print "Failed to add service: " . GetError() . "\n";
   }
  print "finished.\n";
 } # sub Install

sub Remove
 {
  print "WARNING: Be sure to stop the service\n";
  if( Win32::Daemon::DeleteService($ModelHash{name}))
```

```
   {
    print "Successfully removed.\n";
   }
  else
   {
    print "Failed to remove service: " . GetError() . "\n";
   }
  print "finished.\n";
 } # sub Remove

sub GetError
 {
  return( Win32::FormatMessage( Win32::Daemon::GetLastError() ) );
 }

sub Log
 {
  ($sec,$min,$hour,$mday,$mon,$year,$wday,$yday,$isdst) = localtime(time);
  $time = sprintf("%02d%02d%02d%02d%02d",$mon+1,$mday,$year+1900,$hour,$min);
  open(LOG, ">>$LogDir\\Model.log");
  print LOG "$time>$_[0]\n";
  close(LOG);
 }
```

### 7.1.3   Login Nodes

Login nodes are a mechanism to provide remote users with a consistent interface and tools to your cluster. Typically, login nodes have compilers, debuggers, programming environments such as Interix or Cygwin, and scheduler interface tools. Login nodes usually are accessible via telnet or the Windows Terminal Server (with or without Citrix Metaframe, depending on whether you have clients accessing the cluster from a non-Windows platform). In many environments login nodes are not necessary, and simply installing scheduler interface commands on the users' workstations in the same Windows domain is sufficient.

### 7.1.4   Compute Nodes

Chapter 3 of this book provides a complete description of compute node hardware options and their effect on performance. Typically, compute nodes have relatively little software installed on them. The usual software includes runtime libraries, message-passing software, and applications such as Matlab, Mathematica, SAS, and scripting languages, as needed.

## 7.2  Basic Windows 2000 Cluster Installation Procedure

We assume here that you have already installed a Windows 2000 domain along with
Active Directory. You now are ready to install the cluster.

1. *Set up your Windows 2000 domain.* This step involves adding software and
making necessary configuration changes so that the resources in the Windows domain will work the way compute nodes work in a cluster. Note that if the cluster is
already part of your Windows 2000 domain, you do not have to establish a separate
dedicated domain for a Windows 2000 cluster.

2. *Set up your file server.* This step is necessary so that, when you are ready
to install the login and compute nodes, you will be able to refer to this resource.
Recall that the file server can be accessed remotely via UNC or by mapping a drive
to a share, either manually or using the Perl script provided earlier in this chapter.

3. *Install your compute nodes.* You can install each node manually, one by
one, but this process is both time consuming and error prone. Alternatively, you
can use a commercial package such as Symantec Ghost, Imagecast, or PCRDist
that provides a mechanism to create a "node image," which you then use to install
all the cluster compute nodes identically and in parallel. Details of creating and
"pushing" node images are specific to the package you choose. Here, therefore, we
simply describe the logical steps that you should follow in installing the cluster
nodes.

- Install one node completely, including drivers, software, and configuration customizations; however, do not install a scheduling system yet. If you have a *heterogeneous* cluster, you should install one node of each hardware configuration.

- Use the tool called *sysprep* to remove all operating system and software information specific to that node, for example, Microsoft Security IDs and hostnames.
  (The *sysprep* tool is distributed on every Microsoft Windows Server CD.) Configuring your compute nodes to obtain an IP address via DHCP means that all
  networking information in the node image is identical from node to node. The following Web site provides a Web cast of how to use *sysprep*: support.microsoft.
  com/servicedesks/Webcasts/SO\_Projects/so4/SOBLURB4.ASP.

- Create a node image using one of the several packages available. Then, "push"
  this image to all nodes with the same hardware configuration. Tools such as Ghost
  do this via network broadcast, so all machines that are booted in an appropriate
  state to accept an image (again tool specific) can read and install this image
  simultaneously.

- Boot each node and, as it comes up, make local customizations such as its hostname. Then add the machine to your Windows 2000 domain. At this point you should have all your compute nodes set up and running as members of your Windows 2000 domain. (We note that this technique can be used for any Windows 2000 domain members, not just cluster nodes. It is a convenient way to rapidly deploy new desktop machines, for example.)

4. *Install a scheduling system.* Many scheduling systems are available; Chapter 15 provides a good overview of the Maui scheduler, for instance. Scheduler installation can also include modifying access rights and permissions in the Windows 2000 domain. You can make these modifications through normal user and group interactions with Active Directory.

5. *Install the login node or the interface commands.* Successful completion of this step will enable your users to begin using the cluster. As noted in Section 7.1.3, login nodes may not be needed. Instead, you may simply need to install commands or graphical interfaces that allow users to check the cluster resources and job queues and to submit or remove jobs from the queues.

## 7.3  Off and Running

This chapter provides enough information for you to set up and begin using a reasonably large Windows 2000 high-performance cluster. Although other strategies are available, the general process and procedure described here are sufficient for most types of installation.

# 8 How Fast Is My Beowulf?

*David Bailey*

One of the first questions that a user of a new Beowulf-type system asks is "How fast does my system run?" Performance is more than just a curiosity for cluster systems. It is arguably the central motivation for building a clustered system in the first place—a single node is not sufficient for the task at hand. Thus the measurement of performance, as well as comparisons of performance between various available system designs and constructions, is of paramount importance.

## 8.1 Metrics

Many different metrics for system performance exist, varying greatly in their meaningfulness and ease of measurement. We discuss here some of the more widely used metrics.

1. **Theoretical peak performance**. This statistic is merely the maximum aggregate performance of the system. For scientific users, theoretical peak performance means the maximum aggregate floating-point operations per second, usually calculated as

$$P = N * C * F * R,$$

where $P$ is the performance, $N$ is the number of nodes, $C$ is the number of CPUs per node, $F$ is the number of floating-point operations per clock period, and $R$ is the clock rate, measured in cycles per second. $P$ is typically given in Mflops or Gflops. For nonscientific applications, integer operations are counted instead of floating-point operations per second, and rates are typically measured in Mops and Gops, variantly given as Mips and Gips. For nonhomogeneous systems, $P$ is calculated as the total of the theoretical peak performance figures for each homogeneous subsystem.

The advantage of this metric is that is very easy to calculate. What's more, there is little disputing the result: the relevant data is in many cases publicly available. The disadvantage of this metric is that by definition it is unattainable by ordinary application programs. Indeed, a growing concern of scientific users—in particular, users of parallel and distributed systems—is that the typical gap between peak and sustained performance seems to be increasing, not decreasing.

2. **Application performance.** This statistic is the number of operations performed while executing an application program, divided by the total run time. As with theoretical peak performance, it is typically given in Mflops, Gflops, Mops, or Gops. This metric, if calculated for an application program that reasonably closely

resembles the program that the user ultimately intends to run on the system, is obviously a much more meaningful metric than theoretical peak performance. The metric is correspondingly harder to use, however, because you must first port the benchmark program to the cluster system, often a laborious and time-consuming task. Moreover, you must determine fairly accurately the number of floating-point (or integer) operations actually performed by the code. Along this line, you should ascertain that the algorithms used in the code are really the most efficient available for this task, or you should use a floating-point operation count that corresponds to that of an efficient algorithm implementation; otherwise, the results can be questioned. One key difficulty with this metric is the extent to which the source code has been "tuned" for optimal performance on the given system: comparing results that on one system are based on a highly tuned implementation to those on another system where the application has not be highly tuned can be misleading. Nonetheless, if used properly, this metric can be very useful.

3. **Application run time.** This statistic simply means the total wall-clock run time for performing a given application. One advantage of this statistic is that it frees you from having to count operations performed. Also, it avoids the potential distortion of using a code to assess performance whose operation count is larger than it needs be. In many regards, this is the ultimate metric, in the sense that it is precisely the ultimate figure of merit for an application running on a system. The disadvantage of this metric is that unless you are comparing two systems both of which have run exactly the same application, it is hard to meaningfully compare systems based solely on comparisons of runtime performance. Further, the issue of tuning also is present here: In comparing performance between systems, you have to ensure that both implementations have been comparably tuned.

4. **Scalability.** Users often cite scalability statistics when describing the performance of their system. Scalability is usually computed as

$$S = \frac{T(1)}{T(N)},$$

where $T(1)$ is the wall clock run time for a particular program on a single processor and $T(N)$ is the run time on $N$ processors. A scalability figure close to $N$ means that the program scales well. That is, the parallel implementation is very efficient, and the parallel overhead very low, so that nearly a linear speedup has been achieved. Scalability statistics can often provide useful information. For example, they can help you determine an optimal number of processors for a given application. But they can also be misleading, particularly if cited in the absence of application performance statistics. For example, an impressive speedup statistic may be due to a very low value of $T(N)$, which appears in the denominator, but it may also be due to a large value of $T(1)$—in other words, an inefficient one-processor implementation. Indeed, researchers working with parallel systems commonly note that their speedup statistic worsens when they accelerate their parallel program by clever tuning. Also, it is often simply impossible to compute this statistic because, while a benchmark test program may run on all or most of the processors in a system, it may require too much memory to run on a single node.

5. **Parallel efficiency.** A variant of the scalability metric is parallel efficiency, which is usually defined to be $P(N)/N$. Parallel efficiency statistics near one are ideal. This metric suffers from the same potential difficulties as the scalability metric.

6. **Percentage of peak.** Sometimes application performance statistics are given in terms of the percentage of theoretical peak performance. Such statistics are useful in highlighting the extent to which an application is using the full computational power of the system. For example, a low percentage of peak may indicate a mismatch of the architecture and the application, deserving further study to determine the source of the difficulty. However, a percentage-of-peak figure by itself is not too informative. An embarrassingly parallel application can achieve a high percentage of peak, but this is not a notable achievement. In general, percentage-of-peak figures beg the question "What percentage of peak is a realistic target for a given type of application?"

7. **Latency and bandwidth.** Many users are interested in the latency (time delay) and bandwidth (transfer rate) of the interprocessor communications network, since the network is one of the key elements of the system design. These metrics have the advantage of being fairly easy to determine. The disadvantage is that the network often performs differently under highly loaded situations from what the latency and bandwidth figures by themselves reveal. And, needless to say, these metrics characterize only the network and give no information on the computational speed of individual processors.

8. **System utilization.** One common weakness of the cited metrics is that they tend to ignore system-level effects. These effects include competition between two different tasks running in the system, competition between I/O-intensive tasks and non-I/O-intensive tasks, inefficiencies in job schedulers, and job startup delays. To address this issue, some Beowulf system users have measured the performance of

a system on a long-term throughput basis, as a contrast to conventional benchmark performance testing.

Clearly, no single type of performance measurement—much less a single figure of merit—is simultaneously easy to determine and completely informative. In one sense, only one figure of merit matters, as emphasized above: the wall clock run time for your particular application on your particular system. But this is not easy to determine before a purchase or upgrade decision has been made. And even if you can make such a measurement, it is not clear how to compare your results with the thousands of other Beowulf system users around the world, not to mention other types of systems and clusters.

These considerations have led many users of parallel and cluster systems to compare performance based on a few standard benchmark programs. In this way, you can determine whether your particular system design is as effective (as measured by a handful of benchmarks) as another. Such comparisons might not be entirely relevant to your particular application, but with some experience you can find one or more well-known benchmarks that give performance figures that are well correlated with your particular needs.

## 8.2    Ping-Pong Test

One of the most widely used measurements performed on cluster systems is the Ping-Pong test, one of several test programs that measure the latency and bandwidth of the interprocessor communications network. There are a number of tools for testing TCP performance, including `netperf` and `netpipe` (see `www.netperf.org` and `www.scl.ameslab.gov/netpipe`). Ping-Pong tests that are appropriate for application developers measure the performance of the user API and are typically written in C and assume that the MPI communications library is installed on the system. More details on downloading and running these are given in Section 10.10.

## 8.3    The LINPACK Benchmark

The LINPACK benchmark dates back to the early 1980s, when Jack Dongarra (then at Argonne National Laboratory) began collecting performance results of systems, based on their speed in solving a $100 \times 100$ linear system using Fortran routines from the LINPACK library. While a problem of this size is no longer a supercomputer-class exercise, it is still useful for assessing the computational performance of a single-processor system. In particular, it is a reasonable way to measure the performance of a single node of a Beowulf-type system. One can obtain the LINPACK source code, plus instructions for running the LINPACK benchmark, from the `www.netlib.org/benchmark`.

More recently, Dongarra has released the "highly parallel computing" benchmark. This benchmark was developed for medium-to-large parallel and distributed systems and has been tabulated on hundreds of computer systems [2, Table 3]. Unlike the basic LINPACK benchmark, the scalable version does not specify a matrix size. Instead, the user is invited to solve the largest problem that can reasonably be run on the available system, given limitations of memory. Further, the user is not restricted to running a fixed source code, as with the single-processor version. Instead, almost any reasonable programming language and parallel computation library can be run, including assembly-coded library routines if desired.

A portable implementation of the highly parallel LINPACK benchmark, called the High Performance LINPACK (HPL) benchmark, is available. More details on downloading and running the HPL benchmark are given in Section 10.10.3.

During the past ten years, Dongarra and Strohmaier have compiled a running list of the world's so-called Top500 computers, based on the scalable LINPACK benchmark. The current listing is available from the `www.top500.org`. One of the top-ranking systems is the ASCI Red system at Sandia National Laboratories in Albuquerque, New Mexico. The ASCI Red system is a Pentium-based cluster system, although not truly a "Beowulf" system because it has a custom-designed interprocessor network. With an Rmax rating of 2.379 Tflops, it currently ranks third in the Top500 list (based on the June 2001 listing).

The LINPACK benchmarks are fairly easy to download and run. Once a timing figure is obtained, the calculation of performance is very easy. Most significant, there is a huge collection of results for comparison: it is very easy to determine how your system stacks up against other similar systems.

The principal disadvantage of the LINPACK benchmarks, both single processor and parallel, is that they tend to overestimate the performance that real-world scientific applications can expect to achieve on a given system. This is because the LINPACK codes are "dense matrix" calculations, which have very favorable data locality characteristics. It is not uncommon for the scalable LINPACK benchmark, for example, to achieve 30 percent or more of the theoretical peak performance potential of a system. Real scientific application codes, in contrast, seldom achieve more than 10 percent of the peak figure on modern distributed-memory parallel systems such as Beowulf systems.

## 8.4   The NAS Parallel Benchmark Suite

The NAS Parallel Benchmark (NPB) suite was designed at NASA Ames Research Center in 1990 to typify high-end aeroscience computations. This suite consists of eight individual benchmarks, including five general computational kernels and three simulated computational fluid dynamics applications:

**EP:** An "embarrassingly parallel" calculation, it requires almost no interprocessor communication.

**MG:** A multigrid calculation, it tests both short- and long-distance communication.

**CG:** A conjugate gradient calculation, it tests irregular communication.

**FT:** A three-dimensional fast Fourier transform calculation, it tests massive all-to-all communication.

**IS:** An integer sort, it involves integer data and irregular communication.

**LU:** A simulated fluid dynamics application, it uses the LU approach.

**SP:** A simulated fluid dynamics application, it uses the SP approach.

**BT:** A simulated fluid dynamics application, it uses the BT approach.

The original NPB suite was a "paper-and-pencil" specification—the specific calculations to be performed for each benchmark were specified in a technical document, even down to the detail of how to generate the initial data. Some straightforward one-processor sample program codes were provided in the original release, but it was intended that those implementing this suite would use one of several vendor-specific parallel programming models available at the time (1990). The original NPB problem set was deemed Class A size. Subsequently some larger problem sets were defined: Class B, which are about four times as large as the Class A problems, and Class C, which are about four times as large as Class B problems. The small single-processor sample codes are sometimes referred to as the Class W size.

Since the original NPB release, implementations of the NPB using MPI and also OpenMP have been provided by the NASA team. These are available at `www.nas.nasa.gov/Software/NPB/`.

As with the LINPACK benchmark, the NPB suite can be used to measure the performance of either a single node of a Beowulf system or the entire system. In particular, the Class W problems can easily be run on a single-processor system. For a Beowulf system with, say, 32 processors, the Class A problems are an appropriate test. The Class B problems are appropriate for systems with roughly 32–128 processors. The Class C problems can be used for systems with up to 256 CPUs.

Unfortunately, almost the entire NASA research team that designed and championed the NPB suite has now left NASA. As a result, NASA is no longer actively supporting and promoting the benchmarks. Thus, there probably will not be any larger problem sets developed. Further, NASA is no longer actively collecting results.

The NPB suite does, however, continue to attract attention from the parallel computing research community. This is because the suite reflects real-world parallel scientific computation to a significantly greater degree than do most other available benchmarks.

We recommend that users of Beowulf-type systems use the MPI version of the NPB suite. Instructions for downloading, installing, and running the suite are given at the NPB Web site.

# II PARALLEL PROGRAMMING

# 9 Parallel Programming with MPI

*William Gropp and Ewing Lusk*

Parallel computation on a Beowulf is accomplished by dividing a computation into parts and making use of multiple processes, each executing on a separate processor, to carry out these parts. Sometimes an ordinary program can be used by all the processes, but with distinct input files or parameters. In such a situation, no communication occurs among the separate tasks. When the power of a parallel computer is needed to attack a large problem with a more complex structure, however, such communication is necessary.

One of the most straightforward approaches to communication is to have the processes coordinate their activities by sending and receiving messages, much as a group of people might cooperate to perform a complex task. This approach to achieving parallelism is called *message passing*.

In this chapter and the next, we show how to write parallel programs using MPI, the Message Passing Interface. MPI is a message-passing library specification. All three parts of this description are significant.

- MPI addresses the message-passing model of parallel computation, in which processes with separate address spaces synchronize with one another and move data from the address space of one process to that of another by sending and receiving messages.[1]
- MPI specifies a library interface, that is, a collection of subroutines and their arguments. It is not a language; rather, MPI routines are called from programs written in conventional languages such as Fortran, C, and C++.
- MPI is a specification, not a particular implementation. The specification was created by the MPI Forum, a group of parallel computer vendors, computer scientists, and users who came together to cooperatively work out a community standard. The first phase of meetings resulted in a release of the standard in 1994 that is sometimes referred to as MPI-1. Once the standard was implemented and in wide use a second series of meetings resulted in a set of extensions, referred to as MPI-2. MPI refers to both MPI-1 and MPI-2.

As a specification, MPI is defined by a standards document, the way C, Fortran, or POSIX are defined. The MPI standards documents are available at `www.mpi-forum.org` and may be freely downloaded. The MPI-1 and MPI-2 standards are also available as journal issues [10, 11] and in annotated form as books

---

[1] Processes may be single threaded, with one program counter, or multithreaded, with multiple program counters. MPI is for communication among processes rather than threads. Signal handlers can be thought of as executing in a separate thread.

in this series [14, 4]. Implementations of MPI are available for almost all parallel computers, from clusters to the largest and most powerful parallel computers
in the world. In Section 9.8 we provide a summary of the most popular cluster
implementations.

A goal of the MPI Forum was to create a powerful, flexible library that could be
implemented efficiently on the largest computers and provide a tool to attack the
most difficult problems in parallel computing. It does not always do the simplest
things in the simplest way but comes into its own as more complex functionality is
needed. In this chapter and the next we work through a set of examples, starting
with the simplest.

## 9.1 Hello World in MPI

To see what an MPI program looks like, we start with the classic "hello world"
program. MPI specifies only the library calls to be used in a C, Fortran, or C++
program; consequently, all of the capabilities of the language are available. The
simplest "Hello World" program is shown in Figure 9.1.

```
#include "mpi.h"
#include <stdio.h>

int main( int argc, char *argv[] )
{
    MPI_Init( &argc, &argv );
    printf( "Hello World\n" );
    MPI_Finalize();
    return 0;
}
```

**Figure 9.1**
Simple "Hello World" program in MPI.

All MPI programs must contain one call to `MPI_Init` and one to `MPI_Finalize`.
All other[2] MPI routines must be called after `MPI_Init` and before `MPI_Finalize`.
All C and C++ programs must also include the file 'mpi.h'; Fortran programs must
either use the MPI module or include `mpif.h`.

The simple program in Figure 9.1 is not very interesting. In particular, all processes print the same text. A more interesting version has each process identify

---

[2]There are a few exceptions, including `MPI_Initialized`.

```
#include "mpi.h"
#include <stdio.h>

int main( int argc, char *argv[] )
{
    int rank, size;

    MPI_Init( &argc, &argv );
    MPI_Comm_rank( MPI_COMM_WORLD, &rank );
    MPI_Comm_size( MPI_COMM_WORLD, &size );
    printf( "Hello World from process %d of %d\n", rank, size );
    MPI_Finalize();
    return 0;
}
```

**Figure 9.2**
A more interesting version of "Hello World".

itself. This version, shown in Figure 9.2, illustrates several important points. Of particular note are the variables `rank` and `size`. Because MPI programs are made up of communicating processes, each process has its own set of variables. In this case, each process has its own address space containing its own variables `rank` and `size` (and `argc`, `argv`, etc.). The routine `MPI_Comm_size` returns the number of processes in the MPI job in the second argument. Each of the MPI processes is identified by a number, called the *rank*, ranging from zero to the value of `size` minus one. The routine `MPI_Comm_rank` returns in the second argument the rank of the process. The output of this program might look something like the following:

```
Hello World from process 0 of 4
Hello World from process 2 of 4
Hello World from process 3 of 4
Hello World from process 1 of 4
```

Note that the output is not ordered from processes 0 to 3. MPI does not specify the behavior of other routines or language statements such as `printf`; in particular, it does not specify the order of output from print statements.

### 9.1.1  Compiling and Running MPI Programs

The MPI standard does not specify how to compile and link programs (neither do C or Fortran). However, most MPI implementations provide tools to compile and link programs.

The MPICH implementation of MPI provides instructions on setting up a makefile or project file for use with Microsoft Visual Studio. In version 1.2.1, these are

**Include Path:** '<MPICH home>\include'

**Switches:** /MTd for the debug version and /MT for the release version

**Libraries:** 'mpich.lib' (contains MPI-1, all PMPI routines, and MPI-IO); 'mpe.lib' contains the profiling interface to MPI-1

**Library Path:** '<MPICH home>\lib'

**Include path:** '<MPICH home>\include'

Running an MPI program (in most implementations) also requires a special program, particularly when parallel programs are started by a batch system as described in Chapter 13. Many implementations provide a program mpirun that can be used to start MPI programs. For example, the command

```
mpirun -np 4 helloworld
```

runs the program helloworld using four processes. Most MPI implementations will attempt to run each process on a different processor; most MPI implementations provide a way to select particular processors for each MPI process. In MPICH, mpirun should be run from within a console process.

The name and command-line arguments of the program that starts MPI programs were not specified by the original MPI standard, just as the C standard does not specify how to start C programs. However, the MPI Forum did recommend, as part of the MPI-2 standard, an mpiexec command and standard command-line arguments to be used in starting MPI programs. By 2002, most MPI implementations should provide mpiexec. This name was selected because no MPI implementation was using it (many are using mpirun, but with incompatible arguments). The syntax is almost the same as for the MPICH version of mpirun; instead of using -np to specify the number of processes, the switch -n is used:

```
mpiexec -n 4 helloworld
```

The MPI standard defines additional switches for mpiexec; for more details, see Section 4.1, "Portable MPI Process Startup", in the MPI-2 standard.

### 9.1.2    Adding Communication to Hello World

The code in Figure 9.2 does not guarantee that the output will be printed in any particular order. To force a particular order for the output, and to illustrate how data is communicated between processes, we add communication to the "Hello World" program. The revised program implements the following algorithm:

```
Find the name of the processor that is running the process
If the process has rank > 0, then
    send the name of the processor to the process with rank 0
Else
    print the name of this processor
    for each rank,
        receive the name of the processor and print it
Endif
```

This program is shown in Figure 9.3. The new MPI calls are to `MPI_Send` and `MPI_Recv` and to `MPI_Get_processor_name`. The latter is a convenient way to get the name of the processor on which a process is running. `MPI_Send` and `MPI_Recv` can be understood by stepping back and considering the two requirements that must be satisfied to communicate data between two processes:

1.  Describe the data to be sent or the location in which to receive the data

2.  Describe the destination (for a send) or the source (for a receive) of the data.

In addition, MPI provides a way to tag messages and to discover information about the size and source of the message. We will discuss each of these in turn.

**Describing the Data Buffer.**    A data buffer typically is described by an address and a length, such as "`a,100`," where `a` is a pointer to 100 bytes of data. For example, the Unix `write` call describes the data to be written with an address and length (along with a file descriptor). MPI generalizes this to provide two additional capabilities: describing noncontiguous regions of data and describing data so that it can be communicated between processors with different data representations. To do this, MPI uses three values to describe a data buffer: the address, the (MPI) datatype, and the number or *count* of the items of that datatype. For example, a buffer containing four C `int`s is described by the triple "`a, 4, MPI_INT`." There are predefined MPI datatypes for all of the basic datatypes defined in C, Fortran, and C++. The most common datatypes are shown in Table 9.1.

```c
#include "mpi.h"
#include <stdio.h>

int main( int argc, char *argv[] )
{
    int  numprocs, myrank, namelen, i;
    char processor_name[MPI_MAX_PROCESSOR_NAME];
    char greeting[MPI_MAX_PROCESSOR_NAME + 80];
    MPI_Status status;

    MPI_Init( &argc, &argv );
    MPI_Comm_size( MPI_COMM_WORLD, &numprocs );
    MPI_Comm_rank( MPI_COMM_WORLD, &myrank );
    MPI_Get_processor_name( processor_name, &namelen );

    sprintf( greeting, "Hello, world, from process %d of %d on %s",
             myrank, numprocs, processor_name );

    if ( myrank == 0 ) {
        printf( "%s\n", greeting );
        for ( i = 1; i < numprocs; i++ ) {
            MPI_Recv( greeting, sizeof( greeting ), MPI_CHAR,
                      i, 1, MPI_COMM_WORLD, &status );
            printf( "%s\n", greeting );
        }
    }
    else {
        MPI_Send( greeting, strlen( greeting ) + 1, MPI_CHAR,
                  0, 1, MPI_COMM_WORLD );
    }

    MPI_Finalize( );
    return( 0 );
}
```

**Figure 9.3**
A more complex "Hello World" program in MPI. Only process 0 writes to stdout; each process sends a message to process 0.

| | C | | Fortran | |
| | MPI type | | | MPI type |
|---|---|---|---|---|
| int | `MPI_INT` | INTEGER | `MPI_INTEGER` |
| double | `MPI_DOUBLE` | DOUBLE PRECISION | `MPI_DOUBLE_PRECISION` |
| float | `MPI_FLOAT` | REAL | `MPI_REAL` |
| long | `MPI_LONG` | | |
| char | `MPI_CHAR` | CHARACTER | `MPI_CHARACTER` |
| | | LOGICAL | `MPI_LOGICAL` |
| — | `MPI_BYTE` | — | `MPI_BYTE` |

**Table 9.1**
The most common MPI datatypes. C and Fortran types on the same row are often but not always the same type. The type `MPI_BYTE` is used for raw data bytes and does not cooorespond to any particular datatype. The C++ MPI datatypes have the same name as the C datatype, but without the `MPI_` prefix, for example, `MPI::INT`.

**Describing the Destination or Source.**   The destination or source is specified by using the rank of the process. MPI generalizes the notion of destination and source rank by making the rank relative to a group of processes. This group may be a subset of the original group of processes. Allowing subsets of processes and using relative ranks make it easier to use MPI to write component-oriented software (more on this in Section 10.4). The MPI object that defines a group of processes (and a special communication context that will be discussed in Section 10.4) is called a *communicator*. Thus, sources and destinations are given by two parameters: a rank and a communicator. The communicator `MPI_COMM_WORLD` is predefined and contains all of the processes started by `mpirun` or `mpiexec`. As a source, the special value `MPI_ANY_SOURCE` may be used to indicate that the message may be received from any rank of the MPI processes in this MPI program.

**Selecting among Messages.**   The "extra" argument for `MPI_Send` is a nonnegative integer *tag* value. This tag allows a program to send one extra number with the data. `MPI_Recv` can use this value either to select which message to receive (by specifying a specific tag value) or to use the tag to convey extra data (by specifying the *wild card* value `MPI_ANY_TAG`). In the latter case, the tag value of the received message is stored in the `status` argument (this is the last parameter to `MPI_Recv` in the C binding). This is a structure in C, an integer array in Fortran, and a class in C++. The tag and rank of the sending process can be accessed by referring to the appropriate element of `status` as shown in Table 9.2.

| C | Fortran | C++ |
|---|---|---|
| status.MPI_SOURCE | status(MPI_SOURCE) | status.Get_source() |
| status.MPI_TAG | status(MPI_TAG) | status.Get_tag() |

**Table 9.2**
Accessing the source and tag after an MPI_Recv.

**Determining the Amount of Data Received.** The amount of data received can be found by using the routine MPI_Get_count. For example,

```
MPI_Get_count( &status, MPI_CHAR, &num_chars );
```

returns in num_chars the number of characters sent. The second argument should be the same MPI datatype that was used to receive the message. (Since many applications do not need this information, the use of a routine allows the implementation to avoid computing num_chars unless the user needs the value.)

Our example provides a maximum-sized buffer in the receive. It is also possible to find the amount of memory needed to receive a message by using MPI_Probe, as shown in Figure 9.4.

```
char *greeting;
int num_chars, src;
MPI_Status status;
...
MPI_Probe( MPI_ANY_SOURCE, 1, MPI_COMM_WORLD, &status );
MPI_Get_count( &status, MPI_CHAR, &num_chars );
greeting = (char *)malloc( num_chars );
src      = status.MPI_SOURCE;
MPI_Recv( greeting, num_chars, MPI_CHAR,
          src, 1, MPI_COMM_WORLD, &status );
```

**Figure 9.4**
Using MPI_Probe to find the size of a message before receiving it.

MPI guarantees that messages are ordered and that an MPI_Recv after an MPI_Probe will receive the message that the probe returned information on as long as the same message selection criteria (source rank, communicator, and message tag) are used. Note that in this example, the source for the MPI_Recv is specified as status.MPI_SOURCE, not MPI_ANY_SOURCE, to ensure that the message received is the same as the one about which MPI_Probe returned information.

## 9.2    Manager/Worker Example

We now begin a series of examples illustrating approaches to parallel computations that accomplish useful work. While each parallel application is unique, a number of paradigms have emerged as widely applicable, and many parallel algorithms are variations on these patterns.

One of the most universal is the "manager/worker" or "task parallelism" approach. The idea is that the work that needs to be done can be divided by a "manager" into separate pieces and the pieces can be assigned to individual "worker" processes. Thus the manager executes a different algorithm from that of the workers, but all of the workers execute the same algorithm. Most implementations of MPI (including MPICH) allow MPI processes to be running different programs (executable files), but it is often convenient (and in some cases required) to combine the manager and worker code into a single program with the structure shown in Figure 9.5.

```
#include "mpi.h"

int main( int argc, char *argv[] )
{
    int numprocs, myrank;

    MPI_Init( &argc, &argv );
    MPI_Comm_size( MPI_COMM_WORLD, &numprocs );
    MPI_Comm_rank( MPI_COMM_WORLD, &myrank );

    if ( myrank == 0 )          /* manager process */
        manager_code ( numprocs );
    else                        /* worker process */
        worker_code ( );
    MPI_Finalize( );
    return 0;
}
```

**Figure 9.5**
Framework of the matrix-vector multiply program.

Sometimes the work can be evenly divided into exactly as many pieces as there are workers, but a more flexible approach is to have the manager keep a pool of units of work larger than the number of workers, and assign new work dynamically to workers as they complete their tasks and send their results back to the manager. This approach, called *self-scheduling*, works well in the presence of tasks of varying sizes and/or workers of varying speeds.

We illustrate this technique with a parallel program to multiply a matrix by a vector. (A Fortran version of this same program can be found in [6].) This program is not a particularly good way to carry out this operation, but it illustrates the approach and is simple enough to be shown in its entirety. The program multiplies a square matrix a by a vector b and stores the result in c. The units of work are the individual dot products of the rows of a with the vector b. Thus the manager, code for which is shown in Figure 9.6, starts by initializing a. The manager then sends out initial units of work, one row to each worker. We use the MPI tag on each such message to encode the row number we are sending. Since row numbers start at 0 but we wish to reserve 0 as a tag with the special meaning of "no more work to do", we set the tag to one greater than the row number. When a worker sends back a dot product, we store it in the appropriate place in c and send that worker another row to work on. Once all the rows have been assigned, workers completing a task are sent a "no more work" message, indicated by a message with tag 0.

The code for the worker part of the program is shown in Figure 9.7. A worker initializes b, receives a row of a in a message, computes the dot product of that row and the vector b, and then returns the answer to the manager, again using the tag to identify the row. A worker repeats this until it receives the "no more work" message, identified by its tag of 0.

This program requires at least two processes to run: one manager and one worker. Unfortunately, adding more workers is unlikely to make the job go faster. We can analyze the cost of computation and communication mathematically and see what happens as we increase the number of workers. Increasing the number of workers will decrease the amount of computation done by each worker, and since they work in parallel, this should decrease total elapsed time. On the other hand, more workers mean more communication, and the cost of communicating a number is usually much greater than the cost of an arithmetical operation on it. The study of how the total time for a parallel algorithm is affected by changes in the number of processes, the problem size, and the speed of the processor and communication network is called *scalability analysis*. We analyze the matrix-vector program as a simple example.

First, let us compute the number of floating-point operations. For a matrix of size $n$, we have to compute $n$ dot products, each of which requires $n$ multiplications and $n-1$ additions. Thus the number of floating-point operations is $n \times (n + (n-1)) = n \times (2n-1) = 2n^2 - n$. If $T_{calc}$ is the time it takes a processor to do one floating-point

```
#define SIZE 1000
#define MIN( x, y ) ((x) < (y) ? x : y)

void manager_code( int numprocs )
{
    double a[SIZE][SIZE], c[SIZE];

    int i, j, sender, row, numsent = 0;
    double dotp;
    MPI_Status status;

    /* (arbitrary) initialization of a */
    for (i = 0; i < SIZE; i++ )
        for ( j = 0; j < SIZE; j++ )
            a[i][j] = ( double ) j;

    for ( i = 1; i < MIN( numprocs, SIZE ); i++ ) {
        MPI_Send( a[i-1], SIZE, MPI_DOUBLE, i, i, MPI_COMM_WORLD );
        numsent++;
    }
    /* receive dot products back from workers */
    for ( i = 0; i < SIZE; i++ ) {
        MPI_Recv( &dotp, 1, MPI_DOUBLE, MPI_ANY_SOURCE, MPI_ANY_TAG,
                  MPI_COMM_WORLD, &status );
        sender = status.MPI_SOURCE;
        row    = status.MPI_TAG - 1;
        c[row] = dotp;
        /* send another row back to this worker if there is one */
        if ( numsent < SIZE ) {
            MPI_Send( a[numsent], SIZE, MPI_DOUBLE, sender,
                      numsent + 1, MPI_COMM_WORLD );
            numsent++;
        }
        else                          /* no more work */
            MPI_Send( MPI_BOTTOM, 0, MPI_DOUBLE, sender, 0,
                      MPI_COMM_WORLD );
    }
}
```

**Figure 9.6**
The matrix-vector multiply program, manager code.

```
void worker_code( void )
{
    double b[SIZE], c[SIZE];
    int i, row, myrank;
    double dotp;
    MPI_Status status;

    for ( i = 0; i < SIZE; i++ ) /* (arbitrary) b initialization */
        b[i] = 1.0;

    MPI_Comm_rank( MPI_COMM_WORLD, &myrank );
    if ( myrank <= SIZE ) {
        MPI_Recv( c, SIZE, MPI_DOUBLE, 0, MPI_ANY_TAG,
                  MPI_COMM_WORLD, &status );
        while ( status.MPI_TAG > 0 ) {
            row = status.MPI_TAG - 1;
            dotp = 0.0;
            for ( i = 0; i < SIZE; i++ )
                dotp += c[i] * b[i];
            MPI_Send( &dotp, 1, MPI_DOUBLE, 0, row + 1,
                      MPI_COMM_WORLD );
            MPI_Recv( c, SIZE, MPI_DOUBLE, 0, MPI_ANY_TAG,
                      MPI_COMM_WORLD, &status );
        }
    }
}
```

**Figure 9.7**
The matrix-vector multiply program, worker code.

operation, then the total computation time is $(2n^2 - n) \times T_{calc}$. Next, we compute the number of communications, defined as sending one floating-point number. (We ignore for this simple analysis the effect of message lengths.) Leaving aside the cost of communicating b (perhaps it is computed locally in a preceding step), we have to send each row of a and receive back one dot product answer. So the number of floating-point numbers communicated is $(n \times n) + n = n^2 + n$. If $T_{comm}$ is the time to communicate one number, we get $(n^2 + n) \times T_{comm}$ for the total communication time. Thus the ratio of communication time to computation time is

$$\left( \frac{n^2 + n}{2n^2 - n} \right) \times \left( \frac{T_{comm}}{T_{calc}} \right).$$

In many computations the ratio of communication to computation can be reduced almost to 0 by making the problem size larger. Our analysis shows that this is not the case here. As $n$ gets larger, the term on the left approaches $\frac{1}{2}$. Thus we can expect communication costs to prevent this algorithm from showing good speedups, even on large problem sizes.

The situation is better in the case of matrix-*matrix* multiplication, which could be carried out by a similar algorithm. We would replace the vectors **b** and **c** by matrices, send the entire matrix **b** to the workers at the beginning of the computation, and then hand out the rows of **a** as work units, just as before. The workers would compute an entire row of the product, consisting of the dot products of the row of **a** with all of the column of **b**, and then return a row of **c** to the manager.

Let us now do the scalability analysis for the matrix-matrix multiplication. Again we ignore the initial communication of **b**. The number of operations for one dot product is $n + (n + 1)$ as before, and the total number of dot products calculated is $n^2$. Thus the total number of operations is $n^2 \times (2n - 1) = 2n^3 - n^2$. The number of numbers communicated has gone up to $(n \times n) + (n \times n) = 2n^2$. So the ratio of communication time to computation time has become

$$\left( \frac{2n^2}{2n^3 - n^2} \right) \times \left( \frac{T_{comm}}{T_{calc}} \right),$$

which does tend to 0 as $n$ gets larger. Thus, for large matrices the communication costs play less of a role.

Two other difficulties with this algorithm might occur as we increase the size of the problem and the number of workers. The first is that as messages get longer, the workers waste more time waiting for the next row to arrive. A solution to this problem is to "double buffer" the distribution of work, having the manager send two rows to each worker to begin with, so that a worker always has some work to do while waiting for the next row to arrive.

Another difficulty for larger numbers of processes can be that the manager can become overloaded so that it cannot assign work in a timely manner. This problem can most easily be addressed by increasing the size of the work unit, but in some cases it is necessary to parallelize the manager task itself, with multiple managers handling subpools of work units.

A more subtle problem has to do with *fairness*: ensuring that all worker processes are fairly serviced by the manager. MPI provides several ways to ensure fairness; see [6, Section 7.1.4].

## 9.3    Two-Dimensional Jacobi Example with One-Dimensional Decomposition

A common use of parallel computers in scientific computation is to approximate the solution of a partial differential equation (PDE). One of the most common PDEs, at least in textbooks, is the Poisson equation (here shown in two dimensions):

$$\frac{\partial^2 u}{\partial x^2} + \frac{\partial^2 u}{\partial y^2} = f(x,y) \text{ in } \Gamma \tag{9.3.1}$$

$$u = g(x,y) \text{ on } \partial\Gamma \tag{9.3.2}$$

This equation is used to describe many physical phenomena, including fluid flow and electrostatics. The equation has two parts: a differential equation applied everywhere within a domain $\Gamma$ (9.3.1) and a specification of the value of the unknown $u$ along the boundary of $\Gamma$ (the notation $\partial\Gamma$ means "the boundary of $\Gamma$"). For example, if this equation is used to model the equilibrium distribution of temperature inside a region, the boundary condition $g(x,y)$ specifies the applied temperature along the boundary, $f(x,y)$ is zero, and $u(x,y)$ is the temperature within the region. To simplify the rest of this example, we will consider only a simple domain $\Gamma$ consisting of a square (see Figure 9.8).

To compute an approximation to $u(x,y)$, we must first reduce the problem to finite size. We cannot determine the value of $u$ everywhere; instead, we will approximate $u$ at a finite number of points $(x_i, y_j)$ in the domain, where $x_i = i \times h$ and $y_j = j \times h$. (Of course, we can define a value for $u$ at other points in the domain by interpolating from these values that we determine, but the approximation is defined by the value of $u$ at the points $(x_i, y_j)$.) These points are shown as black disks in Figure 9.8. Because of this regular spacing, the points are said to make up a *regular mesh*. At each of these points, we approximate the partial derivatives with finite differences. For example,

$$\frac{\partial^2 u}{\partial x^2}(x_i, y_j) \approx \frac{u(x_{i+1}, y_j) - 2u(x_i, y_j) + u(x_{i-1}, y_j)}{h^2}.$$

If we now let $u_{i,j}$ stand for our approximation to solution of Equation 9.3.1 at the point $(x_i, y_j)$, we have the following set of simultaneous linear equations for the values of $u$:

$$\frac{u_{i+1,j} - 2u_{i,j} + u_{i-1,j}}{h^2} +$$

$$\frac{u_{i,j+1} - 2u_{i,j} + u_{i,j-1}}{h^2} = f(x_i, y_j). \tag{9.3.3}$$

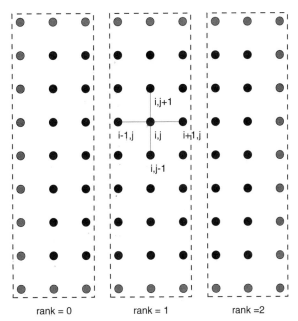

**Figure 9.8**
Domain and $9 \times 9$ computational mesh for approximating the solution to the Poisson problem.

For values of $u$ along the boundary (e.g., at $x = 0$ or $y = 1$), the value of the boundary condition $g$ is used. If $h = 1/(n + 1)$ (so there are $n \times n$ points in the interior of the mesh), this gives us $n^2$ simultaneous linear equations to solve.

Many methods can be used to solve these equations. In fact, if you have this particular problem, you should use one of the numerical libraries described in Table 10.1. In this section, we describe a very simple (and inefficient) algorithm because, from a parallel computing perspective, it illustrates how to program more effective and general methods. The method that we use is called the *Jacobi* method for solving systems of linear equations. The Jacobi method computes successive approximations to the solution of Equation 9.3.3 by rewriting the equation as follows:

$$u_{i+1,j} \quad - \quad 2u_{i,j} + u_{i-1,j} + u_{i,j+1} - 2u_{i,j} + u_{i,j-1} = h^2 f(x_i, y_j)$$

$$u_{i,j} \quad = \quad \frac{1}{4}(u_{i+1,j} + u_{i-1,j} + u_{i,j+1} + u_{i,j-1} - h^2 f_{i,j}). \tag{9.3.4}$$

Each step in the Jacobi iteration computes a new approximation to $u_{i,j}^{N+1}$ in terms of the surrounding values of $u^N$:

$$u_{i,j}^{N+1} = \frac{1}{4}(u_{i+1,j}^N + u_{i-1,j}^N + u_{i,j+1}^N + u_{i,j-1}^N - h^2 f_{i,j}). \tag{9.3.5}$$

This is our algorithm for computing the approximation to the solution of the Poisson problem. We emphasize that the Jacobi method is a poor numerical method but that the same communication patterns apply to many finite difference, volume, or element discretizations solved by iterative techniques.

In the uniprocessor version of this algorithm, the solution $u$ is represented by a two-dimensional array u[max_n][max_n], and the iteration is written as follows:

```
double u[NX+2][NY+2], u_new[NX+2][NY+2], f[NX+2][NY+2];
int    i, j;
...
for (i=1;i<=NX;i++)
   for (j=1;j<=NY;j++)
      u_new[i][j] = 0.25 * (u[i+1][j] + u[i-1][j] +
                            u[i][j+1] + u[i][j-1] - h*h*f[i][j]);
```

Here, we let u[0][j], u[n+1][j], u[i][0], and u[i][n+1] hold the values of the boundary conditions $g$ (these correspond to $u(0,y)$, $u(1,y)$, $u(x,0)$, and $u(x,1)$ in Equation 9.3.1). To parallelize this method, we must first decide how to decompose the data structure u and u_new across the processes. Many possible decompositions exist. One of the simplest is to divide the domain into strips as shown in Figure 9.8.

Let the local representation of the array u be ulocal; that is, each process declares an array ulocal that contains the part of u held by that process. No process has all of u; the data structure representing u is *decomposed* among all of the processes. The code that is used on each process to implement the Jacobi method is

```
for (i=i_start;i<=i_end;i++)
   for (j=1;j<=NY;j++)
      ulocal_new[i-i_start][j] =
         0.25 * (ulocal[i-i_start+1][j] + ulocal[i-i_start-1][j] +
                 ulocal[i-i_start][j+1] + ulocal[i-i_start][j-1] -
                 h*h*flocal[i-i_start][j]);
```

where i_start and i_end describe the strip on this process (in practice, the loop would be from zero to i_end-i_start; we use this formulation to maintain the correspondence with the uniprocessor code). We have defined ulocal so that ulocal[0][j] corresponds to u[i_start][j] in the uniprocessor version of this code. Using variable names such as ulocal that make it obvious which variables are part of a distributed data structure is often a good idea.

From this code, we can see what data we need to communicate. For `i=i_start` we need the values of `u[i_start-1][j]`, and for `i=i_end` we need `u[i_end+1][j]`. These values belong to the adjacent processes and must be communicated. In addition, we need a location in which to store these values. We could use a separate array, but for regular meshes the most common approach is to use *ghost* or *halo* cells, where extra space is set aside in the `ulocal` array to hold the values from neighboring processes. In this case, we need only a single column of neighboring data, so we will let `u_local[1][j]` correspond to `u[i_start][j]`. This changes the code for a single iteration of the loop to

```
exchange_nbrs( ulocal, i_start, i_end, left, right );
for (i_local=1; i_local<=i_end-i_start+1; i_local++)
  for (j=1; j<=NY; j++)
    ulocal_new[i_local][j] =
        0.25 * (ulocal[i_local+1][j] + ulocal[i_local-1][j] +
                ulocal[i_local][j+1] + ulocal[i_local][j-1] -
                h*h*flocal[i_local][j]);
```

where we have converted the `i` index to be relative to the start of `ulocal` rather than `u`. All that is left is to describe the routine `exchange_nbrs` that exchanges data between the neighboring processes. A very simple routine is shown in Figure 9.9.

We note that ISO/ANSI C (unlike Fortran) does not allow runtime dimensioning of multidimensional arrays. To keep these examples simple in C, we use compile-time dimensioning of the arrays. An alternative in C is to pass the arrays a one-dimensional arrays and compute the appropriate offsets.

The values `left` and `right` are used for the ranks of the left and right neighbors, respectively. These can be computed simply by using the following:

```
int rank, size, left, right;
...
MPI_Comm_rank( MPI_COMM_WORLD, &rank );
MPI_Comm_size( MPI_COMM_WORLD, &size );
left  = rank - 1;
right = rank + 1;
if (left < 0)      left  = MPI_PROC_NULL;
if (right >= size) right = MPI_PROC_NULL;
```

The special rank `MPI_PROC_NULL` indicates the edges of the mesh. If `MPI_PROC_NULL` is used as the source or destination rank in an MPI communication call, the

```
void exchange_nbrs( double ulocal[][NY+2], int i_start, int i_end,
                    int left, int right )
{
    MPI_Status status;
    int c;

    /* Send and receive from the left neighbor */
    MPI_Send( &ulocal[1][1], NY, MPI_DOUBLE, left, 0,
             MPI_COMM_WORLD );
    MPI_Recv( &ulocal[0][1], NY, MPI_DOUBLE, left, 0,
             MPI_COMM_WORLD, &status );

    /* Send and receive from the right neighbor */
    c = i_end - i_start + 1;
    MPI_Send( &ulocal[c][1], NY, MPI_DOUBLE, right, 0,
             MPI_COMM_WORLD );
    MPI_Recv( &ulocal[c+1][1], NY, MPI_DOUBLE, right, 0,
             MPI_COMM_WORLD, &status );
}
```

**Figure 9.9**
A simple version of the neighbor exchange code. See the text for a discussion of the limitations
of this routine.

operation is ignored. MPI also provides routines to compute the neighbors in a regular mesh of arbitrary dimension and to help an application choose a decomposition
that is efficient for the parallel computer.

The code in `exchange_nbrs` will work with most MPI implementations for small
values of n but, as described in Section 10.3, is not good practice (and will fail for
values of NY greater than an implementation-defined threshold). A better approach
in MPI is to use the `MPI_Sendrecv` routine when exchanging data between two
processes, as shown in Figure 9.10.

In Sections 10.3 and 10.7, we discuss other implementations of the exchange
routine that can provide higher performance. MPI support for more scalable decompositions of the data is described in Section 10.3.2.

## 9.4   Collective Operations

A *collective* operation is an MPI function that is called by all processes belonging to a communicator. (If the communicator is `MPI_COMM_WORLD`, this means all

```
/* Better exchange code.  */
void exchange_nbrs( double ulocal[][NY+2], int i_start, int i_end,
                    int left, int right )
{
    MPI_Status status;
    int c;

    /* Send and receive from the left neighbor */
    MPI_Sendrecv( &ulocal[1][1], NY, MPI_DOUBLE, left, 0,
                  &ulocal[0][1], NY, MPI_DOUBLE, left, 0,
                  MPI_COMM_WORLD, &status );

    /* Send and receive from the right neighbor */
    c = i_end - i_start + 1;
    MPI_Sendrecv( &ulocal[c][1], NY, MPI_DOUBLE, right, 0,
                  &ulocal[c+1][1], NY, MPI_DOUBLE, right, 0,
                  MPI_COMM_WORLD, &status );
}
```

**Figure 9.10**
A better version of the neighbor exchange code.

processes, but MPI allows collective operations on other sets of processes as well.)
Collective operations involve communication and also sometimes computation, but
since they describe particular patterns of communication and computation, the
MPI implementation may be able to optimize them beyond what is possible by
expressing them in terms of MPI point-to-point operations such as `MPI_Send` and
`MPI_Recv`. The patterns are also easier to express with collective operations.

   Here we introduce two of the most commonly used collective operations and show
how the communication in a parallel program can be expressed entirely in terms
of collective operations with no individual `MPI_Sends` or `MPI_Recvs` at all. The
program shown in Figure 9.11 computes the value of $\pi$ by numerical integration.
Since

$$\int_0^1 \frac{1}{1+x^2} dx = \arctan(x)\big|_0^1 = \arctan(1) - \arctan(0) = \arctan(1) = \frac{\pi}{4},$$

we can compute $\pi$ by integrating the function $f(x) = 4/(1 + x^2)$ from 0 to 1.
We compute an approximation by dividing the interval [0,1] into some number of
subintervals and then computing the total area of these rectangles by having each
process compute the areas of some subset. We could do this with a manager/worker

algorithm, but here we preassign the work. In fact, each worker can compute its set of tasks, and so the "manager" can be a worker, too, instead of just managing the pool of work. The more rectangles there are, the more work there is to do and the more accurate the resulting approximation of $\pi$ is. To experiment, let us make the number of subintervals a command-line argument. (Although the MPI standard does not guarantee that any process receives command-line arguments, in most implementations, especially for Beowulf clusters, one can assume that at least the process with rank 0 can use `argc` and `argv`, although they may not be meaningful until after `MPI_Init` is called.) In our example, process 0 sets $n$, the number of subintervals, to `argv[1]`. Once a process knows $n$, it can claim approximately $\frac{1}{n}$ of the work by claiming every $n$th rectangle, starting with the one numbered by its own rank. Thus process $j$ computes the areas of rectangles $j$ , $j + n$ , $j + 2n$, and so on.

Not all MPI implementations make the command-line arguments available to *all* processes, however, so we start by having process 0 send $n$ to each of the other processes. We could have a simple loop, sending $n$ to each of the other processes one at a time, but this is inefficient. If we know that the same message is to be delivered to all the other processes, we can ask the MPI implementation to do this in a more efficient way than with a series of `MPI_Send`s and `MPI_Recv`s.

Broadcast (`MPI_Bcast`) is an example of an MPI *collective* operation. A collective operation must be called by all processes in a communicator. This allows an implementation to arrange the communication and computation specified by a collective operation in a special way. In the case of `MPI_Bcast`, an implementation is likely to use a tree of communication, sometimes called a spanning tree, in which process 0 sends its message to a second process, then both processes send to two more, and so forth. In this way most communication takes place in parallel, and all the messages have been delivered in $\log_2 n$ steps.

The precise semantics of `MPI_Bcast` is sometimes confusing. The first three arguments specify a message with (address, count, datatype) as usual. The fourth argument (called the *root* of the broadcast) specifies which of the processes owns the data that is being sent to the other processes. In our case it is process 0. `MPI_Bcast` acts like an `MPI_Send` on the root process and like an `MPI_Recv` on all the other processes, but the call itself looks the same on each process. The last argument is the communicator that the collective call is *over*. All processes in the communicator must make this same call. Before the call, $n$ is valid only at the root; after `MPI_Bcast` has returned, all processes have a copy of the value of $n$.

Next, each process, including process 0, adds up the areas of its rectangles into the local variable `mypi`. Instead of sending these values to one process and having

```c
#include "mpi.h"
#include <stdio.h>
#include <math.h>
double f(double a) { return (4.0 / (1.0 + a*a)); }

int main(int argc,char *argv[])
{
  int  n, myid, numprocs, i;
  double PI25DT = 3.141592653589793238462643;
  double mypi, pi, h, sum, x;
  double startwtime = 0.0, endwtime;

  MPI_Init(&argc,&argv);
  MPI_Comm_size(MPI_COMM_WORLD,&numprocs);
  MPI_Comm_rank(MPI_COMM_WORLD,&myid);
  if (myid == 0) {
      startwtime = MPI_Wtime();
      n = atoi(argv[1]);
  }
  MPI_Bcast(&n, 1, MPI_INT, 0, MPI_COMM_WORLD);
  h   = 1.0 / (double) n;
  sum = 0.0;
  for (i = myid + 1; i <= n; i += numprocs) {
      x = h * ((double)i - 0.5);
      sum += f(x);
  }
  mypi = h * sum;
  MPI_Reduce(&mypi, &pi, 1, MPI_DOUBLE, MPI_SUM, 0, MPI_COMM_WORLD);
  if (myid == 0) {
      endwtime = MPI_Wtime();
      printf("pi is approximately %.16f, Error is %.16f\n",
             pi, fabs(pi - PI25DT));
      printf("wall clock time = %f\n", endwtime-startwtime);
  }
  MPI_Finalize();
  return 0;
}
```

**Figure 9.11**
Computing $\pi$ using collective operations.

that process add them up, however, we use another collective operation, `MPI_-Reduce`. `MPI_Reduce` performs not only collective communication but also collective computation. In the call

```
MPI_Reduce( &mypi, &pi, 1, MPI_DOUBLE, MPI_SUM, 0,
            MPI_COMM_WORLD);
```

the sixth argument is again the root. All processes call `MPI_Reduce`, and the root process gets back a result in the second argument. The result comes from performing an arithmetic operation, in this case summation (specified by the fifth argument), on the data items on all processes specified by the first, third, and fourth arguments.

Process 0 concludes by printing out the answer, the difference between this approximation and a previously computed accurate value of $\pi$, and the time it took to compute it. This illustrates the use of `MPI_Wtime`.

`MPI_Wtime` returns a double-precision floating-point number of seconds. This value has no meaning in itself, but the *difference* between two such values is the wall-clock time between the two calls. Note that calls on two different processes are not guaranteed to have any relationship to one another, unless the MPI implementation promises that the clocks on different processes are synchronized (see `MPI_WTIME_-IS_GLOBAL` in any of the MPI books).

The routine `MPI_Allreduce` computes the same result as `MPI_Reduce` but returns the result to all processes, not just the root process. For example, in the Jacobi iteration, it is common to use the two-norm of the difference between two successive iterations as a measure of the convergence of the solution.

```
...
norm2local = 0.0;
for (ii=1; ii<i_end-i_start+1; ii++)
    for (jj=1; jj<NY; jj++)
        norm2local += ulocal[ii][jj] * ulocal[ii][jj];
MPI_Allreduce( &norm2local, &norm2, 1, MPI_DOUBLE,
               MPI_COMM_WORLD, MPI_SUM );
norm2 = sqrt( norm2 );
```

Note that `MPI_Allreduce` is not a routine for computing the norm of a vector. It merely combines values contributed from each process in the communicator.

## 9.5 Parallel Monte Carlo Computation

One of the types of computation that is easiest to parallelize is the *Monte Carlo* family of algorithms. In such computations, a random number generator is used to create a number of independent trials. Statistics done with the outcomes of the trials provide a solution to the problem.

We illustrate this technique with another computation of the value of $\pi$. If we select points at random in the unit square $[0,1] \times [0,1]$ and compute the percentage of them that lies inside the quarter circle of radius 1, then we will be approximating $\frac{\pi}{4}$. (See [6] for a more detailed discussion together with an approach that does not use a parallel random number generator.) We use the SPRNG parallel random number generator (`sprng.cs.fsu.edu`). The code is shown in Figure 9.12.

The defaults in SPRNG make it extremely easy to use. Calls to the `sprng` function return a random number between 0.0 and 1.0, and the stream of random numbers on the different processes is independent. We control the *grain size* of the parallelism by the constant `BATCHSIZE`, which determines how much computation is done before the processes communicate. Here a million points are generated, tested, and counted before we collect the results to print them. We use `MPI_Bcast` to distribute the command-line argument specifying the number of batches, and we use `MPI_Reduce` to collect at the end of each batch the number of points that fell inside the quarter circle, so that we can print the increasingly accurate approximations to $\pi$.

## 9.6 Installing MPICH under Windows 2000

The MPICH implementation of MPI [5] is one of the most popular versions of MPI. Thanks to support from Microsoft, an open-source version is available for Windows NT and Windows 2000. This implementation supports TCP/IP, VIA, and shared-memory communication. This release is available at `www.mcs.anl.gov/mpi/mpich/mpich-nt`, which also contains complete installation instructions for the current version.

This implementation includes

- all source code for MPICH,
- simple example programs like the ones in this chapter,
- performance benchmarking programs,
- the MPE profiling library, and
- the Jumpshot performance visualization system.

```
#include "mpi.h"
#include <stdio.h>
#define SIMPLE_SPRNG               /* simple interface  */
#define USE_MPI                    /* use MPI           */
#include "sprng.h"                 /* SPRNG header file */
#define BATCHSIZE 1000000

int main( int argc, char *argv[] )
{
    int i, j, numin = 0, totalin, total, numbatches, rank, numprocs;
    double x, y, approx, pi = 3.141592653589793238462643;

    MPI_Init( &argc, &argv );
    MPI_Comm_size( MPI_COMM_WORLD, &numprocs );
    MPI_Comm_rank( MPI_COMM_WORLD, &rank );
    if ( rank == 0 ) {
        numbatches = atoi( argv[1] );
    }
    MPI_Bcast( &numbatches, 1, MPI_INT, 0, MPI_COMM_WORLD );
    for ( i = 0; i < numbatches; i++ ) {
        for ( j = 0; j < BATCHSIZE; j++ ) {
            x = sprng( ); y = sprng( );
            if ( x * x + y * y  < 1.0 )
                numin++;
        }
        MPI_Reduce( &numin, &totalin, 1, MPI_INT, MPI_SUM, 0,
                    MPI_COMM_WORLD );
        if ( rank == 0 ) {
            total = BATCHSIZE * ( i + 1 ) * numprocs;
            approx = 4.0 * ( (double) totalin / total );
            printf( "pi = %.16f; error = %.16f, points = %d\n",
                    approx, pi - approx, total );
        }
    }
    MPI_Finalize( );
}
```

**Figure 9.12**
Computing $\pi$ using the Monte Carlo method.

The distribution is available in several forms. The one appropriate for most users is 'mpich.nt.1.2.1.zip', which contains everything you need to compile and run MPI programs.

The various distributions are as follows:

**Full source tree:** 'mpich.nt.1.2.1.src.exe' is a self-extracting WinZip archive.

**Binary distribution:** 'mpich.nt.1.2.1.zip' contains the runtime DLLs, services to start MPI programs, the Visual C++ software developers kit (SDK), and the gcc SDK. An SDK is needed to compile applications but not to run them. You should use setup.exe to install the DLLs and at least one job launcher on all machines that will be used to run MPI processes.

**Software Developers Kit:** 'mpich.nt.1.2.1.zip' contains the SDK, which includes libraries and include files to compile an MPI application using Microsoft Visual C++ and/or Visual Fortran 6.

**gcc Software Developers Kit:** 'mpich.nt.1.2.1.zip' contains the gcc SDK, which includes libraries and include files to compile an MPI application using gcc and the Cygnus tools.

**Using MPIRun.** The easiest way to run an MPI program is with

```
MPIRun -np 2 myapp.exe
```

The MPIRun program accepts several other arguments; see the documentation for a complete list. The most commonly used are as follows:

-env name=value to pass environment variables to the program. A typical use of this is to pass environment variables that MPICH itself uses. For example,

```
MPIRun -np 2 -env "MPICH_USE_POLLING=1|MPICH_SINGLETHREAD=1" mpptest.exe
```

is appropriate for getting the lowest latency in message passing. See the documentation under "Subtle Configuration Options" for more details on the environment variables that affect MPICH.

-localonly n to run $n$ processes on the local machine, using shared memory to communicate between processes. This is often helpful when debugging an MPI program.

The most flexible way to run a program is with a configuration file. The command-line `mpirun file.cfg` uses the specified configuration file ('file.cfg') to run the parallel program. This format allows MPMD (Multiple Program Multiple Data) programs.

Two tools help in running MPICH programs:

- `MPIConfig` attempts to find the machines in your cluster and saves their names in the registry. This tool provides a graphical user interface for finding and modifying the machines available for MPI programs. Using `MPIConfig` allows `MPIRun` to accept the `-np` argument to select the number of processes.
- `MPIRegister` allows you to provide your account name and password only once when running MPI programs. Without this, `MPIRun` will prompt for a username and password.

Here is a configuration file that starts a manager process ('manager.exe') and five worker processes:

```
exe d:\Projects\Me\worker.exe
hosts
roadrunner 1 d:\projects\Me\manager.exe
roadrunner 5
```

## 9.7  Tools

A number of tools are available for developing, testing, and tuning MPI programs. Although they are distributed with MPICH, they can be used with other MPI implementations as well.

### 9.7.1  Profiling Libraries

The MPI Forum decided not to standardize any particular tool but rather to provide a general mechanism for intercepting calls to MPI functions, which is the sort of capability that tools need. The MPI standard requires that any MPI implementation provide two entry points for each MPI function: its normal `MPI_` name and a corresponding `PMPI` version. This strategy allows a user to write a custom version of `MPI_Send`, for example, that carries out whatever extra functions might be desired, calling `PMPI_Send` to perform the usual operations of `MPI_Send`. When the user's custom versions of MPI functions are placed in a library and the library precedes the usual MPI library in the link path, the user's custom code will be invoked around all MPI functions that have been replaced.

MPICH provides three such "profiling libraries" and some tools for creating more. These libraries are easily used by passing an extra argument to MPICH's `mpicc` command for compiling and linking.

`-mpilog` causes a file to be written containing timestamped events. The log file can be examined with tools such as Jumpshot (see below).

`-mpitrace` causes a trace of MPI calls, tagged with process rank in `MPI_COMM_-WORLD` to be written to `stdout`.

`-mpianim` shows a simple animation of message traffic while the program is running.

The profiling libraries are part of the MPE subsystem of MPICH, which is separately distributable and works with any MPI implementation.

### 9.7.2  Visualizing Parallel Program Behavior

The detailed behavior of a parallel program is surprisingly difficult to predict. It is often useful to examine a graphical display that shows the exact sequence of states that each process went through and what messages were exchanged at what times and in what order. The data for such a tool can be collected by means of a profiling library. One tool for looking at such log files is Jumpshot [17]. A screenshot of Jumpshot in action is shown in Figure 9.13.

The horizontal axis represents time, and there is a horizontal line for each process. The states that processes are in during a particular time interval are represented by colored rectangles. Messages are represented by arrows. It is possible to zoom in for microsecond-level resolution in time.

## 9.8  MPI Implementations for Clusters

Many implementations of MPI are available for clusters; Table 9.3 lists some of the available implementations. These range from commercially supported software to supported, freely available software to distributed research project software.

## 9.9  MPI Routine Summary

This section provide a quick summary of the MPI routines used in this chapter for C, Fortran, and C++. Although these are only a small fraction of the routines available in MPI, they are sufficient for many applications.

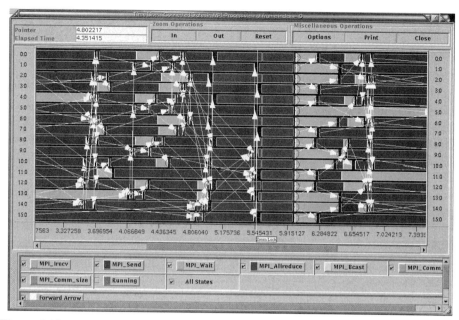

**Figure 9.13**
Jumpshot displaying message traffic

| Name | URL |
|------|-----|
| MPICH | www.mcs.anl.gov/mpi/mpich |
| MPI-FM | www-csag.ucsd.edu/projects/comm/mpi-fm.html |
| MPI/Pro | www.mpi-softtech.com |
| MP-MPICH | www.lfbs.rwth-aachen.de/users/joachim/MP-MPICH/ |
| WMPI | www.criticalsoftware.com |

**Table 9.3**
Some MPI implementations for Windows.

**C Routines.**

int **MPI_Init**(int *argc, char ***argv)

int **MPI_Comm_size**(MPI_Comm comm, int *size)

int **MPI_Comm_rank**(MPI_Comm comm, int *rank)

int **MPI_Bcast**(void *buf, int count, MPI_Datatype datatype, int root,
                  MPI_Comm comm)

int **MPI_Reduce**(void *sendbuf, void *recvbuf, int count, MPI_Datatype datatype,
            MPI_Op op, int root, MPI_Comm comm)

int **MPI_Finalize**()

double **MPI_Wtime**()

int **MPI_Send**(void *buf, int count, MPI_Datatype datatype, int dest, int tag,
            MPI_Comm comm)

int **MPI_Recv**(void *buf, int count, MPI_Datatype datatype, int source, int tag,
            MPI_Comm comm, MPI_Status *status)

int **MPI_Probe**(int source, int tag, MPI_Comm comm, MPI_Status *status)

int **MPI_Sendrecv**(void *sendbuf, int sendcount,MPI_Datatype sendtype, int dest,
            int sendtag, void *recvbuf, int recvcount, MPI_Datatype recvtype,
            int source, MPI_Datatype recvtag, MPI_Comm comm,
            MPI_Status *status)

int **MPI_Allreduce**(void *sendbuf, void *recvbuf, int count, MPI_Datatype datatype,
            MPI_Op op, MPI_Comm comm)

**Fortran routines.**
**MPI_INIT**(ierror)
          integer ierror

**MPI_COMM_SIZE**(comm, size, ierror)
          integer comm, size, ierror

**MPI_COMM_RANK**(comm, rank, ierror)
          integer comm, rank, ierror

**MPI_BCAST**(buffer, count, datatype, root, comm, ierror)
              <type> buffer(*)
          integer count, datatype, root, comm, ierror

**MPI_REDUCE**(sendbuf, recvbuf, count, datatype, op, root, comm, ierror)
              <type> sendbuf(*), recvbuf(*)
          integer count, datatype, op, root, comm, ierror

**MPI_FINALIZE**(ierror)
          integer ierror

double precision **MPI_WTIME**()

**MPI_SEND**(buf, count, datatype, dest, tag, comm, ierror)
                      &lt;type&gt; buf(*)
                      integer count, datatype, dest, tag, comm, ierror

**MPI_RECV**(buf, count, datatype, source, tag, comm, status, ierror)
                      &lt;type&gt; buf(*)
                      integer count, datatype, source, tag, comm,
                          status(MPI_STATUS_SIZE), ierror

**MPI_PROBE**(source, tag, comm, status, ierror)
                      logical  flag
                      integer  source, tag, comm, status(MPI_STATUS_SIZE), ierror

**MPI_SENDRECV**(sendbuf, sendcount, sendtype, dest, sendtag, recvbuf,recvcount,
                  recvtype, source, recvtag, comm, status, ierror)
                  &lt;type&gt; sendbuf(*), recvbuf(*)
                  integer  sendcount, sendtype, dest, sendtag, recvcount,  recvtype,
                      source, recvtag, comm, status(MPI_STATUS_SIZE), ierror

**MPI_ALLREDUCE**(sendbuf, recvbuf, count, datatype, op, comm, ierror)
                      &lt;type&gt; sendbuf(*), recvbuf(*)
                      integer count, datatype, op, comm, ierror

**C++ routines.**
**void MPI::Init**(int& argc, char**& argv)

**void MPI::Init**()

**int MPI::Comm::Get_rank**() const

**int MPI::Comm::Get_size**() const

**void MPI::Intracomm::Bcast**(void* buffer, int count,  const Datatype& datatype,
                  int root) const

**void MPI::Intracomm::Reduce**(const void* sendbuf, void* recvbuf,  int count,
                  const Datatype& datatype, const Op& op,  int root) const

**void MPI::Finalize**()

**double MPI::Wtime**()

**int MPI::Status::Get_source**() const

**int MPI::Status::Get_tag**() const

**void MPI::Comm::Recv**(void* buf, int count,  const Datatype& datatype,
          int source, int tag,  Status& status) const

**void MPI::Comm::Recv**(void* buf, int count,  const Datatype& datatype,
          int source, int tag) const

**void MPI::Comm::Send**(const void* buf, int count, const  Datatype& datatype,
          int dest, int tag) const

**void MPI::Comm::Probe**(int source,int tag, Status& status) const

**void MPI::Comm::Sendrecv**(const void *sendbuf, int sendcount,
          const  Datatype& sendtype, int dest, int sendtag, void *recvbuf,
          int recvcount, const Datatype& recvtype, int source, int recvtag,
          Status& status) const

**void MPI::Intracomm::Allreduce**(const void* sendbuf, void* recvbuf,  int count,
          const Datatype& datatype, const Op& op) const

# 10 Advanced Topics in MPI Programming

*William Gropp and Ewing Lusk*

In this chapter we continue our exploration of parallel programming with MPI. We describe capabilities that are more specific to MPI rather than part of the message-passing programming model in general. We cover the more advanced features of MPI sometimes called MPI-2, such as dynamic process management, parallel I/O, and remote memory access.

## 10.1 Dynamic Process Management in MPI

A new aspect of the MPI-2 standard is the ability of an MPI program to create new MPI processes and communicate with them. (In the original MPI specification, the number of processes was fixed at startup.) MPI calls this capability (together with related capabilities such as connecting two independently started MPI jobs) *dynamic process management*. Three main issues are introduced by this collection of features:

- maintaining simplicity and flexibility;
- interacting with the operating system, a parallel process manager, and perhaps a job scheduler; and
- avoiding race conditions that could compromise correctness.

The key to avoiding race conditions is to make creation of new processes a collective operation, over both the processes creating the new processes and the new processes being created.

### 10.1.1 Intercommunicators

Recall that an MPI communicator consists of a group of processes together with a communication context. Strictly speaking, the communicators we have dealt with so far are *intracommunicators*. There is another kind of communicator, called an *intercommunicator*. An intercommunicator binds together a communication context and *two* groups of processes, called (from the point of view of a particular process) the *local* group and the *remote* group. Processes are identified by rank in group, but ranks in an intercommunicator always refer to the processes in the remote group. That is, an MPI_Send using an intercommunicator sends a message to the process with the destination rank in the *remote* group of the intercommunicator. Collective operations are also defined for intercommunicators; see [7, Chapter 7] for details.

## 10.1.2    Spawning New MPI Processes

We are now in a position to explain exactly how new MPI processes are created by an already running MPI program. The MPI function that does this is `MPI_Comm_-spawn`. Its key features are the following.

- It is collective over the communicator of processes initiating the operation (called the *parents*) and also collective with the calls to `MPI_Init` in the processes being created (called the *children*). That is, the `MPI_Comm_spawn` does not return in the parents until it has been called in all the parents and `MPI_Init` has been called in all the children.
- It returns an intercommunicator in which the local group contains the parents and the remote group contains the children.
- The new processes, which must call `MPI_Init`, have their own `MPI_COMM_WORLD`, consisting of all the processes created by this one collective call to `MPI_Comm_spawn`.
- The function `MPI_Comm_get_parent`, called by the children, returns an inter-communicator with the children in the local group and the parents in the remote group.
- The collective function `MPI_Intercomm_merge` may be called by parents and children to create a normal (intra)communicator containing all the processes, both old and new, but for many communication patterns this is not necessary.

## 10.1.3    Revisiting Matrix-Vector Multiplication

Here we illustrate the use of `MPI_Comm_spawn` by redoing the matrix-vector multiply program of Section 9.2. Instead of starting with a fixed number of processes, we compile separate executables for the manager and worker programs, start the manager with

```
mpiexec -n 1 manager <number-of-workers>
```

and then let the manager create the worker processes dynamically. The program for the manager is shown in Figure 10.1, and the code for the workers is shown in Figure 10.2. Here we assume that only the manager has the matrix a and the vector b and broadcasts them to the workers after the workers have been created.

Let us consider in detail the call in the manager that creates the worker processes.

```
MPI_Spawn( "worker", MPI_ARGV_NULL, numworkers, MPI_INFO_NULL,
           0, MPI_COMM_SELF, &workercomm, MPI_ERRCODES_IGNORE );
```

It has eight arguments. The first is the name of the executable to be run by the new processes. The second is the null-terminated argument vector to be passed to

```
#include "mpi.h"
#include <stdio.h>
#define SIZE 10000

int main( int argc, char *argv[] )
{
    double a[SIZE][SIZE], b[SIZE], c[SIZE];
    int i, j, row, numworkers;
    MPI_Status status;
    MPI_Comm workercomm;

    MPI_Init( &argc, &argv );
    if ( argc != 2 || !isnumeric( argv[1] ))
        printf( "usage: %s <number of workers>\n", argv[0] );
    else
        numworkers = atoi( argv[1] );

    MPI_Spawn( "worker", MPI_ARGV_NULL, numworkers, MPI_INFO_NULL,
               0, MPI_COMM_SELF, &workercomm, MPI_ERRCODES_IGNORE );
    ...
    /* initialize a and b */
    ...
    /* send b to each worker */
    MPI_Bcast( b, SIZE, MPI_DOUBLE, MPI_ROOT, workercomm );
    ...
    /* then normal manager code as before*/
    ...
    MPI_Finalize();
    return 0;
}
```

**Figure 10.1**
Dynamic process matrix-vector multiply program, manager part.

all of the new processes; here we are passing no arguments at all, so we specify the special value MPI_ARGV_NULL. Next is the number of new processes to create. The fourth argument is an MPI "Info" object, which can be used to specify special environment- and/or implementation-dependent parameters, such as the names of the nodes to start the new processes on. In our case we leave this decision to the MPI implementation or local process manager, and we pass the special value

MPI_INFO_NULL. The next argument is the "root" process for this call to MPI_-Comm_spawn; it specifies which process in the communicator given in the following argument is supplying the valid arguments for this call. The communicator we are using consists here of just the one manager process, so we pass MPI_COMM_SELF. Next is the address of the new intercommunicator to be filled in, and finally an array of error codes for examining possible problems in starting the new processes. Here we use MPI_ERRCODES_IGNORE to indicate that we will not be looking at these error codes.

Code for the worker processes that are spawned is shown in Figure 10.2. It is essentially the same as the worker subroutine in the preceding chapter but is an MPI program in itself. Note the use of intercommunicator broadcast in order to receive the vector b from the parents. We free the parent intercommunicator with MPI_Comm_free before exiting.

### 10.1.4    More on Dynamic Process Management

For more complex examples of the use of MPI_Comm_spawn, including how to start processes with different executables or different argument lists, see [7, Chapter 7]. MPI_Comm_spawn is only the most basic of the functions provided in MPI for dealing with a dynamic MPI environment. By querying the attribute MPI_UNIVERSE_SIZE, you can find out how many processes can be usefully created. Separately started MPI computations can find each other and connect with MPI_Comm_connect and MPI_Comm_accept. Processes can exploit non-MPI connections to "bootstrap" MPI communication. These features are explained in detail in [7].

## 10.2    Fault Tolerance

Communicators are a fundamental concept in MPI. Their sizes are fixed at the time they are created, and the efficiency and correctness of collective operations rely on this fact. Users sometimes conclude from the fixed size of communicators that MPI provides no mechanism for writing fault-tolerant programs. Now that we have introduced intercommunicators, however, we are in a position to discuss how this topic might be addressed and how you might write a manager-worker program with MPI in such a way that it would be fault tolerant. In this context we mean that if one of the worker processes terminates abnormally, instead of terminating the job you will be able to carry on the computation with fewer workers, or perhaps dynamically replace the lost worker.

The key idea is to create a separate (inter)communicator for each worker and

```
#include "mpi.h"

int main( int argc, char *argv[] )
{
    int numprocs, myrank;
    double b[SIZE], c[SIZE];
    int i, row, myrank;
    double dotp;
    MPI_Status status;
    MPI_Comm parentcomm;

    MPI_Init( &argc, &argv );
    MPI_Comm_size( MPI_COMM_WORLD, &numprocs );
    MPI_Comm_rank( MPI_COMM_WORLD, &myrank );

    MPI_Comm_get_Parentp &parentcomm );

    MPI_Bcast( b, SIZE, MPI_DOUBLE, 0, parentcomm );

    ...
    /* same as worker code from original matrix-vector multiply */
    ...

    MPI_Comm_free(parentcomm );
    MPI_Finalize( );
    return 0;
}
```

**Figure 10.2**
Dynamic process matrix-vector multiply program, worker part.

use it for communications with that worker rather than use a communicator that contains all of the workers. If an implementation returns "invalid communicator" from an MPI_Send or MPI_Recv call, then the manager has lost contact only with one worker and can still communicate with the other workers through the other, still-intact communicators. Since the manager will be using separate communicators rather than separate ranks in a larger communicator to send and receive message from the workers, it might be convenient to maintain an array of communicators and a parallel array to remember which row has been last sent to a worker, so that if that worker disappears, the same row can be assigned to a different worker.

Figure 10.3 shows these arrays and how they might be used. What we are doing

```
/* highly incomplete */

MPI_Comm worker_comms[MAX_WORKERS];
int last_row_sent[MAX_WORKERS];

rc = MPI_Send( a[numsent], SIZE, MPI_DOUBLE, 0, numsent+1,
               worker_comms[sender] );
if ( rc != MPI_SUCCESS ) {
    /* Check that error class is one we can recover from */
    ...
    MPI_Comm_spawn( "worker" , ... );
```

**Figure 10.3**
Fault-tolerant manager.

with this approach is recognizing that two-party communication can be made fault tolerant, since one party can recognize the failure of the other and take appropriate action. A normal MPI communicator is not a two-party system and cannot be made fault tolerant without changing the semantics of MPI communication. If, however, the communication in an MPI program can be expressed in terms of intercommunicators, which are inherently two-party (the local group and the remote group), then fault tolerance can be achieved.

Note that while the MPI standard, through the use of intercommunicators, makes it possible to write an implementation of MPI that encourages fault-tolerant programming, the MPI standard itself does not require MPI implementations to continue past an error. This is a "quality of implementation" issue and allows the MPI implementor to trade performance for the ability to continue after a fault. As this section makes clear, however, there is nothing in the MPI standard that stands in the way of fault tolerance, and the two primary MPI implementations for Beowulf clusters, MPICH and LAM/MPI, both endeavor to support some style of fault tolerance for applications.

## 10.3 Revisiting Mesh Exchanges

The discussion of the mesh exchanges for the Jacobi problem in Section 9.3 concentrated on the algorithm and data structures, particularly the ghost-cell exchange. In this section, we return to that example and cover two other important issues: the use of blocking and nonblocking communications and communicating noncontiguous data.

### 10.3.1   Blocking and Nonblocking Communication

Consider the following simple code (note that this is similar to the simple version of `exchange_nbrs` in Section 9.3):

```
if (rank == 0) {
    MPI_Send( sbuf, n, MPI_INT, 1, 0, MPI_COMM_WORLD );
    MPI_Recv( rbuf, n, MPI_INT, 1, 0, MPI_COMM_WORLD, &status );
}
else if (rank == 1) {
    MPI_Send( sbuf, n, MPI_INT, 0, 0, MPI_COMM_WORLD );
    MPI_Recv( rbuf, n, MPI_INT, 0, 0, MPI_COMM_WORLD, &status );
}
```

What happens with this code? It looks like process 0 is sending a message to process 1 and that process 1 is sending a message to process 0. But more is going on here. Consider the steps that the MPI implementation must take to make this code work:

1.   Copy the data from the `MPI_Send` into a temporary, system-managed buffer.

2.   Once the `MPI_Send` completes (on each process), start the `MPI_Recv`. The data that was previously copied into a system buffer by the `MPI_Send` operation can now be delivered into the user's buffer (`rbuf` in this case).

This approach presents two problems, both related to the fact that data must be copied into a system buffer to allow the `MPI_Send` to complete. The first problem is obvious: any data motion takes time and reduces the performance of the code. The second problem is more subtle and important: the amount of available system buffer space always has a limit. For values of `n` in the above example that exceed the available buffer space, the above code will *hang*: neither `MPI_Send` will complete, and the code will wait forever for the other process to start an `MPI_Recv`. This is true for *any* message-passing system, not just MPI. The amount of buffer space available for buffering a message varies among MPI implementations, ranging from many megabytes to as little as 128 bytes.

How can we write code that sends data among several processes and that does not rely on the availability of system buffers? One approach is to carefully order the send and receive operations so that each send is guaranteed to have a matching

receive. For example, we can swap the order of the `MPI_Send` and `MPI_Recv` in the
code for process 1:

```
if (rank == 0) {
    MPI_Send( sbuf, n, MPI_INT, 1, 0, MPI_COMM_WORLD );
    MPI_Recv( rbuf, n, MPI_INT, 1, 0, MPI_COMM_WORLD, &status );
}
else if (rank == 1) {
    MPI_Recv( rbuf, n, MPI_INT, 0, 0, MPI_COMM_WORLD, &status );
    MPI_Send( sbuf, n, MPI_INT, 0, 0, MPI_COMM_WORLD );
}
```

However, this can be awkward to implement, particularly for more complex communication patterns; in addition, it does not address the extra copy that may be performed by `MPI_Send`.

The approach used by MPI, following earlier message-passing systems as well as nonblocking sockets (see [6, Chapter 9]), is to split the send and receive operations into two steps: one to initiate the operation and one to complete the operation. Other operations, including other communication operations, can be issued between the two steps. For example, an MPI receive operation can be initiated by a call to `MPI_Irecv` and completed with a call to `MPI_Wait`. Because the routines that initiate these operations do not wait for them to complete, they are called *nonblocking* operations. The "I" in the routine name stands for "immediate"; this indicates that the routine may return immediately without completing the operation. The arguments to `MPI_Irecv` are the same as for `MPI_Recv` except for the last (`status`) argument. This is replaced by an `MPI_Request` value; it is a *handle* that is used to identify an initiated operation. To complete a nonblocking operation, the request is given to `MPI_Wait`, along with a `status` argument; the `status` argument serves the same purpose as `status` for an `MPI_Recv`. Similarly, the nonblocking counterpart to `MPI_Send` is `MPI_Isend`; this has the same arguments as `MPI_Send` with the addition of an `MPI_Request` as the last argument (in C). Using these routines, our example becomes the following:

```
if (rank == 0) {
    MPI_Request req1, req2;
    MPI_Isend( sbuf, n, MPI_INT, 1, 0, MPI_COMM_WORLD, &req1 );
    MPI_Irecv( rbuf, n, MPI_INT, 1, 0, MPI_COMM_WORLD, &req2 );
    MPI_Wait( &req1, &status );
    MPI_Wait( &req2, &status );
```

```
    }
    else if (rank == 1) {
        MPI_Request req1, req2;
        MPI_Irecv( rbuf, n, MPI_INT, 0, 0, MPI_COMM_WORLD, &req1 );
        MPI_Isend( sbuf, n, MPI_INT, 0, 0, MPI_COMM_WORLD, &req2 );
        MPI_Wait( &req1, &status );
        MPI_Wait( &req2, &status );
    }
```

The buffer sbuf provided to MPI_Isend must not be modified until the operation is
completed with MPI_Wait. Similarly, the buffer rbuf provided to MPI_Irecv must
not be modified or read until the MPI_Irecv is completed.

The nonblocking communication routines allow the MPI implementation to wait
until the message can be sent directly from one user buffer to another (e.g., from
sbuf to rbuf) without requiring any copy or using any system buffer space.

Because it is common to start multiple nonblocking operations, MPI provides
routines to test or wait for completion of any one, all, or some of the requests. For
example, MPI_Waitall waits for all requests in an array of requests to complete.
Figure 10.4 shows the use of nonblocking communication routines for the Jacobi
example.[1]

MPI nonblocking operations are not the same as asynchronous operations. The
MPI standard does not require that the data transfers overlap computation with
communication. MPI specifies only the semantics of the operations, not the details
of the implementation choices. The MPI nonblocking routines are provided primarily for correctness (avoiding the limitations of system buffers) and performance
(avoidance of copies).

### 10.3.2   Communicating Noncontiguous Data in MPI

The one-dimensional decomposition used in the Jacobi example (Section 9.3) is
simple but does not scale well and can lead to performance problems. We can
analyze the performance of the Jacobi following the discussion in Section 9.2. Let
the time to communicate $n$ bytes be

$$T_{comm} = s + rn,$$

where $s$ is the *latency* and $r$ is the (additional) time to communicate one byte.
The time to compute one step of the Jacobi method, using the one-dimensional
decomposition in Section 9.3, is

---

[1]On many systems, calling MPI_Isend before MPI_Irecv will improve performance.

```
void exchange_nbrs( double ulocal[][NY+2], int i_start, int i_end,
                    int left, int right )
{
    MPI_Status  statuses[4];
    MPI_Request requests[4];
    int c;

    /* Begin send and receive from the left neighbor */
    MPI_Isend( &ulocal[1][1], NY, MPI_DOUBLE, left, 0,
               MPI_COMM_WORLD, &requests[0] );
    MPI_Irecv( &ulocal[0][1], NY, MPI_DOUBLE, left, 0,
               MPI_COMM_WORLD, &requests[1] );

    /* Begin send and receive from the right neighbor */
    c = i_end - i_start + 1;
    MPI_Isend( &ulocal[c][1], NY, MPI_DOUBLE, right, 0,
               MPI_COMM_WORLD, &requests[2] );
    MPI_Irecv( &ulocal[c+1][1], NY, MPI_DOUBLE, right, 0,
               MPI_COMM_WORLD, &requests[3] );

    /* Wait for all communications to complete */
    MPI_Waitall( 4, requests, statuses );
}
```

**Figure 10.4**
Nonblocking exchange code for the Jacobi example.

$$\frac{5n}{p}f + 2(s + rn),$$

where $f$ is the time to perform a floating-point operation and $p$ is the number of processes. Note that the cost of communication is independent of the number of processes; eventually, this cost will dominate the calculation. Hence, a better approach is to use a two-dimensional decomposition, as shown in Figure 10.5.

The time for one step of the Jacobi method with a two-dimensional decomposition is just

$$\frac{5n}{p}f + 4\left(s + r\frac{n}{\sqrt{p}}\right).$$

This is faster than the one-dimensional decomposition as long as

$$n > \frac{2}{1 - 4/\sqrt{p}}\frac{s}{r}$$

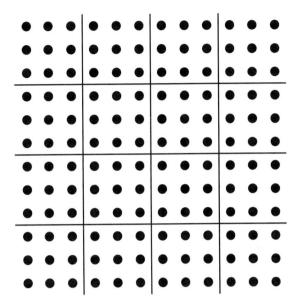

**Figure 10.5**
Domain and $9 \times 9$ computational mesh for approximating the solution to the Poisson problem
using a two-dimensional decomposition.

(assuming $p \geq 16$). To implement this decomposition, we need to communicate
data to four neighbors, as shown in Figure 10.6.

The left and right edges can be sent and received by using the same code as
for the one-dimensional case. The top and bottom edges have noncontiguous data.
For example, the top edge needs to send the tenth, sixteenth, and twenty-second
element. There are four ways to move this data:

1. Each value can be sent separately. Because of the high latency of message
passing, this approach is inefficient and normally should not be used.

2. The data can be copied into a temporary buffer using a simple loop, for
example,

```
for (i=0; i<3; i++) {
    tmp[i] = u_local[i][6];
}
MPI_Send( tmp, 3, MPI_DOUBLE, .. );
```

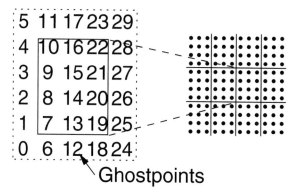

**Figure 10.6**
Locations of mesh points in `ulocal` for a two-dimensional decomposition.

This is a common approach and, for some systems and MPI implementations, may be the most efficient.

3.   MPI provides two routines to pack and unpack a buffer. These routines are `MPI_Pack` and `MPI_Unpack`. A buffer created with these routines should be sent and received with MPI datatype `MPI_PACKED`. We note, however, that these routines are most useful for complex data layouts that change frequently within a program.

4.   MPI provides a way to construct new datatypes representing any data layout. These routines can be optimized by the MPI implementation, in principle providing better performance than the user can achieve using a simple loop [16]. In addition, using these datatypes is crucial to achieving high performance with parallel I/O.

MPI provides several routines to create datatypes representing common patterns of memory. These new datatypes are called *derived* datatypes. For this case, `MPI_-Type_vector` is what is needed to create a new MPI datatype representing data values separated by a constant *stride*. In this case, the stride is `NY+2`, and the number of elements is `i_end-i_start+1`.

```
MPI_Type_vector( i_end - i_start + 1, 1, NY+2,
                 MPI_DOUBLE, &vectype );
MPI_Type_commit( &vectype );
```

The second argument is a *block count* and is the number of the basic datatype items (`MPI_DOUBLE` in this case); this is useful particularly in multicomponent PDE problems. The routine `MPI_Type_commit` must be called to *commit* the MPI datatype;

this call allows the MPI implementation to optimize the datatype (the optimization is not included as part of the routines that create MPI datatypes because some complex datatypes are created recursively from other derived datatypes).

Using an MPI derived datatype representing a strided data pattern, we can write a version of `exchange_nbr` for a two-dimensional decomposition of the mesh; the code is shown in Figure 10.7. Note that we use the same derived datatype `vectype` for the sends and receives at the top and bottom by specifying the first element into which data is moved in the array `u_local` in the MPI calls.

When a derived datatype is no longer needed, it should be freed with `MPI_Type_free`. Many other routines are available for creating datatypes; for example, `MPI_Type_indexed` is useful for scatter-gather patterns, and `MPI_Type_create_struct` can be used for an arbitrary collection of memory locations.

## 10.4   Motivation for Communicators

Communicators in MPI serve two purposes. The most obvious purpose is to describe a collection of processes. This feature allows collective routines, such as `MPI_Bcast` or `MPI_Allreduce`, to be used with any collection of processes. This capability is particularly important for hierarchical algorithms, and also facilitates dividing a computation into subtasks, each of which has its own collection of processes. For example, in the manager-worker example in Section 9.2, it may be appropriate to divide each task among a small collection of processes, particularly if this causes the problem description to reside only in the fast memory cache. MPI communicators are perfect for this; the MPI routine `MPI_Comm_split` is the only routine needed when creating new communicators. Using ranks relative to a communicator for specifying the source and destination of messages also facilitates dividing parallel tasks among smaller but still parallel subtasks, each with its own communicator.

A more subtle but equally important purpose of the MPI communicator involves the *communication context* that each communicator contains. This context is essential for writing software libraries that can be safely and robustly combined with other code, both other libraries and user-specific application code, to build complete applications. Used properly, the communication context guarantees that messages are received by appropriate routines *even if other routines are not as careful*. Consider the example in Figure 10.8 (taken from [6, Section 6.1.2]). In this example, there are two routines, provided by separate libraries or software modules. One, `SendRight`, sends a message to the right neighbor and receives from the left. The other, `SendEnd`, sends a message from process 0 (the leftmost) to the last process

```
void exchange_nbrs2d( double ulocal[][NY+2],
                      int i_start, int i_end, int j_start, int j_end,
                      int left, int right, int top, int bottom,
                      MPI_Datatype vectype )
{
    MPI_Status  statuses[8];
    MPI_Request requests[8];
    int c;

    /* Begin send and receive from the left neighbor */
    MPI_Isend( &ulocal[1][1], NY, MPI_DOUBLE, left, 0,
               MPI_COMM_WORLD, &requests[0] );
    MPI_Irecv( &ulocal[0][1], NY, MPI_DOUBLE, left, 0,
               MPI_COMM_WORLD, &requests[1] );

    /* Begin send and receive from the right neighbor */
    c = i_end - i_start + 1;
    MPI_Isend( &ulocal[c][1], NY, MPI_DOUBLE, right, 0,
               MPI_COMM_WORLD, &requests[2] );
    MPI_Irecv( &ulocal[c+1][1], NY, MPI_DOUBLE, right, 0,
               MPI_COMM_WORLD, &requests[3] );

    /* Begin send and receive from the top neighbor */
    MPI_Isend( &ulocal[1][NY], 1, vectype, top, 0,
               MPI_COMM_WORLD, &requests[4] );
    MPI_Irecv( &ulocal[1][NY+1], 1, vectype, top, 0,
               MPI_COMM_WORLD, &requests[5] );

    /* Begin send and receive from the bottom neighbor */
    MPI_Isend( &ulocal[1][1], 1, vectype, bottom, 0,
               MPI_COMM_WORLD, &requests[6] );
    MPI_Irecv( &ulocal[1][0], 1, vectype, bottom, 0,
               MPI_COMM_WORLD, &requests[7] );

    /* Wait for all communications to complete */
    MPI_Waitall( 8, requests, statuses );
}
```

**Figure 10.7**
Nonblocking exchange code for the Jacobi problem for a two-dimensional decomposition of the mesh.

(the rightmost). Both of these routines use MPI_ANY_SOURCE instead of a particular source in the MPI_Recv call. As Figure 10.8 shows, the messages can be confused, causing the program to receive the wrong data. How can we prevent this situation? Several approaches will *not* work. One is to avoid the use of MPI_ANY_SOURCE. This fixes this example, but only if both SendRight and SendEnd follow this rule. The approach may be adequate (though fragile) for code written by a single person or team, but it isn't adequate for libraries. For example, if SendEnd was written by a commercial vendor and did not use MPI_ANY_SOURCE, but SendRight, written by a different vendor or an inexperienced programmer, did use MPI_ANY_SOURCE, then the program would still fail, and it would look like SendEnd was at fault (because the message from SendEnd was received first).

Another approach that does not work is to use message tags to separate messages. Again, this can work if one group writes all of the code and is very careful about allocating message tags to different software modules. However, using MPI_ANY_-TAG in an MPI receive call can still bypass this approach. Further, as shown in Figure 6.5 in [6], even if MPI_ANY_SOURCE and MPI_ANY_TAG are not used, it is still possible for separate code modules to receive the wrong message.

The communication context in an MPI communicator provides a solution to these problems. The routine MPI_Comm_dup creates a new communicator from an input communicator that contains the same processes (in the same rank order) but with a new communication context. MPI messages sent in one communication context can be received only in that context. Thus, any software module or library that wants to ensure that all of its messages will be seen only within that library needs only to call MPI_Comm_dup at the beginning to get a new communicator. All well-written libraries that use MPI create a private communicator used only within that library.

Enabling the development of libraries was one of the design goals of MPI. In that respect MPI has been very successful. Many libraries and applications now use MPI, and, because of MPI's portability, most of these run on Beowulf clusters. Table 10.1 provides a partial list of libraries that use MPI to provide parallelism. More complete descriptions and lists are available at www.mcs.anl.gov/mpi/libraries and at sal.kachinatech.com/C/3.

## 10.5   More on Collective Operations

One of the strengths of MPI is its collection of scalable collective communication and computation routines. Figure 10.9 shows the capabilities of some of the most important collective communication routines. As an example of their utility, we

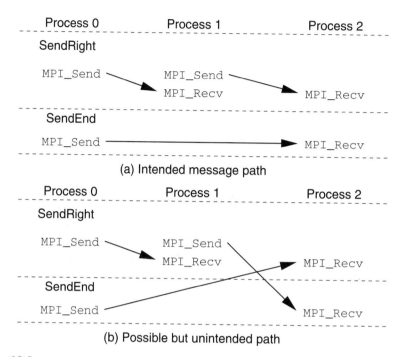

**Figure 10.8**
Two possible message-matching patterns when MPI_ANY_SOURCE is used in the MPI_Recv calls (from [6]).

consider a simple example.

Suppose we want to gather the names of all of the nodes that our program is running on, and we want all MPI processes to have this list of names. This is an easy task using MPI_Allgather:

```
char my_hostname[MAX_LEN], all_names[MAX_PROCS][MAX_LEN];
MPI_Allgather( my_hostname, MAX_LEN, MPI_CHAR,
               all_names, MAX_LEN, MPI_CHAR, MPI_COMM_WORLD );
```

This code assumes that no hostname is longer than MAX_LEN characters (including the trailing null). A better code would check this:

```
char my_hostname[MAX_LEN], all_names[MAX_PROCS][MAX_LEN];
MPI_Allreduce( &my_name_len, &max_name_len, 1, MPI_INT, MPI_MAX,
               MPI_COMM_WORLD );
if (max_name_len > MAX_LEN) {
```

| Library | Description | URL |
|---|---|---|
| PETSc | Linear and nonlinear solvers for PDEs | `www.mcs.anl.gov/petsc` |
| Aztec | Parallel iterative solution of sparse linear systems | `www.cs.sandia.gov/CRF/` `aztec1.html` |
| Cactus | Framework for PDE solutions | `www.cactuscode.org` |
| FFTW | Parallel FFT | `www.fftw.org` |
| PPFPrint | Parallel print | `www.llnl.gov/sccd/lc/` `ptcprint` |
| HDF | Parallel I/O for Hierarchical Data Format (HDF) files | `hdf.ncsa.uiuc.edu/Parallel_` `HDF` |
| NAG | Numerical library | `www.nag.co.uk/numeric/fd/` `FDdescription.asp` |
| ScaLAPACK | Parallel linear algebra | `www.netlib.org/scalapack` |
| SPRNG | Scalable pseudorandom number generator | `sprng.cs.fsu.edu` |

**Table 10.1**
A sampling of libraries that use MPI.

```
        printf( "Error: names too long (%d)", max_name_len );
    }
    MPI_Allgather( my_hostname, MAX_LEN, MPI_CHAR,
                   all_names, MAX_LEN, MPI_CHAR, MPI_COMM_WORLD );
```

Both of these approaches move more data than necessary, however. An even better approach is to first gather the size of each processor's name and then gather exactly the number of characters needed from each processor. This uses the "v" (for vector) version of the allgather routine, `MPI_Allgatherv`, as shown in Figure 10.10.

This example provides a different way to accomplish the action of the example in Section 9.3. Many parallel codes can be written with MPI collective routines instead of MPI point-to-point communication; such codes often have a simpler logical structure and can benefit from scalable implementations of the collective communications routines.

## 10.6 Parallel I/O

MPI-2 provides a wide variety of parallel I/O operations, more than we have space to cover here. See [7, Chapter 3] for a more thorough discussion of I/O in MPI.

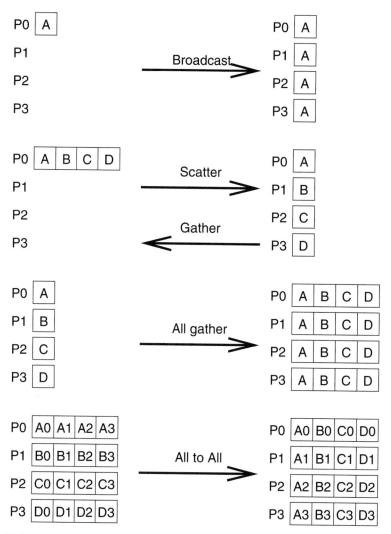

**Figure 10.9**
Schematic representation of collective data movement in MPI.

The fundamental idea in MPI's approach to parallel I/O is that a file is opened collectively by a set of processes that are all given access to the same file. MPI thus associates a communicator with the file, allowing a flexible set of both individual and collective operations on the file.

```
mylen = strlen(my_hostname) + 1;   /* Include the trailing null */
MPI_Allgather( &mylen, 1, MPI_INT, all_lens, 1, MPI_INT,
               MPI_COMM_WORLD );
totlen = all_lens[size-1];
for (i=0; i<size-1; i++) {
    displs[i+1] = displs[i] + all_lens[i];
    totlen      += all_lens[i];
}
all_names = (char *)malloc( totlen );
if (!all_names) MPI_Abort( MPI_COMM_WORLD, 1 );
MPI_Allgatherv( my_hostname, mylen, MPI_CHAR,
                all_names, all_lens, displs, MPI_CHAR,
                MPI_COMM_WORLD );
/* Hostname for the jth process is &all_names[displs[j]] */
```

**Figure 10.10**
Using MPI_Allgather and MPI_Allgatherv.

### 10.6.1  A Simple Example

We first provide a simple example of how processes write contiguous blocks of data into the same file in parallel. Then we give a more complex example, in which the data in each process is not contiguous but can be described by an MPI datatype.

For our first example, let us suppose that after solving the Poisson equation as we did in Section 9.3, we wish to write the solution to a file. We do not need the values of the ghost cells, and in the one-dimensional decomposition the set of rows in each process makes up a contiguous area in memory, which greatly simplifies the program. The I/O part of the program is shown in Figure 10.11.

Recall that the data to be written from each process, not counting ghost cells but including the boundary data, is in the array ulocal[i][j] for i=i_start to i_end and j=0 to NY+1.

Note that the type of an MPI file object is MPI_File. Such file objects are opened and closed much the way normal files are opened and closed. The most significant difference is that opening a file is a collective operation over a group of processes specified by the communicator in the first argument of MPI_File_open. A single process can open a file by specifying the single-process communicator MPI_COMM_SELF. Here we want all of the processes to share the file, and so we use MPI_COMM_WORLD.

In our discussion of dynamic process management, we mentioned MPI_Info ob-

```
MPI_File outfile;
size = NX * (NY + 2);
MPI_File_open( MPI_COMM_WORLD, "solutionfile",
               MPI_MODE_CREATE | MPI_MODE_WRONLY,
               MPI_INFO_NULL, &outfile );
MPI_File_set_view( outfile,
               rank * (NY+2) * (i_end - i_start) * sizeof(double),
               MPI_DOUBLE, MPI_DOUBLE, "native", MPI_INFO_NULL );
MPI_File_write( outfile, &ulocal[1][0], size, MPI_DOUBLE,
               MPI_STATUS_IGNORE );
MPI_File_close( &outfile );
```

**Figure 10.11**
Parallel I/O of Jacobi solution. Note that this choice of file view works only for a single output step; if output of multiple steps of the Jacobi method are needed, the arguments to MPI_File_set_view must be modified.

jects. An MPI info object is a collection of key=value pairs that can be used to encapsulate a variety of special-purpose information that may not be applicable to all MPI implementations. In this section we will use MPI_INFO_NULL whenever this type of argument is required, since we have no special information to convey. For details about MPI_Info, see [7, Chapter 2].

The part of the file that will be seen by each process is called the file *view* and is set for each process by a call to MPI_File_set_view. In our example the call is

```
MPI_File_set_view( outfile, rank * (NY+2) * ( ... ),
               MPI_DOUBLE, MPI_DOUBLE, "native", MPI_INFO_NULL )
```

The first argument identifies the file; the second is the displacement (in bytes) into the file of where the process's view of the file is to start. Here we simply multiply the size of the data to be written by the process's rank, so that each process's view starts at the appropriate place in the file. The type of this argument is MPI_Offset, which can be expected to be a 64-bit integer on systems that support large files.

The next argument is called the *etype* of the view; it specifies the unit of data in the file. Here it is just MPI_DOUBLE, since we will be writing some number of doubles. The next argument is called the *filetype*; it is a flexible way of describing noncontiguous views in the file. In our case, with no noncontiguous units to be written, we can just use the etype, MPI_DOUBLE. In general, any MPI predefined or derived datatype can be used for both etypes and filetypes. We explore this use in more detail in the next example.

The next argument is a string defining the *data representation* to be used. The native representation says to represent data on disk exactly as it is in memory, which provides the fastest I/O performance, at the possible expense of portability. We specify that we have no extra information by providing `MPI_INFO_NULL` for the final argument.

The call to `MPI_File_write` is then straightforward. The data to be written is a contiguous array of doubles, even though it consists of several rows of the (distributed) matrix. On each process it starts at `&ulocal[0][1]` so the data is described in (address, count, datatype) form, just as it would be for an MPI message. We ignore the status by passing `MPI_STATUS_IGNORE`. Finally we (collectively) close the file with `MPI_File_close`.

## 10.6.2  A More Complex Example

Parallel I/O requires more than just calling `MPI_File_write` instead of write. The key idea is to identify the object (across processes), rather than the contribution from each process. We illustrate this with an example of a regular distributed array.

The code in Figure 10.12 writes out an array that is distributed among processes with a two-dimensional decomposition. To illustrate the expressiveness of the MPI interface, we show a complex case where, as in the Jacobi example, the distributed array is surrounded by ghost cells. This example is covered in more depth in Chapter 3 of *Using MPI 2* [7], including the simpler case of a distributed array without ghost cells.

This example may look complex, but each step is relatively simple.

1.  Set up a communicator that represents a virtual array of processes that matches the way that the distributed array is distributed. This approach uses the `MPI_Cart_create` routine and uses `MPI_Cart_coords` to find the coordinates of the calling process in this array of processes. This particular choice of process ordering is important because it matches the ordering required by `MPI_Type_create_subarray`.

2.  Create a *file view* that describes the part of the file that this process will write to. The MPI routine `MPI_Type_create_subarray` makes it easy to construct the MPI datatype that describes this region of the file. The arguments to this routine specify the dimensionality of the array (two in our case), the global size of the array, the local size (that is, the size of the part of the array on the calling process), the location of the local part (`start_indices`), the ordering of indices (column major is `MPI_ORDER_FORTRAN` and row major is `MPI_ORDER_C`), and the basic datatype.

```
/* no. of processes in vertical and horizontal dimensions
   of process grid */
dims[0] = 2;   dims[1] = 3;
periods[0] = periods[1] = 1;
MPI_Cart_create(MPI_COMM_WORLD, 2, dims, periods, 0, &comm);
MPI_Comm_rank(comm, &rank);
MPI_Cart_coords(comm, rank, 2, coords);
/* global indices of the first element of the local array */

/* no. of rows and columns in global array*/
gsizes[0] = m;   gsizes[1] = n;

lsizes[0] = m/dims[0];   /* no. of rows in local array */
lsizes[1] = n/dims[1];   /* no. of columns in local array */

start_indices[0] = coords[0] * lsizes[0];
start_indices[1] = coords[1] * lsizes[1];
MPI_Type_create_subarray(2, gsizes, lsizes, start_indices,
                         MPI_ORDER_C, MPI_FLOAT, &filetype);
MPI_Type_commit(&filetype);

MPI_File_open(comm, "/pfs/datafile",
              MPI_MODE_CREATE | MPI_MODE_WRONLY,
              MPI_INFO_NULL, &fh);
MPI_File_set_view(fh, 0, MPI_FLOAT, filetype, "native",
                  MPI_INFO_NULL);

/* create a derived datatype that describes the layout of the local
   array in the memory buffer that includes the ghost area. This is
   another subarray datatype! */
memsizes[0] = lsizes[0] + 8; /* no. of rows in allocated array */
memsizes[1] = lsizes[1] + 8; /* no. of columns in allocated array */
start_indices[0] = start_indices[1] = 4;
/* indices of the first element of the local array in the
   allocated array */
MPI_Type_create_subarray(2, memsizes, lsizes, start_indices,
                         MPI_ORDER_C, MPI_FLOAT, &memtype);
MPI_Type_commit(&memtype);
MPI_File_write_all(fh, local_array, 1, memtype, &status);
MPI_File_close(&fh);
```

**Figure 10.12**
C program for writing a distributed array that is also noncontiguous in memory because of a ghost area (derived from an example in [7]).

3.  Open the file for writing (`MPI_MODE_WRONLY`), and set the file view with the datatype we have just constructed.

4.  Create a datatype that describes the data to be written. We can use `MPI_-Type_create_subarray` here as well to define the part of the local array that does *not* include the ghost points. If there were no ghost points, we could instead use `MPI_FLOAT` as the datatype with a count of `lsizes[0]*lsizes[1]` in the call to `MPI_File_write_all`.

5.  Perform a collective write to the file with `MPI_File_write_all`, and close the file.

By using MPI datatypes to describe both the data to be written and the destination of the data in the file with a collective file write operation, the MPI implementation can make the best use of the I/O system. The result is that file I/O operations performed with MPI I/O can achieve hundredfold improvements in performance over using individual Unix I/O operations [15].

## 10.7  Remote Memory Access

The message-passing programming model requires that both the sender and the receiver (or all members of a communicator in a collective operation) participate in moving data between two processes. An alternative model where one process controls the communication, called one-sided communication, can offer better performance and in some cases a simpler programming model. MPI-2 provides support for this one-sided approach. The MPI-2 model was inspired by the work on the bulk synchronous programming (BSP) model [9] and the Cray SHMEM library used on the massively parallel Cray T3D and T3E computers [1].

In one-sided communication, one process may *put* data directly into the memory of another process, without that process using an explicit receive call. For this reason, this also called *remote memory access* (RMA).

Using RMA involves four steps:

1.  Describe the memory into which data may be put.

2.  Allow access to the memory.

3.  Begin put operations (e.g., with `MPI_Put`).

4.  Complete all pending RMA operations.

The first step is to describe the region of memory into which data may be placed by an `MPI_Put` operation (also accessed by `MPI_Get` or updated by `MPI_-Accumulate`). This is done with the routine `MPI_Win_create`:

```
MPI_Win win;
double ulocal[MAX_NX][NY+2];

MPI_Win_create( ulocal, (NY+2)*(i_end-i_start+3)*sizeof(double),
            sizeof(double), MPI_INFO_NULL, MPI_COMM_WORLD, &win );
```

The input arguments are, in order, the array `ulocal`, the size of the array in bytes, the size of a basic unit of the array (`sizeof(double)` in this case), a "hint" object, and the communicator that specifies which processes may use RMA to access the array. `MPI_Win_create` is a collective call over the communicator. The output is an MPI *window object* `win`. When a window object is no longer needed, it should be freed with `MPI_Win_free`.

RMA operations take place between two sentinels. One begins a period where access is allowed to a window object, and one ends that period. These periods are called *epochs*.[2] The easiest routine to use to begin and end epochs is `MPI_Win_-fence`. This routine is collective over the processes that created the window object and both ends the previous epoch and starts a new one. The routine is called a "fence" because all RMA operations before the fence complete before the fence returns, and any RMA operation initiated by another process (in the epoch begun by the matching fence on that process) does not start until the fence returns. This may seem complex, but it is easy to use. In practice, `MPI_Win_fence` is needed only to separate RMA operations into groups. This model closely follows the BSP and Cray SHMEM models, though with the added ability to work with any subset of processes.

Three routines are available for initiating the transfer of data in RMA. These are `MPI_Put`, `MPI_Get`, and `MPI_Accumulate`. All are nonblocking in the same sense MPI point-to-point communication is nonblocking (Section 10.3.1). They complete at the end of the epoch that they start in, for example, at the closing `MPI_Win_-fence`. Because these routines specify both the source and destination of data, they have more arguments than do the point-to-point communication routines. The arguments can be easily understood by taking them a few at a time.

---

[2]MPI has two kinds of epochs for RMA: an *access epoch* and an *exposure epoch*. For the example used here, the epochs occur together, and we refer to both of them as just epochs.

1.   The first three arguments describe the *origin* data; that is, the data on the calling process. These are the usual "buffer, count, datatype" arguments.

2.   The next argument is the rank of the *target* process. This serves the same function as the destination of an `MPI_Send`. The rank is relative to the communicator used when creating the MPI window object.

3.   The next three arguments describe the destination buffer. The `count` and `datatype` arguments have the same meaning as for an `MPI_Recv`, but the buffer location is specified as an offset from the beginning of the memory specified to `MPI_Win_create` on the target process. This offset is in units of the displacement argument of the `MPI_Win_create` and is usually the size of the basic datatype.

4.   The last argument is the MPI window object.

Note that there are no MPI requests; the `MPI_Win_fence` completes all preceding RMA operations. `MPI_Win_fence` provides a collective synchronization model for RMA operations in which all processes participate. This is called *active target* synchronization.

With these routines, we can create a version of the mesh exchange that uses RMA instead of point-to-point communication. Figure 10.13 shows one possible implementation.

Another form of access requires no MPI calls (not even a fence) at the target process. This is called *passive target* synchronization. The origin process uses `MPI_-Win_lock` to begin an access epoch and `MPI_Win_unlock` to end the access epoch.[3] Because of the passive nature of this type of RMA, the local memory (passed as the first argument to `MPI_Win_create`) should be allocated with `MPI_Alloc_mem` and freed with `MPI_Free_mem`. For more information on passive target RMA operations, see [7, Chapter 6]. Also note that as of 2001, few MPI implementations support passive target RMA operation. More implementations are expected to support these operations in 2002.

A more complete discussion of remote memory access can be found in [7, Chapters 5 and 6]. Note that MPI implementations are just beginning to provide the RMA routines described in this section. Most current RMA implementations emphasize functionality over performance. As implementations mature, however, the performance of RMA operations will also improve.

---

[3]The names `MPI_Win_lock` and `MPI_Win_unlock` are really misnomers; think of them as begin-RMA and end-RMA.

```
void exchang_nbrs( double u_local[][NY+2], int i_start, int i_end,
                   int left, int right, MPI_Win win )
{
    MPI_Aint left_ghost_disp, right_ghost_disp;
    int      c;

    MPI_Win_fence( 0, win );
    /* Put the left edge into the left neighbors rightmost
       ghost cells.  See text about right_ghost_disp */
    right_ghost_disp = 1 + (NY+2) * (i_end-i_start+2);
    MPI_Put( &u_local[1][1], NY, MPI_DOUBLE,
             left, right_ghost_disp, NY, MPI_DOUBLE, win );
    /* Put the right edge into the right neighbors leftmost ghost
       cells */
    left_ghost_disp = 1;
    c = i_end - i_start + 1;
    MPI_Put( &u_local[c][1], NY, MPI_DOUBLE,
             right, left_ghost_disp, NY, MPI_DOUBLE, win );

    MPI_Win_fence( 0, win )
}
```

**Figure 10.13**
Neighbor exchange using MPI remote memory access.

## 10.8   Using C++ and Fortran 90

MPI-1 defined bindings to C and Fortran 77. These bindings were very similar; the only major difference was the handling of the error code (returned in C, set through the last argument in Fortran 77). In MPI-2, a binding was added for C++, and an MPI module was defined for Fortran 90.

The C++ binding provides a lightweight model that is more than just a C++ version of the C binding but not a no-holds-barred object-oriented model. MPI objects are defined in the MPI namespace. Most MPI objects have corresponding classes, such as Datatype for MPI_Datatype. Communicators and requests are slightly different. There is an abstract base class Comm for general communicators with four derived classes: Intracomm, Intercomm, Graphcomm, and Cartcomm. Most communicators are Intracomms; GraphComm and CartComm are derived from Intracomm. Requests have two derived classes: Prequest for persistent requests and Grequest for generalized requests (new in MPI-2). Most MPI operations are methods on the appropriate objects; for example, most point-to-point and collective communications are methods on the communicator. A few routines, such as `Init` and `Finalize`, stand alone. A simple MPI program in C++ is shown in Figure 10.14.

```
#include "mpi.h"
#include <iostream.h>

int main( int argc, char *argv[] )
{
    int data;
    MPI::Init();

    if (MPI::COMM_WORLD.Get_rank() == 0) {
        // Broadcast data from process 0 to all others
        cout << "Enter an int" << endl;
        data << cin;
    }
    MPI::COMM_WORLD.Bcast( data, 1, MPI::INT, 0 );

    MPI::Finalize();
    return 0;
}
```

**Figure 10.14**
Simple MPI program in C++.

The C++ binding for MPI has a few quirks. One is that the multiple completion operations such as `MPI::Waitall` are methods on requests, even though there is no unique request to use for these methods. Another is the C++ analogue to `MPI_-Comm_dup`. In the C++ binding, `MPI::Comm` is an abstract base class (ABC). Since it is impossible to create an instance of an abstract base class, there can be no general "dup" function that returns a new `MPI::Comm`. Since it is possible in C++ to create a reference to an ABC, however, MPI defines the routine (available only in the C++ binding) `MPI::Clone` that returns a reference to a new communicator.

Two levels of Fortran 90 support are provided in MPI. The basic support provides an '`mpif.h`' include file. The extended support provides an `MPI` module. The module makes it easy to detect the two most common errors in Fortran MPI programs: forgetting to provide the variable for the error return value and forgetting to declare status as an array of size `MPI_STATUS_SIZE`. There are a few drawbacks.

Fortran derived datatypes cannot be directly supported (the Fortran 90 language
provides no way to handle an arbitrary type). Often, you can use the first element
of the Fortran 90 derived type. Array sections should not be used in receive operations, particularly nonblocking communication (see Section 10.2.2 in the MPI-2
standard for more information). Another problem is that while Fortran 90 enables
the user to define MPI interfaces in the MPI module, a different Fortran 90 interface
file must be used for each combination of Fortran datatype and array dimension
(scalars are different from arrays of dimension one, etc.). This leads to a Fortran 90
MPI module library that is often (depending on the Fortran 90 compiler) far larger
than the entire MPI library. However, particularly during program development,
the MPI module is very helpful.

## 10.9    MPI, OpenMP, and Threads

The MPI standard was carefully written to be a thread-safe specification. That
means that the design of MPI doesn't include concepts such as "last message" or
"current pack buffer" that are not well defined when multiple threads are present.
MPI implementations can choose whether to provide thread-safe *implementations*.
Allowing this choice is particularly important because thread safety usually comes
at the price of performance due to the extra overhead required to ensure that
internal data structures are not modified inconsistently by two different threads.
Most early MPI implementations were not thread safe.

MPI-2 introduced four levels of thread safety that an MPI implementation could
provide. The lowest level, `MPI_THREAD_SINGLE`, allows only single threaded programs. The next level, `MPI_THREAD_FUNNELED`, allows multiple threads provided
that all MPI calls are made in a single thread; most MPI implementations provide
`MPI_THREAD_FUNNELED`. The next level, `MPI_THREAD_SERIALIZED`, allows many user
threads to make MPI calls, but only one thread at a time. The highest level of
support, `MPI_THREAD_MULTIPLE`, allows any thread to call any MPI routine.

Understanding the level of thread support is important when combining MPI with
approaches to thread-based parallelism. OpenMP [12] is a popular and powerful
language for specifying thread-based parallelism. While OpenMP provides some
tools for general threaded parallelism, one of the most common uses is to parallelize
a loop. If the loop contains no MPI calls, then OpenMP may be combined with
MPI. For example, in the Jacobi example, OpenMP can be used to parallelize the
loop computation:

```
exchange_nbrs( u_local, i_start, i_end, left, right );
```

```
#pragma omp for
for (i_local=1; i<=i_end-i_start+1; i++)
  for (j=1; j<=NY; j++)
    ulocal_new[i_local][j] =
        0.25 * (ulocal[i_local+1][j] + ulocal[i_local-1][j] +
                ulocal[i_local][j+1] + ulocal[i_local][j-1] -
                h*h*flocal[i_local][j]);
```

This exploits the fact that MPI was designed to work well with other tools, leveraging improvements in compilers and threaded parallelism.

## 10.10   Measuring MPI Performance

Many tools have been developed for measuring performance. The best is always your own application, but a number of tests are available that can give a more general overview of the performance of MPI on a cluster. Measuring communication performance is actually quite tricky; see [8] for a discussion of some of the issues in making reproducible measurements of performance. That paper describes the methods used in the mpptest program for measuring MPI performance.

### 10.10.1   mpptest

The mpptest program allows you to measure many aspects of the performance of any MPI implementation. The most common MPI performance test is the Ping-Pong test (see Section 8.2). The mpptest program provides Ping-Pong tests for the different MPI communication modes, as well as providing a variety of tests for collective operations and for more realistic variations on point-to-point communication, such as halo communication (like that in Section 9.3) and communication that does not reuse the same memory locations (thus benefiting from using data that is already in memory cache). The mpptest program can also test the performance of some MPI-2 functions, including MPI_Put and MPI_Get.

**Using mpptest.** The mpptest program is distributed with MPICH in the directory 'examples/perftest'. You can also download it separately from www.mcs.anl.gov/mpi/perftest.

### 10.10.2   SKaMPI

The SKaMPI test suite [13] is a comprehensive test of MPI performance, covering virtually all of the MPI-1 communication functions.

One interesting feature of the SKaMPI benchmarks is the online tables showing the performance of MPI implementations on various parallel computers, ranging from Beowulf clusters to parallel vector supercomputers.

### 10.10.3   High Performance LINPACK

Perhaps the best known benchmark in technical computing is the LINPACK Benchmark, discussed in Section 8.3. The version of this benchmark that is appropriate for clusters is the High Performance LINPACK (HPL). Obtaining and running this benchmark is relatively easy, though getting good performance can require a significant amount of effort. In addition, as pointed out in Section 8.3, while the LINPACK benchmark is widely known, it tends to significantly overestimate the achieveable performance for many applications.

The HPL benchmark depends on another library, the basic linear algebra subroutines (BLAS), for much of the computation. Thus, to get good performance on the HPL benchmark, you must have a high-quality implementation of the BLAS. Fortunately, several sources of these routines are available. You can often get implementations of the BLAS from the CPU vendor directly, sometimes at no cost.

**HPL.**   Download the HPL package from `www.netlib.org/benchmark/hpl`:

```
% tar zxf hpl.tgz
% cd hpl
```

Create a 'Make.<archname>' in the 'hpl' directory. Consider an `archname` like `Win2k_P4_CBLAS_p4` for a Windows 2000 system on Pentium 4 processors, using the C version of the BLAS constructed by ATLAS, and using the `ch_p4` device from the MPICH implementation of MPI. To create this file, look at the samples in the 'hpl/makes' directory, for example,

```
% copy makes\Make.Linux_PII_CBLAS_gm Make.Win2k_P4_CBLAS_p4
```

Edit this file, changing `ARCH` to the name you selected (e.g., `Win2k_P4_CBLAS_p4`), and set `LAdir` to the location of the ATLAS libraries. Then do the following:

```
% make arch=<thename>
% cd bin\<thename>
% mpirun -np 4 xhpl.exe
```

Check the output to make sure that you have the right answer. The file 'HPL.dat' controls the actual test parameters. The version of 'HPL.dat' that comes with the hpl package is appropriate for testing hpl. To run hpl for performance requires modifying 'HPL.dat'. The file 'hpl/TUNING' contains some hints on setting the values in this file for performance. Here are a few of the most important:

1. Change the problem size to a large value. Don't make it too large, however, since the total computational work grows as the cube of the problem size (doubling the problem size increases the amount of work by a factor of eight). Problem sizes of around 5,000–10,000 are reasonable.

2. Change the block size to a modest size. A block size of around 64 is a good place to start.

3. Change the processor decomposition and number of nodes to match your configuration. In most cases, you should try to keep the decomposition close to square (e.g., $P$ and $Q$ should be about the same value), with $P \geq Q$.

4. Experiment with different values for RFACT and PFACT. On some systems, these parameters can have a significant effect on performance. For one large cluster, setting both to right was preferable.

## 10.11   MPI-2 Status

MPI-2 is a significant extension of the MPI-1 standard. Unlike the MPI-1 standard, where complete implementations of the entire standard were available when the standard was released, complete implementations of all of MPI-2 have been slow in coming. As of June 2001, there are few complete implementations of MPI-2 and none for Beowulf clusters. Most MPI implementations include the MPI-IO routines, in large part because of the ROMIO implementation of these routines. Significant parts of MPI-2 are available, however, including the routines described in this book. Progress continues in both the completeness and performance of MPI-2 implementations, and we expect full MPI-2 implementations to appear in 2002.

## 10.12   MPI Routine Summary

This section provides a quick summary in C, Fortran, C++, and other MPI routines used in this chapter. Although these are only a small fraction of the routines available in MPI, they are sufficient for many applications.

**C Routines.**

int **MPI_Irecv**(void* buf, int count, MPI_Datatype datatype, int source, int tag,
                MPI_Comm comm, MPI_Request *request)

int **MPI_Wait**(MPI_Request *request, MPI_Status *status)

int **MPI_Test**(MPI_Request *request, int *flag, MPI_Status *status)

int **MPI_Waitall**(int count, MPI_Request *array_of_requests,
                MPI_Status *array_of_statuses)

int **MPI_Win_create**(void *base, MPI_Aint size, int disp_unit, MPI_Info info,
                MPI_Comm comm, MPI_Win *win)

int **MPI_Win_free**(MPI_Win *win)

int **MPI_Put**(void *origin_addr, int origin_count, MPI_Datatype origin_datatype,
                int target_rank, MPI_Aint target_disp, int target_count,
                MPI_Datatype target_datatype, MPI_Win win)

int **MPI_Get**(void *origin_addr, int origin_count, MPI_Datatype origin_datatype,
                int target_rank, MPI_Aint target_disp, int target_count,
                MPI_Datatype target_datatype, MPI_Win win)

int **MPI_Win_fence**(int assert, MPI_Win win)

int **MPI_File_open**(MPI_Comm comm, char *filename, int amode, MPI_Info info,
                MPI_File *fh)

int **MPI_File_set_view**(MPI_File fh, MPI_Offset disp, MPI_Datatype etype,
                MPI_Datatype filetype, char *datarep, MPI_Info info)

int **MPI_File_read**(MPI_File fh, void *buf, int count, MPI_Datatype datatype,
                MPI_Status *status)

int **MPI_File_write**(MPI_File fh, void *buf, int count, MPI_Datatype datatype,
                MPI_Status *status)

int **MPI_File_read_all**(MPI_File fh, void *buf, int count, MPI_Datatype datatype,
                MPI_Status *status)

int **MPI_File_write_all**(MPI_File fh, void *buf, int count, MPI_Datatype datatype,
                MPI_Status *status)

int **MPI_File_close**(MPI_File *fh)

int **MPI_Comm_spawn**(char *command, char *argv[], int maxprocs, MPI_Info info,
              int root, MPI_Comm comm, MPI_Comm *intercomm,
              int array_of_errcodes[])

int **MPI_Comm_get_parent**(MPI_Comm *parent)


**Fortran routines.**

**MPI_ISEND**(buf, count, datatype, dest, tag, comm, request, ierror)
              <type> buf(*)
              integer  count, datatype, dest, tag, comm, request, ierror

**MPI_IRECV**(buf, count, datatype, source, tag, comm, request,ierror)
              <type> buf(*)
              integer  count, datatype, source, tag, comm, request, ierror

**MPI_WAIT**(request, status, ierror)
              integer  request,status(MPI_STATUS_SIZE), ierror

**MPI_TEST**(request, flag, status, ierror)
              logical  flag
              integer  request, status(MPI_STATUS_SIZE), ierror

**MPI_WAITALL**(count, array_of_requests, array_of_statuses,ierror)
              integer  count, array_of_requests(*),
                   array_of_statuses(MPI_STATUS_SIZE,*), ierror

**MPI_WIN_CREATE**(base, size, disp_unit, info, comm, win, ierror)
              <type> base(*)
              integer(kind=MPI_ADDRESS_KIND) size
              integer disp_unit, info, comm, win, ierror

**MPI_WIN_FREE**(win, ierror)
              integer win, ierror

**MPI_PUT**(origin_addr, origin_count, origin_datatype, target_rank, target_disp,
              target_count, target_datatype, win, ierror)
              <type> origin_addr(*)
              integer(kind=MPI_ADDRESS_KIND) target_disp

        integer origin_count, origin_datatype, target_rank, target_count,
            target_datatype, win, ierror

**MPI_GET**(origin_addr, origin_count, origin_datatype,target_rank, target_disp,
            target_count, target_datatype, win, ierror)
            <type> origin_addr(*)
            integer(kind=MPI_ADDRESS_KIND) target_disp
            integer origin_count, origin_datatype, target_rank, target_count,
                target_datatype, win, ierror

**MPI_WIN_FENCE**(assert, win, ierror)
            integer assert, win, ierror

**MPI_FILE_OPEN**(comm, filename, amode, info, fh, ierror)
            character*(*) filename
            integer comm, amode, info, fh, ierror

**MPI_FILE_SET_VIEW**(fh, disp, etype, filetype, datarep, info, ierror)
            integer fh, etype, filetype, info, ierror
            character*(*) datarep
            integer(kind=MPI_OFFSET_KIND) disp

**MPI_FILE_READ**(fh, buf, count, datatype, status, ierror)
            <type> buf(*)
            integer fh, count, datatype, status(MPI_STATUS_SIZE), ierror

**MPI_FILE_WRITE**(fh, buf, count, datatype, status, ierror)
            <type> buf(*)
            integer fh, count, datatype, status(MPI_STATUS_SIZE), ierror

**MPI_FILE_READ_ALL**(fh, buf, count, datatype, status, ierror)
            <type> buf(*)
            integer fh, count, datatype, status(MPI_STATUS_SIZE), ierror

**MPI_FILE_WRITE_ALL**(fh, buf, count, datatype, status, ierror)
            <type> buf(*)
            integer fh, count, datatype, status(MPI_STATUS_SIZE), ierror

**MPI_FILE_CLOSE**(fh, ierror)
            integer fh, ierror

**MPI_COMM_SPAWN**(command, argv, maxprocs, info, root, comm, intercomm,
                array_of_errcodes, ierror)
                character*(*) command, argv(*)
                integer info, maxprocs, root, comm, intercomm, array_of_errcodes(*),
                    ierror

**MPI_COMM_GET_PARENT**(parent, ierror)
                integer parent, ierror


C++ **routines.**
**Request MPI::Comm::Isend**(const void* buf, int count,
                const Datatype& datatype, int dest, int tag) const

**Request MPI::Comm::Irecv**(void* buf, int count, const Datatype& datatype,
                int source, int tag) const

**void MPI::Request::Wait**(Status& status)

**void MPI::Request::Wait**()

**bool MPI::Request::Test**(Status& status)

**bool MPI::Request::Test**()

**void MPI::Request::Waitall**(int count, Request array_of_requests[],
                Status array_of_statuses[])

**void MPI::Request::Waitall**(int count, Request array_of_requests[])

**MPI::Win MPI::Win::Create**(const void* base, Aint size, int disp_unit,
                const Info& info, const Intracomm& comm)

**void MPI::Win::Free**()

**void MPI::Win::Put**(const void* origin_addr, int
                origin_count, const Datatype& origin_datatype, int target_rank, Aint
                target_disp, int target_count, const Datatype& target_datatype) const

**void MPI::Win::Get**(void *origin_addr, int
                origin_count, const MPI::Datatype& origin_datatype, int target_rank,
                MPI::Aint target_disp, int target_count,
                const MPI::Datatype& target_datatype) const

**void MPI::Win::Fence**(int assert) const

**MPI::File MPI::File::Open**(const MPI::Intracomm& comm, const char* filename,
  int amode, const MPI::Info& info)

**MPI::Offset MPI::File::Get_size** const

**void MPI::File::Set_view**(MPI::Offset disp, const MPI::Datatype& etype,
  const MPI::Datatype& filetype, const char* datarep,
  const MPI::Info& info)

**void MPI::File::Read**(void* buf, int count, const MPI::Datatype& datatype,
  MPI::Status& status)

**void MPI::File::Read**(void* buf, int count, const MPI::Datatype& datatype)

**void MPI::File::Write**(void* buf, int count, const MPI::Datatype& datatype,
  MPI::Status& status)

**void MPI::File::Write**(void* buf, int count, const MPI::Datatype& datatype)

**void MPI::File::Read_all**(void* buf, int count, const MPI::Datatype& datatype,
  MPI::Status& status)

**void MPI::File::Read_all**(void* buf, int count, const MPI::Datatype& datatype)

**void MPI::File::Write_all**(const void* buf, int count,
  const MPI::Datatype& datatype, MPI::Status& status)

**void MPI::File::Write_all**(const void* buf, int count, const MPI::Datatype& datatype)

**void MPI::File::Close**

**MPI::Intercomm MPI::Intracomm::Spawn**(const char* command,
  const char* argv[], int maxprocs, const MPI::Info& info, int root,
  int array_of_errcodes[]) const

**MPI::Intercomm MPI::Intracomm::Spawn**(const char* command,
  const char* argv[], int maxprocs, const MPI::Info& info, int root) const

**MPI::Intercomm MPI::Comm::Get_parent**()

# 11 Parallel Programming with PVM

*Al Geist and Stephen Scott*

PVM (Parallel Virtual Machine) is an outgrowth of an ongoing computing research project involving Oak Ridge National Laboratory, the University of Tennessee, and Emory University. The general goals of this project are to investigate issues in, and develop solutions for, heterogeneous concurrent computing. PVM is an integrated set of software tools and libraries that emulates a general-purpose, flexible, heterogeneous parallel computing framework on interconnected computers of varied architecture. The overall objective of the PVM system is to enable such a collection of computers to be used cooperatively for a concurrent or parallel computation. This chapter provides detailed descriptions and discussions of the concepts, logistics, and methodologies involved in programming with PVM.

## 11.1 Overview

PVM is based on the following principles:

- **User-configured host pool:** The application's computational tasks execute on a set of machines that are selected by the user for a given run of the PVM program. Both single-CPU machines and hardware multiprocessors (including shared-memory and distributed-memory computers) may be part of the host pool. The host pool may be altered by adding and deleting machines during operation (an important feature for fault tolerance). When PVM is used on Beowulf clusters, the nodes make up the host pool.
- **Translucent access to hardware:** Application programs may view the hardware environment as an attributeless collection of virtual processing elements or may exploit the capabilities of specific machines in the host pool by positioning certain computational tasks on the most appropriate computers.
- **Process-based computation:** The unit of parallelism in PVM is a task, an independent sequential thread of control that has communication and computation capabilities. No process-to-processor mapping is implied or enforced by PVM; in particular, multiple tasks may execute on a single processor.
- **Explicit message-passing model:** Collections of computational tasks, each performing a part of an application's workload, cooperate by explicitly sending to and receiving messages from one another. PVM dynamically allocates space for message buffers so message size is limited only by the amount of available memory.
- **Heterogeneity support:** The PVM system supports heterogeneity in terms of machines, networks, and applications. With regard to message passing, PVM

permits messages containing more than one datatype to be exchanged between machines having different data representations.

• **Multiprocessor support:** PVM uses the native message-passing facilities on multiprocessors to take advantage of the underlying hardware. For example, on the IBM SP, PVM transparently uses IBM's MPI to move data. On the SGI Origin, PVM uses shared memory to move data.

The PVM system is composed of two parts. The first part is a daemon, called `pvmd3` and sometimes abbreviated `pvmd`, that resides on all the computers making up the virtual machine. (An example of a daemon program is the mail program that runs in the background and handles all the incoming and outgoing electronic mail on a computer.) The daemon `pvmd3` is designed so any user with a valid login can install this daemon on a machine. To run a PVM application, you first create a virtual machine by starting up PVM (Section 11.7.2 details how this is done). You can then start the PVM application on any of the hosts. Multiple users can configure virtual machines that overlap the same cluster nodes, and each user can execute several PVM applications simultaneously.

The second part of the system is a library of PVM interface routines. It contains a functionally complete repertoire of primitives that are needed for cooperation between tasks of an application. This library contains user-callable routines for message passing, spawning processes, coordinating tasks, and modifying the virtual machine.

The PVM computing model is based on the notion that an application consists of several tasks each responsible for a part of the application's computational workload. Sometimes an application is parallelized along its functions. That is, each task performs a different function, for example, input, problem setup, solution, output, or display. This is often called functional parallelism. A more common method of parallelizing an application is called data parallelism. In this method all the tasks are the same, but each one knows and solves only a small part of the data. This is also referred to as the SPMD (single program, multiple data) model of computing. PVM supports either or a mixture of both these methods. Depending on their functions, tasks may execute in parallel and may need to synchronize or exchange data.

The PVM system currently supports C, C++, and Fortran languages. These language interfaces have been included based on the observation that the predominant majority of target applications are written in C and Fortran, with an emerging trend in experimenting with object-based languages and methodologies. Third-party groups have created freely available Java, Perl, Python, and IDL interfaces to PVM.

The C and C++ language bindings for the PVM user interface library are implemented as functions, following the general conventions used by most C systems. To elaborate, function arguments are a combination of value parameters and pointers as appropriate, and function result values indicate the outcome of the call. In addition, macro definitions are used for system constants, and global variables such as errno and pvm_errno are the mechanism for discriminating between multiple possible outcomes. Application programs written in C and C++ access PVM library functions by linking against an archival library (libpvm3.a) that is part of the standard distribution.

Fortran language bindings are implemented as subroutines rather than as functions. This approach was taken because some compilers on the supported architectures would not reliably interface Fortran functions with C functions. One immediate implication of this is that an additional argument is introduced into each PVM library call for status results to be returned to the invoking program. Another difference is that library routines for the placement and retrieval of typed data in message buffers are unified, with an additional parameter indicating the datatype. Apart from these differences (and the standard naming prefixes $pvm\_$ for C, and $pvmf$ for Fortran), a one-to-one correspondence exists between the two language bindings. Fortran interfaces to PVM are implemented as library stubs that in turn invoke the corresponding C routines, after casting and/or dereferencing arguments as appropriate. Thus, Fortran applications are required to link against the stubs library (libfpvm3.a) as well as the C library.

All PVM tasks are identified by an integer task identifier *tid*. Messages are sent to tids and received from tids. Since tids must be unique across the entire virtual machine, they are supplied by the local pvmd and are not user chosen. Although PVM encodes information into each tid, the user is expected to treat the tids as opaque integer identifiers. PVM contains several routines that return tid values so that the user application can identify other tasks in the system.

In some applications it is natural to think of a *group* of tasks. And there are cases where you would like to identify your tasks by the numbers 0 to $(p - 1)$, where $p$ is the number of tasks. PVM includes the concept of user-named groups. When a task joins a group, it is assigned a unique "instance" number in that group. Instance numbers start at 0 and count up. In keeping with the PVM philosophy, the group functions are designed to be very general and transparent to the user. For example, any PVM task can join or leave any group at any time without having to inform any other task in the affected groups, groups can overlap, and tasks can broadcast messages to groups of which they are not a member. To use any of the group functions, a program must be linked with `libgpvm3.a`.

The general paradigm for application programming with PVM is as follows. You write one or more sequential programs in C, C++, or Fortran 77 that contain embedded calls to the PVM library. Each program corresponds to a task making up the application. These programs are compiled for each architecture in the host pool, and the resulting object files are placed at a location accessible from machines in the host pool. To execute an application, you typically start one copy of one task (typically the "manager" or "initiating" task) by hand from a machine within the host pool. This process subsequently starts other PVM tasks eventually resulting in a collection of active tasks that then compute locally and exchange messages with each other to solve the problem.

Note that while this scenario is typical, as many tasks as appropriate may be started manually. As mentioned earlier, tasks interact through explicit message passing, identifying each other with a system-assigned, opaque tid.

```
#include "pvm3.h"

main()
{
        int cc, tid, msgtag;
        char buf[100];

        printf("i'm t%x\n", pvm_mytid());

        cc = pvm_spawn("hello_other", (char**)0, 0, "", 1, &tid);

        if (cc == 1) {
                msgtag = 1;
                pvm_recv(tid, msgtag);
                pvm_upkstr(buf);
                printf("from t%x: %s\n", tid, buf);
        } else
                printf("can't start hello_other\n");

        pvm_exit();
}
```

**Figure 11.1**
PVM program 'hello.c'.

Shown in Figure 11.1 is the body of the PVM program 'hello.c', a simple example that illustrates the basic concepts of PVM programming. This program is intended to be invoked manually; after printing its task id (obtained with pvm_mytid()), it initiates a copy of another program called 'hello_other.c' using the pvm_spawn() function. A successful spawn causes the program to execute a blocking receive using pvm_recv. After receiving the message, the program prints the message sent by its counterpart, as well its task id; the buffer is extracted from the message using pvm_upkstr. The final pvm_exit call dissociates the program from the PVM system.

```
#include "pvm3.h"

main()
{
        int ptid, msgtag;
        char buf[100];

        ptid = pvm_parent();

        strcpy(buf, "hello, world from ");
        gethostname(buf + strlen(buf), 64);
        msgtag = 1;
        pvm_initsend(PvmDataDefault);
        pvm_pkstr(buf);
        pvm_send(ptid, msgtag);

        pvm_exit();
}
```

**Figure 11.2**
PVM program 'hello_other.c'.

Figure 11.2 is a listing of the "slave," or spawned program; its first PVM action is to obtain the task id of the "master" using the pvm_parent call. This program then obtains its hostname and transmits it to the master using the three-call sequence: pvm_initsend to initialize the (transparent) send buffer; pvm_pkstr to place a string in a strongly typed and architecture independent manner into the send buffer; and pvm_send to transmit it to the destination process specified by *ptid*, "tagging" the message with the number 1.

## 11.2   Program Examples

In this section we discuss several complete PVM programs in detail. The first example, forkjoin.c, shows how to spawn off processes and synchronize with them. We then discuss a Fortran dot product program PSDOT.F and a matrix multiply example. Lastly, we show how PVM can be used to compute heat diffusion through a wire.

## 11.3   Fork/Join

The fork/join example demonstrates how to spawn off PVM tasks and synchronize with them. The program spawns several tasks, three by default. The children then synchronize by sending a message to their parent task. The parent receives a message from each of the spawned tasks and prints out information about the message from the child tasks.

This program contains the code for both the parent and the child tasks. Let's examine it in more detail. The very first thing the program does is call pvm_mytid(). In fork/join we check the value of mytid; if it is negative, indicating an error, we call pvm_perror() and exit the program. The pvm_perror() call will print a message indicating what went wrong with the last PVM call. In this case the last call was pvm_mytid(), so pvm_perror() might print a message indicating that PVM hasn't been started on this machine. The argument to pvm_perror() is a string that will be prepended to any error message printed by pvm_perror(). In this case we pass argv[0], which is the name of the program as it was typed on the command-line. The pvm_perror() function is modeled after the Unix perror() function.

Assuming we obtained a valid result for mytid, we now call pvm_parent(). The pvm_parent() function will return the tid of the task that spawned the calling task. Since we run the initial forkjoin program from a command prompt, this initial task will not have a parent; it will not have been spawned by some other PVM task but will have been started manually by the user. For the initial fork/join task the result of pvm_parent() will not be any particular task id but an error code, PvmNoParent. Thus we can distinguish the parent fork/join task from the children by checking whether the result of the pvm_parent() call is equal to PvmNoParent. If this task is the parent, then it must spawn the children. If it is not the parent, then it must send a message to the parent.

Let's examine the code executed by the parent task. The number of tasks is taken from the command-line as argv[1]. If the number of tasks is not legal then we

exit the program, calling `pvm_exit()` and then returning. The call to `pvm_exit()`
is important because it tells PVM this program will no longer be using any of the
PVM facilities. (In this case the task exits and PVM will deduce that the dead task
no longer needs its services. Regardless, it is good style to exit cleanly.) Assuming
the number of tasks is valid, fork/join will then attempt to spawn the children.

The `pvm_spawn()` call tells PVM to start `ntask` tasks named `argv[0]`. The
second parameter is the argument list given to the spawned tasks. In this case
we don't care to give the children any particular command-line arguments, so this
value is null. The third parameter to spawn, `PvmTaskDefault`, is a flag telling PVM
to spawn the tasks in the default location. Had we been interested in placing the
children on a specific machine or a machine of a particular architecture, we would
have used `PvmTaskHost` or `PvmTaskArch` for this flag and specified the host or
architecture as the fourth parameter. Since we don't care where the tasks execute,
we use `PvmTaskDefault` for the flag and `null` for the fourth parameter. Finally,
`ntask` tells `spawn` how many tasks to start, and the integer array `child` will hold
the task ids of the newly spawned children. The return value of `pvm_spawn()`
indicates how many tasks were successfully spawned. If `info` is not equal to `ntask`,
then some error occurred during the spawn. In case of an error, the error code is
placed in the task id array, child, instead of the actual task id; `forkjoin` loops over
this array and prints the task ids or any error codes. If no tasks were successfully
spawned, then the program exits.

For each child task, the parent receives a message and prints out information
about that message. The `pvm_recv()` call receives a message from any task as long
as the tag for that message is `JOINTAG`. The return value of `pvm_recv()` is an integer
indicating a message buffer. This integer can be used to find out information about
message buffers. The subsequent call to `pvm_bufinfo()` does just this; it gets the
length, tag, and task id of the sending process for the message indicated by `buf`. In
`forkjoin` the messages sent by the children contain a single integer value, the task
id of the child task. The `pvm_upkint()` call unpacks the integer from the message
into the `mydata` variable. As a sanity check, `forkjoin` tests the value of `mydata`
and the task id returned by `pvm_bufinfo()`. If the values differ, the program has
a bug, and an error message is printed. Finally, the information about the message
is printed, and the parent program exits.

The last segment of code in `forkjoin` will be executed by the child tasks. Before data is placed in a message buffer, the buffer must be initialized by calling
`pvm_initsend()`. The parameter `PvmDataDefault` indicates that PVM should do
whatever data conversion is needed to assure that the data arrives in the correct
format on the destination processor. In some cases this may result in unneces-

sary data conversions. If you are sure no data conversion will be needed since the
destination machine uses the same data format, then you can use PvmDataRaw as
a parameter to pvm_initsend(). The pvm_pkint() call places a single integer,
mytid, into the message buffer. It is important to make sure the corresponding
unpack call exactly matches the pack call. Packing an integer and unpacking it
as a float will not work correctly. There should be a one-to-one correspondence
between pack and unpack calls. Finally, the message is sent to the parent task
using a message tag of JOINTAG.

```
/*
    Fork Join Example
    Demonstrates how to spawn processes and exchange messages
*/

/* defines and prototypes for the PVM library */
#include <pvm3.h>

/* Maximum number of children this program will spawn */
#define MAXNCHILD    20
/* Tag to use for the joing message */
#define JOINTAG      11

int
main(int argc, char* argv[])
{

    /* number of tasks to spawn, use 3 as the default */
    int ntask = 3;
    /* return code from pvm calls */
    int info;
    /* my task id */
    int mytid;
    /* my parents task id */
    int myparent;
    /* children task id array */
    int child[MAXNCHILD];
    int i, mydata, buf, len, tag, tid;

    /* find out my task id number */
    mytid = pvm_mytid();

    /* check for error */
    if (mytid < 0) {
        /* print out the error */
```

```
        pvm_perror(argv[0]);
        /* exit the program */
        return -1;
        }
/* find my parent's task id number */
myparent = pvm_parent();

/* exit if there is some error other than PvmNoParent */
if ((myparent < 0) && (myparent != PvmNoParent)
    && (myparent != PvmParentNotSet)) {
    pvm_perror(argv[0]);
    pvm_exit();
    return -1;
    }

/* if i don't have a parent then i am the parent */
if (myparent == PvmNoParent || myparent == PvmParentNotSet) {
    /* find out how many tasks to spawn */
    if (argc == 2) ntask = atoi(argv[1]);

    /* make sure ntask is legal */
    if ((ntask < 1) || (ntask > MAXNCHILD)) { pvm_exit(); return 0; }

    /* spawn the child tasks */
    info = pvm_spawn(argv[0], (char**)0, PvmTaskDefault, (char*)0,
        ntask, child);
    /* print out the task ids */
    for (i = 0; i < ntask; i++)
        if (child[i] < 0) /* print the error code in decimal*/
            printf(" %d", child[i]);
        else  /* print the task id in hex */
            printf("t%x\t", child[i]);
    putchar('\n');

    /* make sure spawn succeeded */
    if (info == 0) { pvm_exit(); return -1; }

    /* only expect responses from those spawned correctly */
    ntask = info;

    for (i = 0; i < ntask; i++) {
        /* recv a message from any child process */
        buf = pvm_recv(-1, JOINTAG);
        if (buf < 0) pvm_perror("calling recv");
```

```
                info = pvm_bufinfo(buf, &len, &tag, &tid);
                if (info < 0) pvm_perror("calling pvm_bufinfo");
                info = pvm_upkint(&mydata, 1, 1);
                if (info < 0) pvm_perror("calling pvm_upkint");
                if (mydata != tid) printf("This should not happen!\n");
                printf("Length %d, Tag %d, Tid t%x\n", len, tag, tid);
                }
        pvm_exit();
        return 0;
        }

    /* i'm a child */
    info = pvm_initsend(PvmDataDefault);
    if (info < 0) {
        pvm_perror("calling pvm_initsend"); pvm_exit(); return -1;
        }
    info = pvm_pkint(&mytid, 1, 1);
    if (info < 0) {
        pvm_perror("calling pvm_pkint"); pvm_exit(); return -1;
        }
    info = pvm_send(myparent, JOINTAG);
    if (info < 0) {
        pvm_perror("calling pvm_send"); pvm_exit(); return -1;
        }
    pvm_exit();
    return 0;
}
```

Figure 11.3 shows the output of running fork/join. Notice that the order the messages were received is nondeterministic. Since the main loop of the parent processes messages on a first-come first-served basis, the order of the prints are determined simply by the time it takes messages to travel from the child tasks to the parent.

## 11.4   Dot Product

Here we show a simple Fortran program, PSDOT, for computing a dot product. The program computes the dot product of two arrays, X and Y. First PSDOT calls PVMFMYTID() and PVMFPARENT(). The PVMFPARENT call will return PVMNOPARENT if the task wasn't spawned by another PVM task. If this is the case, then PSDOT task is the master and must spawn the other worker copies of PSDOT. PSDOT then asks the user for the number of processes to use and the

```
% forkjoin
t10001c t40149  tc0037
Length 4, Tag 11, Tid t40149
Length 4, Tag 11, Tid tc0037
Length 4, Tag 11, Tid t10001c
% forkjoin 4
t10001e t10001d t4014b  tc0038
Length 4, Tag 11, Tid t4014b
Length 4, Tag 11, Tid tc0038
Length 4, Tag 11, Tid t10001d
Length 4, Tag 11, Tid t10001e
```

**Figure 11.3**
Output of fork/join program.

length of vectors to compute. Each spawned process will receive $n/nproc$ elements
of X and Y, where $n$ is the length of the vectors and $nproc$ is the number of processes
being used in the computation. If $nproc$ does not divide $n$ evenly, then the master
will compute the dot product on extra the elements. The subroutine SGENMAT
randomly generates values for X and Y. PSDOT then spawns $nproc - 1$ copies of
itself and sends each new task a part of the X and Y arrays. The message contains
the length of the subarrays in the message and the subarrays themselves. After
the master spawns the worker processes and sends out the subvectors, the master
then computes the dot-product on its portion of X and Y. The master process then
receives the other local dot products from the worker processes. Notice that the
PVMFRECV call uses a wild card ($-1$) for the task id parameter. This indicates
that a message from *any* task will satisfy the receive. Using the wild card in this
manner results in a race condition. In this case the race condition does not cause a
problem since addition is commutative. In other words, it doesn't matter in which
order we add up the partial sums from the workers. Unless one is certain that the
race will not affect the program adversely, race conditions should be avoided.

Once the master receives all the local dot products and sums them into a global
dot product, it then calculates the entire dot product locally. These two results
are then subtracted and the difference between the two values is printed. A small
difference can be expected due to the variation in floating-point roundoff errors.

If the PSDOT program is a worker, then it receives a message from the master
process containing subarrays of X and Y. It calculates the dot product of these
subarrays and sends the result back to the master process. In the interests of
brevity we do not include the SGENMAT and SDOT subroutines.

```
      PROGRAM PSDOT
*
* PSDOT performs a parallel inner (or dot) product, where the vectors
* X and Y start out on a master node, which then sets up the virtual
* machine, farms out the data and work, and sums up the local pieces
* to get a global inner product.
*
*       .. External Subroutines ..
      EXTERNAL PVMFMYTID, PVMFPARENT, PVMFSPAWN, PVMFEXIT, PVMFINITSEND
      EXTERNAL PVMFPACK, PVMFSEND, PVMFRECV, PVMFUNPACK, SGENMAT
*
*       .. External Functions ..
      INTEGER ISAMAX
      REAL SDOT
      EXTERNAL ISAMAX, SDOT
*
*       .. Intrinsic Functions ..
      INTRINSIC MOD
*
*       .. Parameters ..
      INTEGER MAXN
      PARAMETER ( MAXN = 8000 )
      INCLUDE 'fpvm3.h'
*
*       .. Scalars ..
      INTEGER N, LN, MYTID, NPROCS, IBUF, IERR
      INTEGER I, J, K
      REAL LDOT, GDOT
*
*       .. Arrays ..
      INTEGER TIDS(0:63)
      REAL X(MAXN), Y(MAXN)
*
*     Enroll in PVM and get my and the master process' task ID number
*
      CALL PVMFMYTID( MYTID )
      CALL PVMFPARENT( TIDS(0) )
*
*     If I need to spawn other processes (I am master process)
*
      IF ( TIDS(0) .EQ. PVMNOPARENT ) THEN
*
*         Get starting information
*
```

```
      WRITE(*,*) 'How many processes should participate (1-64)?'
      READ(*,*) NPROCS
      WRITE(*,2000) MAXN
      READ(*,*) N
      TIDS(0) = MYTID
      IF ( N .GT. MAXN ) THEN
         WRITE(*,*) 'N too large.  Increase parameter MAXN to run'//
     $             'this case.'
         STOP
      END IF
*
*     LN is the number of elements of the dot product to do
*     locally.  Everyone has the same number, with the master
*     getting any left over elements.  J stores the number of
*     elements rest of procs do.
*
      J = N / NPROCS
      LN = J + MOD(N, NPROCS)
      I = LN + 1
*
*     Randomly generate X and Y
*     Note: SGENMAT() routine is not provided here
*
      CALL SGENMAT( N, 1, X, N, MYTID, NPROCS, MAXN, J )
      CALL SGENMAT( N, 1, Y, N, I, N, LN, NPROCS )
*
*     Loop over all worker processes
*
      DO 10 K = 1, NPROCS-1
*
*        Spawn process and check for error
*
         CALL PVMFSPAWN( 'psdot', 0, 'anywhere', 1, TIDS(K), IERR )
         IF (IERR .NE. 1) THEN
            WRITE(*,*) 'ERROR, could not spawn process #',K,
     $                '. Dying . . .'
            CALL PVMFEXIT( IERR )
            STOP
         END IF
*
*        Send out startup info
*
         CALL PVMFINITSEND( PVMDEFAULT, IBUF )
         CALL PVMFPACK( INTEGER4, J, 1, 1, IERR )
```

```
            CALL PVMFPACK( REAL4, X(I), J, 1, IERR )
            CALL PVMFPACK( REAL4, Y(I), J, 1, IERR )
            CALL PVMFSEND( TIDS(K), 0, IERR )
            I = I + J
   10    CONTINUE
*
*        Figure master's part of dot product
*        SDOT() is part of the BLAS Library (compile with -lblas)
*
         GDOT = SDOT( LN, X, 1, Y, 1 )
*
*        Receive the local dot products, and
*        add to get the global dot product
*
         DO 20 K = 1, NPROCS-1
            CALL PVMFRECV( -1, 1, IBUF )
            CALL PVMFUNPACK( REAL4, LDOT, 1, 1, IERR )
            GDOT = GDOT + LDOT
   20    CONTINUE
*
*        Print out result
*
         WRITE(*,*) ' '
         WRITE(*,*) '<x,y> = ',GDOT
*
*        Do sequential dot product and subtract from
*        distributed dot product to get desired error estimate
*
         LDOT = SDOT( N, X, 1, Y, 1 )
         WRITE(*,*) '<x,y> : sequential dot product.  <x,y>^ : '//
     $             'distributed dot product.'
         WRITE(*,*) '| <x,y> - <x,y>^ | = ',ABS(GDOT - LDOT)
         WRITE(*,*) 'Run completed.'
*
*     If I am a worker process (i.e. spawned by master process)
*
      ELSE
*
*        Receive startup info
*
         CALL PVMFRECV( TIDS(0), 0, IBUF )
         CALL PVMFUNPACK( INTEGER4, LN, 1, 1, IERR )
         CALL PVMFUNPACK( REAL4, X, LN, 1, IERR )
         CALL PVMFUNPACK( REAL4, Y, LN, 1, IERR )
```

```
*
*          Figure local dot product and send it in to master
*
           LDOT = SDOT( LN, X, 1, Y, 1 )
           CALL PVMFINITSEND( PVMDEFAULT, IBUF )
           CALL PVMFPACK( REAL4, LDOT, 1, 1, IERR )
           CALL PVMFSEND( TIDS(0), 1, IERR )
        END IF
*
        CALL PVMFEXIT( 0 )
*
1000    FORMAT(I10,' Successfully spawned process #',I2,', TID =',I10)
2000    FORMAT('Enter the length of vectors to multiply (1 -',I7,'):')
        STOP
*
*          End program PSDOT
*
        END
```

## 11.5  Matrix Multiply

In this example we program a matrix multiply algorithm described by Fox et al. in [3]. The mmult program can be found at the end of this section. The mmult program will calculate $C = AB$ where $C$, $A$, and $B$ are all square matrices. For simplicity we assume that $m \times m$ tasks are used to calculate the solution. Each task calculates a subblock of the resulting matrix $C$. The block size and the value of $m$ are given as a command-line argument to the program. The matrices $A$ and $B$ are also stored as blocks distributed over the $m^2$ tasks. Before delving into the details of the program, let us first describe the algorithm at a high level.

In our grid of $m \times m$ tasks, each task ($t_{ij}$, where $0 \leq i, j < m$), initially contains blocks $C_{ij}$, $A_{ij}$, and $B_{ij}$. In the first step of the algorithm the tasks on the diagonal ($t_{ij}$ where $i = j$) send their block $A_{ii}$ to all the other tasks in row $i$. After the transmission of $A_{ii}$, all tasks calculate $A_{ii} \times B_{ij}$ and add the result into $C_{ij}$. In the next step, the column blocks of $B$ are rotated. That is, $t_{ij}$ sends its block of $B$ to $t_{(i-1)j}$. (Task $t_{0j}$ sends its $B$ block to $t_{(m-1)j}$). The tasks now return to the first step, $A_{i(i+1)}$ is multicast to all other tasks in row $i$, and the algorithm continues. After $m$ iterations the $C$ matrix contains $A \times B$, and the $B$ matrix has been rotated back into place.

Let us now go over the matrix multiply as it is programmed in PVM. In PVM there is no restriction on which tasks may communicate with which other tasks.

However, for this program we would like to think of the tasks as a two-dimensional conceptual torus. In order to enumerate the tasks, each task joins the group `mmult`. Group ids are used to map tasks to our torus. The first task to join a group is given the group id of zero. In the `mmult` program, the task with group id zero spawns the other tasks and sends the parameters for the matrix multiply to those tasks. The parameters are $m$ and $bklsize$, the square root of the number of blocks and the size of a block, respectively. After all the tasks have been spawned and the parameters transmitted, `pvm_barrier()` is called to make sure all the tasks have joined the group. If the barrier is not performed, later calls to `pvm_gettid()` might fail, since a task may not have yet joined the group.

After the barrier, the task ids for the other tasks are stored in the `row` in the array `myrow`. Specifically, the program calculates group ids for all the tasks in the row, and we ask PVM for the task id for the corresponding group id. Next the program allocates the blocks for the matrices using `malloc()`. (In an actual application program we would expect that the matrices would already be allocated.) Then the program calculates the row and column of the block of $C$ it will be computing; this is based on the value of the group id. The group ids range from 0 to $m - 1$ inclusive. Thus, the integer division of $(mygid/m)$ will give the task's row and $(mygid \bmod m)$ will give the column if we assume a row major mapping of group ids to tasks. Using a similar mapping, we calculate the group id of the task directly *above* and *below* in the torus and store their task ids in `up` and `down`, respectively.

Next the blocks are initialized by calling `InitBlock()`. This function simply initializes $A$ to random values, $B$ to the identity matrix, and $C$ to zeros. This will allow us to verify the computation at the end of the program by checking that $A = C$.

Finally we enter the main loop to calculate the matrix multiply. First the tasks on the diagonal multicast their block of A to the other tasks in their row. Note that the array `myrow` actually contains the task id of the task doing the multicast. Recall that `pvm_mcast()` will send to all the tasks in the tasks array except the calling task. This works well in the case of `mmult`, since we don't want to have to needlessly handle the extra message coming into the multicasting task with an extra `pvm_recv()`. Both the multicasting task and the tasks receiving the block calculate the $AB$ for the diagonal block and the block of $B$ residing in the task.

After the subblocks have been multiplied and added into the $C$ block, we now shift the $B$ blocks vertically. This is done by packing the block of $B$ into a message and sending it to the `up` task id and then receiving a new $B$ block from the `down` task id.

Note that we use different message tags for sending the $A$ blocks and the $B$ blocks as well as for different iterations of the loop. We also fully specify the task ids when doing a `pvm_recv()`. It's tempting to use wild cards for the fields of `pvm_recv()`; however, such use can be dangerous. For instance, had we incorrectly calculated the value for `up` and used a wild card for the `pvm_recv()` instead of `down`, it is possible that we would be sending messages to the wrong tasks without knowing it. In this example we fully specify messages, thereby reducing the possibility of receiving a message from the wrong task or the wrong phase of the algorithm.

Once the computation is complete, we check to see that $A = C$ just to verify that the matrix multiply correctly calculated the values of $C$. This step would not be done in a matrix multiply library routine, for example.

You do not have to call `pvm_lvgroup()` because PVM will realize that the task has exited and will remove it from the group. It is good form, however, to leave the group before calling `pvm_exit()`. The reset command from the PVM console will reset all the PVM groups. The `pvm_gstat` command will print the status of any groups that currently exist.

```
/*
    Matrix Multiply
*/

/* defines and prototypes for the PVM library */
#include <pvm3.h>
#include <stdio.h>

/* Maximum number of children this program will spawn */
#define MAXNTIDS    100
#define MAXROW      10

/* Message tags */
#define ATAG        2
#define BTAG        3
#define DIMTAG      5

void
InitBlock(float *a, float *b, float *c, int blk, int row, int col)
{
    int len, ind;
    int i,j;

    srand(pvm_mytid());
    len = blk*blk;
```

```
    for (ind = 0; ind < len; ind++)
        { a[ind] = (float)(rand()%1000)/100.0; c[ind] = 0.0; }
    for (i = 0; i < blk; i++) {
        for (j = 0; j < blk; j++) {
            if (row == col)
                b[j*blk+i] = (i==j)? 1.0 : 0.0;
            else
                b[j*blk+i] = 0.0;
        }
    }
}

void
BlockMult(float* c, float* a, float* b, int blk)
{
    int i,j,k;

    for (i = 0; i < blk; i++)
        for (j = 0; j < blk; j ++)
            for (k = 0; k < blk; k++)
                c[i*blk+j] += (a[i*blk+k] * b[k*blk+j]);
}

int
main(int argc, char* argv[])
{

    /* number of tasks to spawn, use 3 as the default */
    int ntask = 2;
    /* return code from pvm calls */
    int info;
    /* my task and group id */
    int mytid, mygid;
    /* children task id array */
    int child[MAXNTIDS-1];
    int i, m, blksize;
    /* array of the tids in my row */
    int myrow[MAXROW];
    float *a, *b, *c, *atmp;
    int row, col, up, down;

    /* find out my task id number */
    mytid = pvm_mytid();
    pvm_setopt(PvmRoute, PvmRouteDirect);
```

```
/* check for error */
if (mytid < 0) {
    /* print out the error */
    pvm_perror(argv[0]);
    /* exit the program */
    return -1;
    }

/* join the mmult group */
mygid = pvm_joingroup("mmult");
if (mygid < 0) {
    pvm_perror(argv[0]); pvm_exit(); return -1;
    }

/* if my group id is 0 then I must spawn the other tasks */
if (mygid == 0) {
    /* find out how many tasks to spawn */
    if (argc == 3) {
        m = atoi(argv[1]);
        blksize = atoi(argv[2]);
        }
    if (argc < 3) {
        fprintf(stderr, "usage: mmult m blk\n");
        pvm_lvgroup("mmult"); pvm_exit(); return -1;
        }

    /* make sure ntask is legal */
    ntask = m*m;
    if ((ntask < 1) || (ntask >= MAXNTIDS)) {
        fprintf(stderr, "ntask = %d not valid.\n", ntask);
        pvm_lvgroup("mmult"); pvm_exit(); return -1;
        }
    /* no need to spawn if there is only one task */
    if (ntask == 1) goto barrier;

    /* spawn the child tasks */
    info = pvm_spawn("mmult", (char**)0, PvmTaskDefault, (char*)0,
        ntask-1, child);

    /* make sure spawn succeeded */
    if (info != ntask-1) {
        pvm_lvgroup("mmult"); pvm_exit(); return -1;
        }
```

```
        /* send the matrix dimension */
        pvm_initsend(PvmDataDefault);
        pvm_pkint(&m, 1, 1);
        pvm_pkint(&blksize, 1, 1);
        pvm_mcast(child, ntask-1, DIMTAG);
        }
    else {
        /* recv the matrix dimension */
        pvm_recv(pvm_gettid("mmult", 0), DIMTAG);
        pvm_upkint(&m, 1, 1);
        pvm_upkint(&blksize, 1, 1);
        ntask = m*m;
        }

    /* make sure all tasks have joined the group */

    info = pvm_barrier("mmult",ntask);
    if (info < 0) pvm_perror(argv[0]);

    /* find the tids in my row */
    for (i = 0; i < m; i++)
        myrow[i] = pvm_gettid("mmult", (mygid/m)*m + i);

    /* allocate the memory for the local blocks */
    a = (float*)malloc(sizeof(float)*blksize*blksize);
    b = (float*)malloc(sizeof(float)*blksize*blksize);
    c = (float*)malloc(sizeof(float)*blksize*blksize);
    atmp = (float*)malloc(sizeof(float)*blksize*blksize);
    /* check for valid pointers */
    if (!(a && b && c && atmp)) {
        fprintf(stderr, "%s: out of memory!\n", argv[0]);
        free(a); free(b); free(c); free(atmp);
        pvm_lvgroup("mmult"); pvm_exit(); return -1;
        }

    /* find my block's row and column */
    row = mygid/m; col = mygid % m;
    /* calculate the neighbor's above and below */
    up = pvm_gettid("mmult", ((row)?(row-1):(m-1))*m+col);
    down = pvm_gettid("mmult", ((row == (m-1))?col:(row+1)*m+col));

    /* initialize the blocks */
    InitBlock(a, b, c, blksize, row, col);
```

```
    /* do the matrix multiply */
    for (i = 0; i < m; i++) {
        /* mcast the block of matrix A */
        if (col == (row + i)%m) {
            pvm_initsend(PvmDataDefault);
            pvm_pkfloat(a, blksize*blksize, 1);
            pvm_mcast(myrow, m, (i+1)*ATAG);
            BlockMult(c,a,b,blksize);
            }
        else {
            pvm_recv(pvm_gettid("mmult", row*m + (row +i)%m), (i+1)*ATAG);
            pvm_upkfloat(atmp, blksize*blksize, 1);
            BlockMult(c,atmp,b,blksize);
            }
        /* rotate the columns of B */
        pvm_initsend(PvmDataDefault);
        pvm_pkfloat(b, blksize*blksize, 1);
        pvm_send(up, (i+1)*BTAG);
        pvm_recv(down, (i+1)*BTAG);
        pvm_upkfloat(b, blksize*blksize, 1);
        }

    /* check it */
    for (i = 0 ; i < blksize*blksize; i++)
        if (a[i] != c[i])
            printf("Error a[%d] (%g) != c[%d] (%g) \n", i, a[i],i,c[i]);

    printf("Done.\n");
    free(a); free(b); free(c); free(atmp);
    pvm_lvgroup("mmult");
    pvm_exit();
    return 0;
}
```

## 11.6   One-Dimensional Heat Equation

Here we present a PVM program that calculates heat diffusion through a substrate, in this case a wire. Consider the one-dimensional heat equation on a thin wire:

$$\frac{\partial A}{\partial t} = \frac{\partial^2 A}{\partial x^2} \qquad\qquad (11.6.1)$$

and a discretization of the form

$$\frac{A_{i+1,j} - A_{i,j}}{\triangle t} = \frac{A_{i,j+1} - 2A_{i,j} + A_{i,j-1}}{\triangle x^2}, \tag{11.6.2}$$

giving the explicit formula

$$A_{i+1,j} = A_{i,j} + \frac{\triangle t}{\triangle x^2}(A_{i,j+1} - 2A_{i,j} + A_{i,j-1}). \tag{11.6.3}$$

The initial and boundary conditions are

$A(t,0) = 0$, $A(t,1) = 0$ for all $t$
$A(0,x) = \sin(\pi x)$ for $0 \leq x \leq 1$.
The pseudocode for this computation is as follows:

```
for i = 1:tsteps-1;
    t = t+dt;
    a(i+1,1)=0;
    a(i+1,n+2)=0;
    for j = 2:n+1;
        a(i+1,j)=a(i,j) + mu*(a(i,j+1)-2*a(i,j)+a(i,j-1));
    end;
end
```

For this example we use a master/worker programming model. The master, heat.c, spawns five copies of the program heatslv. The workers compute the heat diffusion for subsections of the wire in parallel. At each time step the workers exchange boundary information, in this case the temperature of the wire at the boundaries between processors.

Let's take a closer look at the code. In heat.c the array solution will hold the solution for the heat diffusion equation at each time step. First the heatslv tasks are spawned. Next, the initial dataset is computed. Notice the ends of the wires are given initial temperature values of zero.

The main part of the program is then executed four times, each with a different value for $\triangle t$. A timer is used to compute the elapsed time of each compute phase. The initial datasets are sent to the heatslv tasks. The left and right neighbor task ids are sent along with the initial dataset. The heatslv tasks use these to communicate boundary information. Alternatively, we could have used the PVM group calls to map tasks to segments of the wire. By using this approach we would have avoided explicitly communicating the task ids to the slave processes.

After sending the initial data, the master process waits for results. When the results arrive, they are integrated into the solution matrix, the elapsed time is calculated, and the solution is written to the output file.

Once the data for all four phases have been computed and stored, the master program prints out the elapsed times and kills the slave processes.

```
/*
heat.c

    Use PVM to solve a simple heat diffusion differential equation,
    using 1 master program and 5 slaves.

    The master program sets up the data, communicates it to the slaves
    and waits for the results to be sent from the slaves.
    Produces xgraph ready files of the results.

*/

#include "pvm3.h"
#include <stdio.h>
#include <math.h>
#include <time.h>
#define SLAVENAME "heatslv"
#define NPROC 5
#define TIMESTEP 100
#define PLOTINC 10
#define SIZE 1000

int num_data = SIZE/NPROC;

main()
{   int mytid, task_ids[NPROC], i, j;
    int left, right, k, l;
    int step = TIMESTEP;
    int info;

    double init[SIZE], solution[TIMESTEP][SIZE];
    double result[TIMESTEP*SIZE/NPROC], deltax2;
    FILE *filenum;
    char *filename[4][7];
    double deltat[4];
    time_t t0;
    int etime[4];
```

```
    filename[0][0] = "graph1";
    filename[1][0] = "graph2";
    filename[2][0] = "graph3";
    filename[3][0] = "graph4";

    deltat[0] = 5.0e-1;
    deltat[1] = 5.0e-3;
    deltat[2] = 5.0e-6;
    deltat[3] = 5.0e-9;

/* enroll in pvm */
    mytid = pvm_mytid();

/* spawn the slave tasks */
    info = pvm_spawn(SLAVENAME,(char **)0,PvmTaskDefault,"",
        NPROC,task_ids);
/* create the initial data set */
    for (i = 0; i < SIZE; i++)
        init[i] = sin(M_PI * ( (double)i / (double)(SIZE-1) ));
    init[0] = 0.0;
    init[SIZE-1] = 0.0;

/* run the problem 4 times for different values of delta t */
    for (l = 0; l < 4; l++) {
        deltax2 = (deltat[l]/pow(1.0/(double)SIZE,2.0));
        /* start timing for this run */
        time(&t0);
        etime[l] = t0;
/* send the initial data to the slaves. */
/* include neighbor info for exchanging boundary data */
        for (i = 0; i < NPROC; i++) {
            pvm_initsend(PvmDataDefault);
            left = (i == 0) ? 0 : task_ids[i-1];
            pvm_pkint(&left, 1, 1);
            right = (i == (NPROC-1)) ? 0 : task_ids[i+1];
            pvm_pkint(&right, 1, 1);
            pvm_pkint(&step, 1, 1);
            pvm_pkdouble(&deltax2, 1, 1);
            pvm_pkint(&num_data, 1, 1);
            pvm_pkdouble(&init[num_data*i], num_data, 1);
            pvm_send(task_ids[i], 4);
            }

/* wait for the results */
```

```
        for (i = 0; i < NPROC; i++) {
            pvm_recv(task_ids[i], 7);
            pvm_upkdouble(&result[0], num_data*TIMESTEP, 1);
/* update the solution */
            for (j = 0; j < TIMESTEP; j++)
                for (k = 0; k < num_data; k++)
                    solution[j][num_data*i+k] = result[wh(j,k)];
            }

/* stop timing */
        time(&t0);
        etime[1] = t0 - etime[1];

/* produce the output */
        filenum = fopen(filename[1][0], "w");
        fprintf(filenum,"TitleText: Wire Heat over Delta Time: %e\n",
            deltat[1]);
        fprintf(filenum,"XUnitText: Distance\nYUnitText: Heat\n");
        for (i = 0; i < TIMESTEP; i = i + PLOTINC) {
            fprintf(filenum,"\"Time index: %d\n",i);
            for (j = 0; j < SIZE; j++)
                fprintf(filenum,"%d %e\n",j, solution[i][j]);
            fprintf(filenum,"\n");
            }
        fclose (filenum);
    }

/* print the timing information */
    printf("Problem size: %d\n",SIZE);
    for (i = 0; i < 4; i++)
        printf("Time for run %d: %d sec\n",i,etime[i]);

/* kill the slave processes */
    for (i = 0; i < NPROC; i++) pvm_kill(task_ids[i]);
    pvm_exit();
}

int wh(x, y)
int x, y;
{
    return(x*num_data+y);
}
```

The heatslv programs do the actual computation of the heat diffusion through the wire. The worker program consists of an infinite loop that receives an initial

dataset, iteratively computes a solution based on this dataset (exchanging boundary information with neighbors on each iteration), and sends the resulting partial
solution back to the master process. As an alternative to using an infinite loop in
the worker tasks, we could send a special message to the slave ordering it to exit.
Instead, we simply use the infinite loop in the worker tasks and kill them off from
the master program. A third option would be to have the workers execute only
once, exiting after processing a single dataset from the master. This would require
placing the master's spawn call inside the main `for` loop of `heat.c`. While this
option would work, it would needlessly add overhead to the overall computation.

For each time step and before each compute phase, the boundary values of the
temperature matrix are exchanged. The left-hand boundary elements are first sent
to the left neighbor task and received from the right neighbor task. Symmetrically,
the right-hand boundary elements are sent to the right neighbor and then received
from the left neighbor. The task ids for the neighbors are checked to make sure no
attempt is made to send or receive messages to nonexistent tasks.

```
/*

heatslv.c

    The slaves receive the initial data from the host,
    exchange boundary information with neighbors,
    and calculate the heat change in the wire.
    This is done for a number of iterations, sent by the master.

*/

#include "pvm3.h"
#include <stdio.h>

int num_data;

main()
{
    int mytid, left, right, i, j, master;
    int timestep;

    double *init, *A;
    double leftdata, rightdata, delta, leftside, rightside;

/* enroll in pvm */
    mytid = pvm_mytid();
```

```
      master = pvm_parent();

/* receive my data from the master program */
  while(1) {
    pvm_recv(master, 4);
    pvm_upkint(&left, 1, 1);
    pvm_upkint(&right, 1, 1);
    pvm_upkint(&timestep, 1, 1);
    pvm_upkdouble(&delta, 1, 1);
    pvm_upkint(&num_data, 1, 1);
    init = (double *) malloc(num_data*sizeof(double));
    pvm_upkdouble(init, num_data, 1);

/* copy the initial data into my working array */

    A = (double *) malloc(num_data * timestep * sizeof(double));
    for (i = 0; i < num_data; i++) A[i] = init[i];

/* perform the calculation */

  for (i = 0; i < timestep-1; i++) {
    /* trade boundary info with my neighbors */
    /*  send left, receive right     */
    if (left != 0) {
        pvm_initsend(PvmDataDefault);
        pvm_pkdouble(&A[wh(i,0)],1,1);
        pvm_send(left, 5);
        }
    if (right != 0) {
        pvm_recv(right, 5);
        pvm_upkdouble(&rightdata, 1, 1);
    /* send right, receive left */
        pvm_initsend(PvmDataDefault);
        pvm_pkdouble(&A[wh(i,num_data-1)],1,1);
        pvm_send(right, 6);
        }
    if (left != 0) {
        pvm_recv(left, 6);
        pvm_upkdouble(&leftdata,1,1);
        }

/* do the calculations for this iteration */

    for (j = 0; j < num_data; j++) {
```

```
        leftside = (j == 0) ? leftdata : A[wh(i,j-1)];
        rightside = (j == (num_data-1)) ? rightdata : A[wh(i,j+1)];
        if ((j==0)&&(left==0))
            A[wh(i+1,j)] = 0.0;
        else if ((j==(num_data-1))&&(right==0))
            A[wh(i+1,j)] = 0.0;
        else
            A[wh(i+1,j)]=
                A[wh(i,j)]+delta*(rightside-2*A[wh(i,j)]+leftside);
        }
    }

/* send the results back to the master program */

    pvm_initsend(PvmDataDefault);
    pvm_pkdouble(&A[0],num_data*timestep,1);
    pvm_send(master,7);
    }

/* just for good measure */
    pvm_exit();
}

int wh(x, y)
int x, y;
{
    return(x*num_data+y);
}
```

In this section we have given a variety of example programs written in both Fortran and C. These examples demonstrate various ways of writing PVM programs. Some divide the application into two separate programs while others use a single program with conditionals to handle spawning and computing phases. These examples show different styles of communication, both among worker tasks and between worker and master tasks. In some cases messages are used for synchronization, and in others the master processes simply kill of the workers when they are no longer needed. We hope that these examples will help you understand how to write better PVM programs and to evaluate the design tradeoffs involved.

## 11.7   Using PVM

This section describes how to set up the PVM software package, how to configure a simple virtual machine, and how to compile and run the example programs supplied with PVM. The first part describes the straightforward use of PVM and the most common problems in setting up and running PVM. The latter part describes some of the more advanced options available for customizing your PVM environment.

### 11.7.1   Setting Up PVM

One of the reasons for PVM's popularity is that it is simple to set up and use.

PVM must be installed by a user with Administrator access. It then can be made available to all users of the machine providing the Administrator has not restricted access to any of the PVM installed files.

The Windows version of PVM is distributed as a WinZip file that contains an `InstallShield` self-extracting executable. Compilers to be used with PVM should already be installed, since the PVM installation process will confirm compiler location and configuration. With this basic information, a user can successfully install PVM by simply clicking *Next* throughout the installation process. One option in the Windows installation process asks whether this is a server or a client installation. For a Windows-based cluster there must be at least one server installation of PVM. This is because a server installation includes all PVM sources and libraries, while a client installation points to a server installation from which it may access the appropriate PVM programs. Of course it is acceptable to do server installations for all nodes of the cluster and thus avoid the need and associated cost of the clients accessing programs via the network during run time.

By default, the installation will put the PVM system in the directory `C:\Program Files\PVM3.4`. (A *Browse* button is available, however, if you wish to specify an alternative location. Select *Next* to continue on to select the location for PVM to use for temporary runtime files. The most common location is `C:\TEMP`. Enter this location, and press *Next* to continue to the Setup Type screen. Selecting the *Typical* installation will ensure that a complete installation is performed. Press *Next* to continue to the C compiler specification screen. Select the C compiler choice from the screen, and press *Next* to continue. If *None* is selected, the Fortran compiler specification screen will be next. If an installed compiler is selected, the destination screen appearing next will contain the correct location for the compiler's `include` and `lib` directories. Press *Next* to continue to the Fortran compiler specification screen. If a compiler is selected that is not installed, you will be given a warning message and asked for the location where the compiler's `include` and `lib` directories are located. Enter this information, and press *Next* to continue to the Fortran compiler specification screen.

The Fortran compiler specification is similar to the C selection above. The installation adds program icons to the appropriate program folder. Simply accept the default, `PVM 3.4`, and press *Next* to continue. The screen displays the current settings just selected. When you press *Next*, the InstallShield process begins copying files and displays the progress on the status bar. This may take a minute or two depending on system performance. When file copying is finished, you will be notified that PVM registry values are going to be added to the system. Press *OK* to continue. If there is not enough space to build PVM, you will be asked whether it is ok to increase environment space in `CONFIG.SYS`. Press *Yes* to continue. The next screen states that the setup is complete and provides the options to view the ReadMe and Help files and to start the PVM daemon process on this machine. These can be skipped for now, since both can be done later. Press *Finish* to proceed to the final setup screen. The machine must reboot before PVM is ready for use.

**Windows Networking Files.** `LMHOSTS` and `HOSTS` both are files used by the Microsoft TCP/IP for Windows. These two files contain cluster node names and IP information so that Windows networking may locally resolve machine and host names. Both files are located in the `C:\WINNT\system32\drivers\etc` directory. Sample files are placed in this location when a Windows system is first built. The sample files contain additional information regarding instruction options. Only those necessary for the PVM installation will be discussed here.

`LMHOSTS` contains mappings of IP addresses to computer names. Each entry is on an individual line, with the IP address followed by the corresponding computer name and then `#PRE`, which causes the entry to be preloaded into the name cache. There must be at least one blank space between each entry on a line.

```
# Filename: LMHOSTS
134.123.10.30     node1     #PRE
134.123.10.31     node2     #PRE
134.123.10.32     node3     #PRE
134.123.10.33     node4     #PRE
```

`HOSTS` contains the mappings of IP addresses to hostnames. Each entry is on an individual line, with the IP address in the first column followed by the corresponding hostname. There must be at least one blank space between each entry on a line.

```
# Filename: HOSTS
```

```
134.123.10.30      node1.epm.ornl.org
134.123.10.31      node2.epm.ornl.org
134.123.10.32      node3.epm.ornl.org
134.123.10.33      node4.epm.ornl.org
```

**Other Required Software.** While it is possible to run PVM programs on a single machine without the need for any additional software, most people use PVM to run parallel applications across multiple Windows machines. To do this requires an RSH or SSH package that will enable remote machine access. Two commercial RSH packages have been tested with PVM: the Ataman package from `www.ataman.com` and Winrshd from `www.winrshd.com`.

### 11.7.2   Starting PVM

Before we go over the steps to compile and run parallel PVM programs, you should be sure you can start up PVM and configure a virtual machine. On any host on which PVM has been installed you can type

```
> pvm
```

and you should get back a PVM console prompt signifying that PVM is now running on this host. You can add hosts to your virtual machine by typing at the console prompt

```
pvm> add hostname
```

You also can delete hosts (except the one you are on) from your virtual machine by typing

```
pvm> delete hostname
```

If you get the message "Can't Start `pvmd`," PVM will run autodiagnostics and report the reason found.

To see what the present virtual machine looks like, you can type

```
pvm> conf
```

To see what PVM tasks are running on the virtual machine, you type

```
pvm> ps -a
```

Of course, you don't have any tasks running yet. If you type "quit" at the console prompt, the console will quit, but your virtual machine and tasks will continue to run. At any command prompt on any host in the virtual machine you can type

```
> pvm
```

and you will get the message "pvm already running" and the console prompt. When you are finished with the virtual machine you should type

```
pvm> halt
```

This command kills any PVM tasks, shuts down the virtual machine, and exits the console. This is the recommended method to stop PVM because it makes sure that the virtual machine shuts down cleanly.

You should practice starting and stopping and adding hosts to PVM until you are comfortable with the PVM console. A full description of the PVM console and its many command options is given in Sections 11.8 and 11.9.

If you don't wish to type in a bunch of hostnames each time, there is a hostfile option. You can list the hostnames in a file one per line and then type

```
> pvm hostfile
```

PVM will then add all the listed hosts simultaneously before the console prompt appears. Several options can be specified on a per host basis in the hostfile; see Section 11.9 if you wish to customize your virtual machine for a particular application or environment.

PVM may also be started in other ways. The functions of the console and a performance monitor have been combined in a graphical user interface called XPVM, which is available from the PVM web site. If XPVM has been installed at your site, then it can be used to start PVM. To start PVM with this interface type:

```
> xpvm
```

The menu button labeled "hosts" will pull down a list of hosts you can add. By clicking on a hostname it is added and an icon of the machine appears in an animation of the virtual machine. A host is deleted if you click on a hostname that is already in the virtual machine. On startup XPVM reads the file $HOME\.xpvm_hosts, which is a list of hosts to display in this menu. Hosts without leading "&" are added all at once at start up.

The quit and halt buttons work just like the PVM console. If you quit XPVM and then restart it, XPVM will automatically display what the running virtual machine looks like. Practice starting and stopping and adding hosts with XPVM. If there are errors they should appear in the window where you started XPVM.

### 11.7.3   Running PVM Programs

In this section you will learn how to compile and run the example programs supplied with the PVM software. These example programs make useful templates on which to base your own PVM programs. PVM itself and all the example programs are built using the C/C++ Microsoft Visual Studio 6. The Fortran compiler used is the Compaq Fortran version 6. Since PVM's origins are from the UNIX world, PVM comes with a `make.bat` file that implements all the make file scripts necessary to build both PVM itself as well as all supplied example codes. Simply click on the `PVM Compile Shell` icon on your desktop and it will launch a `DOS` shell window with the correct paths and resources allocated for this purpose. It starts in the `$HOME\PVM3.4` directory. From here simply type `make` and it will display a selection of command-line options to do everything from removing the current PVM installation and rebuilding to doing the same for only the supplied examples. It is up to you, the user, to decide if you want to build your applications using the `make` technique or directly in the Microsoft Visual Studio style. Note that UNIX `make` files are not directly portable to the Windows environment.

From one window start up PVM and configure some hosts. These examples are designed to run on any number of hosts, including one. In another window, `cd` to the location of the PVM executables and type

```
> master
```

The program will ask about the number of tasks. This number does not have to match the number of hosts in these examples. Try several combinations.

The first example illustrates the ability to run a PVM program from a prompt on any host in the virtual machine. This is how you would run a serial `a.out` program on a workstation. Te next example, which is also a master/slave model called `hitc`, shows how to spawn PVM jobs from the PVM console and also from XPVM.

The model `hitc` illustrates dynamic load balancing using the pool of tasks paradigm. In this paradigm, the master program manages a large queue of tasks, always sending idle slave programs more work to do until the queue is empty. This paradigm is effective in situations where the hosts have very different computational powers because the least-loaded or more powerful hosts do more of the work and all the hosts stay busy until the end of the problem.

Since `hitc` does not require any user input, it can be spawned directly from the PVM console. Start the PVM console, and add a few hosts. At the PVM console prompt, type

```
pvm> spawn -> hitc
```

The "->" spawn option causes all the print statements in `hitc` and in the slaves to appear in the console window. This can be a useful feature when debugging your first few PVM programs. You may wish to experiment with this option by placing print statements in `hitc.f` and `hitc_slave.f` and recompiling.

To get an idea of XPVM's real-time animation capabilities, you again can use `hitc`. Start up XPVM, and build a virtual machine with four hosts. Click on the "tasks" button and select "spawn" from the menu. Type "hitc" where XPVM asks for the command, and click on "start". You will see the host icons light up as the machines become busy. You will see the `hitc_slave` tasks get spawned and see all the messages that travel between the tasks in the *Space Time* display. Several other views are selectable from the XPVM "views" menu. The "task output" view is equivalent to the "->" option in the PVM console. It causes the standard output from all tasks to appear in the window that pops up.

Programs that are spawned from XPVM (and the PVM console) are subject to one restriction: they must not contain any interactive input, such as asking for how many slaves to start up or how big a problem to solve. This type of information can be read from a file or put on the command-line as arguments, but there is nothing in place to get user input from the keyboard to a potentially remote task.

## 11.8   PVM Console Details

The PVM console, called `pvm`, is a standalone PVM task that allows you to interactively start, query, and modify the virtual machine. The console may be started and stopped multiple times on any of the hosts in the virtual machine without affecting PVM or any applications that may be running.

When the console is started, `pvm` determines whether PVM is already running and, if not, automatically executes `pvmd` on this host, passing `pvmd` the command-line options and hostfile. Thus, PVM need not be running to start the console.

```
pvm [-n<hostname>] [hostfile]
```

The $-n$ option is useful for specifying another name for the master `pvmd` (in case hostname doesn't match the IP address you want). This feature becomes very useful with Beowulf clusters because the nodes of the cluster sometime are on their own network. In this case the front-end node will have two hostnames: one for the cluster and one for the external network. The $-n$ option lets you specify the cluster name directly during PVM atartup.

Once started, the console prints the prompt

`pvm>`

and accepts commands from standard input. The available commands are as follows:

**add** followed by one or more hostnames, adds these hosts to the virtual machine.

**alias** defines or lists command aliases.

**conf** lists the configuration of the virtual machine including hostname, `pvmd` task ID, architecture type, and a relative speed rating.

**delete** followed by one or more hostnames, deletes these hosts from the virtual machine. PVM processes still running on these hosts are lost .

**echo** echoes arguments.

**halt** kills all PVM processes including console and then shuts down PVM. All daemons exit.

**help** can be used to get information about any of the interactive commands. The `help` command may be followed by a command name that will list options and flags available for this command.

**id** prints console task id.

**jobs** lists running jobs.

**kill** can be used to terminate any PVM process.

**mstat** shows status of specified hosts.

**ps -a** lists all processes currently on the virtual machine, their locations, their task IDs, and their parents' task IDs.

**pstat** shows status of a single PVM process.

**quit** exits the console, leaving daemons and PVM jobs running.

**reset** kills all PVM processes except consoles, and resets all the internal PVM tables and message queues. The daemons are left in an idle state.

**setenv** displays or sets environment variables.

**sig** followed by a signal number and tid, sends the signal to the task.

**spawn** starts a PVM application. Options include the following:

**-count** shows the number of tasks; default is 1

**-(host)** spawn on host; default is any

**-(PVM_ARCH)** spawn of hosts of type PVM_ARCH

**-?** enable debugging

**->** redirect task output to console

**->file** redirect task output to file

**->>file** redirect task output append to file

**-** trace job; display output on console

**-file** trace job; output to file

**unalias** undefines command alias.

**version** prints version of PVM being used.

PVM supports the use of multiple consoles. It is possible to run a console on any host in an existing virtual machine and even multiple consoles on the same machine. It is possible to start up a console in the middle of a PVM application and check on its progress.

## 11.9    Host File Options

As noted earlier, only one person at a site needs to install PVM, but each PVM user can have his own hostfile, which describes his personal virtual machine.

The hostfile defines the initial configuration of hosts that PVM combines into a virtual machine. It also contains information about hosts that you may wish to add to the configuration later.

The hostfile in its simplest form is just a list of hostnames one to a line. Blank lines are ignored, and lines that begin with a # are comment lines. This approach allows you to document the hostfile and also provides a handy way to modify the initial configuration by commenting out various hostnames.

```
# Configuration used for my PVM run
node4
node6
node9
node10
node11
```

Several options can be specified on each line after the hostname. The options are separated by white space.

**lo= userid** allows you to specify another login name for this host; otherwise, your login name on the startup machine is used.

**so=pw** causes PVM to prompt you for a password on this host. This is useful when you have a different userid and password on a remote system. PVM uses **rsh** by default to start up remote **pvmds**, but when **pw** is specified, PVM will use **rexec()** instead.

**dx= location of pvmd** allows you to specify a location other than the default for this host. This is useful if you wish to use your own copy of **pvmd**.

**ep= paths to user executables** allows you to specify a series of paths to search down to find the requested files to spawn on this host. Multiple paths are separated by a colon.

**sp= value** specifies the relative computational speed of the host compared with other hosts in the configuration. The range of possible values is 1 to 1,000,000, with 1,000 as the default.

**bx= location of debugger** specifies which debugger script to invoke on this host if debugging is requested in the spawn routine. Note that the environment variable PVM_DEBUGGER can also be set.

**wd= working_directory** specifies a working directory in which all spawned tasks on this host will execute. The default is $HOME.

**so=ms** specifies that a slave **pvmd** will be started manually on this host. This is useful if **rsh** and **rexec** network services are disabled but IP connectivity exists. When using this option you will see the following in the **tty** of the **pvmd3**:

```
[t80040000] ready   Fri Aug 27 18:47:47 1993
*** Manual startup ***
Login to "honk" and type:
pvm3/lib/pvmd -S -d0 -nhonk 1 80a9ca95:0cb6 4096 2 80a95c43:0000
Type response:
```

On **honk**, after typing the given line, you should see

```
ddpro<2312> arch<ALPHA> ip<80a95c43:0a8e> mtu<4096>
```

which you should relay back to the master **pvmd**. At that point, you will see

> Thanks

and the two **pvmds** should be able to communicate.

If you wish to set any of the above options as defaults for a series of hosts, you can place these options on a single line with a * for the hostname field. The defaults will be in effect for all the following hosts until they are overridden by another set-defaults line.

Hosts that you don't want in the initial configuration but may add later can be specified in the hostfile by beginning those lines with an &. An example hostfile displaying most of these options is shown below.

```
# Comment lines start with a # (blank lines ignored)
gstws
ipsc dx=/usr/geist/pvm3/lib/I860/pvmd3
ibm1.scri.fsu.edu lo=gst so=pw


# set default options for following hosts with *
* ep=$sun/problem1:~/nla/mathlib
sparky
#azure.epm.ornl.gov
midnight.epm.ornl.gov


# replace default options with new values
* lo=gageist so=pw ep=problem1
thud.cs.utk.edu
speedy.cs.utk.edu


# machines for adding later are specified with &
# these only need listing if options are required
&sun4    ep=problem1
&castor  dx=/usr/local/bin/pvmd3
&dasher.cs.utk.edu lo=gageist
&elvis   dx=~/pvm3/lib/SUN4/pvmd3
```

## 11.10   XPVM

It is often useful and always reassuring to be able to see the present configuration of the virtual machine and the status of the hosts. It would be even more useful if you could also see what your program is doing—what tasks are running, where messages are being sent, and the like. The PVM GUI called XPVM was developed to display this information and more.

XPVM combines the capabilities of the PVM console, a performance monitor, and a call-level debugger in single, easy-to-use graphical user interface. XPVM is available from Netlib (`www.netlib.org`) in the directory `pvm3/xpvm`. The XPVM source is also available for compiling on other machines.

XPVM is written entirely in C using the TCL/TK toolkit and runs as just another PVM task. If you want to build XPVM from the source, you must first obtain and install the TCL/TK software on your system. TCL and TK were developed by John Ousterhout and can be obtained from `www.scriptics.com`. The TCL and XPVM source distributions each contain a README file that describes the most up-to-date installation procedure for each package, respectively.

Figure 11.4 shows a snapshot of XPVM in use.

Like the PVM console, XPVM will start PVM if it is not already running or just attach to the local `pvmd` if it is. The console can take an optional hostfile argument, whereas XPVM always reads `$HOME\.xpvm_hosts` as its hostfile. If this file does not exist, XPVM just starts PVM on the local host (or attaches to the existing PVM). In typical use, the hostfile `.xpvm_hosts` contains a list of hosts prepended with an &. These hostnames then get added to the *Hosts* menu for addition and deletion from the virtual machine by clicking on them.

The top row of buttons performs console-like functions. The *Hosts* button displays a menu of hosts. Clicking on a host toggles whether it is added or deleted from the virtual machine. At the bottom of the menu is an option for adding a host not listed. The *Tasks* button brings up a menu whose most used selection is *spawn*. Selecting spawn brings up a window where the executable name, spawn flags, starting place, number of copies to start, and so forth can be set. By default XPVM turns on tracing in all tasks (and their children) that are started inside XPVM. Clicking on *Start* in the spawn window starts the task, which will then appear in the Space-time view. The *Reset* button has a menu for resetting PVM (i.e., kill all PVM tasks) or resetting different parts of XPVM. The *Quit* button exits XPVM while leaving PVM running. If XPVM is being used to collect trace information, the information will not be collected if XPVM is stopped. The *Halt* button is to be used when you are through with PVM. Clicking on this button kills

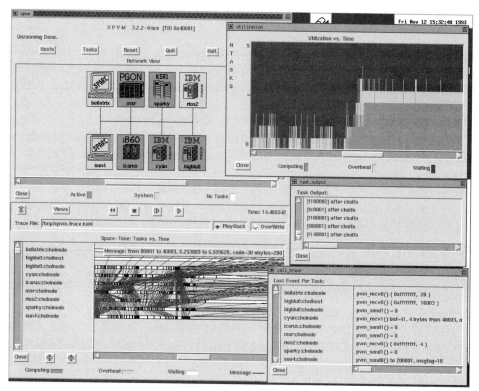

**Figure 11.4**
Snapshot of XPVM interface during use

all running PVM tasks, shuts down PVM cleanly, and exits the XPVM interface.
The *Help* button brings up a menu of topics for which information is available.

While an application is running, XPVM collects and displays the information in
real time. Although XPVM updates the views as fast as it can, there are cases
when XPVM cannot keep up with the events and falls behind the actual run time.

In the middle of the XPVM interface are tracefile controls. Here you can specify
a tracefile; a default tracefile in \tmp is initially displayed. There are buttons to
specify whether the specified tracefile is to be played back or overwritten by a
new run. XPVM saves trace events in a file using the "self-defining data format"
(SDDF) described in Dan Reed's Pablo trace displaying package (other packages
such as Pablo can be used to analyze the PVM traces).

XPVM can play back its own SDDF files. The tape playerlike buttons allow
you to rewind the tracefile, stop the display at any point, and step through the

execution. A time display specifies the number of seconds from when the trace display began.

The *Views* button allows you to open or close any of several views presently supplied with XPVM. These views are described below.

During startup, XPVM joins a group called `xpvm`. This is done so tasks that are started outside the XPVM interface can get the tid of XPVM by doing `tid = pvm_gettid( xpvm, 0 )`. This tid would be needed if you wanted to manually turn on tracing inside such a task and pass the events back to XPVM for display. The expected TraceCode for these events is 666.

### 11.10.1  Network View

The *Network* view displays the present virtual machine configuration and the activity of the hosts. Each host is represented by an icon that includes the `PVM_ARCH` and hostname inside the icon. In the current release of XPVM, the icons are arranged arbitrarily on both sides of a bus network. In future releases the view will be extended to visualize network activity as well. At that time you will be able to specify the network topology to display.

These icons are illuminated in different colors to indicate their status in executing PVM tasks. Green implies that at least one task on that host is busy executing useful work. Yellow indicates that no tasks are executing user computation but at least one task is busy executing PVM system routines. When there are no tasks on a given host, its icon is left uncolored or white. The specific colors used in each case are user customizable.

You can tell at a glance how well the virtual machine is being utilized by your PVM application. If all the hosts are green most of the time, then machine utilization is good. The Network view does not display activity due to other users' PVM jobs or other processes that may be running on the hosts.

In future releases the view will allow you to click on a multiprocessor icon and get information about the number of processors, number of PVM tasks, and the like that are running on the host.

### 11.10.2  Space-Time View

The *Space-time* view displays the activities of individual PVM tasks that are running on the virtual machine. Listed on the left-hand side of the view are the executable names of the tasks preceded by the host they are running on. The task list is sorted by host so that it is easy to see whether tasks are being clumped on one host. This list also shows the task to host mappings (which are not available in the Network view).

The Space-time view combines three different displays. The first is like a Gantt chart. Beside each listed task is a horizontal bar stretching out in the "time" direction. The color of this bar at any time indicates the state of the task. Green indicates that user computations are being executed. Yellow marks the times when the task is executing PVM routines. White indicates when a task is waiting for messages. The bar begins at the time when the task starts executing and ends when the task exits normally. The specific colors used in each case are user customizable.

The second display overlays the first display with the communication activity among tasks. When a message is sent between two tasks, a red line is drawn starting at the sending task's bar at the time the message is sent and ending at the receiving task's bar when the message is received. Note that this is not the time the message arrived, but rather the time the task called `pvm_recv()`. Visually, the patterns and slopes of the red lines combined with white "waiting" regions reveal a lot about the communication efficiency of an application.

The third display appears only when you click on interesting features of the Space-time view with the left mouse button. A small "pop-up" window appears, giving detailed information regarding specific task states or messages. If a task bar is clicked on, the state begin and end times are displayed along with the last PVM system call information. If a message line is clicked on, the window displays the send and receive time as well as the number of bytes in the message and the message tag.

When the mouse is moved inside the Space-time view, a blue vertical line tracks the cursor, and the time corresponding to this vertical line is displayed as Query time at the bottom of the display. This vertical line also appears in the other "something vs. time" views so you can correlate a feature in one view with information given in another view.

You can zoom into any area of the Space-time view by dragging the vertical line with the middle mouse button. The view will unzoom back one level when the right mouse button is clicked. Often, very fine communication or waiting states are visible only when the view is magnified with the zoom feature. As with the Query time, the other views also zoom along with the Space-time view.

### 11.10.3   Other Views

XPVM is designed to be extensible. New views can be created and added to the *Views* menu. At present, there are three other views: Utilization, Call Trace, and Task Output. Unlike the Network and Space-time views, these views are closed by default. Since XPVM attempts to draw the views in real time, the fewer open views the faster XPVM can draw.

The Utilization view shows the number of tasks computing, in overhead, or waiting for each instant. It is a summary of the Space-time view for each instant. Since the number of tasks in a PVM application can change dynamically, the scale on the Utilization view will change dynamically when tasks are added, but not when they exit. When this happens, the displayed portion of the Utilization view is completely redrawn to the new scale.

The Call Trace view provides a textual record of the last PVM call made in each task. The list of tasks is the same as in the Space-time view. As an application runs, the text changes to reflect the most recent activity in each task. This view is useful as a call-level debugger to identify where a PVM program's execution hangs.

XPVM automatically tells all tasks it spawns to redirect their standard output back to XPVM when the Task Output view is opened. This view gives you the option of redirecting the output into a file. If you type a file name in the "Task Output" box, the output is printed in the window and into the file.

As with the trace events, a task started outside XPVM can be programmed to send standard output to XPVM for display by using the options in **pvm_setopt()**. XPVM expects the OutputCode to be set to 667.

# 12 Fault-Tolerant and Adaptive Programs with PVM

*Al Geist and Jim Kohl*

The use of Beowulf clusters has expanded rapidly in the past several years. Originally created by researchers to do scientific computing, today these clusters are being used in business and commercial settings where the requirements and expectations are quite different. For example, at a large Web hosting company the reliability and robustness of their applications are often more important than their raw performance.

A number of factors must be considered when you are developing applications for Beowulf clusters. In the preceding chapters the basic methods of message passing were illustrated so that you could create your own parallel programs. This chapter describes the issues and common methods for making parallel programs that are fault tolerant and adaptive.

*Fault tolerance* is the ability of an application to continue to run or make progress even if a hardware or software problem causes a node in the cluster to fail. It is also the ability to tolerate failures within the application itself. For example, one task inside a parallel application may get an error and abort. Because Beowulf clusters are built from commodity components that are designed for the desktop rather than heavy-duty computing, failures of components inside a cluster are higher than in a more expensive multiprocessor system that has an integrated RAS (Reliability, Availability, Serviceability) system.

While fault-tolerant programs can be thought of as adaptive, the term "adaptive programs" is used here more generally to mean parallel (or serial) programs that dynamically change their characteristics to better match the application's needs and the available resources. Examples include an application that adapts by adding or releasing nodes of the cluster according to its present computational needs and an application that creates and kills tasks based on what the computation needs.

In later chapters you will learn about Condor and other resource management tools that automatically provide some measure of fault tolerance and adaptability to jobs submitted to them. This chapter teaches the basics of how to write such tools yourself.

PVM is based on a dynamic computing model in which cluster nodes can be added and deleted from the computation on the fly and parallel tasks can be spawned or killed during the computation. PVM doesn't have nearly as rich a set of message-passing features as MPI; but, being a virtual machine model, PVM has a number of features that make it attractive for creating dynamic parallel programs. For this reason, PVM will be used to illustrate the concepts of fault tolerance and adaptability in this chapter.

## 12.1    Considerations for Fault Tolerance

A computational biologist at Oak Ridge National Laboratory wants to write an parallel application that runs 24/7 on his Beowulf cluster. The application involves calculations for the human genome and is driven by a constant stream of new data arriving from researchers all around the world. The data is not independent since new data helps refine and extend previously calculated sequences. How can he write such a program?

A company wants to write an application to process a constant stream of sales orders coming in from the Web. The program needs to be robust, since down time costs not only the lost revenue stream but also wages of workers who are idle. The company has recently purchased a Beowulf cluster to provide a reliable cost effective solution. But how do they write the fault-tolerant parallel program to run on the cluster?

When you are developing algorithms that must be reliable the first consideration is the hardware. The bad news is that your Beowulf cluster will have failures; it will need maintenance. It is not a matter of *whether* some node in the cluster will fail but *when*. Experience has shown that the more nodes the cluster has, the more likely one will fail within a given time. How often a hardware failure occurs varies widely between clusters. Some have failures every week; others run for months. It is not uncommon for several nodes to fail at about the same time with similar hardware problems. Evaluate your particular cluster under a simulated load for a couple of weeks to get data on expected mean time between failures (MTBF). If the MTBF is many times longer than your average application run time, then it may not make sense to restructure the application to be fault tolerant. In most cases it is more efficient simply to rerun a failed application if it has a short run time.

The second consideration is the fault tolerance of the underlying software environment. If the operating system is not stable, then the hardware is the least of your problems. The PVM system sits between the operating system and the application and, among other things, monitors the state of the virtual machine. The PVM system is designed to be fault tolerant and to reconfigure itself automatically when a failure is detected. It was discovered early in the PVM project that it doesn't help your fault-tolerant application if the underlying failure detection system crashes during a failure. The PVM failure detection system is responsible for detecting problems and notifying running applications about the problem. It makes no attempt to recover a parallel application automatically.

The third consideration is the application. Not every parallel application can recover from a failure; recovery depends on the design of the application and the nature of the failure. For example, in the manager/worker programs of the preceding chapters, if the node that fails was running a worker, then recovery is possible; but if the node was running the manager, then key data may be lost that can't be recovered.

At the least, any parallel program can be made fault tolerant by restarting it automatically from the beginning if a failure in detected.

Recovery of parallel programs is complicated because data in messages may be in flight when the recovery begins. There is a race condition. If the data did not arrive, then it will need to be resent as part of the recovery. But if the data managed to be received just before the recovery, then there isn't an outstanding receive call, and the data shouldn't be resent.

File I/O is another problem that complicates recovery. File pointers may need to be reset to the last checkpoint to avoid getting a repeated set of output data in the file.

Despite all these issues, a few common methods can be used to improve the fault tolerance of many parallel applications.

## 12.2  Building Fault-Tolerant Parallel Applications

From the application's view three steps must be performed for fault tolerance: notification, recovery, and continue.

The PVM system has a monitoring and notification feature built into it. Any or all tasks in an application can asked to be notified of specific events. These include the exiting of a task within the application. The requesting task can specify a particular task or set of tasks or can ask to be notified if any task within the application fails. In the last case the notification message contains the ID of the task that failed. There is no need for the notified task and the failed task ever to have communicated in order to detect the failure.

The failure or deletion of a node in the cluster is another notify event that can be specified. Again the requesting application task can specify a particular node, set of nodes, or all nodes. And, as before, the notification message returns the ID of the failed node(s).

The addition of one or more cluster nodes to the application's computational environment is also an event that PVM can notify an application about. In this case no ID can be specified, and the notification message returns the ID of the new node(s).

```
int info = pvm_notify( int EventType, int msgtag, int cnt, int *ids )
```

The `EventType` options are `PvmTaskExit`, `PvmHostDelete`, or `PvmHostAdd`. A separate notify call must be made for each event type that the application wishes to be notified about. The `msgtag` argument specifies what message tag the task will be using to listening for events. The `cnt` argument is the number task or node IDs in the ids list for which notification is requested.

Given the flexibility of the `pvm_notify` command, there are several options for how the application can be designed to receive notification from the PVM system. The first option is designing a separate watcher task. One or more of these watcher tasks are spawned across the cluster and often have the additional responsibility of managing the recovery phase of the application. The advantage of this approach is that the application code can remain cleaner. Note that in the manager/worker scheme the manager often assumes the additional duty as watcher.

A second option is for the application tasks to watch each other. A common method is to have each task watch its neighbor in a logical ring. Thus each task just watches one or two other tasks. Another common, but not particularly efficient, method is to have every task watch all the other tasks. Remember that the PVM system is doing the monitoring, not the application tasks. So the monitoring overhead is the same with all these options. The difference is the number of notification messages that get sent in the event of a failure.

Recovery is very dependent on the type of parallel algorithm used in the application. The most commonly used options are restart from the beginning, roll back to the last checkpoint, or reassign the work of a failed task.

The first option is the simplest to implement but the most expensive in the amount of calculation that must be redone. This option is used by many batch systems because it requires no knowledge of the application. It guarantees that the application will complete even if failures occur, although it does not guarantee how long this will take. On average the time is less than twice the normal run time. For short-running applications this is the best option.

For longer-running applications, checkpointing is a commonly used option. With this option you must understand the parallel application and modify it so that the application can restart from a input data file. You then have to modify the application to write out such a data file periodically. In the event of a failure, only computations from the last checkpoint are lost. The application restarts itself from the last successful data file written out. How often checkpoints are written out depends on the size of the restart file and how long the application is going to run. For large, scientific applications that run for days, checkpointing is typically done every few hours.

Note that if a failure is caused by the loss of a cluster node, then the application cannot be restarted until the node is repaired or is replaced by another node in the cluster. The restart file is almost always written out assuming that the same number of nodes are available during the restart.

In the special case where an application is based on a manager/worker scheme, it is often possible to reassign the job sent to the failed worker to another worker or to spawn a replacement worker to take its place. Manager/worker is a very popular parallel programming scheme for Beowulf clusters, so this special case arises often. Below is an example of a fault-tolerant manager/worker program.

```c
/* Fault Tolerant Manager / Worker Example
 * using notification and task spawning.
 * example1.c
 */

#include <stdio.h>
#include <math.h>
#include <pvm3.h>

#define NWORK        4
#define NPROB        10000
#define MSGTAG       123

int main()
{
    double sum = 0.0, result, input = 1.0;
    int tids[NWORK], numt, probs[NPROB], sent=0, recvd=0;
    int aok=0, cc, bufid, done=0, i, j, marker, next, src;

    /* If I am a Manager Task */
    if ( (cc = pvm_parent()) == PvmNoParent || cc == PvmParentNotSet ) {

        /* Spawn NWORK Worker Tasks */
        numt = pvm_spawn( "example1", (char **) NULL, PvmTaskDefault,
                (char *) NULL, NWORK, tids );

        /* Set Up Notify for Spawned Tasks */
        pvm_notify( PvmTaskExit, MSGTAG, numt, tids );

        /* Send Problem to Spawned Workers */
        for ( i=0 ; i < NPROB ; i++ ) probs[i] = -1;
        for ( i=0 ; i < numt ; i++ ) {
            pvm_initsend( PvmDataDefault );
```

```
        pvm_pkint( &aok, 1, 1 );   /* Valid Problem Marker */
        input = (double) (i + 1);
        pvm_pkdouble( &input, 1, 1 );
        pvm_send( tids[i], MSGTAG );
        probs[i] = i;  sent++;  /* Next Problem */
    }

    /* Collect Results / Handle Failures */
    do {
        /* Receive Result */
        bufid = pvm_recv( -1, MSGTAG );
        pvm_upkint( &marker, 1, 1 );

        /* Handle Notify */
        if ( marker > 0 ) {
            /* Find Failed Task Index */
            for ( i=0, next = -1 ; i < numt ; i++ )
                if ( tids[i] == marker )
                    /* Find Last Problem Sent to Task */
                    for ( j=(sent-1) ; j > 0 ; j-- )
                        if ( probs[j] == i ) {
                            /* Spawn Replacement Task */
                            if ( pvm_spawn( "example1", (char **) NULL,
                                    PvmTaskDefault, (char *) NULL, 1,
                                    &(tids[i]) ) == 1 ) {
                                pvm_notify( PvmTaskExit, MSGTAG, 1,
                                        &(tids[i]) );
                                next = i;  sent--;
                            }
                            probs[j] = -1; /* Reinsert Prob */
                            break;
                        }
        } else {
            /* Get Source Task & Accumulate Solution */
            pvm_upkdouble( &result, 1, 1 );
            sum += result;
            recvd++;
            /* Get Task Index */
            pvm_bufinfo( bufid, (int *) NULL, (int *) NULL, &src );
            for ( i=0 ; i < numt ; i++ )
                if ( tids[i] == src ) next = i;
        }

        /* Send Another Problem */
```

```
        if ( next >= 0 ) {
            for ( i=0, input = -1.0 ; i < NPROB ; i++ )
                if ( probs[i] < 0 ) {
                    input = (double) (i + 1);
                    probs[i] = next;  sent++;  /* Next Problem */
                    break;
                }
            pvm_initsend( PvmDataDefault );
            pvm_pkint( &aok, 1, 1 );  /* Valid Problem Marker */
            pvm_pkdouble( &input, 1, 1 );
            pvm_send( tids[next], MSGTAG );
            if ( input < 0.0 ) tids[next] = -1;
        }

    } while ( recvd < sent );

    printf( "Sum = %lf\n", sum );
}

/* If I am a Worker Task */
else if ( cc > 0 ) {
    /* Notify Me If Manager Fails */
    pvm_notify( PvmTaskExit, MSGTAG, 1, &cc );
    /* Solve Problems Until Done */
    do {
        /* Get Problem from Master */
        pvm_recv( -1, MSGTAG );
        pvm_upkint( &aok, 1, 1 );
        if ( aok > 0 )  /* Master Died */
            break;
        pvm_upkdouble( &input, 1, 1 );
        if ( input > 0.0 ) {
            /* Compute Result */
            result = sqrt( ( 2.0 * input ) - 1.0 );
            /* Send Result to Master */
            pvm_initsend( PvmDataDefault );
            pvm_pkint( &aok, 1, 1 );     /* Ask for more... */
            pvm_pkdouble( &result, 1, 1 );
            pvm_send( cc, MSGTAG );
        } else
            done = 1;
    } while ( !done );
}
```

```
    pvm_exit();

    return( 0 );
}
```

This example illustrates another useful function: `pvm_spawn()`. The ability to spawn a replacement task is a powerful capability in fault tolerance. It is also a key function in adaptive programs, as we will see in the next section.

```
int numt = pvm_spawn( char *task, char **argv, int flag,
                      char *node, int ntasks, int *tids )
```

The routine `pvm_spawn()` starts up `ntasks` copies of an executable file `task` on the virtual machine. The PVM virtual machine is assumed to be running on the Beowulf cluster. Here `argv` is a pointer to an array of arguments to `task` with the end of the array specified by NULL. If task takes no arguments then `argv` is NULL. The `flag` argument is used to specify options and is a sum of the following options:

`PvmTaskDefault`: has PVM choose where to spawn processes

`PvmTaskHost`: uses a `where` argument to specify a particular host or cluster node to spawn on

`PvmTaskArch`: uses a `where` argument to specify an architecture class to spawn on

`PvmTaskDebug`: starts up these processes under debugger

`PvmTaskTrace`: uses PVM calls to generate trace data

`PvmMppFront`: starts process on MPP front-end/service node

`PvmHostComp`: starts process on complementary host set

For example, `flag = PvmTaskHost + PvmHostCompl` spawns tasks on every node but the specified node (which may be the manager, for instance).

On return, `numt` is set to the number of tasks successfully spawned or an error code if no tasks could be started. If tasks were started, then `pvm_spawn()` returns a vector of the spawned tasks' `tids`. If some tasks could not be started, the corresponding error codes are placed in the last $(ntask - numt)$ positions of the vector.

In the example above, `pvm_spawn()` is used by the manager to start all the worker tasks and also is used to replace workers who fail during the computation. This type of fault-tolerant method is useful for applications that run continuously with a steady stream of new work coming in, as was the case in our two initial examples. Both used a variation on the above PVM example code for their solution.

## 12.3   Adaptive Programs

In this section, we use some more of the PVM virtual machine functions to illustrate how cluster programs can be extended to adapt not only to faults but also to many other metrics and circumstances. The first example demonstrates a parallel application that dynamically adapts the size of the virtual machine through adding and releasing nodes based on the computational needs of the application. Such a feature is used every day on a 128-processor Beowulf cluster at Oak Ridge National Laboratory that is shared by three research groups.

```
int numh = pvm_addhosts( char **hosts, int nhost, int *infos)
int numh = pvm_delhosts( char **hosts, int nhost, int *infos)
```

The PVM addhosts and delhosts routines add or delete a set of hosts in the virtual machine. In a Beowulf cluster this corresponds to adding or deleting nodes from the computation; numh is returned as the number of nodes successfully added or deleted. The argument infos is an array of length nhost that contains the status code for each individual node being added or deleted. This allows you to check whether only one of a set of hosts caused a problem, rather than trying to add or delete the entire set of hosts again.

```
/*
 * Adaptive Host Allocation Example adds and removes cluster nodes
 * from computation on the fly for different computational phases
 */

#include <stdio.h>
#include <pvm3.h>

static char *host_set_A[] = { "msr", "nova", "sun4" };
static int nhosts_A = sizeof( host_set_A ) / sizeof( char ** );

static char *host_set_B[] = { "davinci", "nimbus" };
static int nhosts_B = sizeof( host_set_B ) / sizeof( char ** );

#define MAX_HOSTS    255
#define MSGTAG       123

double phase1( int prob ) {
    return( (prob == 1) ? 1 : ((double) prob * phase1( prob - 1 )) ); }

double phase2( int prob ) {
```

```
        return( (prob == 1) ? 1 : ((double) prob + phase2( prob - 1 )) ); }

int main( int argc, char **argv )
{
    double sum1 = 0.0, sum2 = 0.0, result;
    int status[MAX_HOSTS], prob, cc, i;
    char *args[3], input[16];

    /* If I am the Manager Task */
    if ( (cc = pvm_parent()) == PvmNoParent || cc == PvmParentNotSet ) {

        /* Phase #1 of computation - Use Host Set A */
        pvm_addhosts( host_set_A, nhosts_A, status );

        /* Spawn Worker Tasks - One Per Host */
        args[0] = "phase1";  args[1] = input;  args[2] = (char *) NULL;
        for ( i=0, prob=0 ; i < nhosts_A ; i++ )
            if ( status[i] > 0 ) {  /* Successful Host Add */
                sprintf( input, "%d", prob++ );
                pvm_spawn( "example2", args, PvmTaskDefault | PvmTaskHost,
                        host_set_A[i], 1, (int *) NULL );
            }
        /* Collect Results */
        for ( i=0 ; i < prob ; i++ ) {
            pvm_recv( -1, MSGTAG );
            pvm_upkdouble( &result, 1, 1 );
            sum1 += result;
        }

        /* Remove Host Set A after Phase #1 */
        for ( i=0 ; i < nhosts_A ; i++ )
            if ( status[i] > 0 )  /* Only Delete Successful Hosts */
                pvm_delhosts( &(host_set_A[i]), 1, (int *) NULL );

        /* Phase #2 of Computation - Use Host Set B */
        pvm_addhosts( host_set_B, nhosts_B, status );

        /* Spawn Worker Tasks - One Per Host (None Locally) */
        args[0] = "phase2";
        for ( i=0, prob=0 ; i < nhosts_B ; i++ )
            if ( status[i] > 0 ) {  /* Successful Host Add */
                sprintf( input, "%d", prob++ );
                pvm_spawn( "example2", args, PvmTaskDefault | PvmTaskHost,
                        host_set_B[i], 1, (int *) NULL );
```

```
        }
        /* Collect Results */
        for ( i=0 ; i < prob ; i++ ) {
            pvm_recv( -1, MSGTAG );
            pvm_upkdouble( &result, 1, 1 );
            sum2 += result;
        }

        /* Remove Host Set B from Phase #2 */
        for ( i=0 ; i < nhosts_B ; i++ )
            if ( status[i] > 0 )   /* Only Delete Successful Hosts */
                pvm_delhosts( &(host_set_B[i]), 1, (int *) NULL );

        /* Done */
        printf( "sum1 (%lf) / sum2 (%lf) = %lf\n", sum1, sum2, sum1/sum2);
    }

    /* If I am a Worker Task */
    else if ( cc > 0 ) {
        /* Compute Result */
        prob = atoi( argv[2] );
        if ( !strcmp( argv[1], "phase1" ) )
            result = phase1( prob + 1 );
        else if ( !strcmp( argv[1], "phase2" ) )
            result = phase2( 100 * ( prob + 1 ) );
        /* Send Result to Master */
        pvm_initsend( PvmDataDefault );
        pvm_pkdouble( &result, 1, 1 );
        pvm_send( cc, MSGTAG );
    }

    pvm_exit();

    return( 0 );
}
```

One of the main difficulties of writing libraries for message-passing applications is that messages sent inside the application may get intercepted by the message-passing calls inside the library. The same problem occurs when two applications want to cooperate, for example, a performance monitor and a scientific application or an airframe stress application coupled with an aerodynamic flow application. Whenever two or more programmers are writing different parts of the overall message-passing application, there is the potential that a message will be inadvertently received by the wrong part of the application. The solution to this problem is communication context. As described earlier in the MPI chapters, communication context in MPI is handled cleanly through the MPI communicator.

In PVM 3.4, pvm_recv() requests a message from a particular source with a user-chosen message tag (either or both of these fields can be set to accept anything). In addition, communication context is a third field that a receive must match on before accepting a message; the context cannot be specified by a wild card. By default there is a base context that is a predefined and is similar to the default MPI_COMM_WORLD communicator in MPI.

PVM has four routines to manage communication contexts.

```
new_context = pvm_newcontext()
old_context = pvm_setcontext( new_context )
info        = pvm_freecontext( context )
context     = pvm_getcontext()
```

Pvm_newcontext() returns a systemwide unique context tag generated by the local daemon (in a way similar to the way the local daemon generates systemwide unique task IDs). Since it is a local operation, pvm_newcontext is very fast. The returned context can then be broadcast to all the tasks that are cooperating on this part of the application. Each of the tasks calls pvm_setcontext, which switches the active context and returns the old context tag so that it can be restored at the end of the module by another call to pvm_setcontext. Pvm_freecontext and pvm_getcontext are used to free memory associated with a context tag and to get the value of the active context tag, respectively.

Spawned tasks inherit the context of their parent. Thus, if you wish to add context to an existing parallel routine already written in PVM, you need to add only four lines to the source:

```
int mycxt, oldcxt;
/* near the beginning of the routine set a new context */
mycxt = pvm_newcontext();
oldcxt = pvm_setcontext( mycxt );

/* spawn slave tasks to help */
/* slave tasks require no source code change */
/* leave all the PVM calls in master unchanged */

/* just before exiting the routine restore previous context */
```

```
    mycxt = pvm_setcontext( oldcxt );
    pvm_freecontext( mycxt );

    return;
```

PVM has always had message handlers internally, which were used for controlling the virtual machine. In PVM 3.4 the ability to define and delete message handlers was raised to the user level so that parallel programs can be written that can add new features while the program is running.

The two new message handler functions are

```
    mhid = pvm_addmhf( src, tag, context, *function );
           pvm_delmhf( mhid );
```

Once a message handler has been added by a task, whenever a message arrives at this task with the specified source, message tag, and communication context, the specified function is executed. The function is passed the message so that it may unpack the message if desired. PVM places no restrictions on the complexity of the function, which is free to make system calls or other PVM calls. A message handler ID is returned by the add routine, which is used in the delete message handler routine.

There is no limit on the number of handlers you can set up, and handlers can be added and deleted dynamically by each application task independently.

By setting up message handlers, you can now write programs that can dynamically change the features of the underlying virtual machine. For example, message handlers could be added that implement active messages; the application then could use this form of communication rather than the typical send/receive. Similar opportunities exist for almost every feature of the virtual machine.

The ability of the application to adapt features of the virtual machine to meet its present needs is a powerful capability that has yet to be fully exploited in Beowulf clusters.

```
/* Adapting available Virtual Machine features with
 * user redefined message handlers.
 */
#include <stdio.h>
#include <pvm3.h>

#define NWORK             4
#define MAIN_MSGTAG     123
#define CNTR_MSGTAG     124
```

```
int counter = 0;

int handler( int mid ) {
    int ack, incr, src;

    /* Increment Counter */
    pvm_upkint( &incr, 1, 1 );
    counter += incr;
    printf( "counter = %d\n", counter );

    /* Acknowledge Counter Task */
    pvm_bufinfo( mid, (int *) NULL, (int *) NULL, &src );
    pvm_initsend( PvmDataDefault );
    ack = ( counter > 1000 ) ? -1 : 1;
    pvm_pkint( &ack, 1, 1 );
    pvm_send( src, CNTR_MSGTAG );

    return( 0 );
}

int main( int argc, char **argv )
{
    int ack, cc, ctx, bufid, incr=1, iter=1, max, numt, old, value=1, src;
    char *args[2];

    /* If I am a Manager Task */
    if ( (cc = pvm_parent()) == PvmNoParent || cc == PvmParentNotSet ) {

        /* Generate New Message Context for Counter Task messages */
        ctx = pvm_newcontext();

        /* Register Message Handler Function for Independent Counter */
        pvm_addmhf( -1, CNTR_MSGTAG, ctx, handler );

        /* Spawn 1 Counter Task */
        args[0] = "counter";  args[1] = (char *) NULL;
        old = pvm_setcontext( ctx );  /* Set Message Context for Task */
        if ( pvm_spawn( "example3", args, PvmTaskDefault,
                (char *) NULL, 1, (int *) NULL ) != 1 )
            counter = 1001;  /* Counter Failed to Spawn, Trigger Exit */
        pvm_setcontext( old );  /* Reset to Base Message Context */

        /* Spawn NWORK Worker Tasks */
```

```
        args[0] = "worker";
        numt = pvm_spawn( "example3", args, PvmTaskDefault,
                (char *) NULL, NWORK, (int *) NULL );

        /* Increment & Return Worker Values */
        do {
            /* Get Value */
            bufid = pvm_recv( -1, MAIN_MSGTAG );
            pvm_upkint( &value, 1, 1 );
            max = ( value > max ) ? value : max;
            printf( "recvd value = %d\n", value );

            /* Send Reply */
            pvm_bufinfo( bufid, (int *) NULL, (int *) NULL, &src );
            if ( counter <= 1000 ) value += iter++;
                else { value = -1; numt--; }  /* Tell Workers to Exit */
            pvm_initsend( PvmDataDefault );
            pvm_pkint( &value, 1, 1 );
            pvm_send( src, MAIN_MSGTAG );
        } while ( numt > 0 );

        printf( "Max Value = %d\n", max );
    }

    /* If I am a Worker Task */
    else if ( cc > 0 && !strcmp( argv[1], "worker" ) ) {
        /* Grow Values Until Done */
        do {
            /* Send Value to Master */
            value *= 2;
            pvm_initsend( PvmDataDefault );
            pvm_pkint( &value, 1, 1 );
            pvm_send( cc, MAIN_MSGTAG );
            /* Get Incremented Value from Master */
            pvm_recv( cc, MAIN_MSGTAG );
            pvm_upkint( &value, 1, 1 );
        } while ( value > 0 );
    }

    /* If I am a Counter Task */
    else if ( cc > 0 && !strcmp( argv[1], "counter" ) ) {
        /* Grow Values Until Done */
        do {
            /* Send Counter Increment to Master */
```

```
        pvm_initsend( PvmDataDefault );
        pvm_pkint( &incr, 1, 1 );
        pvm_send( cc, CNTR_MSGTAG );
        incr *= 2;
        /* Check Ack from Master */
        pvm_recv( cc, CNTR_MSGTAG );
        pvm_upkint( &ack, 1, 1 );
    } while ( ack > 0 );
}

pvm_exit();

return( 0 );
}
```

In a typical message-passing system, messages are transient, and the focus is on making their existence as brief as possible by decreasing latency and increasing bandwidth. But there are a growing number of situations in the parallel applications seen today in which programming would be much easier if there was a way to have persistent messages. This is the purpose of the *Message Box* feature in PVM. The Message Box is an internal tuple space in the virtual machine.

Four functions make up the Message Box:

```
index = pvm_putinfo( name, msgbuf, flag )
        pvm_recvinfo( name, index, flag )
        pvm_delinfo( name, index, flag )
        pvm_getmboxinfo( pattern, matching_names, info )
```

Tasks can use regular PVM pack routines to create an arbitrary message and then use pvm_putinfo() to place this message into the Message Box with an associated name. Copies of this message can be retrieved by any PVM task that knows the name. If the name is unknown or is changing dynamically, then pvm_getmboxinfo() can be used to find the list of names active in the Message Box. The flag defines the properties of the stored message, such as who is allowed to delete this message, whether this name allows multiple instances of messages, and whether a *put* to the same name can overwrite the message.

The Message Box has been used for many other purposes. For example, the PVM group server functionality has all been implemented in the new Message Box functions; the Cumulvs computational steering tool uses the Message Box to query for the instructions on how to attach to a remote distributed simulation; and performance monitors leave their findings in the Message Box for other tools to use.

The capability to have persistent messages in a parallel computing opens up many new application possibilities not only in high-performance computing but also in collaborative technologies.

```c
/* Example using persistent messages to adapt to change
 * Monitor tasks are created and killed as needed
 * Information is exchanged between these tasks using persistent messages
 */

#include <stdio.h>
#include <sys/time.h>
#include <pvm3.h>

#define MSGBOX          "load_stats"

int main()
{
    int cc, elapsed, i, index, load, num;
    struct timeval start, end;
    double value;

    /* If I am a Manager Task */
    if ( (cc = pvm_parent()) == PvmNoParent || cc == PvmParentNotSet ) {

        /* Periodically Spawn Load Monitor, Check Current System Load */
        do {
            /* Spawn Load Monitor Task */
            if ( pvm_spawn( "example4", (char **) NULL, PvmTaskDefault,
                    (char *) NULL, 1, (int *) NULL ) != 1 ) {
                perror( "spawning load monitor" );  break;
            }
            sleep( 1 );

            /* Check System Load (Microseconds Per Megaflop) */
            for ( i=0, load=0.0, num=0 ; i < 11 ; i++ )
                if ( pvm_recvinfo( MSGBOX, i, PvmMboxDefault ) >= 0 ) {
                    pvm_upkint( &elapsed, 1, 1 );
                    load += elapsed;  num++;
                }
            if ( num )
                printf( "Load Avg = %lf usec/Mflop\n",
                        (double) load / (double) num );
            sleep( 5 );
        } while ( 1 );
    }
```

```
/* If I am a Load Monitor Task */
else if ( cc > 0 ) {
    /* Time Simple Computation */
    gettimeofday( &start, (struct timezone *) NULL );
    for ( i=0, value=1.0 ; i < 1000000 ; i++ )
        value *= 1.2345678;
    gettimeofday( &end, (struct timezone *) NULL );
    elapsed = (end.tv_usec - start.tv_usec)
            + 1000000 * (end.tv_sec - start.tv_sec);

    /* Dump Into Next Available Message Mbox */
    pvm_initsend( PvmDataDefault );
    pvm_pkint( &elapsed, 1, 1 );
    index = pvm_putinfo( MSGBOX, pvm_getsbuf(),
            PvmMboxDefault | PvmMboxPersistent
                | PvmMboxMultiInstance | PvmMboxOverWritable );

    /* Free Next Mbox Index for Next Instance (Only Save 10) */
    pvm_delinfo( MSGBOX, (index + 1) % 11, PvmMboxDefault );
}

pvm_exit();

return( 0 );
}
```

# III MANAGING CLUSTERS

# 13 Cluster Workload Management

*James Patton Jones, David Lifka, Bill Nitzberg, and Todd Tannenbaum*

A Beowulf cluster is a powerful (and attractive) tool. But managing the workload can present significant challenges. It is not uncommon to run hundreds or thousands of jobs or to share the cluster among many users. Some jobs may run only on certain nodes because not all the nodes in the cluster are identical; for instance, some nodes have more memory than others. Some nodes temporarily may not be functioning correctly. Certain users may require priority access to part or all of the cluster. Certain jobs may have to be run at certain times of the day or only after other jobs have completed. Even in the simplest environment, keeping track of all these activities and resource specifics while managing the ever-increasing web of priorities is a complex problem. Workload management software attacks this problem by providing a way to monitor and manage the flow of work through the system, allowing the *best* use of cluster resources as defined by a supplied policy.

Basically, workload management software maximizes the delivery of resources to jobs, given competing user requirements and local policy restrictions. Users package their work into sets of jobs, while the administrator (or system owner) describes local use policies (e.g., Tom's jobs always go first). The software monitors the state of the cluster, schedules work, enforces policy, and tracks usage.

A quick note on terminology: Many terms have been used to describe this area of management software. All of the following topics are related to workload management: distributed resource management, batch queuing, job scheduling, and, resource and task scheduling.

## 13.1  Goal of Workload Management Software

The goal of workload management software is to make certain the submitted jobs ultimately run to completion by utilizing cluster resources according to a supplied policy. But in order to achieve this goal, workload management systems usually must perform some or all of the following activities:

- Queuing
- Scheduling
- Monitoring
- Resource management
- Accounting

The typical relationship between users, resources, and these workload management activities is depicted in Figure 13.1. As shown in this figure, workload management software sits between the cluster users and the cluster resources. First, users submit jobs to a queue in order to specify the work to be performed. (Once a job has been submitted, the user can request status information about that job at any time.) The jobs then wait in the queue until they are scheduled to start on the cluster. The specifics of the scheduling process are defined by the policy rules. At this point, resource management mechanisms handle the details of properly launching the job and perhaps cleaning up any mess left behind after the job either completes or is aborted. While all this is going on, the workload management system is monitoring the status of system resources and accounting for which users are using what resources.

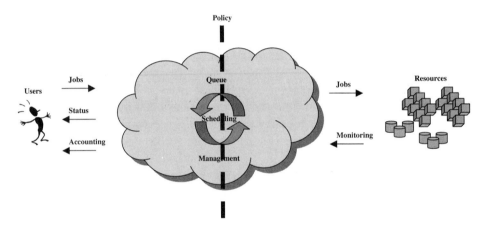

**Figure 13.1**
Activities performed by a workload management system.

## 13.2   Workload Management Activities

Now let us take a look in more detail at each of the major activities performed by a cluster workload management system.

### 13.2.1   Queueing

The first of the five aspects of workload management is *queuing*, or the process of collecting together "work" to be executed on a set of resources. This is also the portion most visible to the user.

The tasks the user wishes to have the computer perform, the work, is submitted to the workload management system in a container called a "batch job". The batch job consists of two primary parts: a set of resource directives (such as the amount of memory or number of CPUs needed) and a description of the task to be executed. This description contains all the information the workload management system needs in order to start a user's job when the time comes. For instance, the job description may contain information such as the name of the file to execute, a list of data files required by the job, and environment variables or command-line arguments to pass to the executable.

Once submitted to the workload management system, the batch jobs are held in a "queue" until the matching resources (e.g., the right kind of computers with the right amount of memory or number of CPUs) become available. Examples of real-life queues are lines at the bank or grocery store. Sometimes you get lucky and there's no wait, but usually you have to stand in line for a few minutes. And on days when the resources (clerks) are in high demand (like payday), the wait is substantially longer.

The same applies to computers and batch jobs. Sometimes the wait is very short, and the jobs run immediately. But more often (and thus the need for the workload management system) resources are oversubscribed, and so the jobs have to wait.

One important aspect of queues is that limits can be set that restrict access to the queue. This allows the cluster manager greater control over the usage policy of the cluster. For example, it may be desirable to have a queue that is available for short jobs only. This would be analogous to the "ten items or fewer express lane" at the grocery store, providing a shorter wait for "quick tasks."

Each of the different workload management systems discussed later in this volume offers a rich variety of queue limits and attributes.

### 13.2.2 Scheduling

The second area of workload management is scheduling, which is simply the process of choosing the *best* job to run. Unlike in our real-life examples of the bank and grocery store (which employ a simple first-come, first-served model of deciding who's next), workload management systems offer a variety of ways by which the *best* job is identified.

As we have discussed earlier, however, *best* can be a tricky goal, and depends on the usage policy set by local management, the available workload, the type and availability of cluster resources, and the types of application being run on the cluster. In general, however, scheduling can be broken into two primary activities: *policy enforcement* and *resource optimization*.

Policy encapsulates how the cluster resources are to be used, addressing such issues as priorities, traffic control, and capability vs. high throughput. Scheduling is then the act of enforcing the policy in the selection of jobs, ensuring the priorities are met and policy goals are achieved.

While implementing and enforcing the policy, the scheduler has a second set of goals. These are resource optimization goals, such as "pack jobs efficiently" or "exploit underused resources."

The difficult part of scheduling, then, is balancing policy enforcement with resource optimization in order to pick the *best* job to run.

Logically speaking, one could think of a scheduler as performing the following loop:

1. Select the best job to run, according to policy and available resources.

2. Start the job.

3. Stop the job and/or clean up after a completed job.

4. Repeat.

The nuts and bolts of scheduling is, of course, choosing and tuning the policy to meet your needs. Although different workload management systems each have their own idiosyncrasies, they typically all provide ways in which their scheduling policy can be customized. Subsequent chapters of this book will discuss the various scheduling policy mechanisms available in several popular workload management systems.

### 13.2.3   Monitoring

Resource monitoring is the third part of any cluster workload management system. It provides necessary information to administrators, users and the scheduling system itself on the status of jobs and resources. There are basically three critical times that resource monitoring comes into play:

1. When nodes are idle, to verify that they are in working order before starting another job on them.

2. When nodes are busy running a job. Users and administrators may want to check memory, CPU, network, I/O, and utilization of other system resources. Such checks often are useful in parallel programming when users wish to verify that they have balanced their workload correctly and are effectively using all the nodes they've been allocated.

3. When a job completes. Here, resource monitoring is used to ensure that there are no remaining processes from the completed job and that the node is still in working order before starting another job on it.

The Microsoft Windows 2000 operating system provides several built-in tools for monitoring. The most common is the *Computer Management* console. It provides system details and allows administrators to monitor services, file I/O, user management information, and many other things. Figure 13.2 shows the Computer Management console.

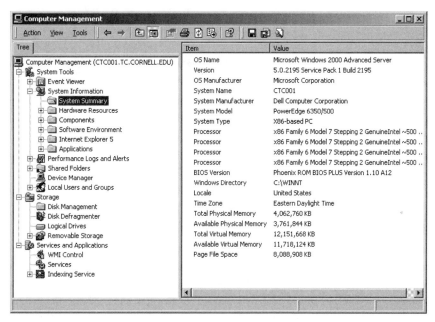

**Figure 13.2**
Windows 2000 Computer Management console.

Another built-in tool is the Performance Monitor. It lets you monitor resource utilization on multiple nodes simultaneously. Figure 13.3 shows the Performance Monitor console.

Both of these tools rely upon Windows Management and Instrumentation (WMI), which is a built-in service that is part of any Windows 2000 installation and is also available for Windows NT. It acts as a COM+ object that allows administrators and users to develop monitoring tools on it using any language, including scripting languages.

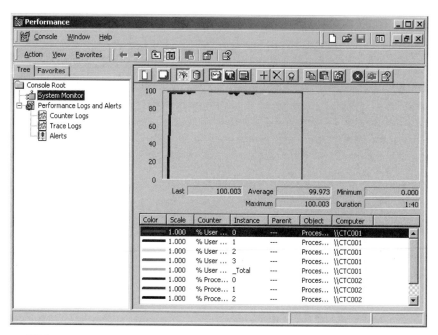

**Figure 13.3**
Windows 2000 Performance Monitor console.

### 13.2.4   Resource Management

The fourth area, resource management, is essentially responsible for the starting, stopping, and cleaning up after jobs that are run on cluster nodes. In a batch system resource management involves running a job for a user, under the identity of the user, on the resources the user was allocated in such a way that the user need not be present at that time.

Starting jobs typically involves some form of secure impersonation. Microsoft Windows 2000, like other operating systems, provides mechanisms for doing this securely. Typically this is handled by the use of services or COM+ objects that can create a user process token for a given user and use it to run a job as that user. Short of a mechanism like this, users typically must supply their username and password at run time to authenticate to the system and start processes as them. This obviously does not work in a batch situation.

Once processes are started, the resource management system has to be able to enumerate those associated with a given job. Windows 2000 provides the *job object* for this purpose. All processes created within a job object can be monitored and stopped by stopping their associated job object. Job objects also provide a way for running multiple jobs per node, since all of a given job's processes are managed within a unique job object.

Many cluster workload management systems provide mechanisms to ensure the successful startup and cleanup of jobs and to maintain node status data internally, so that jobs are started only on nodes that are available and functioning correctly.

In addition, limits may need to be placed on the job and enforced by the workload management system. These limits are yet another aspect of policy enforcement, in addition to the limits on queues and those enacted by the scheduling component.

Another aspect of resource management is providing the ability to remove or add compute resources to the available pool of systems. Clusters are rarely static; systems go down, or new nodes are added. The "registration" of new nodes and the marking of nodes as unavailable are both additional aspects of resource management.

### 13.2.5   Accounting

The fifth aspect of workload management is accounting and reporting. Workload accounting is the process of collecting resource usage data for the batch jobs that run on the cluster. Such data includes the job owner, resources requested by the job, and total amount of resources consumed by the job. Other data about the job may also be available, depending on the specific workload managment system in use.

Cluster workload accounting data can used for a variety of purposes, such as

1.  producing weekly system usage reports,

2.  preparing monthly per user usage reports,

3.  enforcing per project allocations,

4.  tuning the scheduling policy,

5.  calculating future resource allocations,

6.  anticipating future computer component requirements, and

7.  determining areas of improvement within the computer system.

The data for these purposes may be collected as part of the resource monitoring tasks or may be gathered separately. In either case, data is pulled from the available sources in order to meet the objectives of workload accounting. Details of using the workload accounting features of specific workload management systems are discussed in subsequent chapters of this book.

# 14 Condor: A Distributed Job Scheduler

*Todd Tannenbaum, Derek Wright, Karen Miller, and Miron Livny*

**Condor** is a sophisticated and unique distributed job scheduler developed by the Condor research project at the University of Wisconsin-Madison Department of Computer Sciences.

A public-domain version of the Condor software and complete documentation is freely available from the Condor project's Web site at `www.cs.wisc.edu/condor`. Organizations may purchase a commercial version of Condor with an accompanying support contract; for additional information see `www.condorcomputing.com`.

This chapter introduces all aspects of Condor, from its ability to satisfy the needs and desires of both submitters and resource owners, to the management of Condor on clusters. Following an overview of Condor and Condor's ClassAd mechanism is a description of Condor from the user's perspective. The architecture of the software is presented along with overviews of installation and management. The chapter ends with configuration scenarios specific to clusters.

## 14.1 Introduction to Condor

Condor is a specialized workload management system for compute-intensive jobs. Like other full-featured batch systems, Condor provides a job queuing mechanism, scheduling policy, priority scheme, resource monitoring, and resource management. Users submit their jobs to Condor, and Condor places them into a queue, chooses when and where to run them based upon a policy, monitors their progress, and ultimately informs the user upon completion.

While providing functionality similar to that of a more traditional batch queuing system, Condor's novel architecture allows it to succeed in areas where traditional scheduling systems fail. Condor can be used to manage a cluster of dedicated Beowulf nodes. In addition, several unique mechanisms enable Condor to effectively harness wasted CPU power from otherwise idle desktop workstations. Condor can be used to seemlessly combine all of your organization's computational power into one resource.

Condor is the product of the Condor Research Project at the University of Wisconsin-Madison (UW-Madison) and was first installed as a production system in the UW-Madison Department of Computer Sciences nearly ten years ago. This Condor installation has since served as a major source of computing cycles to UW-Madison faculty and students. Today, just in our department alone, Condor manages more than one thousand workstations, including the department's 500-CPU Beowulf cluster. On a typical day, Condor delivers more than 650 CPU-*days* to

UW researchers. Additional Condor installations have been established over the years across our campus and the world. Hundreds of organizations in industry, government, and academia have used Condor to establish compute environments ranging in size from a handful to hundreds of workstations.

### 14.1.1  Features of Condor

Condor's features are extensive. Condor provides great flexibility for both the user submitting jobs and for the owner of a machine that provides CPU time toward running jobs. The following list summarizes some of Condor's capabilities.

**Distributed submission:** There is no single, centralized submission machine. Instead, Condor allows jobs to be submitted from many machines, and each machine contains its own job queue. Users may submit to a cluster from their own desktop machines.

**Job priorities:** Users can assign priorities to their submitted jobs in order to control the execution order of the jobs. A "nice-user" mechanism requests the use of only those machines that would have otherwise been idle.

**User priorities:** Administrators may assign priorities to users using a flexible mechanism that enables a policy of fair share, strict ordering, fractional ordering, or a combination of policies.

**Job dependency:** Some sets of jobs require an ordering because of dependencies between jobs. "Start job X only after jobs Y and Z successfully complete" is an example of a dependency. Enforcing dependencies is easily handled.

**Support for multiple job models:** Condor handles both serial jobs and parallel jobs incorporating PVM, dynamic PVM, and MPI.

**ClassAds:** The ClassAd mechanism in Condor provides an extremely flexible and expressive framework for matching resource requests (jobs) with resource offers (machines). Jobs can easily state both job requirements and job preferences. Likewise, machines can specify requirements and preferences about the jobs they are willing to run. These requirements and preferences can be described in powerful expressions, resulting in Condor's adaptation to nearly any desired policy.

**Job suspend and resume:** Based on policy rules, Condor can ask the operating system to suspend and later resume a job.

**Pools of machines working together:** *Flocking* allows jobs to be scheduled across multiple Condor pools. It can be done across pools of machines owned by different organizations that impose their own policies.

**Authentication and authorization:** Administrators have fine-grained control of access permissions, and Condor can perform strong network authentication using a variety of mechanisms including the Microsoft Windows NT LAN Manager (NTLM) protocol routinely used on Windows NT and Windows 2000, as well as Kerberos and X.509 public key certificates.

**Heterogeneous platforms:** In addition to Windows 2000, Condor has been ported to most of the primary flavors of Unix as well as Windows NT. A single pool can contain multiple platforms. Jobs to be executed under one platform may be submitted from a different platform. As an example, an executable that runs under Windows 2000 may be submitted from a machine running Linux.

**Grid computing:** Condor incorporates many of the emerging Grid-based computing methodologies and protocols. It can interact with resources managed by Globus.

### 14.1.2   Understanding Condor ClassAds

The ClassAd is a flexible representation of the characteristics and constraints of both machines and jobs in the Condor system. *Matchmaking* is the mechanism by which Condor matches an idle job with an available machine. Understanding this unique framework is the key to harness the full flexibility of the Condor system. ClassAds are employed by users to specify which machines should service their jobs. Administrators use them to customize scheduling policy.

**Conceptualizing Condor ClassAds: Just Like the Newspaper.** Condor's ClassAds are analogous to the classified advertising section of the newspaper. Sellers advertise specifics about what they have to sell, hoping to attract a buyer. Buyers may advertise specifics about what they wish to purchase. Both buyers and sellers list constraints that must be satisfied. For instance, a buyer has a maximum spending limit, and a seller requires a minimum purchase price. Furthermore, both want to rank requests to their own advantage. Certainly a seller would rank one offer of $50 higher than a different offer of $25. In Condor, users submitting jobs can be thought of as buyers of compute resources and machine owners are sellers.

All machines in a Condor pool advertise their attributes, such as available RAM memory, CPU type and speed, virtual memory size, current load average, current time and date, and other static and dynamic properties. This machine ClassAd also advertises under what conditions it is willing to run a Condor job and what type of job it prefers. These policy attributes can reflect the individual terms and preferences by which the different owners have allowed their machines to participate in the Condor pool.

After a job is submitted to Condor, a job ClassAd is created. This ClassAd includes attributes about the job, such as the amount of memory the job uses, the name of the program to run, the user who submitted the job, and the time it was submitted. The job can also specify requirements and preferences (or *rank*) for the machine that will run the job. For instance, perhaps you are looking for the fastest floating-point performance available. You want Condor to rank available machines based on floating-point performance. Perhaps you care only that the machine has a minimum of 256 MBytes of RAM. Or, perhaps you will take any machine you can get! These job attributes and requirements are bundled up into a job ClassAd.

Condor plays the role of matchmaker by continuously reading all the job ClassAds and all the machine ClassAds, matching and ranking job ads with machine ads. Condor ensures that the requirements in both ClassAds are satisfied.

**Structure of a ClassAd.** A ClassAd is a set of uniquely named expressions. Each named expression is called an *attribute*. Each attribute has an *attribute name* and an *attribute value*. The attribute value can be a simple integer, string, or floating-point value, such as

```
Memory = 512
OpSys = "LINUX"
NetworkLatency = 7.5
```

An attribute value can also consist of a logical expression that will evaluate to TRUE, FALSE, or UNDEFINED. The syntax and operators allowed in these expressions are similar to those in C or Java, that is, == for equals, != for not equals, && for logical **and**, || for logical **or**, and so on. Furthermore, ClassAd expressions can incorporate attribute names to refer to other attribute values. For instance, consider the following small sample ClassAd:

```
MemoryInMegs = 512
MemoryInBytes = MemoryInMegs * 1024 * 1024
Cpus = 4
BigMachine = (MemoryInMegs > 256) && (Cpus >= 4)
VeryBigMachine = (MemoryInMegs > 512) && (Cpus >= 8)
FastMachine = BigMachine && SpeedRating
```

In this example, `BigMachine` evaluates to TRUE and `VeryBigMachine` evaluates to FALSE. But, because attribute `SpeedRating` is not specified, `FastMachine` would evaluate to UNDEFINED.

Condor provides *meta-operators* that allow you to explicitly compare with the UNDEFINED value by testing both the type and value of the operands. If both the types and values match, the two operands are considered *identical*; =?= is used for meta-equals (or, is-identical-to) and =!= is used for meta-not-equals (or, is-not-identical-to). These operators always return TRUE or FALSE and therefore enable Condor administrators to specify explicit policies given incomplete information.

A complete description of ClassAd semantics and syntax is documented in the Condor manual.

**Matching ClassAds.** ClassAds can be matched with one another. This is the fundamental mechanism by which Condor matches jobs with machines. Figure 14.1 displays a ClassAd from Condor representing a machine and another representing a queued job. Each ClassAd contains a `MyType` attribute, describing what type of resource the ad represents, and a `TargetType` attribute. The `TargetType` specifies the type of resource desired in a match. Job ads want to be matched with machine ads and vice versa.

Each ClassAd engaged in matchmaking specifies a `Requirements` and a `Rank` attribute. In order for two ClassAds to match, the `Requirements` expression in both ads must evaluate to TRUE. An important component of matchmaking is the `Requirements` and `Rank` expression can refer not only to attributes in their own ad but also to attributes in the candidate matching ad. For instance, the `Requirements` expression for the job ad specified in Figure 14.1 refers to `Arch`, `OpSys`, and `Disk`, which are all attributes found in the machine ad.

What happens if Condor finds more than one machine ClassAd that satisfies the constraints specified by `Requirements`? That is where the `Rank` expression comes into play. The `Rank` expression specifies the desirability of the match (where higher numbers mean better matches). For example, the job ad in Figure 14.1 specifies

```
Requirements = ((Arch=="INTEL" && OpSys=="WINNT5") && Disk > DiskUsage)
Rank         = (Memory * 10000) + KFlops
```

In this case, the job requires a computer running the Windows 2000 operating system and more local disk space than it will use. Among all such computers, the user prefers those with large physical memories and fast floating-point CPUs (`KFlops` is a metric of floating-point performance). Since the `Rank` is a user-specified metric, *any* expression may be used to specify the perceived desirability of the match. Condor's matchmaking algorithms deliver the best resource (as defined by the `Rank` expression) while satisfying other criteria.

| Job ClassAd | Machine ClassAd |
|---|---|

**MyType** = "Job"  
**TargetType** = "Machine"  
**Requirements** = ((Arch=="INTEL" && Op-Sys=="WINNT5") && Disk > DiskUsage)  
**Rank** = (Memory * 10000) + KFlops  
**Args** = "-ini ./ies.ini"  
**ClusterId** = 680  
**Cmd** = "c:\home\tannenba\bin\sim-exe.exe"  
**Department** = "CompSci"  
**DiskUsage** = 465  
**StdErr** = "sim.err"  
**ExitStatus** = 0  
**FileReadBytes** = 0.000000  
**FileWriteBytes** = 0.000000  
**ImageSize** = 465  
**StdIn** = "NUL"  
**Iwd** = "\home\tannenba\sim-m\run_55"  
**JobPrio** = 0  
**JobStartDate** = 971403010  
**JobStatus** = 2  
**StdOut** = "sim.out"  
**Owner** = "tannenba"  
**ProcId** = 64  
**QDate** = 971377131  
**RemoteSysCpu** = 0.000000  
**RemoteUserCpu** = 0.000000  
**RemoteWallClockTime** = 2401399.000000  
**TransferFiles** = "NEVER"  
**WantCheckpoint** = FALSE  
**WantRemoteSyscalls** = FALSE  
.  
.  
.

**MyType** = "Machine"  
**TargetType** = "Job"  
**Requirements** = Start  
**Rank** = TARGET.Department==MY.Department  
**Activity** = "Idle"  
**Arch** = "INTEL"  
**ClockDay** = 0  
**ClockMin** = 614  
**CondorLoadAvg** = 0.000000  
**Cpus** = 1  
**CurrentRank** = 0.000000  
**Department** = "CompSci"  
**Disk** = 3076076  
**EnteredCurrentActivity** = 990371564  
**EnteredCurrentState** = 990330615  
**FileSystemDomain** = "cs.wisc.edu"  
**IsInstructional** = FALSE  
**KeyboardIdle** = 15  
**KFlops** = 145811  
**LoadAvg** = 0.220000  
**Machine** = "nostos.cs.wisc.edu"  
**Memory** = 511  
**Mips** = 732  
**OpSys** = "LINUX"  
**Start** = (LoadAvg <= 0.300000) && (KeyboardIdle > (15 * 60))  
**State** = "Unclaimed"  
**Subnet** = "128.105.165"  
**TotalVirtualMemory** = 787144  
.  
.  
.

**Figure 14.1**  
Examples of ClassAds in Condor.

## 14.2   Using Condor

The road to using Condor effectively is a short one. The basics are quickly and easily learned.

### 14.2.1   Roadmap to Using Condor

The following steps are involved in running jobs using Condor:

**Prepare the Job to Run Unattended.** An application run under Condor must be able to execute as a batch job. Condor runs the program unattended and in the background. A program that runs in the background will not be able to perform interactive input and output. Condor can redirect console output (stdout and stderr) and keyboard input (stdin) to and from files. You should create any needed files that contain the proper keystrokes needed for program input. You should also make certain the program will run correctly with the files. Typically programs submitted to Condor will be console-mode programs because `stdin` and `stdout/err` can be redirected. However, GUI-based programs can be submitted to Condor provided they do not block waiting for mouse/keyboard input.

**Select the Condor Universe.** Condor has five runtime environments from which to choose. Each runtime environment is called a *Universe*. Usually the Universe you choose is determined by the type of application you are asking Condor to run. There are three job Universes in total: one for serial jobs (Vanilla), one for parallel MPI jobs (MPI), and one for meta-schedulers (Scheduler). Section 14.2.4 provides more information on each of these Universes.

**Create a Submit Description File.** The details of a job submission are defined in a *submit description* file. This file contains information about the job such as what executable to run, which Universe to use, the files to use for `stdin, stdout,` and `stderr`, requirements and preferences about the machine which should run the program, and where to send e-mail when the job completes. You can also tell Condor how many times to run a program; it is simple to run the same program multiple times with different data sets.

**Submit the Job.** Submit the program to Condor with the `condor_submit` command.

Once a job has been submitted, Condor handles all aspects of running the job. You can subsequently monitor the job's progress with the `condor_q` and `condor_status` commands. You may use `condor_prio` to modify the order in which Condor will run your jobs. If desired, Condor can also record what is being done with your job at every stage in its lifecycle, through the use of a log file specified during submission.

When the program completes, Condor notifies the owner (by e-mail, the user-specified log file, or both) the exit status, along with various statistics including time used and I/O performed. You can remove a job from the queue at any time with `condor_rm`.

### 14.2.2   Submitting a Job

To submit a job for execution to Condor, you use the `condor_submit` command. This command takes as an argument the name of the submit description file, which contains commands and keywords to direct the queuing of jobs. In the submit description file, you define everything Condor needs to execute the job. Items such as the name of the executable to run, the initial working directory, and command-line arguments to the program all go into the submit description file. The `condor_submit` command creates a job ClassAd based on the information, and Condor schedules the job.

The contents of a submit description file can save you considerable time when you are using Condor. It is easy to submit multiple runs of a program to Condor. To run the same program 500 times on 500 different input data sets, the data files are arranged such that each run reads its own input, and each run writes its own output. Every individual run may have its own initial working directory, `stdin`, `stdout`, `stderr`, command-line arguments, and shell environment.

The following examples illustrate the flexibility of using Condor. We assume that the jobs submitted are serial jobs intended for a cluster that has a shared file system across all nodes. Therefore, all jobs use the Vanilla Universe, the simplest one for running serial jobs. The other Condor Universes are explored later.

**Example 1.** Example 1 is the simplest submit description file possible. It queues up one copy of the program 'foo' for execution by Condor. A log file called 'foo.log' is generated by Condor. The log file contains events pertaining to the job while it runs inside of Condor. When the job finishes, its exit conditions are noted in the log file. We recommend that you always have a log file so you know what happened to your jobs. The *queue* statement in the submit description file tells Condor to use all the information specified so far to create a job ClassAd and place the job into the queue. Lines that begin with a pound character (#) are comments and are ignored by `condor_submit`.

```
# Example 1 : Simple submit file
universe = vanilla
executable = foo
log = foo.log
queue
```

**Example 2.** Example 2 queues two copies of the program 'mathematica'. The first copy runs in directory 'run_1', and the second runs in directory 'run_2'. For both queued copies, 'stdin' will be 'test.data', 'stdout' will be 'loop.out', and 'stderr' will be 'loop.error'. Two sets of files will be written, since the files are each written to their own directories. This is a convenient way to organize data for a large group of Condor jobs.

```
# Example 2: demonstrate use of multiple
# directories for data organization.
```

```
universe = vanilla
executable = mathematica
# Give some command line args, remap stdio
arguments = -solver matrix
input = test.data
output = loop.out
error = loop.error
log = loop.log

initialdir = run_1
queue
initialdir = run_2
queue
```

**Example 3.** The submit description file for Example 3 queues 150 runs of program 'foo'. This job requires Condor to run the program on machines that have greater than 128 megabytes of physical memory, and it further requires that the job not be scheduled to run on a specific node. Of the machines that meet the requirements, the job prefers to run on the fastest floating-point nodes currently available to accept the job. It also advises Condor that the job will use up to 180 megabytes of memory when running. Each of the 150 runs of the program is given its own process number, starting with process number 0. Several built-in macros can be used in a submit description file; one of them is the $(Process) macro which Condor expands to be the process number in the job cluster. This causes files 'stdin', 'stdout', and 'stderr' to be 'in.0', 'out.0', and 'err.0' for the first run of the program, 'in.1', 'out.1', and 'err.1' for the second run of the program, and so forth. A single log file will list events for all 150 jobs in this job cluster.

```
# Example 3: Submit lots of runs and use the
# pre-defined $(Process) macro.
universe = vanilla
executable = foo
requirements = Memory > 128  && Machine != "server-node.cluster.edu"
rank = KFlops
image_size = 180

Error   = err.$(Process)
Input   = in.$(Process)
Output  = out.$(Process)
Log = foo.log

queue 150
```

Note that the `requirements` and `rank` entries in the submit description file will become the requirements and rank attributes of the subsequently created ClassAd for this job. These are arbitrary expressions that can reference any attributes of either the machine or the job; see Section 14.1.2 for more on requirements and rank expressions in ClassAds.

### 14.2.3   Overview of User Commands

Once you have jobs submitted to Condor, you can manage them and monitor their progress. Table 14.1 shows several commands available to the Condor user to view the job queue, check the status of nodes in the pool, and perform several other activities. Most of these commands have many command-line options; see the Command Reference chapter of the Condor manual for complete documentation. To provide an introduction from a user perspective, we give here a quick tour showing several of these commands in action.

| Command | Description |
|---|---|
| `condor_history` | View log of Condor jobs completed to date |
| `condor_hold` | Put jobs in the queue in hold state |
| `condor_prio` | Change priority of jobs in the queue |
| `condor_qedit` | Modify attributes of a previously submitted job |
| `condor_q` | Display information about jobs in the queue |
| `condor_release` | Release held jobs in the queue |
| `condor_reschedule` | Update scheduling information to the central manager |
| `condor_rm` | Remove jobs from the queue |
| `condor_run` | Submit a shell command-line as a Condor job |
| `condor_status` | Display status of the Condor pool |
| `condor_submit_dag` | Manage and queue jobs within a specified DAG for interjob dependencies. |
| `condor_submit` | Queue jobs for execution |
| `condor_userlog` | Display and summarize job statistics from job log files |

**Table 14.1**
List of user commands.

When jobs are submitted, Condor will attempt to find resources to service the jobs. A list of all users with jobs submitted may be obtained through `condor_status` with the *-submitters* option. An example of this would yield output similar to the following:

```
C:\>condor_status -submitters
```

| Name | Machine | Running | IdleJobs | HeldJobs |
|------|---------|---------|----------|----------|
| ballard@cs.wisc.edu | bluebird.c | 0 | 11 | 0 |
| nice-user.condor@cs. | cardinal.c | 6 | 504 | 0 |
| wright@cs.wisc.edu | finch.cs.w | 1 | 1 | 0 |
| jbasney@cs.wisc.edu | perdita.cs | 0 | 0 | 5 |

| | RunningJobs | IdleJobs | HeldJobs |
|---|-------------|----------|----------|
| ballard@cs.wisc.edu | 0 | 11 | 0 |
| jbasney@cs.wisc.edu | 0 | 0 | 5 |
| nice-user.condor@cs. | 6 | 504 | 0 |
| wright@cs.wisc.edu | 1 | 1 | 0 |
| Total | 7 | 516 | 5 |

**Checking on the Progress of Jobs.** The condor_q command displays the status of all jobs in the queue. An example of the output from condor_q is

```
C:\>condor_q

-- Schedd: uug.cs.wisc.edu : <128.115.121.12:33102>
 ID      OWNER          SUBMITTED     RUN_TIME ST PRI SIZE CMD
 55574.0   jane          6/23 11:33   4+03:35:28 R  0   25.7 seycplex seymour.d
 55575.0   jane          6/23 11:44   0+23:24:40 R  0   26.8 seycplexpseudo sey
 83193.0   jane          3/28 15:11  48+15:50:55 R  0   17.5 cplexmip test1.mp
 83196.0   jane          3/29 08:32  48+03:16:44 R  0   83.1 cplexmip test3.mps
 83212.0   jane          4/13 16:31  41+18:44:40 R  0   39.7 cplexmip test2.mps

5 jobs; 0 idle, 5 running, 0 held
```

This output contains many columns of information about the queued jobs. The ST column (for status) shows the status of current jobs in the queue. An R in the status column means the the job is currently running. An I stands for idle. The status H is the hold state. In the hold state, the job will not be scheduled to run until it is released (via the condor_release command). The RUN_TIME time reported for a job is the time that job has been allocated to a machine as DAYS+HOURS+MINS+SECS.

Another useful method of tracking the progress of jobs is through the user log. If you have specified a log command in your submit file, the progress of the job may be followed by viewing the log file. Various events such as execution commencement, checkpoint, eviction, and termination are logged in the file along with the time at which the event occurred. Here is a sample snippet from a user log file

```
000 (8135.000.000) 05/25 19:10:03 Job submitted from host: <128.105.146.14:1816>
...
001 (8135.000.000) 05/25 19:12:17 Job executing on host: <128.105.165.131:1026>
...
005 (8135.000.000) 05/25 19:13:06 Job terminated.
        (1) Normal termination (return value 0)
                        Usr 0 00:00:37, Sys 0 00:00:00  -  Run Remote Usage
                        Usr 0 00:00:00, Sys 0 00:00:05  -  Run Local Usage
                        Usr 0 00:00:37, Sys 0 00:00:00  -  Total Remote Usage
                        Usr 0 00:00:00, Sys 0 00:00:05  -  Total Local Usage
        9624  -  Run Bytes Sent By Job
        7146159 -  Run Bytes Received By Job
        9624  -  Total Bytes Sent By Job
        7146159 -  Total Bytes Received By Job
...
```

The `condor_jobmonitor` tool parses the events in a user log file and can use the information to graphically display the progress of your jobs. Figure 14.2 contains a screenshot of `condor_jobmonitor` in action.

You can locate all the machines that are running your job with the `condor_status` command. For example, to find all the machines that are running jobs submitted by breach@cs.wisc.edu, type

```
C:\>condor_status -constraint 'RemoteUser == "breach@cs.wisc.edu"'
```

| Name | Arch | OpSys | State | Activity | LoadAv | Mem | ActvtyTime |
|------|------|-------|-------|----------|--------|-----|------------|
| alfred.cs. | INTEL | LINUX | Claimed | Busy | 0.980 | 64 | 0+07:10:02 |
| biron.cs.w | INTEL | LINUX | Claimed | Busy | 1.000 | 128 | 0+01:10:00 |
| cambridge. | INTEL | LINUX | Claimed | Busy | 0.988 | 64 | 0+00:15:00 |
| falcons.cs | INTEL | LINUX | Claimed | Busy | 0.996 | 32 | 0+02:05:03 |
| happy.cs.w | INTEL | LINUX | Claimed | Busy | 0.988 | 128 | 0+03:05:00 |
| istat03.st | INTEL | LINUX | Claimed | Busy | 0.883 | 64 | 0+06:45:01 |
| istat04.st | INTEL | LINUX | Claimed | Busy | 0.988 | 64 | 0+00:10:00 |
| istat09.st | INTEL | LINUX | Claimed | Busy | 0.301 | 64 | 0+03:45:00 |

...

To find all the machines that are running any job at all, type

```
C:\>condor_status -run
```

| Name | Arch | OpSys | LoadAv | RemoteUser | ClientMachine |
|------|------|-------|--------|------------|---------------|
| adriana.cs | INTEL | LINUX | 0.980 | hepcon@cs.wisc.edu | chevre.cs.wisc. |
| alfred.cs. | INTEL | LINUX | 0.980 | breach@cs.wisc.edu | neufchatel.cs.w |
| amul.cs.wi | INTEL | LINUX | 1.000 | nice-user.condor@cs. | chevre.cs.wisc. |
| anfrom.cs. | INTEL | LINUX | 1.023 | ashoks@jules.ncsa.ui | jules.ncsa.uiuc |
| anthrax.cs | INTEL | LINUX | 0.285 | hepcon@cs.wisc.edu | chevre.cs.wisc. |

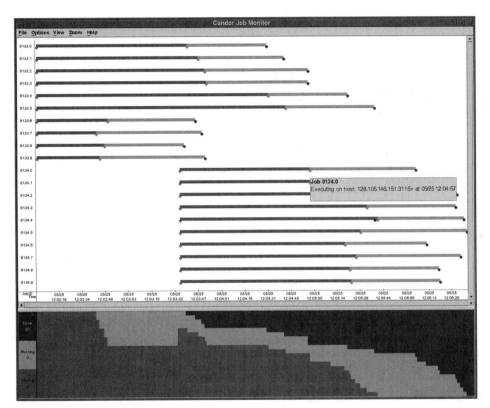

**Figure 14.2**
Condor jobmonitor tool.

```
astro.cs.w INTEL    LINUX       1.000   nice-user.condor@cs. chevre.cs.wisc.
aura.cs.wi INTEL    LINUX       0.996   nice-user.condor@cs. chevre.cs.wisc.
balder.cs. INTEL    LINUX       1.000   nice-user.condor@cs. chevre.cs.wisc.
bamba.cs.w INTEL    LINUX       1.574   dmarino@cs.wisc.edu  riola.cs.wisc.e
bardolph.c INTEL    LINUX       1.000   nice-user.condor@cs. chevre.cs.wisc.
...
```

**Removing a Job from the Queue.**    You can remove a job from the queue at any time using the `condor_rm` command. If the job that is being removed is currently running, the job is killed without a checkpoint, and its queue entry is removed. The following example shows the queue of jobs before and after a job is removed.

```
% condor_q
```

```
-- Submitter: froth.cs.wisc.edu : <128.105.73.44:33847> : froth.cs.wisc.edu
 ID       OWNER            SUBMITTED    RUN_TIME  ST PRI SIZE CMD
 125.0    jbasney          4/10 15:35   0+00:00:00 I  -10 1.2  hello.remote
 132.0    raman            4/11 16:57   0+00:00:00 R  0   1.4  hello

2 jobs; 1 idle, 1 running, 0 held

%  condor_rm 132.0
Job 132.0 removed.

%  condor_q

-- Submitter: froth.cs.wisc.edu : <128.105.73.44:33847> : froth.cs.wisc.edu
 ID       OWNER            SUBMITTED    RUN_TIME  ST PRI SIZE CMD
 125.0    jbasney          4/10 15:35   0+00:00:00 I  -10 1.2  hello.remote

1 jobs; 1 idle, 0 running, 0 held
```

**Changing the Priority of Jobs.** In addition to the priorities assigned to each user, Condor provides users with the capability of assigning priorities to any submitted job. These job priorities are local to each queue and range from $-20$ to $+20$, with higher values meaning better priority.

The default priority of a job is 0. Job priorities can be modified using the condor_prio command. For example, to change the priority of a job to $-15$, type

```
%  condor_q raman

-- Submitter: froth.cs.wisc.edu : <128.105.73.44:33847> : froth.cs.wisc.edu
 ID       OWNER            SUBMITTED    RUN_TIME  ST PRI SIZE CMD
 126.0    raman            4/11 15:06   0+00:00:00 I  0   0.3  hello

1 jobs; 1 idle, 0 running, 0 held

%  condor_prio -p -15 126.0

%  condor_q raman

-- Submitter: froth.cs.wisc.edu : <128.105.73.44:33847> : froth.cs.wisc.edu
 ID       OWNER            SUBMITTED    RUN_TIME  ST PRI SIZE CMD
 126.0    raman            4/11 15:06   0+00:00:00 I  -15 0.3  hello

1 jobs; 1 idle, 0 running, 0 held
```

We emphasize that these *job* priorities are completely different from the *user* priorities assigned by Condor. Job priorities control only which one of *your* jobs should run next; there is no effect whatsoever on whether your jobs will run before another user's jobs.

**Determining Why a Job Does Not Run.**   A specific job may not run for several reasons. These reasons include failed job or machine constraints, bias due to preferences, insufficient priority, and the preemption throttle that is implemented by the `condor_negotiator` to prevent thrashing. Many of these reasons can be diagnosed by using the *-analyze* option of `condor_q`. For example, the following job submitted by user jbasney had not run for several days.

```
% condor_q

-- Submitter: froth.cs.wisc.edu : <128.105.73.44:33847> : froth.cs.wisc.edu
 ID      OWNER            SUBMITTED     RUN_TIME ST PRI SIZE CMD
 125.0   jbasney          4/10 15:35   0+00:00:00 I  -10 1.2  hello.remote

1 jobs; 1 idle, 0 running, 0 held
```

Running `condor_q`'s analyzer provided the following information:

```
%  condor_q 125.0 -analyze

-- Submitter: froth.cs.wisc.edu : <128.105.73.44:33847> : froth.cs.wisc.edu
---
125.000:  Run analysis summary.  Of 323 resource offers,
          323 do not satisfy the request's constraints
            0 resource offer constraints are not satisfied by this request
            0 are serving equal or higher priority customers
            0 are serving more preferred customers
            0 cannot preempt because preemption has been held
            0 are available to service your request

WARNING:  Be advised:
   No resources matched request's constraints
   Check the Requirements expression below:

Requirements = Arch == "INTEL" && OpSys == "IRIX6" &&
  Disk >= ExecutableSize && VirtualMemory >= ImageSize
```

The `Requirements` expression for this job specifies a platform that does not exist. Therefore, the expression always evaluates to FALSE.

While the analyzer can diagnose most common problems, there are some situations that it cannot reliably detect because of the instantaneous and local nature

of the information it uses to detect the problem. The analyzer may report that
resources are available to service the request, but the job still does not run. In
most of these situations, the delay is transient, and the job will run during the next
negotiation cycle.

If the problem persists and the analyzer is unable to detect the situation, the
job may begin to run but immediately terminates and return to the idle state.
Viewing the job's error and log files (specified in the submit command file) and
Condor's SHADOW_LOG file may assist in tracking down the problem. If the cause is
still unclear, you should contact your system administrator.

**Job Completion.**   When a Condor job completes (either through normal means
or abnormal means), Condor will remove it from the job queue (therefore, it will
no longer appear in the output of condor_q) and insert it into the job history file.
You can examine the job history file with the condor_history command. If you
specified a log file in your submit description file, then the job exit status will be
recorded there as well.

By default, Condor will send you an e-mail message when your job completes.
You can modify this behavior with the condor_submit "notification" command.
The message will include the exit status of your job or notification that your job
terminated abnormally.

### 14.2.4   Submitting Different Types of Jobs: Alternative Universes

A Universe in Condor defines an execution environment. Condor supports the
following Universes on Windows 2000:

- Vanilla
- MPI
- Scheduler

The Universe attribute is specified in the submit description file. At the publication time of this book, the Unix port of Condor has several more Universes
available than does Condor on Windows 2000. For instance, Condor on Unix has a
PVM Universe in addition to MPI. The Condor Team intends ultimately to support
all Universes on Windows 2000 as well; in fact, a PVM Universe may already exist
in Condor for Windows 2000 by the time you read this.

**Vanilla Universe.**   The Vanilla Universe is used to run serial (nonparallel) jobs.
The examples provided in the preceding section use the Vanilla Universe. Any
program that runs outside of Condor will run in the Vanilla Universe. Binary
executables as well as batch files are welcome in the Vanilla Universe.

A typical Vanilla Universe job relies on a shared file system between the submit machine and all the nodes in order to allow jobs to access their data. However, if a shared file system is not available, Condor can transfer the files needed by the job to and from the execute machine. See Section 14.2.5 for more details on this.

**MPI Universe.** The MPI Universe allows parallel programs written with MPI to be managed by Condor. To submit an MPI program to Condor, specify the number of nodes to be used in the parallel job. Use the `machine_count` attribute in the submit description file, as in the following example:

```
# Submit file for an MPI job which needs 8 large memory nodes
universe = mpi
executable = my-parallel-job
requirements = Memory >= 512
machine_count = 8
queue
```

Further options in the submit description file allow a variety of parameters, such as the job requirements or the executable to use across the different nodes.

By late 2001, Condor expects your MPI job to be linked with the MPICH implementation of MPI configured with the `ch_p4` device (see Section 9.6). Support for different devices and MPI implementations is expected, however, so check the documentation included with your specific version of Condor for additional information on how your job should be linked with MPI for Condor.

If your Condor pool consists of both dedicated compute machines (that is, Beowulf cluster nodes) and opportunistic machines (that is, desktop workstations), by default Condor will schedule MPI jobs to run on the dedicated resources only.

**Scheduler Universe.** The Scheduler Universe is used to submit a job that will immediately run on the *submit* machine, as opposed to a remote execution machine. The purpose is to provide a facility for job *meta-schedulers* that desire to manage the submission and removal of jobs into a Condor queue. Condor includes one such meta-scheduler that utilizes the Scheduler Universe: the DAGMan scheduler, which can be used to specify complex interdependencies between jobs. See Section 14.2.6 for more on DAGMan.

### 14.2.5   Giving Your Job Access to Its Data Files

Once your job starts on a machine in your pool, how does it access its data files? Condor provides several choices.

Condor can use a shared file system, if one is available and permanently mounted across the machines in the pool. This is usually the case in a Beowulf cluster. But what if your Condor pool includes nondedicated (desktop) machines as well? You could specify a **Requirements** expression in your submit description file to require that jobs run only on machines that actually do have access to a common, shared file system. Or, you could request in the submit description file that Condor transfer your job's data files using the Condor File Transfer mechanism.

When Condor finds a machine willing to execute your job, it can create a temporary subdirectory for your job on the execute machine. The Condor File Transfer mechanism will then send via TCP the job executable(s) and input files from the submitting machine into this temporary directory on the execute machine. After the input files have been transferred, the execute machine will start running the job with the temporary directory as the job's current working directory. When the job completes or is kicked off, Condor File Transfer will automatically send back to the submit machine any output files created or modified by the job. After the files have been sent back successfully, the temporary working directory on the execute machine is deleted.

Condor's File Transfer mechanism has several features to ensure data integrity in a nondedicated environment. For instance, transfers of multiple files are performed atomically.

Condor File Transfer behavior is specified at job submission time using the submit description file and `condor_submit`. Along with all the other job submit description parameters, you can use the following File Transfer commands in the submit description file:

**transfer_input_files** = < **file1, file2, file... >**: Use this parameter to list all the files that should be transferred into the working directory for the job before the job is started.

**transfer_output_files** = < **file1, file2, file... >**: Use this parameter to explicitly list which output files to transfer back from the temporary working directory on the execute machine to the submit machine. Most of the time, however, there is no need to use this parameter. If `transfer_output_files` is not specified, Condor will automatically transfer in the job's temporary working directory all files that have been modified or created by the job.

**transfer_files** = <**ONEXIT | ALWAYS | NEVER**>: If `transfer_files` is set to `ONEXIT`, Condor will transfer the job's output files back to the submitting machine only when the job completes (exits). Specifying `ALWAYS` tells Condor to transfer back the output files when the job completes *or* when Condor kicks off the job (preempts) from a machine prior to job completion. The `ALWAYS` option is specifically intended for fault-tolerant jobs that periodocially write out their state to disk and can restart where they left off. Any output files transferred back to the submit machine when Condor preempts a job will automatically be sent back out again as input files when the job restarts.

### 14.2.6   The DAGMan Scheduler

The DAGMan scheduler within Condor allows the specification of dependencies between a set of programs. A directed acyclic graph (DAG) can be used to represent a set of programs where the input, output, or execution of one or more programs is dependent on one or more other programs. The programs are nodes (vertices) in the graph, and the edges (arcs) identify the dependencies. Each program within the DAG becomes a job submitted to Condor. The DAGMan scheduler enforces the dependencies of the DAG.

An input file to DAGMan identifies the nodes of the graph, as well as how to submit each job (node) to Condor. It also specifies the graph's dependencies and describes any extra processing that is involved with the nodes of the graph and must take place just before or just after the job is run.

A simple diamond-shaped DAG with four nodes is given in Figure 14.3.

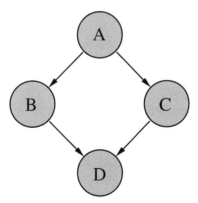

**Figure 14.3**
A directed acyclic graph with four nodes.

A simple input file to DAGMan for this diamond-shaped DAG may be

```
# file name: diamond.dag
Job   A   A.condor
Job   B   B.condor
```

```
Job   C   C.condor
Job   D   D.condor
PARENT A CHILD B C
PARENT B C CHILD D
```

The four nodes are named A, B, C, and D. Lines beginning with the keyword Job identify each node by giving it a name, and they also specify a file to be used as a submit description file for submission as a Condor job. Lines with the keyword **PARENT** identify the dependencies of the graph. Just like regular Condor submit description files, lines with a leading pound character (#) are comments.

The DAGMan scheduler uses the graph to order the submission of jobs to Condor. The submission of a child node will not take place until the parent node has successfully completed. No ordering of siblings is imposed by the graph, and therefore DAGMan does not impose an ordering when submitting the jobs to Condor. For the diamond-shaped example, nodes B and C will be submitted to Condor in parallel.

Each job in the example graph uses a different submit description file. An example submit description file for job A may be

```
# file name: A.condor
executable   = nodeA.exe
output       = A.out
error        = A.err
log          = diamond.log
universe     = vanilla
queue
```

An important restriction for submit description files of a DAG is that each node of the graph use the same log file. DAGMan uses the log file in enforcing the graph's dependencies.

The graph for execution under Condor is submitted by using the Condor tool condor_submit_dag. For the diamond-shaped example, submission would use the command

```
condor_submit_dag diamond.dag
```

## 14.3   Condor Architecture

A Condor pool comprises a single machine that serves as the *central manager* and an arbitrary number of other machines that have joined the pool. Conceptually, the pool is a collection of resources (machines) and resource requests (jobs). The role of Condor is to match waiting requests with available resources. Every part of Condor sends periodic updates to the central manager, the centralized repository of information about the state of the pool. The central manager periodically assesses the current state of the pool and tries to match pending requests with the appropriate resources.

### 14.3.1   The Condor Daemons

In this subsection we describe all the daemons (background server processes) in Condor and the role each plays in the system.

`condor_master`: This daemon's role is to simplify system administration. The `condor_master` is registered by the installation program with the Windows 2000 Service Control Manager as a system service. Windows will automatically start the master at boot time. It is responsible for keeping the rest of the Condor daemons running on each machine in a pool. The master spawns the other daemons and periodically checks the timestamps on the binaries of the daemons it is managing. If it finds new binaries, the master will restart the affected daemons. This allows Condor to be upgraded easily. In addition, if any other Condor daemon on the machine exits abnormally, the `condor_master` will send e-mail to the system administrator with information about the problem and then automatically restart the affected daemon. The `condor_master` also supports various administrative commands to start, stop, or reconfigure daemons remotely. The `condor_master` runs on every machine in your Condor pool.

`condor_startd`: This daemon represents a machine to the Condor pool. It advertises a machine ClassAd that contains attributes about the machine's capabilities and policies. Running the `startd` enables a machine to execute jobs. The `condor_startd` is responsible for enforcing the policy under which remote jobs will be started, suspended, resumed, vacated, or killed. When the `startd` is ready to execute a Condor job, it spawns the `condor_starter`, described below.

`condor_starter`: This program is the entity that spawns the remote Condor job on a given machine. It sets up the execution environment and monitors the job once it is running. The starter detects job completion, sends back status information to the submitting machine, and exits.

`condor_schedd`: This daemon represents jobs to the Condor pool. Any machine that allows users to submit jobs needs to have a `condor_schedd` running. Users submit jobs to the `condor_schedd`, where they are stored in the *job queue*. The various tools to view and manipulate the job queue (such as `condor_submit`, `condor_q`, or `condor_rm`) connect to the `condor_schedd` to do their work.

`condor_shadow`: This program runs on the machine where a job was submitted whenever that job is executing. The shadow serves requests for files to transfer, logs the job's progress, and reports statistics when the job completes.

`condor_collector`: This daemon is responsible for collecting all the information about the status of a Condor pool. All other daemons periodically send ClassAd updates to the collector. These ClassAds contain all the information about the state of the daemons, the resources they represent, or resource requests in the pool (such as jobs that have been submitted to a given `condor_schedd`). The `condor_collector` can be thought of as a dynamic database of ClassAds. The `condor_status` command can be used to query the collector for specific information about various parts of Condor. The Condor daemons also query the collector for important information, such as what address to use for sending commands to a remote machine. The `condor_collector` runs on the machine designated as the central manager.

`condor_negotiator`: This daemon is responsible for all the matchmaking within the Condor system. The negotiator is also responsible for enforcing user priorities in the system.

### 14.3.2   The Condor Daemons in Action

Within a given Condor installation, one machine will serve as the pool's central manager. In addition to the `condor_master` daemon that runs on every machine in a Condor pool, the central manager runs the `condor_collector` and the `condor_negotiator` daemons. Any machine in the installation that should be capable of running jobs should run the `condor_startd`, and any machine that should maintain a job queue and therefore allow users on that machine to submit jobs should run a `condor_schedd`.

Condor allows any machine simultaneously to execute jobs and serve as a submission point by running both a `condor_startd` and a `condor_schedd`. Figure 14.4 displays a Condor pool in which every machine in the pool can both submit and run jobs, including the central manager.

The interface for adding a job to the Condor system is `condor_submit`, which reads a job description file, creates a job ClassAd, and gives that ClassAd to the `condor_schedd` managing the local job queue. This triggers a *negotiation cycle*.

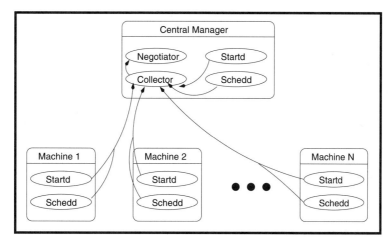

**Figure 14.4**
Daemon layout of an idle Condor pool.

During a negotiation cycle, the `condor_negotiator` queries the `condor_collector` to discover all machines that are willing to perform work and all users with idle jobs. The `condor_negotiator` communicates *in user priority order* with each `condor_schedd` that has idle jobs in its queue, and performs matchmaking to match jobs with machines such that both job and machine ClassAd requirements are satisfied and preferences (rank) are honored.

Once the `condor_negotiator` makes a match, the `condor_schedd` claims the corresponding machine and is allowed to make subsequent scheduling decisions about the order in which jobs run. This hierarchical, distributed scheduling architecture enhances Condor's scalability and flexibility.

When the `condor_schedd` starts a job, it spawns a `condor_shadow` process on the submit machine, and the `condor_startd` spawns a `condor_starter` process on the corresponding execute machine (see Figure 14.5). The shadow transfers the job ClassAd and any data files required to the starter, which spawns the user's application.

When the job completes or is aborted, the `condor_starter` removes every process spawned by the user job, and frees any temporary scratch disk space used by the job. This ensures that the execute machine is left in a clean state and that resources (such as processes or disk space) are not being leaked.

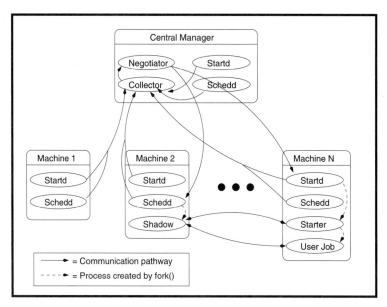

**Figure 14.5**
Daemon layout when a job submitted from Machine 2 is running.

## 14.4   Installing Condor under Windows 2000

The first step toward the installation of Condor is to download the software from the Condor Web site at `www.cs.wisc.edu/condor/downloads`. There is no cost to download or use Condor.

On the Web site you will find complete documentation and release notes for the different versions and platforms supported.

Before you begin the installation, there are several issues you need to consider and actions to perform.

**Location.** On Windows 2000, Condor is installed as a system service. Therefore, it is best to install Condor on the local disk (in `C:\condor`).

**Administrator.** Condor needs an e-mail address for an administrator. Should Condor need assistance, this is where e-mail will be sent.

**Central Manager.** The central manager of a Condor pool does matchmaking and collects information for the pool. Choose a central manager that has a good network connection and is likely to be online all the time (or at least rebooted quickly in the event of a failure).

Once you have decided the answers to these questions you are ready to begin installation. Execute the file obtained by download to start installation. The configuration tool will ask you a short series of questions, mostly related to the issues addressed above. Answer the questions appropriately for your site, and Condor will be installed.

Section 14.5 discusses how to configure and customize your pool for a dedicated cluster.

After Condor is installed, you will want to customize a few security configuration right away. Condor implements security at the host (or machine) level. A set of configuration defaults set by the installation deal with access to the Condor pool by host. Given the distributed nature of the daemons that implement Condor, access to these daemons is naturally host based. Each daemon can be given the ability to allow or deny service (by host) within its configuration. Within the access levels available, *Read*, *Write*, *Administrator*, and *Config* are important to set correctly for each pool of machines.

**Read:** allows a machine to obtain information from Condor. Examples of information that may be read are the status of the pool and the contents of the job queue.

**Write:** allows a machine to provide information to Condor, such as submit a job or join the pool.

**Administrator:** allows a user on the machine to affect privileged operations such as changing a user's priority level or starting and stopping the Condor system from running.

**Config:** allows a user on the machine to change Condor's configuration settings remotely using the `condor_config_val` tool's *-set* and *-rset* options. This has very serious security implications, so we recommend that you not enable Config access to any hosts.

The defaults during installation give all machines read and write access. The central manager is also given administrator access. You will probably wish to change these defaults for your site. Read the Condor Administrator's Manual for details on network authorization in Condor and how to customize it for your wishes.

## 14.5   Configuring Condor

This section describes how to configure and customize Condor for your site. It discusses the configuration files used by Condor, describes how to configure the policy for starting and stopping jobs in your pool, and recommends settings for using Condor on a cluster.

A number of configuration files facilitate different levels of control over how Condor is configured on each machine in a pool. The top-level or global configuration file is shared by all machines in the pool. For ease of administration, this file should be located on a shared file system. In addition, each machine may have multiple local configuration files allowing the local settings to override the global settings. Hence, each machine may have different daemons running, different policies for when to start and stop Condor jobs, and so on.

All of Condor's configuration files should be owned and writable only by Administrator. It is important to maintain strict control over these files because they contain security-sensitive settings.

### 14.5.1   Location of Condor's Configuration Files

Condor has a default set of locations it uses to try to find its top-level configuration file. The locations are checked in the following order:

1.   The file specified in the CONDOR_CONFIG environment variable.

2.   The file specified in the HKEY_LOCAL_MACHINE\Software\Condor registry entry. This entry is set when you run Condor's installation program on Windows.

If a Condor daemon or tool cannot find its global configuration file when it starts, it will print an error message and immediately exit. Once the global configuration file has been read by Condor, however, any other local configuration files can be specified with the LOCAL_CONFIG_FILE macro.

This macro can contain a single entry if you want only two levels of configuration (global and local). If you need a more complex division of configuration values (for example, if you have machines of different platforms in the same pool and desire separate files for platform-specific settings), LOCAL_CONFIG_FILE can contain a list of files.

Condor provides other macros to help you easily define the location of the local configuration files for each machine in your pool. Most of these are special macros that evaluate to different values depending on which host is reading the global configuration file:

- HOSTNAME: The hostname of the local host.
- FULL_HOSTNAME: The fully qualified hostname of the local host.
- OPSYS: The operating system of the local host, such as "LINUX," "WINNT4" (for Windows NT), or "WINNT5" (for Windows 2000). This is primarily useful in heterogeneous clusters with multiple platforms.
- RELEASE_DIR: The directory where Condor is installed on each host. This macro is defined in the global configuration file and is set by Condor's installation program.

By default, the local configuration file is defined as

```
LOCAL_CONFIG_FILE = $(RELEASE_DIR)\condor_config.local
```

### 14.5.2   Recommended Configuration File Layout for a Cluster

Ease of administration is an important consideration in a cluster, particularly if you have a large number of nodes. To make Condor easy to configure, we highly recommend that you install all of your Condor configuration files, even the per-node local configuration files, on a shared file system. That way, you can easily make changes in one place. On Windows 2000, you must use a shared drive that is mapped at boot time for this, instead of drives that are mapped when you log in.

You should use a subdirectory in your release directory for holding all of the local configuration files. On Windows 2000, you will have to create this directory yourself. For the purposes of the following examples, we will assume you have called this subdirectory 'config'.

You should create separate files for each node in your cluster, using the hostname as the first half of the filename, and ".local" as the end. For example, if your cluster nodes are named "n01", "n02" and so on, the files should be called 'n01.local', 'n02.local', and so on. These files should all be placed in your 'config' directory.

In your global configuration file, you should use the following setting to describe the location of your local configuration files:

```
LOCAL_CONFIG_FILE = $(RELEASE_DIR)\config\$(HOSTNAME).local
```

The central manager of your pool needs special settings in its local configuration file. These attributes are set automatically by the Condor installation program. The rest of the local configuration files can be left empty at first.

Having your configuration files laid out in this way will help you more easily customize Condor's behavior on your cluster. We discuss other possible configuration scenarios at the end of this chapter.

**Note:** We recommend that you store all of your Condor configuration files under a version control system, such as CVS. While this is not required, it will help you keep track of the changes you make to your configuration, who made them, when they occurred, and why. In general, it is a good idea to store configuration files under a version control system, since none of the above concerns are specific to Condor.

### 14.5.3   Customizing Condor's Policy Expressions

Certain configuration expressions are used to control Condor's policy for executing, suspending, and evicting jobs. Their interaction can be somewhat complex. Defining an inappropriate policy impacts the throughput of your cluster and the happiness of its users. If you are interested in creating a specialized policy for your pool, we recommend that you read the Condor Administrator's Manual. Only a basic introduction follows.

All policy expressions are ClassAd expressions and are defined in Condor's configuration files. Policies are usually poolwide and are therefore defined in the global configuration file. If individual nodes in your pool require their own policy, however, the appropriate expressions can be placed in local configuration files.

The policy expressions are treated by the `condor_startd` as part of its machine ClassAd (along with all the attributes you can view with `condor_status -long`). They are always evaluated against a job ClassAd, either by the `condor_negotiator` when trying to find a match or by the `condor_startd` when it is deciding what to do with the job that is currently running. Therefore, all policy expressions can reference attributes of a job, such as the memory usage or owner, in addition to attributes of the machine, such as keyboard idle time or CPU load.

Most policy expressions are ClassAd Boolean expressions, so they evaluate to TRUE, FALSE, or UNDEFINED. UNDEFINED occurs when an expression references a ClassAd attribute that is not found in either the machine's ClassAd or the ClassAd of the job under consideration. For some expressions, this is treated as a fatal error, so you should be sure to use the ClassAd meta-operators, described in Section 14.1.2 when referring to attributes which might not be present in all ClassAds.

An explanation of policy expressions requires an understanding of the different stages that a job can go through from initially executing until the job completes or is evicted from the machine. Each policy expression is then described in terms of the step in the progression that it controls.

**The Lifespan of a Job Executing in Condor.**  When a job is submitted to Condor, the `condor_negotiator` performs matchmaking to find a suitable resource to use for the computation. This process involves satisfying both the job and the machine's requirements for each other. The machine can define the exact conditions under which it is willing to be considered available for running jobs. The job can define exactly what kind of machine it is willing to use.

Once a job has been matched with a given machine, there are four states the job can be in: running, suspended, graceful shutdown, and quick shutdown. As soon as the match is made, the job sets up its execution environment and begins running.

While it is executing, a job can be suspended (for example, because of other activity on the machine where it is running). Once it has been suspended, the job can resume execution or can move on to preemption or eviction.

All Condor jobs have two methods for preemption: graceful and quick. Graceful implies that the program told to get off the system, but it is given time to clean up after itself. A quick shutdown involves rapidly killing all processes associated with a job, without giving them any time to execute their own cleanup procedures. The Condor system performs checks to ensure that processes are not left behind once a job is evicted from a given node.

**Condor Policy Expressions.**  Various expressions are used to control the policy for starting, suspending, resuming, and preempting jobs.

**START:** when the `condor_startd` is willing to start executing a job.

**RANK:** how much the `condor_startd` prefers each type of job running on it. The RANK expression is a floating-point instead of a Boolean value. The `condor_startd` will preempt the job it is currently running if there is another job in the system that yields a higher value for this expression.

**WANT_SUSPEND:** controls whether the `condor_startd` should even consider suspending this job or not. In effect, it determines which expression, SUSPEND or PREEMPT, should be evaluated while the job is running. WANT_SUSPEND does not control when the job is actually suspended; for that purpose, you should use the SUSPEND expression.

**SUSPEND:** when the `condor_startd` should suspend the currently running job. If WANT_SUSPEND evaluates to TRUE, SUSPEND is periodically evaluated whenever a job is executing on a machine. If SUSPEND becomes TRUE, the job will be suspended.

**CONTINUE:** if and when the `condor_startd` should resume a suspended job. The CONTINUE expression is evaluated only while a job is suspended. If it evaluates to TRUE, the job will be resumed, and the condor_startd will go back to the Claimed/Busy state.

PREEMPT: when the condor_startd should preempt the currently running job. This expression is evaluated whenever a job has been suspended. If WANT_SUSPEND evaluates to FALSE, PREEMPT is checked while the job is executing.

WANT_VACATE: whether the job should be evicted gracefully or quickly if Condor is preempting a job (because the PREEMPT expression evaluates to TRUE). If WANT_VACATE is FALSE, the condor_startd will immediately kill the job and all of its child processes whenever it must evict the application. If WANT_VACATE is TRUE, the condor_startd performs a graceful shutdown, instead.

KILL: when the condor_startd should give up on a graceful preemption and move directly to the quick shutdown.

PREEMPTION_REQUIREMENTS: used by the condor_negotiator when it is performing matchmaking, not by the condor_startd. While trying to schedule jobs on resources in your pool, the condor_negotiator considers the priorities of the various users in the system (see Section 14.6.3 for more details). If a user with a better priority has jobs waiting in the queue and no resources are currently idle, the matchmaker will consider preempting another user's jobs and giving those resources to the user with the better priority. This process is known as *priority preemption*. The PREEMPTION_REQUIREMENTS expression must evaluate to TRUE for such a preemption to take place.

PREEMPTION_RANK: a floating-point value evaluated by the condor_negotiator. If the matchmaker decides it must preempt a job due to user priorities, the macro PREEMPTION_RANK determines which resource to preempt. Among the set of all resources that make the PREEMPTION_REQUIREMENTS expression evaluate to TRUE, the one with the highest value for PREEMPTION_RANK is evicted.

### 14.5.4   Customizing Condor's Other Configuration Settings

In addition to the policy expressions, you will need to modify other settings to customize Condor for your cluster.

DAEMON_LIST: the comma-separated list of daemons that should be spawned by the condor_master. As described in Section 14.3.1 discussing the architecture of Condor, each host in your pool can play different roles depending on which daemons are started on it. You define these roles using the DAEMON_LIST in the appropriate configuration files to enable or disable the various Condor daemons on each host.

`DedicatedScheduler:` the name of the dedicated scheduler for your cluster. This setting must have the form

```
DedicatedScheduler = "DedicatedScheduler@full.host.name.here"
```

## 14.6 Administration Tools

Condor has a rich set of tools for the administrator. Table 14.2 gives an overview of the Condor commands typically used solely by the system administrator. Of course, many of the "user-level" Condor tools summarized in Table 14.2 can be helpful for cluster administration as well. For instance, the `condor_status` tool can easily display the status for all nodes in the cluster, including dynamic information such as current load average and free virtual memory.

| Command | Description |
|---|---|
| condor_config_val | Query or set a given Condor configuration variable |
| condor_master_off | Shut down Condor and the condor_master |
| condor_off | Shut down Condor daemons |
| condor_on | Start up Condor daemons |
| condor_reconfig | Reconfigure Condor daemons |
| condor_restart | Restart the condor_master |
| condor_stats | Display historical information about the Condor pool |
| condor_userprio | Display and manage user priorities |
| condor_vacate | Vacate jobs that are running on the specified hosts |

**Table 14.2**
Commands reserved for the administrator.

### 14.6.1 Remote Configuration and Control

All machines in a Condor pool can be remotely managed from a centralized location. Condor can be enabled, disabled, or restarted remotely using the `condor_on`, `condor_off`, and `condor_restart` commands, respectively. Additionally, any aspect of Condor's configuration file on a node can be queried or changed remotely via the `condor_config_val` command. Of course, not everyone is allowed to change your Condor configuration remotely. Doing so requires proper authorization, which is set up at installation time (see Section 14.4).

Many aspects of Condor's configuration, including its scheduling policy, can be changed on the fly without requiring the pool to be shut down and restarted. This is accomplished by using the `condor_reconfig` command, which asks the

Condor daemons on a specified host to reread the Condor configuration files and take appropriate action—on the fly if possible.

## 14.6.2    Accounting and Logging

Condor keeps many statistics about what is happening in the pool. Each daemon can be asked to keep a detailed log of its activities; Condor will automatically rotate these log files when they reach a maximum size as specified by the administrator.

In addition to the `condor_history` command, which allows users to view job ClassAds for jobs that have previously completed, the `condor_stats` tool can be used to query for historical usage statistics from a poolwide accounting database. This database contains information about how many jobs were being serviced for each user at regular intervals, as well as how many machines were busy. For instance, `condor_stats` could be asked to display the total number of jobs running at five-minute intervals for a specified user between January 15 and January 30.

The `condor_view` tool takes the raw information obtainable with `condor_stats` and converts it into HTML, complete with interactive charts. Figure 14.6 shows a sample display of the output from `condor_view` in a Web browser. The site administrator, using `condor_view`, can quickly put detailed, real-time usage statistics about the Condor pool onto a Web site.

## 14.6.3    User Priorities in Condor

The job queues in Condor are not strictly first-in, first-out. Instead, Condor implements *priority queuing*. Different users will get different-sized allocations of machines depending on their current user priority, regardless of how many jobs from a competing user are "ahead" of them in the queue. Condor can also be configured to perform *priority preemption* if desired. For instance, suppose user $A$ is using all the nodes in a cluster, when suddenly a user with a superior priority submits jobs. With priority preemption enabled, Condor will preempt the jobs of the lower-priority user in order to immediately start the jobs submitted by the higher-priority user.

Starvation of the lower-priority users is prevented by a fair-share algorithm, which attempts to give all users the same amount of machine allocation time over a specified interval. In addition, the priority calculations in Condor are based on *ratios* instead of absolutes. For example, if Bill has a priority that is twice as good as that of Fred, Condor will not starve Fred by allocating all machines to Bill. Instead, Bill will get, on average, twice as many machines as will Fred because Bill's priority is twice as good.

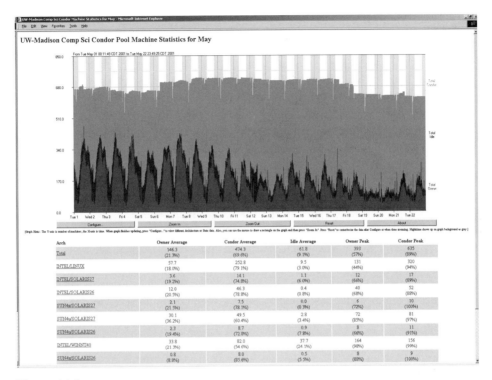

**Figure 14.6**
CondorView displaying machine usage.

The `condor_userprio` command can be used by the administrator to view or edit a user's priority. It can also be used to override Condor's default fair-share policy and explicitly assign users a better or worse priority in relation to other users.

## 14.7   Cluster Setup Scenarios

This section explores different scenarios for how to configure your cluster. Five scenarios are presented, along with a basic idea of what configuration settings you will need to modify or what steps you will need to take for each scenario:

1. A uniformly owned, dedicated compute cluster, with a single front-end node for submission, and support for MPI applications.

2. A cluster of multiprocessor nodes.

3. A cluster of distributively owned nodes. Each node prefers to run jobs submitted by its owner.

4. Desktop submission to the cluster.

5. Expanding the cluster to nondedicated (desktop) computing resources.

Most of these scenarios can be combined. Each scenario builds on the previous one to add further functionality to the basic cluster configuration.

### 14.7.1 Basic Configuration: Uniformly Owned Cluster

The most basic scenario involves a cluster where all resources are owned by a single entity and all compute nodes enforce the same policy for starting and stopping jobs. All compute nodes are dedicated, meaning that they will always start an idle job and they will never preempt or suspend until completion. There is a single front-end node for submitting jobs, and dedicated MPI jobs are enabled from this host.

In order to enable this basic policy, your global configuration file must contain these settings:

```
START = True
SUSPEND = False
CONTINUE = False
PREEMPT = False
KILL = False
WANT_SUSPEND = True
WANT_VACATE = True
RANK = Scheduler =?= $(DedicatedScheduler)
DAEMON_LIST = MASTER, STARTD
```

The final entry listed here specifies that the default role for nodes in your pool is execute-only. The DAEMON_LIST on your front-end node must also enable the condor_schedd. This front-end node's local configuration file will be

```
DAEMON_LIST = MASTER, STARTD, SCHEDD
```

### 14.7.2 Using Multiprocessor Compute Nodes

If any node in your Condor pool is a symmetric multiprocessor machine, Condor will represent that node as multiple virtual machines (VMs), one for each CPU. By default, each VM will have a single CPU and an even share of all shared system resources, such as RAM and swap space. If this behavior satisfies your needs, you do not need to make any configuration changes for SMP nodes to work properly with Condor.

Some sites might want different behavior of their SMP nodes. For example, assume your cluster was composed of dual-processor machines with 1 gigabyte of RAM, and one of your users was submitting jobs with a memory footprint of 700 megabytes. With the default setting, all VMs in your pool would only have 500 megabytes of RAM, and your user's jobs would never run. In this case, you would want to unevenly divide RAM between the two CPUs, to give half of your VMs 750 megabytes of RAM. The other half of the VMs would be left with 250 megabytes of RAM.

There is more than one way to divide shared resources on an SMP machine with Condor, all of which are discussed in detail in the Condor Administrator's Manual. The most basic method is as follows. To divide shared resources on an SMP unevenly, you must define different *virtual machine types* and tell the condor_startd how many virtual machines of each type to advertise. The simplest method to define a virtual machine type is to specify what fraction of all shared resources each type should receive.

For example, if you wanted to divide a two-node machine where one CPU received one-quarter of the shared resources, and the other CPU received the other three-quarters, you would use the following settings:

```
VIRTUAL_MACHINE_TYPE_1 = 1/4
VIRTUAL_MACHINE_TYPE_2 = 3/4
NUM_VIRTUAL_MACHINES_TYPE_1 = 1
NUM_VIRTUAL_MACHINES_TYPE_2 = 1
```

If you want to divide certain resources unevenly but split the rest evenly, you can specify separate fractions for each shared resource. This is described in detail in the Condor Administrator's Manual.

### 14.7.3  Scheduling a Distributively Owned Cluster

Many clusters are owned by more than one entity. Two or more smaller groups might pool their resources to buy a single, larger cluster. In these situations, the group that paid for a portion of the nodes should get priority to run on those nodes.

Each resource in a Condor pool can define its own RANK expression, which specifies the kinds of jobs it would prefer to execute. If a cluster is owned by multiple entities, you can divide the cluster's nodes up into groups, based on ownership. Each node would set Rank such that jobs coming from the group that owned it would have the highest priority.

Assume there is a 60-node compute cluster at a university, shared by three departments: astronomy, math, and physics. Each department contributed the funds for 20 nodes. Each group of 20 nodes would define its own Rank expression. The astronomy department's settings, for example, would be

```
Rank = Department == "Astronomy"
```

The users from each department would also add a Department attribute to all of their job ClassAds. The administrators could configure Condor to add this attribute automatically to all job ads from each site (see the Condor Administrator's Manual for details).

If the entire cluster was idle and a physics user submitted 40 jobs, she would see all 40 of her jobs start running. If, however, a user in math submitted 60 jobs and a user in astronomy submitted 20 jobs, 20 of the physicist's jobs would be preempted, and each group would get 20 machines out of the cluster.

If all of the astronomy department's jobs completed, the astronomy nodes would go back to serving math and physics jobs. The astronomy nodes would continue to run math or physics jobs until either some astronomy jobs were submitted, or all the jobs in the system completed.

### 14.7.4   Submitting to the Cluster from Desktop Workstations

Most organizations that install a compute cluster have other workstations at their site. It is usually desirable to allow these machines to act as front-end nodes for the cluster, so users can submit their jobs from their own machines and have the applications execute on the cluster. Even if there is no shared file system between the cluster and the rest of the computers, Condor's file transfer functionality can enable jobs to migrate between the two and still access their data (see Section 14.2.5 for details on accessing data files).

To enable a machine to submit into your cluster, run the Condor installation program and specify that you want to setup a *submit-only* node. This will set the DAEMON_LIST on the new node to be

```
DAEMON_LIST = MASTER, SCHEDD
```

The installation program will also create all the directories and files needed by Condor.

Note that you can have only one node configured as the dedicated scheduler for your pool. Do not attempt to add a second submit node for MPI jobs.

### 14.7.5 Expanding the Cluster to Nondedicated (Desktop) Computing Resources

One of the most powerful features in Condor is the ability to combine dedicated and opportunistic scheduling within a single system. *Opportunistic scheduling* involves placing jobs on nondedicated resources under the assumption that the resources might not be available for the entire duration of the jobs. Opportunistic scheduling is used for all jobs in Condor with the exception of dedicated MPI applications.

If your site has a combination of jobs and uses applications other than MPI, you should strongly consider adding all of your computing resources, even desktop workstations, to your Condor pool. With suspend and resume capabilities, opportunistic scheduling and matchmaking, Condor can harness the idle CPU cycles of any machine and put them to good use.

To add other computing resources to your pool, run the Condor installation program and specify that you want to configure a node that can both submit and execute jobs. The default installation sets up a node with a policy for starting, suspending, and preempting jobs based on the activity of the machine (for example, keyboard idle time and CPU load). These nodes will not run dedicated MPI jobs, but they will run jobs from any other universe, including PVM.

## 14.8  Conclusion

Condor is a powerful tool for scheduling jobs across platforms, both within and beyond the boundaries of your Beowulf clusters. Through its unique combination of both dedicated and opportunistic scheduling, Condor provides a unified framework for high-throughput computing.

# 15 Maui Scheduler: A Multifunction Cluster Scheduler

*David B. Jackson*

In this chapter we describe the Maui scheduler, a job-scheduling component that can interact with a number of different resource managers.

Like virtually every major development project, Maui grew out of a pressing need. In Maui's case, various computing centers including the Maui High-Performance Computing Center, Pacific Northwest National Laboratory, San Diego Supercomputer Center, and Argonne National Laboratory were investing huge sums of money in new, top-of-the-line hardware, only to be frustrated by the inability to use these new resources in an efficient or controlled manner. While existing resource management systems allowed the basic ability to submit and run jobs, they did not empower the site to maximize the use of the cluster. Sites could not *translate* local mission policies into scheduling behavior, and the scheduling decisions that were made were often quite suboptimal. Worse, the resulting system was often so complex that management, administrators, and users were unable to tell how well the system was running or what could be done to improve it.

Maui was designed to address these issues and has been developed and tested over the years at many leading-edge computing centers. It was built to enable sites to control, understand, and use their clusters effectively. Maui picks up where many scheduling systems leave off, providing a suite of advanced features in the areas of reservations, backfill, fairshare, job prioritization, quality of service, metascheduling, and more.

## 15.1 Overview

Maui is an *external* scheduler, meaning it does not include a resource manager but rather extends the capabilities of the existing resource manager. Maui uses the native scheduling APIs of OpenPBS, PBSPro and Loadleveler to obtain system information and direct cluster scheduling activities. While the underlying resource manager continues to maintain responsibility for managing nodes and tracking jobs, Maui controls the decisions of when, where, and how jobs will run.

System administrators control Maui via a master config file, `maui.cfg`, and text or Web-based administrator commands. On the other hand, end users are not required to learn any new commands or job submission language, and need not even know that Maui has been installed. While Maui provides numerous commands to provide users with additional job information and control, these commands are optional and may be introduced to the users as needed.

## 15.2  Installation and Initial Configuration

The Maui scheduler is available in many of the most popular cluster-building tool-kits, including *Rocks* and *OSCAR*. For the most recent version of Maui, you can download the code from the Maui home page at `supercluster.org/maui`. This site also contains online documentation, FAQs, links to the Maui users mailing list, and other standard open source utilities. To build the code once it has been downloaded, you need simply to issue the standard `configure`, `make`, and `make install`.

### 15.2.1  Basic Configuration

The `configure` script will prompt you for some basic information regarding the `install` directory and desired resource manager type. It then creates the Maui home directory, builds executables in the `bin` subdirectory, and copies these to the `install` directory. Finally, the script creates an initial `maui.cfg` file using templates located in the `samples` subdirectory and user-supplied information. This file is a *flat text* config file used for virtually all scheduler configuration and contains a number of parameters that should be verified, particularly, `SERVERHOST`, `SERVERMODE`, and `ADMIN1`. Initially, these should be set to the name of the host where Maui will run, `NORMAL`, and the user name of the Maui administrator, respectively. At any time when Maui is running, the `schedctl` command can be used with the '`-l`' flag to *list* the value of any parameter whether explicitly set or not, while the '`-m`' flag can be used to dynamically *modify* parameter values. The online `parameters` documentation provides further details about these and all other Maui parameters.

### 15.2.2  Simulation and Testing

With the initial configuration complete, the next step is testing the scheduler to become familiar with its capabilities and to verify basic functionality. Maui can be run in a completely *safe* manner by setting `SERVERMODE` to `TEST`. In *test* mode, Maui contacts the resource manager to obtain up-to-date configuration, node, and job information; however, in this mode, interfaces to start or modify these jobs are disabled. To start Maui, you must make the parameter changes and issue the command `maui`. You may also use commands such as `showq`, `diagnose`, and `checknode` to verify proper scheduler-resource manager communication and scheduler functionality. Full details on the suite of Maui commands are available online or in documentation included with your distribution.

### 15.2.3 Production Scheduling

Once you've taken the scheduler for a test drive and have verified its proper behavior, you can run Maui *live* by disabling the default scheduler and changing the `SERVERMODE` parameter to `NORMAL`. Information on disabling the default resource manager scheduler is provided in the resource manager's documentation and in the online Maui migration guides located at `supercluster.org/documentation/maui`. These changes will allow Maui to start, modify, and cancel jobs according to the specified scheduling policies.

Out of the box, Maui essentially duplicates the behavior of a vanilla cluster scheduler, providing first-in, first-out scheduling with backfill enabled. The parameters documentation explains in detail each of the parameters needed to enable advanced scheduling features. In most cases, each site will require only a small subset of the available parameters to meet local needs.

## 15.3 Advanced Configuration

With the initial configuration and testing completed, you can now configure Maui to end your administration pilgrimage and reach the long-sought cluster mecca—running the right jobs at the right time, in the right way, at the right place. To this end, Maui can be thought of as an integrated scheduling toolkit providing a number of capabilities that may be used individually or together to obtain the desired system behavior. These include

- job prioritization,
- node allocation policies,
- throttling policies,
- fairshare,
- reservations,
- allocation management,
- quality of service,
- backfill,
- node sets, and
- preemption policies.

Each of these is described below. While this coverage will be adequate to introduce and initially configure these capabilities, you should consult the online Maui Administrators Manual for full details. We reiterate that while Maui possesses a wide range of features and associated parameters, most capabilities are disabled by default; thus, a site need configure only the features of interest.

### 15.3.1 Assigning Value: Job Prioritization and Node Allocation

In general, prioritization is the process of determining which of many options best fulfills overall goals. n the case of scheduling, a site will often have multiple, independent goals that may include maximizing system utilization, giving preference to users in specific projects, or making certain that no job sits in the queue for more than a given period of time. One approach to representing a multifaceted set of site goals is to assign weights to the various objectives so an overall value or priority can be associated with each potential scheduling decision. With the jobs prioritized, the scheduler can roughly fulfill site objectives by starting the jobs in priority order.

Maui was designed to allow component and subcomponent weights to be associated with many aspects of a job. To realize this fine-grained control, Maui uses a simple priority-weighting hierarchy where the contribution of a priority factor is calculated as PRIORITY-FACTOR-VALUE * SUBFACTORWEIGHT * FACTORWEIGHT. Component and subcomponent weights are listed in Table 15.1. Values for all weights may be set in the maui.cfg file by using the associated component-weight parameter specified as the name of the weight followed by the string WEIGHT (e.g., SERVICEWEIGHT or PROCWEIGHT).

By default, Maui runs jobs in order of actual submission, using the QUEUETIME. By using priority components, however, you can incorporate additional information, such as current level of service, service targets, resources requested, and historical usage. You can also limit the contribution of any component, by specifying a priority component *cap*, such as RESOURCECAP. A job's priority is equivalent to the sum of all enabled priority factors.

Each component or subcomponent may be used for different purposes. WALLTIME can be used to favor (or disfavor) jobs based on their duration; ACCOUNT can be used to favor jobs associated with a particular project; QUEUETIME can be used to favor those jobs that have been waiting the longest. By mixing and matching priority weights, sites generally obtain the desired job-start behavior. At any time, you can issue the diagnose -p command to determine the impact of the current priority-weight settings on idle jobs.

While most subcomponents are metric based (i.e., number of seconds queued or number of nodes requested), the credential subcomponents are based on priorities specified by the administrator. Maui allows you to use the *CFG parameters to rank

| Component | Subcomponent |
|---|---|
| SERVICE (Level of Service) | QUEUETIME (Current queue time in minutes) |
| | XFACTOR (Current expansion factor) |
| | BYPASS (Number of times jobs were bypassed via backfill) |
| TARGET (Proximity to Service Target - Exponential) | TARGETQUEUETIME (Delta to queue-time target in minutes) |
| | TARGETXFACTOR (Delta to Xfactor target) |
| RESOURCE (Resources Requested) | PROC (Processors) |
| | MEM (Requested memory in MBytes) |
| | SWAP (Requested virtual memory in MBytes) |
| | DISK (Requested local disk in MBytes) |
| | NODE (Requested number of nodes) |
| | WALLTIME (Requested wall time in seconds) |
| | PS (Requested processor-seconds) |
| | PE (Requested processor-equivalents) |
| FS (Fairshare) | FSUSER (User fairshare percentage) |
| | FSGROUP (Group fairshare percentage) |
| | FSACCOUNT (Account fairshare percentage) |
| | FSCLASS (Class fairshare percentage) |
| | FSQOS (QoS fairshare percentage) |
| CRED (Credential) | USER (User priority) |
| | GROUP (Group priority) |
| | ACCOUNT (Account priority) |
| | CLASS (Class priority) |
| | QOS (QoS priority) |

**Table 15.1**
Maui priority components.

jobs by individual job credentials. For example, to favor jobs submitted by users bob and john and members of the group staff, a site might specify the following:

```
USERCFG[bob]        PRIORITY=100
USERCFG[john]       PRIORITY=500
GROUPWEIGHT[staff]  PRIORITY=1000
USERWEIGHT          1
GROUPWEIGHT         1
CREDWEIGHT          1
```

Note that both component and subcomponent weights are specified to enable these credential priorities to take effect. Further details about the use of these component factors, as well as anecdotal usage information, are available in the Maui Administrators Manual.

Complementing the issue of job prioritization is that of node allocation. When the scheduler selects a job to run, it must also determine which resources to allocate to the job. Depending on the use of the cluster, you can specify different policies by using `NODEALLOCATIONPOLICY`. Legal parameter values include the following:

- `MINRESOURCE`: This algorithm selects the nodes with the minimum configured resources which still meet the requirements of the job. The algorithm leaves more richly endowed nodes available for other jobs that may specifically request these additional resources.
- `LASTAVAILABLE`: This algorithm is particularly useful when making reservations for backfill. It determines the earliest time a job can run and then selects the resources available at a time such that, whenever possible, currently idle resources are left unreserved and are thus available for backfilling.
- `NODEPRIORITY`: This policy allows a site to create its own node allocation prioritization scheme, taking into account issues such as installed software or other local node configurations.
- `CPULOAD`: This policy attempts to allocate the most lightly loaded nodes first.

### 15.3.2  Fairness: Throttling Policies and Fairshare

The next issue most often confronting sites is *fairness*. Fairness seems like a simple concept but can be terribly difficult to map onto a cluster. Should all users get to run the same number of jobs or use the same number of nodes? Do these usage constraints cover the present time only or a specified time frame? If historical information is used, what is the metric of consumption? What is the time frame? Does fair consumption necessarily mean equal consumption? How should resources be allocated if user X bought two-thirds of the nodes and user Y purchased the other third? Is fairness based on a static metric, or is it conditional on current resource demand?

While Maui is not able to address all these issues, it does provide some flexible tools that help with 90 percent of the battle. Specifically, these tools are *throttling policies* and *fairshare* used to control immediate and historical usage, respectively.

**Throttling Policies.** The term "throttling policies" is collectively applied to a set of policies that constrain instantaneous resource consumption. Maui supports limits on the number of processors, nodes, proc-seconds, jobs, and processor equivalents allowed at any given time. Limits may be applied on a per user, group, account, QoS, or queue basis via the `*CFG` set of parameters. For example, specifying `USERCFG[bob]` `MAXJOB=3` `MAXPROC=32` will constrain user `bob` to running no more than 3 jobs and 32 total processors at any given time. Specifying `GROUPCFG[DEFAULT]` `MAXNODE=64` will limit each group to using no more than 64 nodes simultaneously unless overriding limits for a particular group are specified. `ACCOUNTCFG`, `QOSCFG`, and `CLASSCFG` round out the *CFG family of parameters providing a means to throttle instantaneous use on accounts, QoS's, and classes, respectively.

With each of the parameters, *hard* and *soft* limits can be used to apply a form of *demand*-sensitive limits. While hard limits cannot be violated under any conditions, soft limits may be violated if no other jobs can run. For example, specifying `USERCFG[DEFAULT]` `MAXNODE=16,24` will allow each user to cumulatively allocate up to 16 nodes while jobs from other users can use available resources. If no other jobs can use these resources, a user may run on up to 24 nodes simultaneously.

Throttling policies are effective in preventing cluster "hogging" by an individual user or group. They also provide a simple mechanism of fairness and cycle distribution. Such policies may lead to lower overall system utilization, however. For instance, resources might go unused if these policies prevent all queued jobs from running. When possible, throttling policies should be set to the highest feasible level, and the cycle distribution should be managed by tools such as fairshare, allocation management systems, and QoS-based prioritization.

**Fairshare.** A typical fairshare algorithm attempts to deliver a fair resource distribution over a given time frame. As noted earlier, however, this general statement leaves much to interpretation. In particular, how is the distribution to be measured, and what time frame should be used?

Maui provides the parameter `FSPOLICY` to allow each site to determine how resource distribution is to be measured, and the parameters `FSINTERVAL`, `FSDEPTH`, and `FSDECAY` to determine how historical usage information is to be weighted.

To control resource distribution, Maui uses fairshare targets that can be applied to users, groups, accounts, queues, and QoS mechanisms with both default and specific targets available. Each target may be one of four different types: *target*, *floor*, *ceiling*, or *cap*. In most cases, Maui adjusts job priorities to meet fairshare targets. With the standard target, Maui attempts to adjust priorities at all times in an attempt to meet the target. In the case of floors, Maui will increase job priority only to maintain *at least* the targeted usage. With ceilings, the converse occurs. Finally, with fairshare caps, job eligibility rather than job priority is adjusted to prevent jobs from running if the cap is exceeded during the specified fairshare interval.

The example below shows a possible fairshare configuration.

```
# maui.cfg
FSPOLICY    DEDICATEDPS
FSDEPTH     7
FSINTERVAL  24:00:00
FSDECAY     0.80

USERCFG[DEFAULT]    FSTARGET=10.0
USERCFG[john]       FSTARGET=25.0+
GROUPCFG[staff]     FSTARGET=20.0-
```

In this case, fairshare usage will track delivered system *processor seconds* over a seven-day period with a 0.8 decay factor. All users will have a fairshare *target* of 10 percent of these processor seconds—with the exception of `john`, who will have a *floor* of 25 percent. Also, the group `staff` will have a fairshare *ceiling* of 20 percent. At any time, you can examine the fairshare status of the system by using the `diagnose -f` command.

### 15.3.3 Managing Resource Access: Reservations, Allocation Managers, and Quality of Service

In managing any cluster system, half of the administrative effort involves configuring it to handle the *steady-state* situation. The other half occurs when a very important user has a special one-time request. Maui provides two features, advance reservations and QoS, to handle many types of such special requests.

**Advance Reservations.** Reservations allow a site to set aside a block of resources for various purposes such as cluster maintenance, special user projects, or benchmarking nodes. In order to create a reservation, a start and end time must be determined, as well as the resources to be reserved and a list of those who can access these resources. Reservations can be created dynamically by scheduler administrators using the `setres` command or managed directly by Maui via config file parameters.

For example, to reserve `nodeA` and `nodeB` for a four-hour maintenance at 2:30 P.M., you could issue the following command:

```
> setres -s 14:30 -d 4:00:00 'node[AB]'
```

A reservation request can specify allocation of particular resources or a given quantity of resources. The following reservation will allocate 20 processors to users `john` and `sam` starting on April 14 at 5:00 P.M.

```
> setres -u john:sam -s 17:00_04/14 TASKS==20
```

With no duration or end time specified, this reservation will default to an infinite length and will remain in place until removed by a scheduler administrator using the `releaseres` command.

Access to reservations is controlled by an access control list (ACL). Reservation access is based on job credentials, such as user or group, and job attributes, such as wall time requested. Reservation ACLs can include multiple access types and individuals. For example, a reservation might reserve resources for users A and B, jobs in class C, and jobs that request less than 30 minutes of wall time. Reservations may also overlap each other if desired, in which case access is granted only if the job meets the access policies of all active reservations.

At many sites, reservations are used on a permanent or periodic basis. In such cases, it is best to use *standing* reservations. Standing reservations allow a site to apply reservations as an ongoing part of cluster policies. The parameter `SRPERIOD` can be set to `DAY`, `WEEK`, or `INFINITE` to indicate the periodicity of the reservation, with additional parameters available to determine what time of the day or week the reservation should be enabled. For example, the following configuration will create a reservation named `development` that, during primetime hours, will set aside 16 nodes for exclusive use by jobs requiring less than 30 minutes.

```
SRPERIOD[development]    DAY
SRDAYS[development]      Mon Tue Wed Thu Fri
SRSTARTTIME[development] 8:00:00
SRENDTIME[development]   17:00:00
SRMAXTIME[development]   00:30:00
SRTASKCOUNT[development] 16
```

At times, a site may want to allow access to a set of resources only if there are no other resources available. Maui enables this conditional usage through reservation *affinity*. When specifying any reservation access list, each access value can be associated with positive, negative, or neutral affinity by using the '+', '-', or '=' characters. If nothing is specified, positive affinity is assumed. For example, consider the following reservation line:

```
SRUSERLIST[special]  bob john steve= bill-
```

With this specification, `bob` and `john`'s jobs receive the default positive affinity and are essentially *attracted* to the reservation. For these jobs, Maui will attempt to use resources in the `special` reservation first, before considering any other resources. Jobs belonging to `steve`, on the other hand, can use these resources but are not attracted to them. Finally, `bill`'s jobs will use resources in the `special` reservation only if no other resources are available. You can get detailed information about reservations by using the `showres` and `diagnose -r` commands.

**Allocation Managers.** Allocation management systems allow a site to control total resource access in real time. While interfaces to support other systems exist, the allocation management system most commonly used with the Maui scheduler is QBank (`http://www.emsl.pnl.gov:80/mscf/docs/qbank-2.9`), provided by Pacific Northwest National Laboratory. This system and others like it allow sites to provide distinct resource allocations much like the creation of a bank account. As jobs run, the resources used are translated into a charge and debited from the appropriate account. In the case of QBank, expiration dates may be associated with allocations, private and shared accounts maintained, per machine allocations created, and so forth.

Within Maui, the allocation manager interface is controlled through a set of `BANK*` parameters such as in the example below:

```
BANKTYPE              QBANK
BANKHOST              bank.univ.edu
BANKCHARGEPOLICY      DEBITSUCCESSFULWC
BANKDEFERJOBONFAILURE TRUE
BANKFALLBACKACCOUNT   freecycle
```

This configuration enables a connection to an allocation manager located on `bank.univ.edu` using the QBank interface. The unit of charge is configured to be *dedicated processor-seconds* and users will be charged only if their job completes successfully. If the job does not have adequate allocations in the specified account, Maui will attempt to redirect the job to use allocations in the `freecycle` account. In many cases, a *fallback* account is configured so as to be associated with lower priorities and/or additional limitations. If the job is not approved by the allocation manager, Maui will defer the job for a period of time and try it again later.

**Quality of Service.** Maui's QoS feature allows sites to control access to special functions, resources, and service levels. Each QoS consists of an access control list controlling which users, groups, accounts, and job queues can access the QoS privileges. Associated with each QoS are special service-related priority weights and service targets. Additionally, each QoS can be configured to span resource partitions, preempt other jobs, and the like.

Maui also enables a site to charge a premium rate for the use of some QoS services. For example, the following configuration will cause user john's jobs to use QoS hiprio by default and allow members of the group bio to access it by request:

```
USERCFG[john]  QLIST=hiprio:normal QDEF=hiprio
GROUPCFG[bio]  QLIST=hiprio:medprio:development QDEF=medprio
QOSCFG[hiprio] PRIORITY=50 QTTARGET=30 FLAGS=PREEMPTOR:IGNMAXJOB \
     MAXPROC=150
```

Jobs using QoS hiprio receive the following privileges and constraints:

- A priority boost of 50 * QOSWEIGHT * DIRECTWEIGHT
- A queue-time target of 30 minutes
- The ability to preempt lower priority PREEMPTEE jobs
- The ability to ignore MAXJOB policy limits defined elsewhere
- A cumulative limit of 150 processors allocated to QoS hiprio jobs

A site may have dozens of QoS objects described and may allow users access to any number of these. Depending on the type of service desired, users may then choose the QoS that best meets their needs.

### 15.3.4  Optimizing Usage: Backfill, Node Sets, and Preemption

The Maui scheduler provides several features to optimize performance in terms of system utilization, job throughput, and average job turnaround time.

**Backfill.** Backfill is a now common method used to improve both system utilization and average job turnaround time by running jobs out of order. Backfill, simply put, enables the scheduler to run any job so long as it does not delay the start of jobs of higher priority. Generally, the algorithm prevents delay of high-priority jobs through some form of reservation. Backfill can be thought of as a process of filling in the resource *holes* left by the high priority jobs. Since holes are being filled, it makes sense that the jobs most commonly backfilled are the ones requiring the least time and/or resources. With backfill enabled, sites typically report system utilization improvements of 10 to 25% and a slightly lower average job queue time.

By default, backfill scheduling is enabled in Maui under control of the parameter BACKFILLPOLICY. While the default configuration generally is adequate, sites may want to adjust the job selection policy, the reservation policy, the depth of reservations, or other aspects of backfill scheduling. You should consult the online documentation for details about associated parameters.

**Allocation Based on Node Set.** While backfill improves the scheduler's performance, this is only half the battle. The efficiency of a cluster, in terms of actual work accomplished, is a function of both scheduling performance and individual job efficiency. In many clusters, job efficiency can vary from node to node as well as with the *node mix* allocated. Since most parallel jobs written in popular languages such as MPI or PVM do not internally load balance their workload, they run only as fast as the slowest node allocated. Consequently, these jobs run most effectively on homogeneous sets of nodes. While many clusters start out as homogeneous, however, they quickly evolve as new generations of compute nodes are integrated into the system. Research has shown that this integration, while improving scheduling performance due to increased scheduler selection, can actually decrease average job efficiency.

A feature called *node sets* allows jobs to request sets of common resources without specifying exactly what resources are required. Node set policy can be specified globally or on a per job basis and can be based on node processor speed, memory, network interfaces, or locally defined node attributes. In addition to forcing jobs onto homogeneous nodes, these policies may also be used to guide jobs to one or more types of nodes on which a particular job performs best, similar to job preferences available in other systems. For example, an I/O-intensive job may run best on a certain range of processor speeds, running slower on slower nodes while wasting cycles on faster nodes. A job may specify `ANYOF:PROCSPEED:450:500:650` to request nodes in the range of 450 to 650 MHz. Alternatively, if a simple procspeed-homogeneous node set is desired, `ONEOF:PROCSPEED` may be specified. On the other hand, a communication-sensitive job may request a network-based node set with the configuration `ONEOF:NETWORK:via:myrinet:ethernet`, in which case Maui will first attempt to locate adequate nodes where all nodes contain VIA network interfaces. If such a set cannot be found, Maui will look for sets of nodes containing the other specified network interfaces. In highly heterogeneous clusters, the use of node sets has been found to improve job throughput by 10 to 15 percent.

**Preemption.** Many sites possess workloads of varying importance. While it may be critical that some jobs obtain resources immediately, other jobs are less sensitive to turnaround time but have an insatiable hunger for compute cycles, consuming every available cycle for years on end. These latter jobs often have turnaround times on the order of weeks or months. The concept of *cycle stealing*, popularized by systems such as Condor, handles such situations well and enables systems to run low-priority preemptible jobs whenever something more pressing is not running. These other systems are often employed on compute farms of desktops where the jobs must vacate whenever interactive system use is detected.

Maui's QoS-based preemption system allows a dedicated, noninteractive cluster to be used in much the same way. Certain QoS objects may be marked with the flag PREEMPTOR and others with the flag PREEMPTEE. With this configuration, low-priority "preemptee" jobs can be started whenever idle resources are available. These jobs will be allowed to run until a "preemptor" job arrives, at which point the preemptee job will be checkpointed if possible and vacated. This strategy allows almost immediate resource access for the preemptor job. Using this approach, a cluster can maintain nearly 100 percent system utilization while still delivering excellent turnaround time to the jobs of greatest value.

Use of the preemption system need not be limited to controlling low-priority jobs. Other uses include optimistic scheduling and development job support.

### 15.3.5   Evaluating System Performance: Diagnostics, Profiling, Testing, and Simulation

High-performance computing clusters are complicated. First, such clusters have an immense array of attributes that affect overall system performance, including processor speed, memory, networks, I/O systems, enterprise services, and application and system software. Second, each of these attributes is evolving over time, as is the usage pattern of the system's users. Third, sites are presented with an equally immense array of buttons, knobs, and levers which they can push, pull, kick, and otherwise manipulate. How does one evaluate the success of a current configuration? And how does one establish a causal effect between pushing one of the many provided buttons and improved system performance when the system is constantly changing in multiple simultaneous dimensions?

To help alleviate this problem, Maui offers several useful features.

**Diagnostics.**   Maui possesses many internal diagnostic functions that both locate problems and present system state information. For example, the *priority* diagnostic aggregates priority relevant information, presenting configuration settings and their impact on the current idle workload; administrators can see the contribution associated with each priority factor on a per job and systemwide average basis. The *node* diagnostic presents significant node-relevant information together with messages regarding any unexpected conditions. Other diagnostics are available for jobs, reservations, QoS, fairshare, priorities, fairness policies, users, groups, and accounts.

**Profiling Current and Historical Usage.** Maui maintains internal statistics and records detailed information about each job as it completes. The `showstats` command provides detailed usage information for users, groups, accounts, nodes, and the system as a whole. The `showgrid` command presents scheduler performance statistics in a job size/duration matrix to aid in analyzing the effectiveness of current policies.

The completed job statistics are maintained in a flat file located in the `stats` directory. These statistics are useful for two primary purposes: driving simulations (described later) and profiling actual system usage. The `profiler` command allows the processing of these historical scheduler statistics and generation of usage reports for specific time frames or for selected users, groups, accounts, or types of jobs.

**Testing.** To test new policies, you can run a `TEST` mode instance of Maui concurrently with the production scheduler. This allows a site to analyze the effects of the new policies on the scheduling behavior of the test instance, while safely running the production workload under tried and true policies. When running an instance of Maui in test mode, it is often best to create a second Maui directory with associated `log` and `stats` subdirectories. To run multiple, concurrent Maui instances, you should take the following into account:

- **Configuration file:** The test version of Maui should have its own `maui.cfg` file to allow specification of the `SERVERMODE` parameter and allow policy differences as needed by the test.
- **User interface port:** To avoid conflicts between different scheduler instances and client commands, the test version of the `maui.cfg` file should specify a unique parameter value for `SERVERPORT`.
- **Log and statistics files:** Both production and test runs will create and update log and statistics files. To avoid file conflicts, each instance of the scheduler should point to different files using the `LOGDIR` and `STATDIR` parameters.
- **Home directory:** When Maui was initially installed, the `configure` script prompted for a home directory where the default `maui.cfg` file could be found. To run multiple instances of Maui, you should override this default by using the `-c` command line flag or by specifying the environment variable `MAUIHOMEDIR`. The latter approach is most often used, with the variable set to the new home directory before starting the test version of the scheduler or running test version client commands.

Once the test version is started, all scheduler behavior will be identical to the production system with the exception that Maui's ability to start, cancel, or otherwise modify jobs is disabled. You can, however, observe Maui's behavior under the new set of policies and validate the scheduler either directly via client commands or indirectly by analyzing the Maui log files.

**Simulation.** Simulation allows a site to specify a workload and resource configuration trace file. These traces, specified via the `SIMWORKLOADTRACEFILE` and `SIMRESOURCETRACEFILE`, can accurately and reproducibly replicate the workload and resources recorded at the site. To run a simulation, an adjusted `maui.cfg` file is created with the policies of interest in place and the parameter `SERVERMODE` set to `SIMULATION`. Once started, Maui can be stepped through simulated time using the `schedctl` command. All Maui commands continue to function as before, allowing interactive querying of status, adjustment to parameters, or even submission or cancellation of jobs.

This feature enables sites to analyze the impact of different scheduling policies on their own workload and system configuration. The effects of new reservations or job prioritizations can be evaluated in a *zero-exposure* environment, allowing sites to determine ideal policies without experimenting on a production system. Sites can also evaluate the impact of additional or modified workloads or changes in available resources. What impact will removing a block of resources for maintenance have on average queue time? How much benefit will a new reservation dedicated exclusively to development jobs have on development job turnaround time? How much pain will it cause nondevelopment jobs? Using simulation makes it easier to obtaining answers to such questions.

This same simulation feature can be used to test a new algorithm against workload and resource traces from various supercomputing centers. Moreover, with the simulator, you can create and plug in modules to emulate the behavior of various job types on different hardware platforms, across bottlenecking networks, or under various data migration conditions.

The capabilities and use of simulation cannot be adequately covered in a chapter of this size. Further information is given in the Simulation section of the Maui Administrators Manual.

## 15.4   Steering Workload and Improving Quality of Information

A good scheduler can improve the use of a cluster significantly, but its effectiveness is limited by the scheduling environment in which it must work and the quality of information it receives. Often, a cluster is underutilized because users overestimate a job's resource requirements. Other times, inefficiencies crop up when users request

job constraints in terms of job duration or processors required that are not easily
packed onto the cluster. Maui provides tools to allow fine tuning of job resource
requirement information and steering of cluster workload so as to allow maximum
utilization of the system.

One such tool is a *feedback* interface, which allows a site to report detailed job
usage statistics to users. This interface provides information about the resources
requested and those actually used. Using the `FEEDBACKPROGRAM` parameter, local
scripts can be executed that use this information to help users improve resource
requirement estimates. For example, a site with nodes with various memory configurations may choose to create a script such as the following that automates the
mailing of notices at job completion:

```
Job 1371 completed successfully}.  Note that it requested nodes
with 512 MBytes of RAM yet used  only 112 MBytes.  Had the job provided a
more accurate estimate, it would have, on average, started 02:27:16
earlier.
```

Such notices can be used to improve memory, disk, processor, and wall-time estimates. Another route that is often used is to set the allocation manager charge
policy so that users are charged for requested resources rather than used resources.

The `showbf` command is designed to help tailor jobs that can run immediately.
This command allows you to specify details about your desired job (such as user,
group, queue, and memory requirements) and returns information regarding the
quantity of available nodes and the duration of their availability.

A final area of user feedback is job scaling. Often, users will submit parallel jobs
that scale only moderately scale, hoping that by requesting more processors, their
job will run faster and provide results sooner. A job's completion time is simply the
sum of its queue time plus its execution time. Users often fail to realize that a larger
job may be more difficult to schedule, resulting in a longer queue time, and may run
less efficiently, with a *sublinear* speedup. The increased queue-time delay, together
with the limitations in execution time improvements, generally results in larger
jobs having a greater average turnaround time than smaller jobs performing the
same work. Maui commands such as `showgrid` can provide real-time job efficiency
and average queue-time stats correlated to job size. The output of the `profiler`
command can also be used to provide per user job efficiency and average queue
time correlated by job size and can alert administrators and users to this problem.

## 15.5  Troubleshooting

When troubleshooting scheduling issues, you should start with Maui's diagnostic and informational commands. The `diagnose` command together with `checknode` and `checkjob` provides detailed state information about the scheduler, including its various facilities, nodes, and jobs. Additionally, each of these commands initiates an extensive internal sanity check in the realm of interest. Results of this check are reported in the form of `WARNING` messages appended to the normal command output. Use of these commands typically identifies or resolves 95 percent of all scheduling issues.

If you need further information, Maui writes out detailed logging information in the directory pointed to by the `LOGFILE` parameter (usually in `${MAUIHOME}/log/maui.log`). Using the `LOGLEVEL` and `LOGFACILITY` parameters, you can control the verbosity and focus of these logs. (Note, however, that these logs can become *very* verbose, so keeping the LOGLEVEL below 4 or so unless actually tracking problems is advised.) These logs contain a number of entries, including the following:

`INFO:` provides status information about normal scheduler operations.

`WARNING:` indicates that an unexpected condition was detected and handled.

`ALERT:` indicates that an unexpected condition occurred that could not be fully handled.

`ERROR:` indicates that problem was detected that prevents Maui from fully operating. This may be a problem with the cluster that is outside of Maui's control or may indicate corrupt internal state information.

`Function header:` indicates when a function is called and the parameters passed.

A simple `grep` through the log file will usually indicate whether any serious issues have been detected and is of significant value when obtaining support or locally diagnosing problems. If neither commands nor logs point to the source of the problem, you may consult the Maui users list (`mauiusers@supercluster.org`) or directly contact Supercluster support at `support@supercluster.org`.

## 15.6  Conclusions

This chapter has introduced some of the key Maui features currently available. With hundreds of sites now using and contributing to this open source project, Maui is evolving and improving faster than ever. To learn about the latest developments and to obtain more detailed information about the capabilities described above, see the Maui home page at `www.supercluster.org/maui`.

# 16 PBS: Portable Batch System

*James Patton Jones*

The Portable Batch System (PBS) is a flexible workload management and job scheduling system originally developed to manage aerospace computing resources at NASA. PBS has since become the leader in supercomputer workload management and an increasingly popular choice for job scheduling on Windows 2000 clusters.

Today, growing enterprises often support hundreds of users running thousands of jobs across different types of machines in different geographical locations. In this distributed heterogeneous environment, it can be extremely difficult for administrators to collect detailed, accurate usage data or to set systemwide resource priorities. As a result, many computing resources are left underused, while others are overused. At the same time, users are confronted with an ever-expanding array of operating systems and platforms. Each year, scientists, engineers, designers, and analysts waste countless hours learning the nuances of different computing environments, rather than being able to focus on their core priorities. PBS addresses these problems for computing-intensive industries such as science, engineering, finance, and entertainment.

PBS allows you to unlock the potential in the valuable assets you already have, while at the same time reducing demands on system administrators, freeing them to focus on other activities. PBS can also help you effectively manage growth by tracking use levels across your systems and enhancing effective utilization of future purchases.

## 16.1 History of PBS

In the past, computers were used in a completely interactive manner. Background jobs were just processes with their input disconnected from the terminal. As the number of processors in computers continued to increase, however, the need to be able to schedule tasks based on available resources rose in importance. The advent of networked compute servers, smaller general systems, and workstations led to the requirement of a networked batch scheduling capability. The first such Unix-based system was the Network Queueing System (NQS) from NASA Ames Research Center in 1986. NQS quickly became the de facto standard for batch queuing.

Over time, distributed parallel systems began to emerge, and NQS was inadequate to handle the complex scheduling requirements presented by such systems. In addition, computer system managers wanted greater control over their compute resources, and users wanted a single interface to the systems. In the early 1990s

NASA needed a solution to this problem, but after finding nothing on the market that adequately addressed their needs, led an international effort to gather requirements for a next-generation resource management system. The requirements and functional specification were later adopted as an IEEE POSIX standard (1003.2d). Next, NASA funded the development of a new resource management system compliant with the standard. Thus the Portable Batch System was born.

PBS was quickly adopted on distributed parallel systems and replaced NQS on traditional supercomputers and server systems. Eventually the entire industry evolved toward distributed parallel systems, taking the form of both special-purpose and commodity clusters. Managers of such systems found that the capabilities of PBS mapped well onto cluster systems.

The latest chapter in the PBS story began when Veridian (the Research and Developement contractor that developed PBS for NASA) released the Portable Batch System Professional Edition (PBS Pro), a complete workload management solution. The cluster administrator can now use the commercial version of this space-age technology to manage the workload on Windows 2000 clusters.

This chapter gives a technical overview of PBS Pro and information on installing, using and managing PBS. However, it is not possible to cover all the details of a software system the size and complexity of PBS in a single chapter. Therefore, we limit this discussion to the recommended configuration for clusters, providing references to the various PBS documentation where additional, detailed information is available.

### 16.1.1 Acquiring PBS

While PBS Pro is bundled in a variety of cluster kits, the best source for the most current release is the official Veridian PBS Pro Web site: www.PBSpro.com. This site offers downloads of the software and documentation, as well as FAQs, discussion lists, and current PBS news. Hardcopy documentation, support services, training and PBS Pro software licenses are available from the PBS Pro Online Store, accessed through the PBS Web site.

### 16.1.2 PBS Features

PBS Pro provides many features and benefits to the cluster administrator. A few of the more important features are the following:

*Enterprisewide resource sharing* provides transparent job scheduling on any PBS system by any authorized user. Jobs can be submitted from any client system, both local and remote, crossing domains where needed.

*Multiple user interfaces* provide a graphical user interface for submitting batch and interactive jobs; querying job, queue, and system status; and monitoring job progress. Also provided is a traditional command line interface.

*Security and access control lists* permit the administrator to allow or deny access to PBS systems on the basis of username, group, host, and/or network domain.

*Job accounting* offers detailed logs of system activities for charge-back or usage analysis per user, per group, per project, and per compute host.

*Automatic file staging* provides users with the ability to specify any files that need to be copied onto the execution host before the job runs and any that need to be copied off after the job completes. The job will be scheduled to run only after the required files have been successfully transferred.

*Parallel job support* works with parallel programming libraries such as MPI, PVM, and HPF. Applications can be scheduled to run within a single multiprocessor computer or across multiple systems.

*System monitoring* includes a graphical user interface for system monitoring. PBS displays node status, job placement, and resource utilization information for both standalone systems and clusters.

*Job interdependency* enables the user to define a wide range of interdependencies between jobs. Such dependencies include execution order, synchronization, and execution conditioned on the success or failure of another specific job (or set of jobs).

*Computational Grid support* provides an enabling technology for meta-computing and computational Grids, including support for the Globus Toolkit.

*Comprehensive API* includes a complete application programming interface for sites that wish to integrate PBS with other applications or to support unique job-scheduling requirements.

*Automatic load-leveling* provides numerous ways to distribute the workload across a cluster of machines, based on hardware configuration, resource availability, keyboard activity, and local scheduling policy.

*Distributed clustering* allows customers to use physically distributed systems and clusters, even across wide area networks.

*Common user environment* offers users a common view of the job submission, job querying, system status, and job tracking over all systems.

*Cross-system scheduling* ensures that jobs do not have to be targeted to a specific computer system. Users may submit their job and have it run on the first available system that meets their resource requirements.

*Job priority* allows users the ability to specify the priority of their jobs; defaults can be provided at both the queue and system level.

*User name mapping* provides support for mapping user account names on one system to the appropriate name on remote server systems. This allows PBS to fully function in environments where users do not have a consistent username across all the resources they have access to.

*Full configurability* makes PBS easily tailored to meet the needs of different sites. Much of this flexibility is due to the unique design of the scheduler module, which permits complete customization.

*Broad platform availability* is achieved through support of Windows 2000 and every major version of Unix and Linux, from workstations and servers to supercomputers. New platforms are being supported with each new release.

*System integration* allows PBS to take advantage of vendor-specific enhancements on different systems (such as supporting `cpusets` on SGI systems and interfacing with the global resource manager on the Cray T3E).

### 16.1.3   PBS Architecture

PBS consists of two major component types: user-level commands and system daemons. A brief description of each is given here to help you make decisions during the installation process.

PBS supplies both command-line programs that are POSIX 1003.2d conforming and a graphical interface. These are used to submit, monitor, modify, and delete jobs. These *client commands* can be installed on any system type supported by PBS and do not require the local presence of any of the other components of PBS. There are three classifications of commands: user commands that any authorized user can use, operator commands, and manager (or administrator) commands. Operator and manager commands require specific access privileges. (See also the security sections of the PBS Administrator Guide.)

The *job server* daemon is the central focus for PBS. Within this document, it is generally referred to as the *Server* or by the execution name `pbs_server`. All commands and the other daemons communicate with the Server via an Internet Protocol (IP) network. The Server's main function is to provide the basic batch services such as receiving or creating a batch job, modifying the job, protecting the job against system crashes, and running the job. Typically, one Server manages a given set of resources.

The *job executor* is the daemon that actually places the job into execution. This daemon, `pbs_mom`, is informally called *MOM* because it is the mother of all executing jobs. (MOM is a reverse-engineered acronym that stands for Machine Oriented Mini-server.) MOM places a job into execution when it receives a copy of the job from a Server. MOM creates a new session as identical to a user login session as possible. For example, if the user's login shell is `csh`, then MOM creates a session in which `.login` is run as well as `.cshrc`. MOM also has the responsibility for returning the job's output to the user when directed to do so by the Server. One MOM daemon runs on each computer that will execute PBS jobs.

The *job scheduler* daemon, `pbs_sched`, implements the site's policy controlling when each job is run and on which resources. The Scheduler communicates with the various MOMs to query the state of system resources and with the Server to learn about the availability of jobs to execute. The interface to the Server is through the same API (discussed below) as used by the client commands. Note that the Scheduler interfaces with the Server with the same privilege as the PBS manager.

## 16.2   Using PBS

From the user's perspective, a workload mangement system enables you to make more efficient use of your time by allowing you to specify the tasks you need run on the cluster. The system takes care of running these tasks and returning the results to you. If the cluster is full, then it holds your tasks and runs them when the resources are available.

With PBS you create a *batch job* that you then submit to PBS. A batch job is a shell script containing the set of commands you want run on the cluster. It also contains directives that specify the resource requirements (such as memory or CPU time) that your job needs. Once you create your PBS job, you can reuse it, if you wish, or you can modify it for subsequent runs. Example job scripts are shown below.

PBS also provides a special kind of batch job called *interactive batch*. This job is treated just like a regular batch job (it is queued up and must wait for resources to become available before it can run). But once it is started, the user's terminal input and output are connected to the job in what appears to be an `rlogin` session. It appears that the user is logged into one of the nodes of the cluster, and the resources requested by the job are reserved for that job. Many users find this feature useful for debugging their applications or for computational steering.

PBS provides two user interfaces: a command-line interface (CLI) and a graphical user interface (GUI). You can use either to interact with PBS: both interfaces have the same functionality.

## 16.2.1   Creating a PBS Job

Previously we mentioned that a PBS job is simply a shell script containing resource
requirements of the job and the command(s) to be executed. Here is what a sample
PBS job might look like the following:

```
#!/bin/sh
#PBS -l walltime=1:00:00
#PBS -l mem=400mb
#PBS -l ncpus=4
#PBS -j oe

cd ${HOME}/PBS/test
mpirun -np 4 myprogram
```

This script would then be submitted to PBS using the *qsub* command.

Let us look at the script for a moment. The first line tells what shell to use to
interpret the script. Lines 2–4 are resource directives, specifying arguments to the
"resource list" ("-l") option of **qsub**. Note that all PBS directives begin with **#PBS**.
These lines tell PBS what to do with your job. Any **qsub** option can also be placed
inside the script by using a **#PBS** directive. However, PBS stops parsing directives
with the first blank line encountered.

Returning to our example above, we see a request for 1 hour of wall-clock time,
400 MBytes of memory and 4 CPUs. The fifth line is a request for PBS to merge
the stdout and stderr file streams of the job into a single file. The last two lines are
the commands the user wants executed: change directory to a particular location,
then execute an MPI program called '**myprogram**'.

This job script could have been created in one of two ways: using a text editor,
or using the *xpbs* graphical interface (see below).

## 16.2.2   Submitting a PBS Job

The command used to submit a job to PBS is **qsub**. For example, say you created a
file containing your PBS job called '**myscriptfile**'. The following example shows
how to submit the job to PBS:

```
% qsub myscriptfile
12322.sol.pbspro.com
```

The second line in the example is the job identifier returned by the PBS server.
This unique identifier can be used to act on this job in the future (before it completes

running). The next section of this chapter discusses using this "job id" in various ways.

The `qsub` command has a number of options that can be specified either on the command-line or in the job script itself. Note that any command-line option will override the same option within the script file.

Table 16.1 lists the most commonly used options to `qsub`. See the PBS User Guide for the complete list and full description of the options.

| Option | Purpose |
|---|---|
| -l list | List of resources needed by job |
| -q queue | Queue to submit job to |
| -N name | Name of job |
| -S shell | Shell to execute job script |
| -p priority | Priority value of job |
| -a datetime | Delay job under after datetime |
| -j oe | Join output and error files |
| -h | Place a hold on job |

**Table 16.1**
PBS commands.

The "`-l resource_list`" option is used to specify the resources needed by the job. Table 16.2 lists all the resources available to jobs running on clusters.

| Resource | Meaning |
|---|---|
| arch | System architecture needed by job |
| cput | CPU time required by all processes in job |
| file | Maximum single file disk space requirements |
| mem | Total amount of RAM memory required |
| ncpus | Number of CPUs (processors) required |
| nice | Requested "nice" (Unix priority) value |
| nodes | Number and/or type of nodes needed |
| pcput | Maximum per-process CPU time required |
| pmem | Maximum per-process memory required |
| wall time | Total wall-clock time needed |
| workingset | Total disk space requirements |

**Table 16.2**
PBS resources.

### 16.2.3    Getting the Status of a PBS Job

Once the job has been submitted to PBS, you can use either the qstat or xpbs commands to check the job status. If you know the job identifier for your job, you can request the status explicitly. Note that unless you have multiple clusters, you need only specify the sequence number portion of the job identifier:

```
% qstat 12322
Job id          Name         User    Time Use S Queue
-------------   ------------  ------  -------- - -----
12322.sol       myscriptfile jjones  00:06:39 R submit
```

If you run the qstat command without specifing a job identifier, then you will receive status on all jobs currently queued and running.

Often users wonder why their job is not running. You can query this information from PBS using the "-s" (status) option of qstat, for example,

```
% qstat 12323
Job id          Name         User    Time Use S Queue
-------------   ------------  ------  -------- - -----
12323.sol       myscriptfile jjones  00:00:00 Q submit
    Requested number of CPUs not currently available.
```

A number of options to qstat change what information is displayed. The PBS User Guide gives the complete list.

### 16.2.4    PBS Command Summary

So far we have seen several of the PBS user commands. Table 16.3 is provided as a quick reference for all the PBS user commands. Details on each can be found in the PBS manual pages and the PBS User Guide.

### 16.2.5    Using the PBS Graphical User Interface

PBS provides two GUI interfaces: a TCL/TK-based GUI called **xpbs** and an optional Web-based GUI.

The GUI xpbs provides a user-friendly point-and-click interface to the PBS commands. To run xpbs as a regular, nonprivileged user, type

```
setenv DISPLAY your_workstation_name:0
xpbs
```

| Command | Purpose |
|---------|---------|
| qalter | Alter job(s) |
| qdel | Delete job(s) |
| qhold | Hold job(s) |
| qmsg | Send a message to job(s) |
| qmove | Move job(s) to another queue |
| qrls | Release held job(s) |
| qrerun | Rerun job(s) |
| qselect | Select a specific subset of jobs |
| qsig | Send a signal to job(s) |
| qstat | Show status of job(s) |
| qsub | Submit job(s) |
| xpbs | Graphical Interface (GUI) to PBS commands |

**Table 16.3**
PBS commands.

To run `xpbs` with the additional purpose of terminating PBS Servers, stopping and starting queues, or running or rerunning jobs, type

```
xpbs -admin
```

Note that you must be identified as a PBS operator or manager in order for the additional "-admin" functions to take effect.

The optional Web-based user interface provides access to all the functionality of `xpbs` via almost any Web browser. To access it, you simply type the URL of your PBS Server host into your browser. The layout and usage are similar to those of `xpbs`. For details, see The PBS User Guide.

### 16.2.6   PBS Application Programming Interface

Part of the PBS package is the PBS Interface Library, or IFL. This library provides a means of building new PBS clients. Any PBS service request can be invoked through calls to the interface library. Users may wish to build a PBS job that will check its status itself or submit new jobs, or they may wish to customize the job status display rather than use the `qstat` command. Administrators may use the interface library to build new control commands.

The IFL provides a user-callable function that corresponds to each PBS client command. There is (approximately) a one-to-one correlation between commands and PBS service requests. Additional routines are provided for network connection management. The user-callable routines are declared in the header file '`PBS_ifl.h`'.

Users request service of a batch server by calling the appropriate library routine and passing it the required parameters. The parameters correspond to the options and operands on the commands. The user must ensure that the parameters are in the correct syntax. Each function will return zero upon success and a nonzero error code on failure. These error codes are available in the header file 'PBS_error.h'. The library routine will accept the parameters and build the corresponding batch request. This request is then passed to the server communication routine. (The PBS API is fully documented in the PBS External Reference Specification.)

## 16.3  Installing PBS

PBS is able to support a wide range of configurations. It may be installed and used to control jobs on a single system or to load balance jobs on a number of systems. It may be used to allocate nodes of a cluster or parallel system to both serial and parallel jobs. It can also deal with a mix of these situations. However, given the topic of this book, we focus on the recommended configuration for clusters. The PBS Administrator Guide explains other configurations.

When PBS is installed on a cluster, a MOM daemon must be on each execution host, and the Server and Scheduler should be installed on one of the systems or on a front-end system.

For Windows 2000 clusters, PBS is provided in a single package that contains

- the *PBS Administrator Guide* in PDF form
- the *PBS User Guide* in PDF form,
- the PBS Pro software, and
- supporting text files: software license, README, release notes, and the like.

The PBS Pro install program will walk you through the installation process. If you are installing from the PBS Pro CD-ROM, insert the CD-ROM into your computer's CD-ROM drive, browse to your CD-ROM drive, and double-click on the Install program icon.

Alternatively, you can download the latest PBS Pro package from the PBS Pro Web site, and save it to your hard drive. From there you can manually run the installation program by typing

```
install.exe
```

The installation program will prompt you for the names of directories for the different parts of PBS and the type of installation (full, server-only, execution host only). Next, you will be prompted for your software license key(s). (See Section 16.1.1 if you do not already have your software license key.)

## 16.4   Configuring PBS

Now that PBS has been installed, the Server and MOMs can be configured and the scheduling policy selected. Note that further configuration of may not be required since PBS Pro comes preconfigured, and the default configuration may completely meet your needs. However, you are advised to read this section to determine whether the defaults are indeed complete for you or whether any of the optional settings may apply.

### 16.4.1   Network Addresses and PBS

PBS makes use of fully qualified host names for identifying the jobs and their location. A PBS installation is known by the host name on which the Server is running. The name used by the daemons or used to authenticate messages is the canonical host name. This name is taken from the primary name field, h_name, in the structure returned by the library call gethostbyaddr(). According to the IETF RFCs, this name must be fully qualified and consistent for any IP address assigned to that host.

### 16.4.2   The Qmgr Command

The PBS manager command, qmgr, provides a command-line administrator interface. The command reads directives from standard input. The syntax of each directive is checked and the appropriate request sent to the Server(s). A qmgr directive takes one of the following forms:

```
command server [names] [attr OP value[,...]]
command queue  [names] [attr OP value[,...]]
command node   [names] [attr OP value[,...]]
```

where command is the command to perform on an object. The qmgr commands are listed in Table 16.4.

The list or print subcommands of qmgr can be executed by the general user. Creating or deleting a queue requires PBS Manager privilege. Setting or unsetting server or queue attributes requires PBS Operator or Manager privilege.

Here are several examples that illustrate using the qmgr command. These and other qmgr commands are fully explained below, along with the specific tasks they accomplish.

| Command | Explanation |
|---------|-------------|
| active  | Set the active objects. |
| create  | Create a new object, applies to queues and nodes. |
| delete  | Destroy an existing object (queues or nodes). |
| set     | Define or alter attribute values of the object. |
| unset   | Clear the value of the attributes of the object. |
| list    | List the current attributes and values of the object. |
| print   | Print all the queue and server attributes. |

**Table 16.4**
qmgr commands.

```
% qmgr
Qmgr: create node mars np=2,ntype=cluster
Qmgr: create node venus properties="inner,moonless"
Qmgr: set node mars properties = inner
Qmgr: set node mars properties += haslife
Qmgr: delete node mars
Qmgr: d n venus
```

Commands can be abbreviated to their minimum unambiguous form (as shown in the last line in the example above). A command is terminated by a new line character or a semicolon. Multiple commands may be entered on a single line. A command may extend across lines by marking the new line character with a backslash. Comments begin with a pound sign and continue to the end of the line. Comments and blank lines are ignored by qmgr. See the qmgr manual page for detailed usage and syntax description.

### 16.4.3   Nodes

Where jobs will be run is determined by an interaction between the Scheduler and the Server. This interaction is affected by the contents of the PBS 'nodes' file and the system configuration onto which you are deploying PBS. Without this list of nodes, the Server will not establish a communication stream with the MOM(s), and MOM will be unable to report information about running jobs or to notify the Server when jobs complete. In a cluster configuration, distributing jobs across the various hosts is a matter of the Scheduler determining on which host to place a selected job.

Regardless of the type of execution nodes, each node must be defined to the Server in the PBS nodes file, (the default location of which is '/usr/spool/PBS/server_-

priv/nodes'). This is a simple text file with the specification of a single node per line in the file. The format of each line in the file is

```
node_name[:ts] [attributes]
```

The node name is the network name of the node (host name), it does not have to be fully qualified (in fact, it is best kept as short as possible). The optional ":ts" appended to the name indicates that the node is a timeshared node.

Nodes can have attributes associated with them. Attributes come in three types: properties, `name=value` pairs, and `name.resource=value` pairs.

Zero or more properties may be specified. The property is nothing more than a string of alphanumeric characters (first character must be alphabetic) without meaning to PBS. Properties are used to group classes of nodes for allocation to a series of jobs.

Any legal node `name=value` pair may be specified in the node file in the same format as on a `qsub` directive: `attribute.resource=value`. Consider the following example:

```
NodeA resource_available.ncpus=3 max_running=1
```

The expression `np=N` may be used as shorthand for `resources_available.ncpus=N`, which can be added to declare the number of virtual processors (VPs) on the node. This syntax specifies a numeric string, for example, `np=4`. This expression will allow the node to be allocated up to N times to one job or more than one job. If `np=N` is not specified for a cluster node, it is assumed to have one VP.

You may edit the nodes list in one of two ways. If the server is not running, you may directly edit the nodes file with a text editor. If the server is running, you should use `qmgr` to edit the list of nodes.

Each item on the line must be separated by white space. The items may be listed in any order except that the host name must always be first. Comment lines may be included if the first nonwhite space character is the pound sign.

The following is an example of a possible nodes file for a cluster called "planets":

```
# The first set of nodes are cluster nodes.
# Note that the properties are provided to
# logically group certain nodes together.
# The last node is a timeshared node.
#
mercury     inner moonless
venus       inner moonless np=1
```

```
earth       inner np=1
mars        inner np=2
jupiter     outer np=18
saturn      outer np=16
uranus      outer np=14
neptune     outer np=12
pluto:ts
```

### 16.4.4  Creating or Adding Nodes

After `pbs_server` is started, the node list may be entered or altered via the `qmgr` command:

```
create node node_name [attribute=value]
```

where the attributes and their associated possible values are shown in Table 16.5.

| Attribute | Value |
|---|---|
| state | `free`, `down`, `offline` |
| properties | any alphanumeric string |
| ntype | `cluster`, `time-shared` |
| `resources_available.ncpus` (np) | number of virtual processors $> 0$ |
| `resources_available` | list of resources available on node |
| `resources_assigned` | list of resources in use on node |
| `max_running` | maximum number of running jobs |
| `max_user_run` | maximum number of running jobs per user |
| `max_group_run` | maximum number of running jobs per group |
| queue | queue name (if any) associated with node |
| reservations | list of reservations pending on the node |
| comment | general comment |

**Table 16.5**
PBS node syntax.

Below are several examples of setting node attributes via `qmgr`:

```
% qmgr
Qmgr: create node mars np=2,ntype=cluster
Qmgr: create node venus properties="inner,moonless"
```

Once a node has been created, its attributes and/or properties can be modified by using the following `qmgr` syntax:

```
set node node_name [attribute[+|-]=value]
```

where attributes are the same as for `create`, for example,

```
% qmgr
Qmgr: set node mars properties=inner
Qmgr: set node mars properties+=haslife
```

Nodes can be deleted via `qmgr` as well, using the `delete node` syntax, as the following example shows:

```
% qmgr
Qmgr: delete node mars
Qmgr: delete node pluto
```

Note that the `busy` state is set by the execution daemon, `pbs_mom`, when a load-average threshold is reached on the node. See `max_load` in MOM's config file. The `job-exclusive` and `job-sharing` states are set when jobs are running on the node.

### 16.4.5 Default Configuration

Server management consist of configuring the Server and establishing queues and their attributes. The default configuration, shown below, sets the minimum server settings and some recommended settings for a typical PBS cluster.

```
% qmgr
Qmgr: print server
# Create queues and set their attributes
#
# Create and define queue workq
#
create queue workq
set queue workq queue_type = Execution
set queue workq enabled = True
set queue workq started = True
#
# Set Server attributes
#
set server scheduling = True
set server default_queue = workq
set server log_events = 511
set server mail_from = adm
set server query_other_jobs = True
set server scheduler_iteration = 600
```

### 16.4.6    Configuring MOM

The execution server daemons, MOMs, require much less configuration than does
the Server. The installation process creates a basic MOM configuration file that
contains the minimum entries necessary in order to run PBS jobs. This section
describes the MOM configuration file and explains all the options available to customize the PBS installation to your site.

The behavior of MOM is controlled via a configuration file that is read upon
daemon initialization (startup) and upon reinitialization (when `pbs_mom` receives a
SIGHUP signal). The configuration file provides several types of runtime information to MOM: access control, static resource names and values, external resources
provided by a program to be run on request via a shell escape, and values to pass to
internal functions at initialization (and reinitialization). Each configuration entry
is on a single line, with the component parts separated by white space. If the line
starts with a pound sign, the line is considered to be a comment and is ignored.

A minimal MOM configuration file should contain the following:

```
$logevent 0x1ff
$clienthost server-hostname
```

The first entry, `$logevent`, specifies the level of message logging this daemon should
perform. The second entry, `$clienthost`, identifies a host that is permitted to
connect to this MOM. You should set the *server-hostname* variable to the name of
the host on which you will be running the PBS Server (`pbs_server`). Advanced
MOM configuration options are described in the PBS Administrator Guide.

### 16.4.7    Scheduler Configuration

Now that the Server and MOMs have been configured, we turn our attention to the
PBS Scheduler. As mentioned previously, the Scheduler is responsible for implementing the local site policy regarding which jobs are run and on what resources.
This section discusses the recommended configuration for a typical cluster. The full
list of tunable Scheduler parameters and detailed explanation of each is provided
in the PBS Administrator Guide.

The PBS Pro Scheduler provides a wide range of scheduling policies. It provides
the ability to sort the jobs in several different ways, in addition to FIFO order. It
also can sort on user and group priority. The queues are sorted by queue priority
to determine the order in which they are to be considered. As distributed, the
Scheduler is configured with the defaults shown in Table 16.6.

| Option | Default Value |
|---|---|
| round_robin | False |
| by_queue | True |
| strict_fifo | False |
| load_balancing | False |
| load_balancing_rr | False |
| fair_share | False |
| help_starving_jobs | True |
| backfill | True |
| backfill_prime | False |
| sort_queues | True |
| sort_by | shortest_job_first |
| smp_cluster_dist | pack |
| preemptive_sched | True |

**Table 16.6**
Default scheduling policy parameters.

Once the Server and Scheduler are configured and running, job scheduling can be initiated by setting the Server attribute scheduling to a value of true:

```
# qmgr -c "set server scheduling=true"
```

The value of scheduling is retained across Server terminations or starts. After the Server is configured, it may be placed into service.

## 16.5   Managing PBS

This section is intended for the PBS administrator: it discusses several important aspects of managing PBS on a day-to-day basis.

During the installation of PBS Pro, the file '/etc/pbs.conf' was created. This configuration file controls which daemons are to be running on the local system. Each node in a cluster should have its own '/etc/pbs.conf' file.

### 16.5.1   Starting PBS Daemons

The daemon processes (pbs_server, pbs_sched, and pbs_mom) must run with the real and effective uid of root. Typically, the daemons are started automatically by the system upon reboot. The boot-time start/stop script for PBS is '/etc/init.d/pbs'. This script reads the '/etc/pbs.conf' file to determine which daemons should be started.

The startup script can also be run by hand to get status on the PBS daemons, and to start/stop all the PBS daemons on a given host. The command line syntax for the startup script is

```
/etc/init.d/pbs [ status | stop | start ]
```

Alternatively, you can start the individual PBS daemons manually, as discussed in the following sections. Furthermore, you may wish to change the options specified to various daemons, as discussed below.

### 16.5.2   Monitoring PBS

The node monitoring GUI for PBS is xpbsmon. It is used for displaying graphically information about execution hosts in a PBS environment. Its view of a PBS environment consists of a list of sites where each site runs one or more Servers and each Server runs jobs on one or more execution hosts (nodes).

The system administrator needs to define the site's information in a global X resources file, 'PBS_LIB/xpbsmon/xpbsmonrc', which is read by the GUI if a personal '.xpbsmonrc' file is missing. A default 'xpbsmonrc' file is created during installation defining (under *sitesInfo resource) a default site name, the list of Servers that run on the site, the set of nodes (or execution hosts) where jobs on a particular Server run, and the list of queries that are communicated to each node's pbs_mom. If node queries have been specified, the host where 'xpbsmon' is running must have been given explicit permission by the pbs_mom daemon to post queries to it; this is done by including a $restricted entry in the MOM's config file.

### 16.5.3   Tracking PBS Jobs

Periodically you (or the user) will want track the status of a job. Or perhaps you want to view all the log file entries for a given job. Several tools allow you to track a job's progress, as Table 16.7 shows.

| Command | Explanation |
|---------|-------------|
| qstat | Shows status of jobs, queues, and servers |
| xpbs | Can alert user when job starts producing output |
| tracejob | Collates and sorts PBS log entries for specified job |

**Table 16.7**
Job-tracking commands.

### 16.5.4  PBS Accounting Logs

The PBS Server daemon maintains an accounting log. The log name defaults to '/usr/spool/PBS/server_priv/accounting/yyyymmdd' where yyyymmdd is the date. The accounting log files may be placed elsewhere by specifying the -A option on the pbs_server command line. The option argument is the full (absolute) path name of the file to be used. If a null string is given, for example

```
# pbs_server -A ""
```

then the accounting log will not be opened, and no accounting records will be recorded.

The accounting file is changed according to the same rules as the log files. If the default file is used, named for the date, the file will be closed and a new one opened every day on the first event (write to the file) after midnight. With either the default file or a file named with the -A option, the Server will close the accounting log and reopen it upon the receipt of a SIGHUP signal. This strategy allows you to rename the old log and start recording anew on an empty file. For example, if the current date is December 1, the Server will be writing in the file '20011201'. The following actions will cause the current accounting file to be renamed 'dec1' and the Server to close the file and starting writing a new '20011201'.

```
# mv 20011201 dec1
# kill -HUP (pbs_server's PID)
```

## 16.6  Troubleshooting

The following is a list of common problems and recommended solutions. Additional information is always available on the PBS Web sites.

### 16.6.1  Clients Unable to Contact Server

If a client command (such as qstat or qmgr) is unable to connect to a Server there are several possible errors to check. If the error return is 15034, *No server to connect to*, check (1) that there is indeed a Server running and (2) that the default Server information is set correctly. The client commands will attempt to connect to the Server specified on the command line if given or, if not given, the Server specified in the default server file, '/usr/spool/PBS/default_server'.

If the error return is 15007, *No permission*, check for (2) as above. Also check that the executable pbs_iff is located in the search path for the client and that it is setuid root. Additionally, try running pbs_iff by typing

```
pbs_iff server_host 15001
```

where `server_host` is the name of the host on which the Server is running and 15001 is the port to which the Server is listening (if started with a different port number, use that number instead of 15001). The executable `pbs_iff` should print out a string of garbage characters and exit with a status of 0. The garbage is the encrypted credential that would be used by the command to authenticate the client to the Server. If `pbs_iff` fails to print the garbage and/or exits with a nonzero status, either the Server is not running or it was installed with a different encryption system from that used for `pbs_iff`.

### 16.6.2   Nodes Down

The PBS Server determines the state of nodes (up or down), by communicating with MOM on the node. The state of nodes may be listed by two commands: `qmgr` and `pbsnodes`.

```
% qmgr
Qmgr: list node @active

% pbsnodes -a
Node jupiter
        state = down, state-unknown
        properties = sparc, mine
        ntype = cluster
```

A node in PBS may be marked **down** in one of two substates. For example, the state above of node "jupiter" shows that the Server has not had contact with MOM on that since the Server came up. Check to see whether a MOM is running on the node. If there is a MOM and if the MOM was just started, the Server may have attempted to poll her before she was up. The Server should see her during the next polling cycle in ten minutes. If the node is still marked **down, state-unknown** after ten minutes, either the node name specified in the Server's node file does not map to the real network hostname or there is a network problem between the Server's host and the node.

If the node is listed as

```
% pbsnodes -a
Node jupiter
        state = down
```

```
properties = sparc, mine
ntype = cluster
```

then the Server has been able to communicate with MOM on the node in the past, but she has not responded recently. The Server will send a `ping` PBS message to every free node each ping cycle (10 minutes). If a node does not acknowledge the ping before the next cycle, the Server will mark the node `down`.

### 16.6.3    Nondelivery of Output

If the output of a job cannot be delivered to the user, it is saved in a special directory '`/usr/spool/PBS/undelivered`' and mail is sent to the user. The typical causes of nondelivery are the following:

- The destination host is not trusted and the user does not have a .rhost file.
- An improper path was specified.
- A directory in the specified destination path is not writable.
- The user's .cshrc on the destination host generates output when executed.

The '`/usr/spool/PBS/spool`' directory on the execution host does not have the correct permissions. This directory must have mode 1777 (`drwxrwxrwxt`).

### 16.6.4    Job Cannot Be Executed

If a user receives a mail message containing a job identifier and the line "Job cannot be executed," the job was aborted by MOM when she tried to place it into execution. The complete reason can be found in one of two places: MOM's log file or the standard error file of the user's job.

If the second line of the message is "See Administrator for help," then MOM aborted the job before the job's files were set up. The reason will be noted in MOM's log. Typical reasons are a bad user/group account or a system error.

If the second line of the message is "See job standard error file," then MOM had already created the job's file, and additional messages were written to standard error.

# 17 MPI Software Technology, Inc., Cluster CoNTroller

*David Lifka*

In 1997, Cornell University was funded by Intel's Technology for Education 2000 program to investigate the use of Intel-based computers for a broad range of research and computing projects (see `www.cs.cornell.edu/tech`2000). The role of the Cornell Theory Center (CTC) in that proposal was to develop a parallel Windows-based cluster and job-scheduling system and to evaluate its feasibility as a high-performance computing platform. Led by David Lifka, CTC developed a Windows job-scheduling system called Cluster CoNTroller.

The original design goal of Cluster CoNTroller was to provide an easy-to-use heterogeneous resource job scheduler that behaved (from the users' perspective) like other parallel scheduling systems and leveraged Windows 2000 technology wherever possible. After several months of using the system, we began to investigate how we could add other parallel programming tools needed by our users, arguably the most important tool being MPI. Since our objective was to use commercially supported tools wherever possible, we began searching for a commercial Windows implementation of MPI. Eventually we decided to partner with MPI Software Technology, Inc. (MSTI) and to license Cluster CoNTroller to them; they in turn agreed to harden Cluster CoNTroller as a product and provide it—together with MPI/Pro, their commercial MPI implementation—to others interested in production-quality cluster computing.

In this chapter we describe the MPI Software Technology, Inc. Cluster CoNTroller. We discuss its components, its configuration, and its strengths. We also work through an example of how to submit a parallel job to the scheduler.

## 17.1 Overview of Cluster CoNTroller

Cluster CoNTroller provides parallel batch and interactive job scheduling for dedicated computational clusters of Windows 2000 workstations or servers. Cluster CoNTroller efficiently manages all types of jobs, from serial to massively parallel, and ensures that they are run in a timely, deterministic fashion, thereby increasing the throughput of computation. Ideal for users who routinely want to run computational science or finance applications in parallel, Cluster CoNTroller is well suited to schedule programs written using MPI/Pro, but it will also support any other type of Windows application.

### 17.1.1  Strengths

At the heart of Cluster CoNTroller is a deterministic heterogeneous scheduling algorithm that allows users to specify hardware and software resource requirements for parallel and serial jobs and to use the resources in batch or interactive mode. In batch mode, the scheduling system runs the user's job as that user on the resources it allocates. In interactive mode, the user logs in, via Telnet, to the nodes allocated and runs a job by hand until the time allotment expires. In both cases, Cluster CoNTroller allocates resources (starts the batch jobs) and then gets out of the way. No polling or resource monitoring occurs during a user's time allocation. Thus, the entire computer and network resource are available to the user. Cluster CoNTroller commands themselves are not resource intensive and generate very low overhead to the cluster resources.

Cluster CoNTroller was designed with flexibility in mind. Cluster CoNTroller commands can easily be adapted via scripting language wrappers to behave in a way specific to different environments. In addition, Cluster CoNTroller can be purchased with a Perl-based scheduling core that can easily be customized for any environment. Further, MPI Software Technology consultants can provide customized scheduling algorithms to meet a customer's specific requirements.

### 17.1.2  Availability

Cluster CoNTroller is sold under a support-only pricing model. You may download Cluster CoNTroller for free from the MSTI Web site, `www.mpi-softtech.com` for up to 16 computers with no support. Support and licenses for additional computers are competitively priced. Microsoft has licensed Cluster CoNTroller and MPI/Pro for up to 16 computers from MSTI and makes it available on their High Performance Resource Kit CD set (see `https://microsoft.order-1.com/cctp`).

## 17.2  Installation Configuration

A Cluster CoNTroller system comprises four basic resource types: login nodes, file servers, scheduler node/domain controller, and compute nodes. In many large installations these resources are supported on dedicated computers, but in smaller configurations it is certainly not necessary.

### 17.2.1  Login Nodes

Login nodes provide remote access to the cluster resources and the Cluster CoNTroller commands. Typically, they provide Telnet and Terminal Server (including

Citrix support for non-Windows clients, if necessary) access. All the scheduler commands, compilers, and user-level cluster monitoring tools usually are available on the login nodes. These nodes are commonly used to compile and link codes to run on the cluster, develop batch scripts, and provide scheduler access for submitting, monitoring, and canceling jobs on the cluster.

Login nodes are useful in a production environment to ensure that all users have access to the necessary software and tools to use the cluster no matter where they are accessing it from. In many smaller, dedicated cluster environments, however, login nodes may not be needed. Instead, individual desktops in the same Windows domain can be configured to interact with the scheduling system.

### 17.2.2 File Servers

File servers under Windows work in a manner different from file servers in a Unix system. Under Windows, remote file access is built into the operating system, without requiring mounted file systems such as NFS. Windows provides two simple-to-use mechanisms to access files remotely. As discussed in Section 7.1.2, Windows "shares" (or shared files or folders) can be accessed via a UNC or by mapping them to a local drive letter via Windows explorer.

The Cornell Theory Center has several file servers each with one terabyte of Small Computer System Interface (SCSI) attached storage that is made available as a single logical volume via Microsoft's Distributed File System, DFS. All cluster nodes map this share as H: via a Windows service so that it is persistent, even if no one is logged in at the console (normally all mapped drives are disconnected when the user logs off). This approach allows users to access their home directory from any cluster node, including the login nodes, for example,

```
c:\ dir h:\users\lifka
```

Section 7.1.2 shows a simple Perl script that runs as a Windows service to map a network drive even after the console is logged out. You can download the module from www.roth.net/perl/.

### 17.2.3 Compute Nodes

Compute nodes are the components on which jobs are actually run. These nodes typically are configured with minimal software (e.g., Telnet, Cygwin, Perl, Python, and MPI). Cluster CoNTroller manages and allocates these compute nodes for the various jobs that are submitted to the cluster.

### 17.2.4   Scheduler Node

The Cluster CoNTroller scheduling service must be run from a Windows domain controller. The scheduler node maintains the job queue and the node status information. It also allocates and deallocates resources via global domain groups and standard builtin Microsoft mechanisms for starting and stopping jobs on cluster nodes within the domain.

### 17.2.5   Security and Management

Unlike many parallel job scheduling systems, Cluster CoNTroller was designed from its conception to work in and leverage security and management features of the Windows operating system. For this reason it scales well and doesn't have any legacy system baggage to make things clumsy in a Windows environment.

For secure file access, Cluster CoNTroller uses NTFS and UNCs. Cluster CoNTroller also uses a specialized Windows service for secure user impersonation. This so-called impersonator service is installed on each compute node. The scheduler node can start this service remotely as the user it wants to impersonate. This means that all secure authentication information is maintained on a secure domain controller where the scheduler resides.

For node access control, Cluster CoNTroller uses global domain groups. This strategy means that all the management is handled only on the scheduling node. To grant a user access to nodes, all that is needed is to add that user to the appropriate group for each node (and vice versa, for removal). This does not require each node to be accessed over the network.

## 17.3   Administrative Features

Cluster CoNTroller has several nice administrative features. The Install Shield installer, for example, makes setting up the cluster easy, even for a novice. The key is simply understanding the various node types and which resources will be used for the nodes. Cluster CoNTroller also provides tools that allow system administrators to list and manage all processes on any cluster node and from the Web, to mark nodes up and down, and to reboot them from a single console.

Once the strongest features of Cluster CoNTroller is the ease with which administrators can customize its behavior for different environments. At its heart Cluster CoNTroller has a deterministic heterogeneous scheduling algorithm that balances utilization with reasonable wait times. MPI Software Technology also offers support for users to build their own scheduler components, using any programming or scripting language, and to develop special-purpose algorithms to meet specific needs.

Many of the Cluster CoNTroller commands are command shell executables that provide a way for wrapper scripts to be used to customize environments or define usage policies. For example, time limits can be enforced at submit time by rejecting jobs that request more time than is allowed at a particular site.

Another useful feature of Cluster CoNTroller is that node features can be redefined on the fly, allowing administrators to allocate portions of the cluster to specific users or groups.

## 17.4   User Commands

Cluster CoNTroller provides easy-to-use text-based user commands to interface with it. With these toolsa users can view the computer resources, their availability, and the jobs running on them remotely. Users can also submit jobs and remove them from the system. These tools can easily be added to scripts and batch files to develop customized tools and interfaces. The basic commands are the following:

- ccq: The ccq command allows users to see the entire job queue. It lists the running jobs in the order that they will complete and the waiting jobs in the order they were submitted. Figure 17.1 shows the output from ccq.

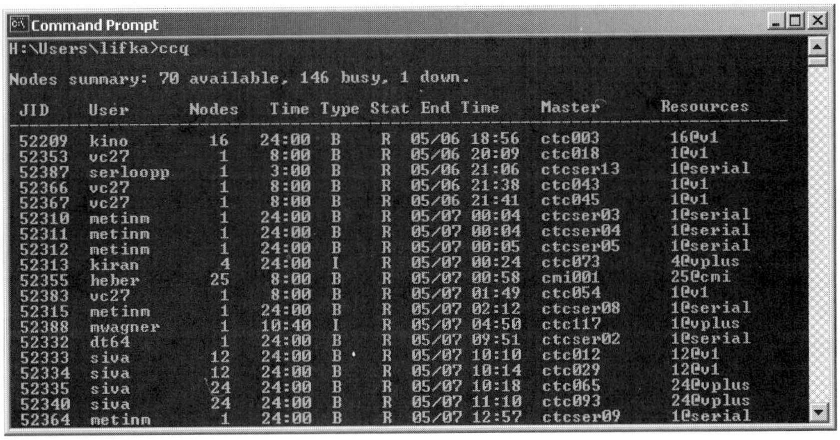

**Figure 17.1**
Output from ccq.

• cctypes: The `cctypes` commands shows the various resource pools that Cluster CoNTroller knows about and the features it can consider for a specific resource request. Figure 17.2 shows the output from the `cctypes` command. Note that there are several different resource types.

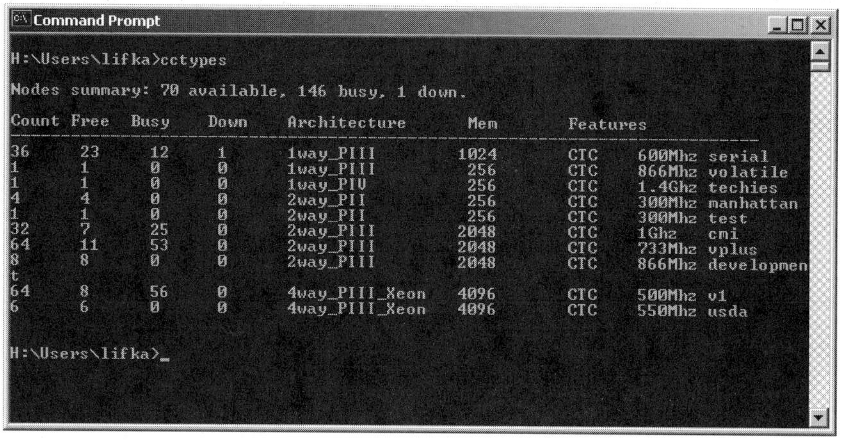

```
Command Prompt

H:\Users\lifka>cctypes

Nodes summary: 70 available, 146 busy, 1 down.

Count Free  Busy   Down   Architecture      Mem     Features
--------------------------------------------------------------------------
36     23    12      1    1way_PIII         1024    CTC    600Mhz serial
1      1     0       0    1way_PIII          256    CTC    866Mhz volatile
1      1     0       0    1way_PIV           256    CTC    1.4Ghz techies
4      4     0       0    2way_PII           256    CTC    300Mhz manhattan
1      1     0       0    2way_PII           256    CTC    300Mhz test
32     7     25      0    2way_PIII         2048    CTC    1Ghz   cmi
64     11    53      0    2way_PIII         2048    CTC    733Mhz vplus
8      8     0       0    2way_PIII         2048    CTC    866Mhz developmen
t
64     8     56      0    4way_PIII_Xeon    4096    CTC    500Mhz v1
6      6     0       0    4way_PIII_Xeon    4096    CTC    550Mhz usda


H:\Users\lifka>_
```

**Figure 17.2**
Output from cctypes.

• ccusage: The `ccusage` command lists each node in the system, its status, and (if it is busy) what userid is using it, the job it associated with it, and the time it will complete. Figure 17.3 shows the output from `ccusage.`

• ccsubmit and ccrm: The `ccsubmit` command allows users to submit a job to the system. The `ccrm` command with a valid jobid in the queue allows a user to remove a job that they submitted. Figure 17.4 shows the output from `ccsubmit` and `ccrm`.

### 17.4.1 Batch File Syntax

The Cluster CoNTroller batch file syntax is actually quite simple. A user must specify four fields:

• rem ccs account: Currently the account keyword must be set to the userid of the user submitting the job. If it is not, the job will be rejected. This field is also a place holder for accounting features in future releases where a user may want to specify a group that they belong to, in order to charge the time the job will be used. An example is `rem ccs account = lifka`.

• rem ccs nodes: This is the number of nodes or separate computers that the user wishes to use for a given job. Note that this is not necessarily the same as the

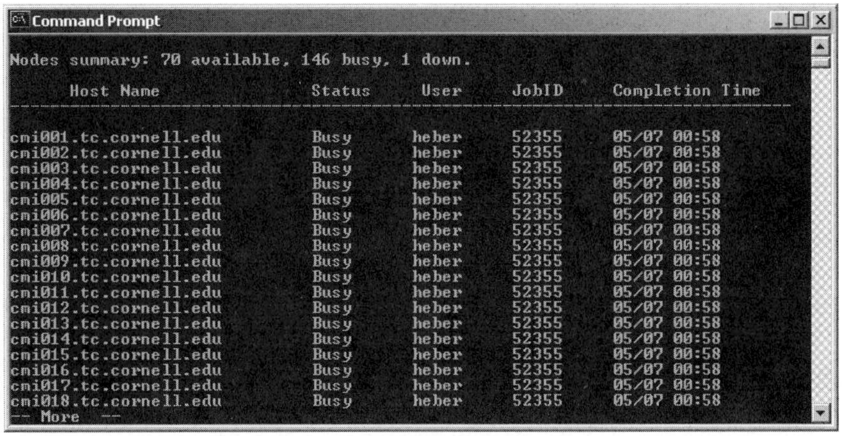

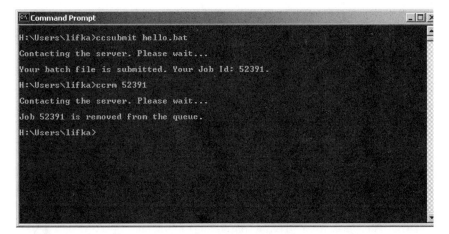

**Figure 17.3**
Output from ccusage.

**Figure 17.4**
Output from ccsubmit and ccrm.

number of processors. Cluster CoNTroller allocates nodes no matter how many processors a node has. For example, if your cluster has nodes with four processors, the fewest nodes you could request is one and the fewest processors is four. An example is `rem ccs nodes = 4`.

• rem ccs minutes: This is the number of minutes a job requires for a given job. Cluster CoNTroller schedules by wall-clock time, not CPU time. This is because it supports interactive jobs (described next) and a user cannot easily gauge CPU time while running interactively but can watch the clock on the wall to know when their time allocation will end.

• rem ccs type: Cluster CoNTroller supports both batch and interactive jobs. If you request a batch job (e.g., `rem ccs type = batch`), the scheduler will run your batch file for you, as you on the master node, or the first node in the set you are allocated. Anything in the batch file you submitted will be run on the master node. This allows you to submit work to the system to be done later, for example over a weekend. If you prefer to log in to the nodes you are allocated and run your jobs by hand (debugging work, for example), you can request interactive time (e.g., `rem ccs type = interactive`). For interactive jobs Cluster CoNTroller gives you access to the nodes and then gets out of the way. When the type you requested is up, Cluster CoNTroller will kill your processes (including Telnet sessions to the nodes) and make the resources available for the next job.

In addition to these four requirements, there is an optional field:

• rem ccs requirements Cluster CoNTroller supports heterogeneous resource scheduling. Hence, if you have multiple types of node resources, you can specifically request them. The `cctypes` command will show you the various types of node resources your cluster has available. Note that if all your nodes are the same, this keyword is not necessary. An example would be `rem ccs requirements = 8@development`. This is interpreted as 8 nodes that have a feature named "development."

All Cluster CoNTroller commands are prefaced in a Windows batch file (.bat extension) with `rem ccs`. These lines are parsed and checked when a user submits a job.

**JobSetup.** The last item in your batch file, following the Cluster CoNTroller directives, is the actual work you want done in batch. Interactive jobs read the Cluster CoNTroller directives to allocate the necessary resources. The batch file is not started on the nodes. Batch jobs actually this batch file on the master node. The example in Figure 17.5 illustrates a batch file that runs a "Hello World" program over two different network interfaces, one after the other.

Let's go through this example line by line. The commands

```
set MPI_COMM=TCP
```

and

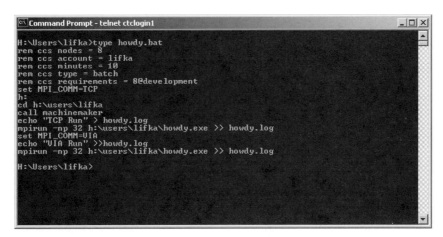

**Figure 17.5**
Batch file runing a "Hello World" program over two network interfaces.

```
set MPI_COMM=VIA
```

tell MPI/Pro to use the Ethernet or Emulex CLAN, respectively, for communication; both are installed on the Cornell Theory Center clusters. Note that this is an MPI/Pro-specific command.
The command

```
h:
```

switches to the shared drive from the local *c:* drive.
The command

```
cd h:\users\lifka
```

moves the user (lifka) into his home directory.
The command

```
call machinemaker
```

runs a script developed at CTC that creates a host file for MPI based on the node that the script is executed on.
The commands

```
echo "TCP Run" > howdy.log
```

and

```
echo "VIA Run" >> howdy.log
```

add text to the log file stating that a particular run is about to begin.
The last command

```
mpirun -np 32 h:\users\lifka\howdy.exe >> howdy.log
```

runs the `howdy.exe program` with 32 processes. These lines are executed in the
order they appear in Figure 17.5.

**Running Parallel Jobs.** Cluster CoNTroller is well integrated with MPI/Pro.
MPI/Pro is able to use the same impersonation mechanisms that Cluster CoN-
Troller uses for batch job startup. This means that it is possible to run MPI/Pro
jobs in batch. The Cornell Theory Center is working with Microsoft to provide a
standard Microsoft mechanism for impersonation so that all parallel libraries and
scheduling systems can be compatible. Of course, all parallel libraries may be used
interactively under Cluster CoNTroller.

### 17.4.2   Lifecycle of a Job

Le us now walk through an example of a typical user experience in submitting a
job to Cluster CoNTroller. For this example we show actual Cluster CoNTroller
interaction at the Cornell Theory Center.

Assume that you would like to run a four-node parallel "Hello World" job.

1.   Determine what resources you need and what you'd like to request. To do
this, you can use `ccq`, `ccusage`, and `cctypes` to provide information about what
nodes are available and what is currently running and waiting.

```
 Command Prompt                                                    _ □ ×
H:\Users\lifka>cctypes

Nodes summary: 78 available, 151 busy, 0 down.

Count Free  Busy  Down    Architecture       Mem       Features
34    31    3     0       1way_PIII          1024      CTC   600Mhz serial
2     2     0     0       1way_PIII          1024      CTC   600Mhz upgrade
1     1     0     0       1way_PIII          256       CTC   866Mhz volatile
1     1     0     0       1way_PIV           256       CTC   1.4Ghz techies
1     1     0     0       2way_PII           256       CTC   300Mhz test
32    0     32    0       2way_PIII          2048      CTC   1Ghz   cmi
64    8     56    0       2way_PIII          2048      CTC   733Mhz vplus
8     7     1     0       2way_PIII          2048      CTC   866Mhz developmen
t
16    16    0     0       2way_PIII          2048      CTC   933Mhz manhattan
64    5     59    0       4way_PIII_Xeon     4096      CTC   500Mhz v1
6     6     0     0       4way_PIII_Xeon     4096      CTC   550Mhz usda


H:\Users\lifka>_
```

2.      After you have verified that the resources you require exist, you can set up your batch file to request these resources. The following batch file asks for 4 nodes of the "development" resource type for 5 minutes.

```
 Command Prompt - vi howdy.bat                                     _ □ ×
rem ccs nodes = 4
rem ccs account = lifka
rem ccs minutes = 5
rem ccs type = batch
rem ccs requirements = 4@development
set MPI_COMM=TCP
h:
cd h:\users\lifka
call notify lifka@tc.cornell.edu "Job started"
call machinemaker
echo "TCP Run" > howdy.log
mpirun -np 8 h:\users\lifka\howdy.exe >> howdy.log
set MPI_COMM=VIA
echo "VIA Run" >>howdy.log
mpirun -np 8 h:\users\lifka\howdy.exe >> howdy.log
ccrelease
~
~
~
~
~
~
~
~
"howdy.bat": 16 lines, 426 characters.
```

3.      To put your job in the queue, you must use **ccsubmit**, which interacts with the JobManager service on the scheduler node to queue the job for you. The JobManager returns a unique job id once the job has been successfully queued.

```
Command Prompt                                              _ □ x
Count Free  Busy  Down   Architecture      Mem      Features
34    31    3     0      1way_PIII         1024     CTC    600Mhz serial
2     2     0     0      1way_PIII         1024     CTC    600Mhz upgrade
1     1     0     0      1way_PIII         256      CTC    866Mhz volatile
1     1     0     0      1way_PIV          256      CTC    1.4Ghz techies
1     1     0     0      2way_PII          256      CTC    300Mhz test
32    0     32    0      2way_PIII         2048     CTC    1Ghz   cmi
64    8     56    0      2way_PIII         2048     CTC    733Mhz vplus
8     7     1     0      2way_PIII         2048     CTC    866Mhz developmen
t
16    16    0     0      2way_PIII         2048     CTC    933Mhz manhattan
64    5     59    0      4way_PIII_Xeon    4096     CTC    500Mhz v1
6     6     0     0      4way_PIII_Xeon    4096     CTC    550Mhz usda

H:\Users\lifka>vi howdy.bat

H:\Users\lifka>ccsubmit howdy.bat

Contacting the server. Please wait...

Your batch file is submitted. Your Job Id: 57170.

H:\Users\lifka>_
```

4.    The scheduler service also running on the scheduling nodes checks the queue of waiting jobs and the available resources and, when there is a match, starts the job via the impersonator service running on the "master node," which is the first node in the set of nodes that are allocated to a job. The impersonator service runs the batch script you submitted with `ccsubmit`, for you, as you.

5.    When the job completes, a `ccrelease` is issued as the last line of the batch file. This tells the scheduler service to initiate a cleanup. You can cancel a running job or remove a queued job with the `ccrm` command at any time as well. If a job runs over its time limit, the scheduler will automatically clear the resources a job occupies.

6.    The scheduler service removes user access to the nodes by removing them from each nodes global domain group and then by starting the nodemanager service on each node to clear any remaining user processes. While this is happening, the job is in the "clearing state" as is shown here:

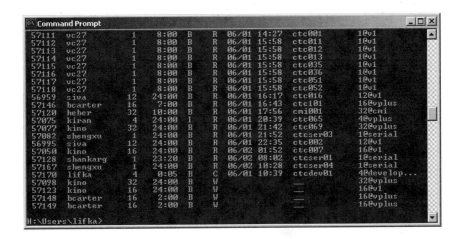

## 17.5   Future Enhancements

Several significant enhancements will be available in future releases of Cluster CoN-
Troller. These include

- complete COM+ support,
- advanced user interface tools using COM+,
- support for multiple jobs per node,
- advanced tools for better accounting of resources, and
- advanced tools for improved cluster administration.

# 18 Cornell Theory Center

*David Lifka*

The Cornell Theory Center (CTC), located at Cornell University, is a center of excellence in high-performance computing and interdisciplinary research. CTC currently operates some of the world's largest Microsoft Windows 2000 clusters. These clusters are used by over one hundred Cornell principal investigators and over six hundred related users. Outside collaborators with Cornell research partners also have access to CTC cluster resources.

## 18.1 CTC Users

CTC has a diverse user community who use the center's computational resources in various modes:

- **Serial mode:** Some user jobs require large amounts of memory, disk, or faster processors. For these users we provide a serial job farm.
- **Master/worker parallelism:** Some users have an efficient serial code and need to explore many data sets simultaneously or need to run different scenarios with the same code. For these users, the master/worker paradigm, sometimes called "task parallelism" or "task farming," is best.
- **Tightly coupled parallelism:** Some users have jobs that require two or more compute servers connected by a high-performance network interconnect. Problems are solved in parallel by dividing the code over the available computers and having the processes communicate necessary data and information over the network. High-bandwidth, low-latency networks often are required for this type of application to perform well. At CTC our parallel compute clusters use CLAN from Emulex Corporation.

Users of the CTC resources conduct research in a wide variety of areas, including the following:

| | |
|---|---|
| Agricultural Economics | Animal Science |
| Astronomy | Biochemistry, Biology |
| Chemical Engineering | Civil/Environmental Engineering |
| Clinical Sciences | Computer Science |
| Design and Environmental Analysis | Ecology and Systematics |
| Electrical Engineering | Geological Sciences |
| Marketing | Mathematics |
| Mechanical/Aerospace Engineering | Neurobiology and Behavior |
| Nuclear Science and Engineering | Physics |
| Plant Breeding and Biometry | Theoretical and Applied Mechanics |

Because of the favorable price/performance of its industry-standard clusters, CTC is able to meet the increasing needs of its growing user community. The center encourages new applications that can benefit from its computing resources.

## 18.2   Systems Overview

Today CTC has several large parallel clusters, as well as associated resources such as file servers and login nodes. In this section we briefly describe the current cluster resources at CTC and their purposes.

### 18.2.1   File Servers

Having a main file system available on whatever resource a user logs into is essential. At CTC we currently have three dedicated file servers each with one terabyte of SCSI attached storage. We use Microsoft's Distributed File System to map the physical disk volumes onto one logical volume that users can map to their local machines and is automatically mapped to every cluster node as the "H:" drive. The three available terabytes store the data and tools that users need to interact with the cluster resources.

| | |
|---|---|
| H:\ | Home, where all main directories are stored |
| H:\ Users | User home directories |
| H:\ CTC Tools | Scheduler commands, help, setup files for various peices of software, and Login.bat |

Whenever a user logs into a CTC resource, `login.bat` is automatically executed. This checks for the existence of a .bashrc or .cshrc file in the user's home directory, thereby enabling us to control path settings and to allow users to set up their own shell environments at login.

### 18.2.2   Login Nodes

The CTC login nodes are two dedicated dual-processor servers that run Citix MetaFrame, Terminal Server, and Seattle Labs SLnet Telnet Service. These machines allow remote users to access the CTC cluster resources from any platform. Users can use these machines to compile codes, develop batch scripts, and interact with the Cluster CoNTroller job scheduling system to submit and monitor jobs.

### 18.2.3   Development Cluster

The development cluster is a small, special-purpose cluster used for quick turnaround testing and debugging runs. It was installed because other cluster resources

were saturated and development time was scarce. It is managed by Cluster CoN-
Troller and allows users up to three-minute jobs in the queue. The development
cluster is configured to have ardware and software similar to that of the large clusters, so that once users have their codes and batch scripts tuned, they can easily
move up to the other clusters for long production runs. The development cluster
nodes have the following configuration:

8 Dell PowerEdge 1550 servers

Dual-processor Pentium III 866 MHz/256 KByte cache

2 GByte RAM/node

27 GByte disk (RAID 0)/node

Giganet CLAN interconnect

### 18.2.4   Serial Nodes

Serial nodes serve two purposes. First, they allow users that have efficient nonparallel codes to run long-running jobs on well-managed resources that have more
memory and/or disk capacity than users typically can afford on their workstations
or laptops. Second, the serial nodes act as a resource pool for Web computing
applications (described later in this chapter). Having serial nodes provides a cost-
effective way of allowing these users to get their work done and keeping the parallel
cluster resources available to those users who need them. The serial nodes are configured with one processor and one gigabyte of RAM, so they are proportionally
as powerful as the SMP-based parallel nodes. The serial nodes were bought in
separate batches. Their configurations are as follows:

26 Dell PowerEdge 2450 servers

Pentium III 600 MHz/256 KBytes cache

1 GByte RAM/node

27 GBytes disk (RAID 0)/node

10 Dell PowerEdge 1550 servers

Pentium III 866 MHz/256 KBytes cache

1 GByte RAM/node

27 GBytes disk (RAID 0)/node

### 18.2.5   General-Purpose Compute Cluster, Velocity I

Velocity I was the first cluster installed at CTC. We configured the the Velocity I
nodes with as much memory, disk and L2 cache as we could, in order to provide
maximum flexibility for our users. For example, we wanted users to be able to use
four processors per node or fewer, to leave more of the shared memory available for

the processes. Today Velocity I is our main general-purpose parallel cluster. New users are first allocated time on this system, and it is used by a large number of users for production computing. Velocity I is configured as follows:

    64 Dell PowerEdge 6350 servers

    Quad Pentium III Xeon 500 MHz processors (SMP)

    4 GBytes RAM/node

    54 GBytes disk/node

    Giganet CLAN interconnect

    100 Mbit switched Ethernet

### 18.2.6    Strategic Application Compute Cluster, Velocity I Plus

Velocity I Plus was the second parallel cluster at CTC. It was installed six months after Velocity I to provide additional computing cycles for strategic parallel applications. Today the primary applications that Velocity I Plus supports are genomics, protein folding, and fracture mechanics. Velocity I Plus was configured with parallel program performance in mind: it has dual processors and a faster front-side bus to improve memory bandwidth over Velocity I Quads. Velocity I Plus has the following configuration:

    64 Dell PowerEdge 2450 servers

    Dual-processor Pentium III 733 MHz/256 KBytes cache

    2 GBytes RAM/node

    27 GBytes disk (RAID 0)/node

    Giganet CLAN interconnect

## 18.3    Dedicated Clusters

The success of the Velocity clusters, along with their impressive price/performance, led other groups at Cornell to have CTC install specialized clusters dedicated to their users and applications.

### 18.3.1    Computational Materials Institute Cluster

As noted earlier, the fracture mechanics group in Cornell's Computational Materials Institute (CMI) make heavy use of Velocity I Plus for multiscale crack propagation simulations. To supplement the Velocity I Plus cluster, the CMI added its own cluster, which is configured as follows:

32 Dell PowerEdge 1550 servers
Dual-processor Pentium III 1 GHz/256 KBytes cache
2 GBytes RAM/node
27 GBytes disk (RAID 0)/node
Giganet CLAN interconnect

### 18.3.2   Social Sciences and Economics Research Cluster

Cornell social scientists installed a high-performance computing platform to support
their SAS analysis of census data. SAS is multithreaded and performs well on the
Quad SMPs. Recently a parallel version of SAS was released that the Cornell
researchers are beginning to use successfully. Because of the secure nature of their
data, the social science research cluster includes its own disk storage and backup
system. The cluster has the following configuration:

8 Dell PowerEdge 6350 servers
Quad-processor SMP 550 MHz Pentium III Xeons
1 GByte RAM/node
54 GBytes disk/node
Gigabit switched Ethernet
3 TBytes Dell Power Vault SCSI attached storage
2 TBytes Dell Power Vault 130T tape library

### 18.3.3   Agricultural Bioinformatics Cluster

Cornell has a large genomics and bioinformatics initiative. We collaborate closely
with the U.S. Department of Agriculture and operate for them a special cluster that
handles plant genomics data and provides cycles for researchers to run the BLAST
code against that data. The Web-based plant genomics databases are served by

4 Dell PowerEdge 6300 servers
Quad-processor SMP 400 MHz Pentium II Xeons
1 GByte RAM
56 GBytes disk

The compute nodes are configured as follows:

8 Dell PowerEdge 6350 servers
Quad-processor SMP 550 MHz Pentium III Xeons
1 GByte RAM
54 GBytes disk
100 Mbit switched Ethernet
Gigabit switched Ethernet

### 18.3.4    Corporate Cluster

Since our move to Windows-based clusters, corporate interest in CTC and our computing environment has grown substantially. We installed a dedicated cluster to provide corporate clients and partners with a place to do performance testing and code development. The corporate cluster currently has the following configuration:

16 Dell PowerEdge 2450 servers
Dual-processor Pentium III 933 MHz/256 KBytes cache
2 GBytes RAM/node
27 GBytes disk (RAID 0)/node

### 18.3.5    Computational Finance Cluster

CTC director Thomas Coleman has a research group focused on computational finance both in Ithaca and in the CTC-Manhattan office in New York City. They use clusters for such activities as portfolio risk analysis. One of the tools they find useful is the Cornell Multitask Toolbox, which enables them to use Matlab for parallel computations on the cluster. The computational finance cluster is configured as follows:

16 Dell PowerEdge 2450 servers
Dual-processor Pentium III 933 MHz/256 KBytes cache
2 GBytes RAM/node
27 GBytes disk (RAID 0)/node
Giganet CLAN interconnect

## 18.4    Other Cluster Resources

In addition to the CTC Windows-based clusters and the dedicated clusters, we are exploring Web-based clusters and a Windows-based CAVE environment. We believe that these resources and the applications we are developing to use them will play a major role in making high-performance computing available to the masses.

### 18.4.1    Web Clusters

As mentioned earlier, we are using the CTC serial nodes as a resource pool for new Web-based computing interfaces. To date, we have two Web-based cluster applications.

The first application, `ser-loopp`, involves protein sequence prediction. The user enter a protein sequence and an e-mail address. This sequence is then submitted to Cluster CoNTroller securely via the IIS Web server. After the `ser-loopp` code has been run against the sequence, results are e-mailed to the user that submitted the sequence. Currently, over 200 node-hours per week are spent on this application; see `ser-loopp.tc.cornell.edu/loopp.html`.

The second application, a fracture mechanics problem, is more sophisticated. Users authenticate to a Web server via IIS. They then upload a model of a material for which they want to perform a crack propagation simulation. The job is automatically submitted to the serial nodes, which generate a mesh for the model with the initial crack inserted. Once that job completes, it submits a parallel job to run the crack propagation simulation code on the Velocity I cluster. After the code has run, the users are notified that their results are available in their user directory on the H: drive.

One advantage of this new computing model is that users don't have to know which operating system or which computer architecture is being used. They can simply focus on their research. On the other hand, there is still a batch queue between the user and the cluster (even though the end users don't see it). To address this issue, we are beginning to investigate Microsoft .Net technology. Our goal is to provide real-time feedback and simulation response.

### 18.4.2   Windows 2000–Based Cave Environment

CTC is working with Microsoft and VRCO to develop the first Windows 2000–based CAVE environment. VRCO provide Windows-based development tools so that users can generate CAVE models on their desktops. We are developing tools and programming interfaces that will make the CAVE easy to use by any CTC cluster user without the help of a visualization expert. We believe that this will lead to application steering and more mainsteam use of what traditionally has been a specialized resource. The CAVE environment computer resources are as follows:

3 Dual-processor Dell Precision 620 workstations

1 GBytes RAM/workstation

Giganet CLAN interconnect

## 18.5   Providing a Consistent User Interface

The Cornell Theory Center believed it essential to make the transition to a Windows computing environment as easy as possible for users. In particular, to help users get their codes running from other programming environments, we had to provide the necessary tools and system interfaces that users were familiar with. In the the first six months that the Velocity I cluster was in production, CTC consultants met with various Cornell user groups to discuss their requirements. These requirements fell into three basic areas: remote access interfaces, programming environment, and application software.

## 18.5.1   Remote Access Mechanisms

Providing remote access to cluster resources is critical. CTC has a complete suite of tools for remote access to meet the needs of our users, who come from a wide variety of platforms (e.g., Unix, Windows, Macintosh). The most popular mechanism for remote access is Telnet; shown below is a typical Telnet session. The Microsoft server allows two simultaneous Telnet sessions per machine. For many of our applications that is sufficient. In the case of login nodes, however, obviously many more sessions are needed. Several Telnet servers are available for Windows 2000; we have been successful with Seattle Lab's "SLnet" product (see `www.seattlelab.com`).

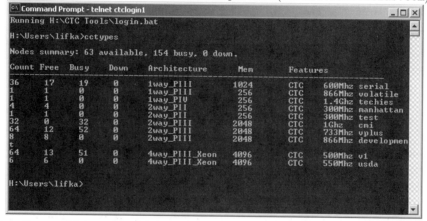

Another useful interface is the Windows Terminal Server. This allow users to open a Windows session, with its native graphical user interface, from a Terminal Server Client. Terminal Server is a feature of Windows 2000 server but works only for Microsoft Windows clients by itself; however, a third-party product, called Citrix MetaFrame, allows non-Windows clients to connect. It also allows access from a Web browser (see `www.citrix.com/`).

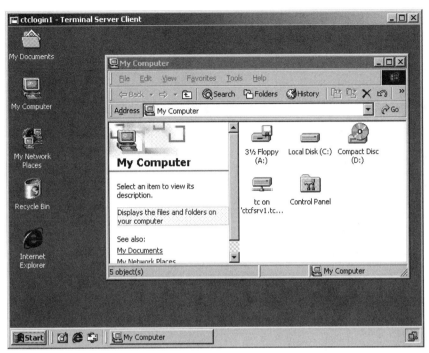

X-Windows is also supported under Windows 2000. If you have applications that require X-Windows, even as simple as xterm, you can compile and run them under Windows using available X libraries such as GNU or commercial systems such as Hummingbird's Exceed. Using X requires that you have a X-Windows client-side application that is capable of displaying the X-Windows.

## 18.5.2 Programming Environment

The principal concern of our users when moving to the Windows environment was whether they would have the necessary tools to build their applications.

Compilers were no problem: a wide variety of excellent compilers are available for Windows. At CTC we support the Microsoft Visual Studio Suite, Compaq Fortran, Intel Vtune Suite, Portland Group, and the GNU compilers. We have found that one compiler may work better than others depending on the application; sometimes, for example, one compiler may not adhere to a language standard but may provide superior optimization. CTC consultants often work with users to find the best compiler solution for their application.

To make moving to the Windows environment easier and more comfortable for users coming from a Unix environment, we found tools such as Cygwin and Interix quite useful. They provide features like Unix shells and utilities like `make`. Users at CTC have been able to port millions of lines of legacy Fortran, C, and C++ to Windows by using Cygwin. Another advantage of Cygwin is that if you need to be able to run your application on multiple platforms or operating systems, you don't have to make significant changes to your code or makefiles. Often, no changes are needed at all.

### 18.5.3   Application Software

Besides compilers and development environments, we provide a broad range of software and libraries for our users. These fall into four basic categories: tools, mathematical libraries, scripting languages, and message passing.

**Tools.**   Following is a list of the tools that we have provided for our users for various applications. Every tool that our users have required has been available in the Windows environment.

| | |
|---|---|
| Abaqus | Finite element modeling |
| Ansys | Finite element modeling |
| Cornell Multitask Toolbox for MATLAB | Parallel Matlab |
| Fidap | Computational fluid dynamics |
| Fluent | Computational fluid dynamics |
| G98W | Computational chemistry |
| Mathematica | Mathematics application |
| Matlab | Mathematics application |
| SAS | Statistics |
| Visualization Toolkit (VTK) | Visualization package |

**Mathematical Libraries.**   As our users moved moved from different platforms, they requested various mathematical libraries. The main libraries we provided are IMSL, LAPACK, the Intel Math Kernel Library, and the NAG Library.

**Scripting Languages.**   Scripting languages allow users to do rapid prototyping and to manage program execution. Under Windows 2000, COM+ and WMI make scripting even more attractive, and the wealth of modules for scripting languages continues to grow. CTC currently supports three scripting languages: ActiveState Perl, Python, and Microsoft Visual Basic.

**Message Passing.**   MPI is the primary message-passing library our users require. We use MPI/Pro from MPI Software Technology, Inc. It has proven to be extremely stable and well supported. We also have a few users who use PVM; however, we do not currenlty support it.

## 18.6   Helping Users Get Started

CTC has a staff of consultants with over ten years' experience in parallel programming and optimization. These consultants work with our users to make sure that they can get their work done in the most efficient way possible. The consultants also are available for porting and development work as needed by the Cornell user community and to outside customers on a contractual basis. To make it easy for users new to the Windows environment to get started without having to have a Windows-based machine, CTC has set up a "Collaboratory"—a large room with ten high-end workstations fully configured with all the software and tools that are installed on the cluster resources. Users can come to the Collaboratory and work with collaborators and CTC consultants to get codes running on the clusters.

## 18.7   Batch and Interactive Job Scheduling

CTC developed the Cluster CoNTroller job scheduling system as part of the research and development under an Intel Technology for Education grant (see `www.cs.cornell.edu/tech2000/`). We licensed this system to MPI Software Technology, Inc., who continues to develop, sell, and support it (see `www.mpi-softtech.com/products/cluster_controller`). Chapter 17 provides further details on Cluster CoNTroller.

## 18.8   CTC Success Story

The move to Windows-based clusters has been successful for CTC and, most important, its users. Windows 2000 is more reliable than the Unix systems we've had in the past; and the Dell servers are quite stable. Indeed, we have been doing a reliability study with Intel for over a year now, looking at everything from hardware to software issues. We had 99.9986% uptime the first three months we ran Windows 2000; and in the past two months on all the cluster resources described in this chapter, we have had 99.99999% uptime.

More information about CTC and its cluster resources is available at the following URLs:

`www.tc.cornell.edu`

`www.ctc-manhattan.com`

`www.tc.cornell.edu/AC3`

# 19 Conclusions

*Thomas Sterling*

This book represents the practical state of the art in hardware and software for Beowulf cluster computing. But it also exemplifies the extreme rate at which commodity clusters are maturing and in so doing, gaining utility across ever-broader domains of application. Only two years ago our first work in this area, *How to Build a Beowulf,* was published by MIT Press. But in the short interval since then, the art and practice of cluster computing have evolved dramatically. Then, such systems were used in rather restrictive ways with limited software support beyond the basic node operating systems and message-passing libraries. System size rarely exceeded a hundred processors. Today, systems exceeding a thousand processors are employed for both technical and commercial computing. But more significant is the array of software tools available and under development to manage the implementation, maintenance, administration, and resource allocation of workloads on Beowulf clusters both large and small. Thus, in the brief period between this offering and our original modest work, Beowulf commodity cluster computing has come of age. Then, Beowulf systems were only a narrow element of the parallel computing domain. Today, they are often the system of choice and are rapidly coming to dominate even the highest end of computing. It is telling that at the most recent Supercomputing conference, the industrial exhibits included more commodity clusters on the floor than all other forms of parallel computing systems combined.

In spite of these enormous gains, Beowulf cluster computing is very much a field in transition. There is no one universally accepted distributed environment or, for that matter, hardware foundation on which the cluster community relies. Of course, the flexibility this implies is part of its strength and invulnerability to vendor changes. Indeed, both hardware and software are in a state of flux, with continued changes foreseen for the next one to three years. It is worth considering where these likely changes will occur.

## 19.1 Future Directions for Hardware Components

Processor technology is witnessing three areas of change. The first is continued growth of processor capability, most notably in clock speed. Predictions to the contrary, clock rates continue to grow. At the time of this writing, the Pentium 4 with a clock rate of 1.7 GHz is available in consumer-grade packages. Memory enhancements and cache size also expand to attempt to match the processor peak performance. The second change is a new generation of 64-bit architecture with the commercial release of the Intel IA-64 64-bit family of processors. The third

area of change is the likely integration of multiple processors per chip in SMP
configurations. Should this trend become reality, then nodes of commodity clusters
could all be SMP structures of two or more processors. All of these advances are
driven by the continued reduction of integration feature size, with logic moving
below 0.18 micron.

Network technology is expected to make significant strides as gigahertz per node
channels become commonplace and costs continue to drop. Myrinet and Ethernet
dominate Beowulf cluster configurations, but other network technologies are having
significant impact. The Quadrics QSW networks are providing a high-bandwidth
framework for the highest end of the Compaq Alpha processor-based systems, and
larger configurations have been proposed that could yield clusters capable of over
100 teraflops peak performance. The VIA architecture continues to make inroads
in the cluster market delivering gigabit per second throughputs and latencies well
below 10 microseconds. Foremost among these is the Emulex cLAN network. But
perhaps the most interesting advance is the emergence of the new industry Infiniband architecture (IBA) standard (well over 1,500 pages). Infiniband provides a
new tightly integrated strategy and technology for all I/O needs including cluster
interconnection networks. Instead of connecting to an intermediary I/O interface
such as PCI, Infiniband will be tied more directly to the processor communications,
increasing I/O bandwidth and reducing latencies down toward a microsecond. Already specified are several levels of bandwidth including the use of optical media
that will work in the 10 Gbps regime. Infiniband is supported by a large industrial consortium and may become the new dominant I/O interface. Products based
on IBA should be available within the next eighteen months. However, in spite
of wide optimism, costs to customers have yet to be determined. It is interesting
to note that the external network bandwidths are approaching the main memory
bandwidths of the processing nodes. With another order of magnitude gain in
bandwidth anticipated in the next few years, it may be that network bandwidth
will cease to be the dominant bottleneck to realizable performance.

Although less widely discussed, significant advances in mass storage are expected.
These are being fueled by the rapidly growing PDA, digital camera, and cellular
phone markets that require high-capacity storage in small, lightweight, and low-
power components. "Matchbox" disk drives will provide multigigabyte capacities
in the near future. For larger units, advanced EIDE drives will provide hundreds
of gigabytes per unit at a cost of less than $10 per gigabyte. For many technical
and commercial problems, mass storage is the bottleneck, both in capacity and
in bandwidth. Commodity clusters provide a rich tradeoff space within which to
configure and operate large disk farms. But reliability and software support for

distributed file spaces continue to offer considerable challenges that have not been fully resolved.

Packaging of systems will continue to evolve and have impact on Beowulf clusters in two important ways. Historically, Beowulfs have taken up a lot of room. Although the very first Beowulf was custom packaged with 16 motherboards in a half-height rack, the majority of systems leveraged the low-cost, high-reliability PC tower packages with power supply. But the density of this class of package is low. For all but the smallest systems, floor space has become a problem. Because the market for Beowulf-class clusters has become significant, however, vendors are providing new packaging options with high-density rack-mounted units available such that 40 or more processors can now be installed in a single floor standing rack. As higher-degree SMPs are built into such units, the number of processors per rack will continue to expand allowing larger systems to be installed in modest machine rooms. But this also leads to the second way future machines will be impacted and that is the scale of the largest Beowulf-clusters. In the near future, the largest systems in the world will be commodity clusters comprising 10,000 processors or more. Within the lifetime of this edition of this book, clusters delivering as much as 100 teraflops may be implemented on this scale.

## 19.2   Future Directions for Software Components

While enormous strides have been made in the area of cluster middleware within the past few years, the general consensus is that continued advances are required to bring this class of system to a level of usability and robustness equivalent to other server technology. Key attributes sought are completeness, commonality, usability, generality, and reliability.

*Completeness* relates to the need for a comprehensive software environment that spans all aspects of the distributed cluster system and supports the major activities associated with the operation of a commodity cluster, large or small. These activities include installation, configuration and initialization, status monitoring and maintenance, administration, and resource scheduling.

*Commonality* is the property of such an environment to be broadly used across the majority of Beowulf clusters throughout the community. Linux, Windows, and MPI all exhibit this property, which has been an important enabler to the wide dissemination of Beowulf systems. To that extent, if you've used one Beowulf, you are likely to be able, with little trouble, to work with any other. But at the middleware level, there is not such uniformity of environments. This is partly intentional and partly due to history. As vendors have successfully advanced into the arena, middleware has been one area in which they could provide product differentiation, to enhance the apparent value of their respective offerings. Historically, low-level tools—especially for monitoring system status, operation, and health—have been developed in house with only limited sharing. As we have seen, however, other tools such as schedulers have seen much wider use.

*Usability* combined with *generality* relates to the ease of system operation through the abstraction presented by the middleware environment. A highly valued attribute, perceived to strongly contribute to usability, is "single-system image." Originally, Beowulf clusters were treated as an ensemble of separate loosely coupled processing systems, each being managed individually. In the earliest days, there would even be some kind of a switchbox connecting the operator's keyboard and monitor to any designated processor node. While this can work for small, dedicated systems, it is untenable for larger, multiuser clusters and undesirable in any case. A system includes a number of name spaces with which the user must contend. Some of these include the user application's global variables, the file space, the set of process IDs and jobs, and I/O. In the worst case, these all need to be dealt with on a per node basis. As systems grow to the scale of a thousand or more processors, this too can prove untenable. Even for much smaller systems, such explicit per node control is prone to operator error. Single-system image is the property by which the entire cluster presents only a single name space for each class of named object for the entire system, independent of the number of processors employed. The user sees one process ID space, one distributed file space, and the same for others. Generality extends the property of usability to include a broad range of operating modes from dedicated single user to multi-user, multiprogram operation.

System reliability is critical to long-term acceptance of Beowulf clusters by the information processing market. Opinions differ widely concerning the actual reliability of Beowulf systems. Infant mortality lasting weeks for moderate-sized systems can be high with fans, power supplies, disk drives, and even memories breaking in a short time interval. After this period, however, systems often experience long stable operation, potentially of many months between required maintenance. After two to three years, age begins to take its toll, and failures begin to escalate. But for very large systems on the order of thousands of processors, single point failures can be significantly more prevalent. For either class of system, rapid detection, diagnosis, repair, restart, and recovery are essential to high availability. Software tools to aid in all facets of reliability are essential as well, but little work has been done in this area, and no accepted general set of tools is in use, although some experimental systems have been explored. One important capability is checkpoint and restart, and some tools exist but involve direct application programmer intervention. Tools for logging and reporting soft errors can be used to identify likely future failures, directing preemptive controlled replacement of system components without disrupting application execution. Much more work is required in this area.

A valuable effort is the collection and integration of a critical subset of existing tools to build a useful environment meeting at least some of the requirements above. OSCAR led out of Oak Ridge National Lab, Rocks being done at the San Diego Supercomputing Center, the integrated tool set at the Cornell Theory Center (CTC), and the integrated software system provided by Scyld are all examples of such efforts. OSCAR is a collaboration of a number of organizations including industry partners and is worth watching as it evolves. The tool set from CTC is one of the most comprehensive to be based on Windows. The Scyld software environment provides a good example of a user level single system image. While most Beowulf cluster software supports full operating systems on every node, each operating semi-independently, the Scyld model is different. By employing a logical structure of a master processor and multiple slave processors, all name spaces are managed through the master processor, presenting a single system image to the user. Processes are controlled by the master but delegated to the slave processors to be executed. The slave node kernels are very limited and lightweight and are downloaded by the master. This can be performed very efficiently, much more quickly than on conventional clusters, and solves the problem of version consistency control. Nevertheless, while the Scyld software environment exhibits many desirable properties, there is a question regarding scalability. A single master processor can create a bottleneck, and the coordination of multiple masters is nontrivial.

With increased prevalence of SMP nodes in cluster systems, means of exploiting this class of tightly coupled unit is called for. OpenMP has been developed as one way to apply these resources within a shared-memory paradigm. But between nodes is still the fragmented name space so typical of most clusters. Ironically, even on systems with distributed shared memory hardware support, the majority of parallel programmers today use MPI with its message-passing model. The underlying mechanisms supporting the MPI implementation take advantage of the shared-memory hardware support, thereby making at least some of its operators more efficient than between cluster nodes, and this is done in a way that is transparent to the user. But a clean way of using shared memory within a node and distributed memory between nodes has not found a satisfactory solution in common practice. A class of programming models sometimes referred to as "put-get" models may provide at least a partial solution. Inspired in part by the Cray T3E programming model, this approach gives the impression of a distributed shared memory but assumes no cache coherence. Within an SMP node, conventional load/store operations are used, but for remote accesses the corresponding get and put operators are used within the same programming model. Examples of this include UPC developed at IDA CCS and the experimental Earth-C developed at the University of Delaware.

## 19.3   Final Thoughts

It is hard to forecast where such a volatile technology as parallel computing will take us, as so many factors and trends influence the final outcome. A decade ago, clusters were in their infancy, and Beowulf was still in the future. A decade from now will see as many changes. Nonetheless, at least some of the possibilities can be considered. Extrapolating both the Top500 list and the Semiconductor Industry Association roadmap implies that the largest computers in the world, in all likelihood commodity clusters, will achieve a peak performance of 1 petaflops by the year 2010. Integrated circuits of a billion devices most likely comprising a number of processors will be capable of a performance on the order of 100 Gflops or more. DRAM densities will grow a factor of a hundred in that same timeframe. And if optical communications are employed to their fullest, per channel bandwidths of 1 Tbps or more are possible. In such a scenario, almost every small Beowulf will be a teraflops machine by 2010.

As long as there is a need for servers of one type or another, there will be the opportunity for performance gains through commodity clusters. But a number of trends in the market are not aligned with a future with clusters. Portable computing devices including personal digital assistants, laptop computers, and soon to be released (probably) electronic books all have built-in human interfaces including screens and keyboards that make them unsuitable for clustering. It is true that their technology push helps reduce cost, power, and size, which can have a positive influence on cluster nodes. But the mass-market products themselves are not likely to be used in clusters generally. Admittedly, there have already been cases of clustering laptops. But these are not cost effective. Desktop (or desk side) computers in their ungainly tower cases may already be becoming extinct. A growing number of users have simply migrated their complete user environment onto their laptops. The laptop is everything, their entire world. With wireless interconnect in the office and home, even cellular Internet connections on the road, and disk capacities that will shortly exceed 100 Gbytes, the desktop is rapidly becoming a dinosaur. But it was from these devices that the first Beowulfs were devised. Beowulf-class systems exploited the existing mass-market devices, and now these may disappear.

But this is no longer a problem because the value of clusters to the market has been proven. Vendors are now manufacturing processor nodes explicitly for the purpose of building high-density clusters. Thus the components are no longer hand-me-downs from other markets but optimized for this purpose. In a sense, the day of Beowulf classic is passing—not yet, but eventually. Commodity clusters were offered as a cheap alternative to MPPs to help offload these more expensive machines of at least part of their workload. But with the next-generation high-bandwidth networks and their tight integration with the processor/memory core, much of the distinction between MPPs and clusters is beginning to disappear. And with efficient implementations of such operations as put and get, a shared memory space (without cache coherence) model may be available, further eroding the distinction between cluster and MPP. If this happens, we will have truly witnessed the convergence of parallel architecture.

And yet, that will not be the end of the story. The programming models described so far are still primitive and require a close and explicit relationship between the physical system and the programmer. In the limit, the programmer should be responsible for describing the application's parallel algorithm, but not responsible for hand manipulating the management of the physical resources and their direct association to the application task and data objects. As processors become ubiquitous in the tens of thousands and the critical resource is recognized to be memory bandwidth, these parallel systems will motivate the development of a new family of programming models where once again, as in the earliest days of computing, the programmer will treat the computer as a single system and not a distributed collection of many machines. We have had only tantalizing glimpses of what such models might contain, but already researchers are considering just such new paradigms. Beowulf cluster computing is leading parallel processing into the future. Each step is an accomplishment in its own right and the foundation for progress to the next.

# A Glossary of Terms

**AMD:** Advanced Micro Devices

**ASIC:** Application Specific Integrated Circuits

**ASMP:** Asymmetric multiprocessing. A system of processing on a multiprocessor system that typically selects one processor to execute operating system code while other processors run only user code.

**ASRAM:** Asynchronous Static Random Access Memory

**ATM:** Asynchronous Transfer Mode; a network and protocol for wide area networks (WAN); while employed as the interconnection medium for some commodity clusters, it has not seen wide use for clusters because it is not optimized for this use and is fairly expensive

**AWE:** Address Windowing Extensions. A mechanism in Windows 2000 that allows a 32-bit application to allocate up to 64 GB of physical memory and then map views, or windows, into its 2-GB virtual address space. Using AWE puts the burden of managing mappings of virtual-to-physical memory on the programmer but solves the immediate need of being able to directly access more physical memory than can be mapped at any one time in a 32-bit process address space.

**BDA:** BIOS Data Area

**Beowulf-class system:** commodity cluster employing personal computers or low-cost SMP servers to achieve excellent price-performance initially developed by the Beowulf project at the NASA Goddard Space Flight Center

**BIOS:** Basic Input Output System

**bit:** the fundamental unit of information representing a two-state value; a digital circuit capable of storing a two-state value

**BLAS:** basic linear algebra subroutines

**bps:** bits per second, a unit measure of data transfer rate

**byte:** a commonly addressed quantity of digital information storage of eight bits reflecting one of 256 distinct values

**CD-ROM:** Compact Disc Read Only Memory

**checked build:** A special debug version of Windows 2000 Professional that is available only as part of the MSDN Professional (or Universal) subscription. (No checked build is available for Windows 2000 Server.) The checked build is created by compiling the Windows 2000 sources with the compile-time flag DEBUG set to TRUE.

**cluster:** in the general sense, any interconnected ensemble of computers capable of independent operation but employed to service a common workload

**CMOS:** Complimentary Metal Oxide Semiconductor

**commodity cluster:** a cluster of commercial computing nodes integrated with a commercial system area network

**Condor:** a software package developed at the University of Wisconson to manage the scheduling of a job workload across a distributed computing system including clusters

**constellation:** a cluster of large DSM, SMP, or MPP computing nodes incorporating more microprocessors per node than there are nodes in the system

**context switch:** The procedure of saving the volatile machine state associated with a running thread, loading another thread's volatile state, and starting the new thread's execution.

**COW:** cluster of workstations; an early project at the University of Wisconsin

**CPU:** Central Processing Unit

**CRC:** Cyclic Redundancy Check

**DDR:** Double Data Rate

**deferred procedure call (DPC) object:** A kernel control object that describes a request to defer interrupt processing to DPC/dispatch level. (See interrupt request levels (IRQLs).) This object isn't visible to user-mode programs but is visible to device drivers and other system code. The most important piece of information the DPC object contains is the address of the system function that the kernel will call when it processes the DPC interrupt.

**device drivers:** Loadable kernel-mode modules (typically ending in .sys) that interface between the I/O system and the relevant hardware. Device drivers on Windows 2000 don't manipulate hardware devices directly, but rather they call parts of the hardware application layer (HAL) to interface with the hardware.

**dispatcher:** A set of routines in the kernel that implement Windows 2000 scheduling. Windows 2000 doesn't have a single "scheduler" module or routine-the code is spread throughout the kernel in which scheduling-related events occur.

**dispatcher objects:** A set of kernel objects that incorporate synchronization capabilities and alter or affect thread scheduling. The dispatcher objects include the kernel thread, mutex (called mutant internally), event, kernel event pair, semaphore, timer, and waitable timer.

**DRAM:** Dynamic Random Access Memory

**driver support routines:** Routines that device drivers call to accomplish their I/O requests.

**DSM:** distributed shared memory multiprocessor, tightly coupled cache coherent multiprocessor with non-uniform memory access

**DVD:** Digital Versatile Disc

**Dynamic linked library (DLL):** A separately loadable module containing executable code that can be shared among processes. Similar to a shared library on Unix.

**EDO:** Extended Data Out

**EEPROM:** Electrically Erasable Programmable Read Only Memory

**EIDE:** Enhanced Integrated Drive Electronics

**Emulex:** vendor, distributor, and developer of the cLAN network for commodity clusters

**environment subsystems:** User processes that expose the native operating system services to user applications, thus providing an operating system environment, or personality. Windows 2000 ships with three environment subsystems: Win32, POSIX, and OS/2 1.2.

**EPIC:** Explicitly Parallel Instruction Computing

**Ethernet:** the first widely used and truly ubiquitous local area network operating at 10 Mbps

**event:** An object with a persistent state (signaled or not signaled) that can be used for synchronization; also, a system occurrence that triggers an action.

**exception:** A synchronous condition that results from the execution of a particular instruction. Running a single program with the same data under the same conditions can reproduce exceptions.

**executive:** The upper layer of Ntoskrnl.exe. (The kernel is the lower layer.) The executive contains the base operating system services, such as the process and thread manager, the virtual memory manager, the memory manager, the security reference monitor, the I/O system, and the cache manager. See also kernel.

**executive objects:** Objects implemented by various components of the executive (such as the process manager, memory manager, I/O subsystem, and so on). The executive objects and object services are primitives that the environment subsystems use to construct their own versions of objects and other resources. Because executive objects are typically created either by an environment subsystem on behalf of a user application or by various components of the operating system as part of their normal operation, many of them contain (encapsulate) one or more kernel objects. See also kernel objects.

**Fast Ethernet:** a cost effective local area network based on the original Ethernet protocol that has become very popular with low end Beowulf-class systems; providing 100 Mbps

**FDD:** Floppy Disk Drive

**free build:** The version of the Windows 2000 system that can be purchased as a retail product. It is built with full compiler optimizations turned on and has internal symbol table information stripped out from the images. See also checked build.

**function driver:** The main device driver that provides the operational interface for its device. It is a required driver unless the device is used raw (an implementation in which I/O is done by the bus driver and any bus filter drivers, such as SCSI PassThru). A function driver is the driver that knows the most about a particular device and is usually the only driver that accesses device-specific registers.

**Gigabit Ethernet:** a LAN that is the successor of Fast Ethernet providing peak bandwidth of 1 Gbps. While employed for some clusters, its use is limited by its relatively high cost

**GNU:** a project resulting in a number of open source and free software tools including the GNU C compiler and Emacs

**GPL:** GNU Public License; a legal framework protecting open source software

**handle:** An object identifier. A process receives a handle to an object when it creates or opens an object by name. Referring to an object by its handle is faster than using its name because the object manager can skip the name lookup and find the object directly.

**handle table:** A table that contains pointers to all the objects that the process has opened a handle to. Handle tables are implemented as a three-level scheme, similar to the way that the x86 memory management unit implements virtual-to-physical address translation.

**hardware abstraction layer (HAL):** A loadable kernel-mode module (Hal.dll) that provides the low-level interface to the hardware platform on which Windows 2000 is running. The HAL hides hardware-dependent details such as I/O interfaces, interrupt controllers, and multiprocessor communication mechanisms-any functions that are architecture-specific and machine-dependent.

**HDD:** Hard Disk Drive

**HDF:** Hierarchical data format, both a file format and high level interface for I/O access in both sequential and parallel applications

**HPL:** High Performance Linpack

**I/O:** Input/Output

**I/O request packet (IRP):** A data structure that controls how the I/O operation is processed at each stage. Most I/O requests are represented by an IRP, which travels from one I/O system component to another.

**I/O system:** The Windows 2000 executive component that accepts I/O requests (from both user-mode and kernel-mode callers) and delivers them, in a different form, to I/O devices.

**IDE:** Integrated Drive Electronics

**interrupt:** An asynchronous event (one that can occur at any time) that is unrelated to what the processor is executing. Interrupts are generated primarily by I/O devices, processor clocks, or timers, and they can be enabled or disabled.

**interrupt object:** A kernel control object that allows device drivers to register interrupt service routines (ISRs) for their devices. An interrupt object contains all the information the kernel needs to associate a device ISR with a particular level of interrupt, including the address of the ISR, the interrupt request level (IRQL) at which the device interrupts, and the entry in the kernel's interrupt dispatch table with which the ISR should be associated.

**IRQ:** Interrupt Request

**job object:** A nameable, securable, shareable object in Windows 2000 that controls certain attributes of processes associated with the job. A job object's basic function is to allow groups of processes to be managed and manipulated as a unit. The job object also records basic accounting information for all processes associated with the job and for all processes that were associated with the job but have since terminated.

**kernel:** The lowest layer in Ntoskrnl.exe. The kernel, a component of the executive, determines how the operating system uses the processor or processors and ensures that they are used prudently. The kernel provides thread scheduling and dispatching, trap handling and exception dispatching, interrupt handling and dispatching, and multiprocessor synchronization. See also executive.

**kernel mode:** A privileged mode of code execution in a processor in which all memory is totally accessible and all CPU instructions can be issued. Operating system code (such as system services and device drivers) runs in kernel mode. See also user mode.

**kernel objects:** A primitive set of objects implemented by the Windows 2000 kernel. These objects aren't visible to user-mode code but are created and used only within the executive. Kernel objects provide fundamental capabilities, such as synchronization, on which executive objects are built. See also executive objects.

**kernel-mode device driver:** The only type of driver that can directly control and access hardware devices.

**kernel-mode graphics driver:** A Win32 subsystem display or print device driver that translates device-independent graphics (GDI) requests into device-specific requests.

**LAN:** Local Area Network; a network employed within a single administrative domain such as a laboratory or office complex, connecting PCs and workstations together to file servers, printers and other peripherals, and to the Internet. Low cost LAN technology has been adopted to provide Beowulf-class systems with inexpensive moderate bandwidth interconnect

**LED:** Light Emitting Diode

**Linux:** the dominant Unix-like cross-platform operating system developed by a broad international community enabled by an open source code framework

**LOBOS:** Lots of Boxes on Shelves

**local procedure call (LPC):** An interprocess communication facility for high-speed message passing (not available through the Win32 API but rather through an internal mechanism available only to Windows 2000 operating system components). LPCs are typically used between a server process and one or more client processes of that server. An LPC connection can be established between two user-mode processes or between a kernel-mode component and a user-mode process.

**local security authority (LSA) server:** A user-mode process running the image \Winnt\System32\Lsass.exe that is responsible for the local system security policy (such as which users are allowed to log on to the machine, password policies, privileges granted to users and groups, and the system security auditing settings), user authentication, and sending security audit messages to the Event Log. The LSA service (Lsasrv - \Winnt\System32\Lsasrv.dll), a library that Lsass loads, implements most of this functionality.

**logon process:** A user-mode process running Winlogon.exe that is responsible for capturing the username and password, sending them to the local security authority server for verification, and creating the initial process in the user's session.

**LPT:** Line Printer

**MAC:** Media Access Controller

**mapped file I/O:** The ability to view a file residing on disk as part of a process's virtual memory. A program can access the file as a large array without buffering data or performing disk I/O. The program accesses memory, and the memory manager uses its paging mechanism to load the correct page from the disk file. If the application writes to its virtual address space, the memory manager writes the changes back to the file as part of normal paging.

**MAU:** Medium Attachment Unit

**Mbps:** 1 million bits per second data transfer rate or bandwidth

**Mega:** prefix meaning 1 million or in the case of storage $2^{20}$

**memory manager:** The Windows 2000 executive component that implements demand-paged virtual memory, giving each process the illusion that it has a 4-GB 32-bit address space (while mapping a subset of that address space to physical memory).

**message passing:** An approach to parallelism based on communicating data between processes running (usually) on separate computers.

**metadata:** Used in the context of file systems, this is the information describing the file, including owner, permissions, and location of data

**MPI:** message passing interface, a community derived logical standard for the transfer of program messages between separate concurrent processes

**MPP:** or Massively Parallel Processors

**MSDN Microsoft Developer Network:** Microsoft's support program for developers. MSDN offers three CD-ROM subscription programs: MSDN Library, Professional, and Universal. For more information, see `msdn.microsoft.com`.

**MTBF:** Mean Time Between Failure

**mutex:** A synchronization mechanism used to serialize access to a resource.

**Myricom:** vendor, distributor, and developer of the Myrinet network for commodity clusters

**network:** the combination of communication channels, switches, and interface controllers that transfer digital messages between Beowulf cluster nodes

**NIC:** network interface controller; usually the combination of hardware and software that matches the network transport layer to the computer node of a cluster

**NIH:** National Institutes of Health

**NOW:** network or workstations, and early influential commodity cluster project at UC Berkeley

**Ntkrnlmp.exe:** The executive and kernel for multiprocessor systems.

**Ntoskrnl.exe:** The executive and kernel for uniprocessor systems.

**object:** In the Windows 2000 executive, a single, run-time instance of a statically defined object type.

**object manager:** The Windows 2000 executive component responsible for creating, deleting, protecting, and tracking objects. The object manager centralizes resource control operations that would otherwise be scattered throughout the operating system.

**paging:** The process of moving memory contents to disk, freeing physical memory so that it can be used for other processes or for the operating system itself. Because most systems have much less physical memory than the total virtual memory in use by the running processes (2 GB or 3 GB for each process), the memory manager transfers, or pages, some of the memory contents to disk.

**PC:** see Personal Computer

**PCI:** the dominant external interface standard for PCs and workstations to support I/O controllers including NICs

**Personal Computer or PC:** mass market microprocessor based computer employed by both commercial and consumer users for everything from games to spreadsheets and internet browsers; emphasizing performance/cost for maximum market share, these nodes are the basis for low cost Beowulf-class clusters

**PLS:** Physical Line Signaling

**Plug and Play (PnP) manager:** A major component of the executive that determines which drivers are required to support a particular device and loads those drivers. The PnP manager retrieves the hardware resource requirements for each device during enumeration. Based on the resource requirements of each device, the PnP manager assigns the appropriate hardware resources such as I/O ports, IRQs, DMA channels, and memory locations. It is also responsible for sending proper event notification for device changes (addition or removal of a device) on the system.

**PnP:** Plug 'n Play

**POST:** Power On Self Test

**power manager:** A major component of the executive that coordinates power events and generates power management I/O notifications to device drivers. When the system is idle, the power manager can be configured to reduce power consumption by putting the CPU to sleep. Changes in power consumption by individual devices are handled by device drivers but are coordinated by the power manager.

**process:** The virtual address space and control information necessary for the execution of a set of thread objects.

**PROM:** Programmable Read Only Memory

**PVFS:** Parallel virtual file system

**PVM:** Parallel Virtual Machine, a library of functions supporting an advanced message-passing semantics

**QSW:** high bandwidth network employed in very large clusters, specifically the SC series developed by Compaq

**Quadrics:** commercial vendor of networking hardware and software. See QSW

**RAM:** Random Access Memory

**RISC:** Reduced Instruction Set Computer

**ROM:** Read Only Memory

**ROMIO:** Portable implementation of MPI-IO interface (not an acronym)

**RTC:** Real Time Clock

**RWCP:** major Japanese initiative to develop robust and sophisticated cluster software environment

**SAN:** System Area Network; a network optimized for use as a dedicated communication medium within a commodity cluster

**SBSRAM:** Synchronous Burst Static Random Access Memory

**Scheduler:** a software tool which is part of the node operating system or system middleware that manages the assignment of tasks to cluster nodes and determines the timing of their execution

**SCI:** Scalable Coherent Interconnect

**SCSI:** Small Computer System Interface

**SDRAM:** Synchronous Dynamic Random Access Memory

**Security Accounts Manager (SAM) service:** A set of subroutines responsible for managing the database that contains the usernames and groups defined on the local machine or for a domain (if the system is a domain controller). The SAM runs in the context of the Lsass process.

**server processes:** User processes that are Windows 2000 services, such as the Event Log and Schedule services. Many add-on server applications, such as Microsoft SQL Server and Microsoft Exchange Server, also include components that run as Windows 2000 services.

**SMP:** Symmetric MultiProcessor, tightly coupled cache coherent multiprocessor with uniform memory access

**SRAM:** Static Random Access Memory

**symmetric multiprocessing:** A multiprocessing operating system in which there is no master processor-the operating system as well as user threads can be scheduled to run on any processor. All the processors share just one memory space.

**thread context:** A thread's volatile registers, the stacks, and the private storage area. Because this information is different for each machine architecture that Windows 2000 runs on, this structure is architecture-specific. In fact, the CONTEXT structure returned by the Win32 GetThreadContext function is the only public data structure in the Win32 API that is machine-dependent.

**TLA:** Three Letter Acronym

**user mode:** The nonprivileged processor mode that applications run in. A limited set of interfaces is available in this mode, and the access to system data is limited. See also kernel mode.

**VGA:** Video Graphics Array

**virtual address space:** A set of virtual memory addresses that a process can use.

**virtual memory manager:** Implements virtual memory, a memory management scheme that provides a large, private address space for each process that can exceed available physical memory.

**WAN:** Wide Area Networks used to connect distant sites, even on a continental scale

**WDM drivers:** Device drivers that adhere to the Windows Driver Model (WDM). WDM includes support for Windows 2000 power management, Plug and Play, and Windows Management Instrumentation (WMI). WDM is implemented on Windows 2000, Windows 98, and Windows Millennium Edition, so WDM drivers are source compatible between these operating systems and in many cases are also binary compatible. There are three types of WDM drivers: bus drivers, function drivers, and filter drivers.

**Win32 services:** A mechanism to start processes at system startup time that provide services not tied to an interactive user. Services are similar to UNIX daemon processes and often implement the server side of client/server applications.

**WMI (Windows Management Instrumentation):** A component of the executive that enables device drivers to publish performance and configuration information and receive commands from the user-mode WMI service. Consumers of WMI information can be on the local machine or remote across the network.

# B  Annotated Reading List

This appendix contains an annotated reading list of books and papers of interest to builders and users of Beowulf clusters.

Ian Foster. *Designing and Building Parallel Programs.* Addison-Wesley, 1995. Also at: `http://www.mcs.anl.gov/dbpp/`. A general introduction to the process of creating parallel applications. It includes short sections on MPI and HPF.

William Gropp, Steven Huss-Lederman, Andrew Lumsdaine, Ewing Lusk, Bill Nitzberg, William Saphir, and Marc Snir. *MPI—The Complete Reference: Volume 2, The MPI-2 Extensions.* MIT Press, Cambridge, MA, 1998. An annotated version of the MPI Standard; this contains additional examples and discussion about MPI-2.

William Gropp, Ewing Lusk, and Anthony Skjellum. *Using MPI: Portable Parallel Programming with the Message Passing Interface,* 2nd edition. MIT Press, 1999. A tutorial introduction to the MPI Standard, with examples in C and Fortran.

William Gropp, Ewing Lusk, and Rajeev Thakur. *Using MPI-2: Advanced Features of the Message-Passing Interface.* MIT Press, Cambridge, MA, 1999. A tutorial introduction to the MPI-2 Standard, with examples in C and Fortran. This is the best place to find information on using MPI I/O in applications.

Brian W. Kernighan and Dennis M. Ritchie. *The C Programming Language.* PTR Prentice Hall, 2nd edition, 1988. The original book describing the C programming language.

John M. May. *Parallel I/O for High Performance Computing.* Morgan Kaufmann, 2001. A thorough introduction to parallel I/O including MPI I/O and higher-level libraries such as HDF.

Evi Nemeth, Garth Snyder, Scott Seebass, and Trent R. Hein. *Unix System Administration Handbook.* Prentice Hall PTR, 3rd edition, 2001. A comprehensive and practical book on Unix system administration, it covers all major varieties of Unix, not just Linux.

Peter S. Pacheco. *Parallel Programming with MPI.* Morgan Kaufman, 1997. A good introductory text on parallel programming using MPI.

Gregory F. Pfister. *In Search of Clusters: The Ongoing Battle in Lowly Parallel Computing, 2nd ed.* Prentice Hall, Englewood Cliffs, NJ, 1995 edition, 1998. A delightful book advocating clusters for many problems, including for commercial computing. It has nice sections on parallel programming and (as part of his argument for clusters) a good discussion of shared-memory systems and the issues of correctness and performance that are often brushed under the rug. See Pfister's annotated bibliography for more books and articles on clusters.

Marc Snir, Steve W. Otto, Steven Huss-Lederman, David W. Walker, and Jack Dongarra. *MPI—The Complete Reference: Volume 1, The MPI Core,* 2nd edition. MIT Press, Cambridge, MA, 1998. An annotated version of the MPI-1 Standard, it contains more examples than the official copy and is a good reference on MPI.

Thomas L. Sterling, John Salmon, Donald J. Becker, and Daniel F. Savarese. *How to Build a Beowulf.* MIT Press, 1999. The original and best-selling Beowulf book.

David Wright, editor. *Beowulf.* Penguin Classics, 1957. A highly regarded translation (into prose) of the Beowulf Epic.

# C Annotated URLs

Below is a sampling of URLs that are helpful for those building or using a Beowulf. This is not an exhaustive list, and we encourage the reader to browse the Web for other sites. A good place to start is the general Beowulf Web sites.

## C.1  General Beowulf Information

`www.beowulf.org`: The original Beowulf Web site.

`beowulf-underground.org`: The Beowulf Underground provides "unsanctioned and unfettered information on building and using Beowulf systems." It is a site that allows the Beowulf community to post brief articles about software, documentation, and announcements related to Beowulf computing. Each article includes links to Web sites and downloads for the various items. A separate commercial and vendor area keeps free software well delineated. Moderators work to keep the material brief and on topic and to prevent abuses. This is the one stop for all things Beowulf.

## C.2  Node and Network Hardware

`www.cs.virginia.edu/stream`: The STREAM Benchmark provides a simple measure of the performance of the memory system on a node. This site also includes results for a wide variety of platforms, from PC nodes suitable for a Beowulf, to workstations, to supercomputers.

`www.tomshardware.com`: Aimed at hobbyists building their own computers, this is a good site for general background on node hardware and includes up-to-date instructions on building your own node.

## C.3  Performance Tools

`www.netlib.org/benchmark/hpl`: Home of the High Performance Linpack Benchmark

## C.4  Parallel Programming and Software

`www.mpi-forum.org`: The official MPI Forum Web site, contains Postscript and HTML versions of the MPI-1 and MPI-2 Standards.

`www.mcs.anl.gov/mpi`: A starting point for information about MPI, including libraries and tools that use MPI and papers about the implementation or use of MPI.

`www.mcs.anl.gov/mpich`: Home of the MPICH implementation of MPI. Download source, documentation, and Unix and Windows versions of MPI from here. Also check the bug list page for patches and announcements of releases.

`www.mcs.anl.gov/mpi/mpptest`: Performance tests for MPI, including a guide for how *not* to measure communication performance.

`www.netlib.org`: A valuable collection of mathematical software and related information.

`www.csm.ornl.gov/pvm`: PVM home page.

`www.mcs.anl.gov/romio`: Home of the ROMIO implementation of the I/O chapter from MPI-2. ROMIO is included in MPICH and LAM but can also be downloaded separately. Information on tuning ROMIO for performance can be found here.

`hdf.ncsa.uiuc.edu`: Home of HDF. Included here are I/O libraries; tools for analyzing, visualizing, and converting scientific data; and software downloads, documentation, and support information.

`www.cs.dartmouth.edu/pario`: Home of the Parallel I/O Archive. This includes a list of projects in parallel I/O, people working in parallel I/O, and conferences on parallel I/O. Its biggest claim to fame is an extensive annotated bibliography of parallel I/O resources.

## C.5   Scheduling and Management

`www.openpbs.org`: The OpenPBS site is the official Web site for the open source version of PBS. Maintained by Veridian, it offers downloads of software, patches, and documentation, and it hosts FAQs, discussion lists, searchable archives, and general PBS community announcements.

`www.pbspro.com`: Focused on the Professional Version of PBS, the PBS Pro Web site includes software downloads, documentation, evaluation versions, beta releases of new software, news, and information for the PBS administrator.

`www.supercluster.org`: The Supercluster Web site contains documentation for the Maui scheduler and Silver metascheduler. It also includes cluster-relevant research in areas of simulation, metascheduling, data staging, allocation management, and resource optimization.

## C.6   Other

`www.vrco.com`: VRCO provides virtual reality-based software including immersive environments for Windows 2000.

`www.seattlelab.com`: Seattle Labs provides remote access tools for Windows 2000 including TelnetD and remote control tools.

`www.citrix.com`: Citrix provides an extension to Window 2000 Terminal server that allows users from non-Windows platforms to remotely access Windows-based systems using the native Windows interface.

`www.cs.cornell.edu/tech2000`: This web site describes the Intel funded Technology for Education 2000 project at Cornell University.

`www.tc.cornell.edu`: This is the home page of the Cornell Theory Center (CTC), a high-performance cluster computing and interdisciplinary computational research center at Cornell University—home to the largest Windows/Intel/Dell cluster complex in the world.

`www.tc.cornell.edu/AC3`: The Advanced Cluster Computing Consortium (AC3) at CTC—a consortium that includes computing manufacturers, software vendors, academics, government agencies, and corporate clients who focus on industry standard IT solutions that maximize the performance, reliability, and usability of Intel-based servers operating Windows 2000.

`www.ctc-manhattan.com`: This is CTC's cluster computing showcase and computational finance solutions center located at 55 Broad St. in Manhattan.

# References

[1] Cray Research. *Application Programmer's Library Reference Manual*, 2nd edition, November 1995. Publication SR-2165.

[2] Jack Dongarra. Performance of various computers using standard linear equations software. Technical Report Number CS-89–85, University of Tennessee, Knoxville TN, 37996, 2001. `http://www.netlib.org/benchmark/performance.ps`.

[3] G. C. Fox, S. W. Otto, and A. J. G. Hey. Matrix algorithms on a hypercube I: Matrix multiplication. *Parallel Computing*, 4:17–31, 1987.

[4] William Gropp, Steven Huss-Lederman, Andrew Lumsdaine, Ewing Lusk, Bill Nitzberg, William Saphir, and Marc Snir. *MPI—The Complete Reference: Volume 2, The MPI-2 Extensions*. MIT Press, Cambridge, MA, 1998.

[5] William Gropp, Ewing Lusk, Nathan Doss, and Anthony Skjellum. A high-performance, portable implementation of the MPI Message-Passing Interface standard. *Parallel Computing*, 22(6):789–828, 1996.

[6] William Gropp, Ewing Lusk, and Anthony Skjellum. *Using MPI: Portable Parallel Programming with the Message Passing Interface*, 2nd edition. MIT Press, Cambridge, MA, 1999.

[7] William Gropp, Ewing Lusk, and Rajeev Thakur. *Using MPI-2: Advanced Features of the Message-Passing Interface*. MIT Press, Cambridge, MA, 1999.

[8] William D. Gropp and Ewing Lusk. Reproducible measurements of MPI performance characteristics. In Jack Dongarra, Emilio Luque, and Tomàs Margalef, editors, *Recent Advances in Parallel Virtual Machine and Message Passing Interface*, volume 1697 of *Lecture Notes in Computer Science*, pages 11–18. Springer Verlag, 1999. 6th European PVM/MPI Users' Group Meeting, Barcelona, Spain, September 1999.

[9] J. M. D. Hill, B. McColl, D. C. Stefanescu, M. W. Goudreau, K. Lang, S. B. Rao, T. Suel, T. Tsantilas, and R. H. Bisseling. BSPlib: The BSP programming library. *Parallel Computing*, 24(14):1947–1980, December 1998.

[10] Message Passing Interface Forum. MPI: A Message-Passing Interface standard. *International Journal of Supercomputer Applications*, 8(3/4):165–414, 1994.

[11] Message Passing Interface Forum. MPI2: A message passing interface standard. *International Journal of High Performance Computing Applications*, 12(1–2):1–299, 1998.

[12] OpenMP Web page. `www.openmp.org`.

[13] R. Reussner, P. Sanders, L. Prechelt, and M Müller. SKaMPI: A detailed, accurate MPI benchmark. In Vassuk Alexandrov and Jack Dongarra, editors, *Recent advances in Parallel Virtual Machine and Message Passing Interface*, volume 1497 of *Lecture Notes in Computer Science*, pages 52–59. Springer, 1998. 5th European PVM/MPI Users' Group Meeting.

[14] Marc Snir, Steve W. Otto, Steven Huss-Lederman, David W. Walker, and Jack Dongarra. *MPI—The Complete Reference: Volume 1, The MPI Core*, 2nd edition. MIT Press, Cambridge, MA, 1998.

[15] Rajeev Thakur, Ewing Lusk, and William Gropp. A case for using MPI's derived datatypes to improve I/O performance. In *Proceedings of SC98: High Performance Networking and Computing*, November 1998.

[16] J. L. Traeff, R. Hempel, H. Ritzdoff, and F. Zimmermann. Flattening on the fly: Efficient handling of MPI derived datatypes. Number 1697 in Lecture Notes in Computer Science, pages 109–116, Berlin, Germany / Heidelberg, Germany / London, UK / etc., 1999. Spring-er-Verlag.

[17] Omer Zaki, Ewing Lusk, William Gropp, and Deborah Swider. Toward scalable performance visualization with Jumpshot. *High Performance Computing Applications*, 13(2):277–288, Fall 1999.

# Index